The New Punitiveness

To Rio de Janeiro: the city which made
this book a possibility

The New Punitiveness

Trends, theories, perspectives

Edited by John Pratt, David Brown, Mark Brown, Simon Hallsworth and Wayne Morrison

WILLAN
PUBLISHING

Published by

Willan Publishing
Culmcott House
Mill Street, Uffculme
Cullompton, Devon
EX15 3AT, UK
Tel: +44(0)1884 840337
Fax: +44(0)1884 840251
e-mail: info@willanpublishing.co.uk
website: www.willanpublishing.co.uk

Published simultaneously in the USA and Canada by

Willan Publishing
c/o ISBS, 920 NE 58th Ave, Suite 300,
Portland, Oregon 97213-3786, USA
Tel: +001(0)503 287 3093
Fax: +001(0)503 280 8832
e-mail: info@isbs.com
website: www.isbs.com

First published 2005

ISBN 1-84392-109-X (Paperback)
      1-84392-110-3 (Hardback)

British Library Cataloguing-in-Publication Data

A catalogue record for this book is available from the British Library

Project managed by Deer Park Productions, Tavistock, Devon
Typeset by GCS, Leighton Buzzard, Bedfordshire, LU7 1AR
Printed and bound by T.J. International, Padstow, Cornwall

Contents

Notes on the editors and contributors

Katja Franko Aas is Senior Researcher at the Institute of Criminology and Sociology of Law, University of Oslo. She has written extensively on punishment and information technologies, including *Sentencing in the Age of Information: from Faust to Macintosh* (Cavendish/Glasshouse 2005). She is currently working on a project about globalization and crime.

Estella Baker is a Senior Lecturer in Law and Deputy Head of the School of Law at the University of Sheffield. Her principal research interests lie in the fields of penology and sentencing, European criminal law and justice, and the relationship between criminal justice and governance.

Ulla V. Bondeson has been Professor of Criminology at the University of Copenhagen since 1980. Previously, she was a professor of sociology and had the chair of sociology of law at Lund University, Sweden. She has been the President of the Scandinavian Research Council for Criminology and is presently Vice-president of the International Society of Criminology. She is a member of the Steering Committee for the Campbell Crime and Justice Group. The American Society of Criminology has honoured her with the Sellin and Glueck Award, and she has written extensively in the field of criminology.

David Brown is Professor at the University of New South Wales, Sydney, teaching criminal law and criminal justice. He has been active in criminal justice movements, issues and debates for three decades and is a regular media commentator and has published widely in the field. He has co-authored or co-edited *The Prison Struggle* (1982), *The Judgments of Lionel Murphy* (1986), *Death in the Hands of the State* (1988), *Criminal Laws* in three editions (1990, 1996, 2001), *Rethinking Law and Order* (1998) and *Prisoners as Citizens* (2002).

Mark Brown teaches criminology at the University of Melbourne. He has written on a number of aspects of corrections and penology, including contemporary understandings of risk and the so-called dangerous offender. Since 1999 he has been engaged in research on the penal history of British India and is currently writing a book focusing on the notorious 'criminal tribes' of north India.

Roy Coleman is Lecturer in Criminology at the University of Liverpool, and was formerly at Liverpool John Moores University. His research interests lie in the areas of social and criminological theory, social control, the uses of street camera surveillance technologies, statecraft, and urban governance. His recent publications include *Reclaiming the Streets: surveillance, social control and the city* (Willan 2004), and articles (with Joe Sim) in the *British Journal of Sociology* and the *International Review of Law, Computers and Technology*.

Simon Hallsworth is Director of the Centre for Social and Evaluation Research at London Metropolitan University. His research interests include examining penal trends in late modernity, and contemporary changes in local crime prevention. His current work includes examining gangs and collective delinquency in Europe. His recent publications include *Street Crime* (Willan 2005). He is currently completing a book for Glasshouse Press entitled *Punitive States*.

Kelly Hannah-Moffat is an Associate Professor in the Department of Sociology, University of Toronto. She worked as a researcher and policy adviser for the Commission of Inquiry into Certain Events at the Prison for Women in Kingston. Her recent publications include 'Losing ground: gender, responsibility and parole risk', in *Social Politics* (2005); and 'Criminogenic need and the transformative risk subject: hybridizations of risk/need in penality' in *Punishment and Society* (2005).

Lyn Hinds is a Lecturer in Criminology in the School of Social Science, University of Queensland, Australia. Her areas of research interest are criminological theory and functionality and variation in punishment.

Mona Lynch is an Associate Professor in the Justice Studies Department at San Jose State University, where she teaches courses on courts, punishment, research methods, and the death penalty. Much of her recent research examines penal/legal discourse and practices in a number of settings, focusing especially on the social and cultural dynamics of contemporary punishment. She is currently writing a book on the recent dramatic developments and shifts in Arizona's penal practices, as they are embedded in the recent social, cultural, and political history of that state.

Jeffrey Meyer graduated from Carleton University in 2004 with a Master of Arts in Sociology. His research focused on analyzing governmental discourses of crime and deviance. He is currently working for Canada Post Corporation as a Parliamentary Relations Officer. Future directions include pursuing doctoral research in political science.

Dawn Moore is an Assistant Professor in the Department of Law and the Criminology, Criminal Justice Institute, Carleton University. She has done activist work and academic writing opposing prison privatization in Canada and concerning prisoners' rights. She also publishes in the field of controlled drugs and substances, and is currently working on a book which aims to critically explore the rise of substance abuse 'programming' for those in conflict with the law in Canada. She has also written on drug-induced sexual assault and is interested in issues of sexual identity and the law.

Wayne Morrison is Director of the External Programme in Laws, University of London and Reader in Laws, Queen Mary College, University of London. His teaching interests are in the area of criminology and jurisprudence, with his main publications being a modernized English edition of *Blackstone's Commentaries on the Laws of England* (Cavendish 2001), *Theoretical Criminology: from modernity to postmodernism* (Cavendish 1995; Chinese edition Law Press of China Ltd 2004) and *Jurisprudence: from the Greeks to postmodernity* (Cavendish 1997; Chinese edition University of Whu Han Press 2003). He is currently working on a text that puts the history of criminological theory in a global and colonial context (*Criminology, Civilisation and the New World Order*, Glasshouse forthcoming).

David Nelken is Distinguished Professor of Legal Institutions and Social Change at the University of Macerata in Italy, and also Distinguished Research Professor at Cardiff Law School and Honorary Visiting Professor of Law at the London School of Economics. His recent publications focus on comparative sociology of law and comparative criminal justice, and include *Contrasting Criminal Justice* (Ashgate 2000) and *Adapting Legal Cultures* (Hart 2001). Former trustee of the Law and Society Association and a vice-president of the RCSL (International Sociological Association), he is a member of the editorial boards of legal, socio-legal, political science, criminology and criminal law journals in five countries.

Mike Nellis is a Senior Lecturer in Criminal Justice Studies in the Department of Sociology at the University of Birmingham. He previously worked as a joint appointment with the University of Sheffield and the South Yorkshire Probation Service, and before that as a youth justice worker. He has written widely on the future of the Probation Service, electronic monitoring, community justice, probation training and prison movies. He is currently researching the GPS tracking pilots in England and Wales.

John Pratt was educated in England at the universities of London (LLB Hons), Keele (MA, Criminology), and Sheffield (PhD). He is now Professor of Criminology at the Institute of Criminology, Victoria University of Wellington, New Zealand. He has taught and lectured at universities in the United Kingdom, continental Europe, North America and Australia. He has undertaken extensive research on the history and sociology of punishment in modern society including *Punishment in a Perfect Society* (1992), *Governing the Dangerous* (1997), *Dangerous Offenders* (2000, joint editor with Mark Brown), *Punishment and Civilization* (2002) and *Crime, Truth and Justice* (2003, joint editor with George Gilligan). He has also been editor of the *Australian and New Zealand Journal of Criminology* since 1997.

Julian Roberts is Reader in Criminology at the University of Oxford. His research interests include sentencing, and public attitudes to crime and criminal justice. His most recent book is *The Virtual Prison: community custody and the evolution of imprisonment* published by Cambridge University Press in 2004.

Mick Ryan is Professor of Penal Politics at the University of Greenwich, London. He has written extensively on criminal justice matters in Europe and North America, most recently, *Penal Policy and Political Culture in England and Wales* (Waterside Press 2003) In the 1980s he was a member of the editorial collective responsible for *The Abolitionist* and later served as Chair of INQUEST the pressure group monitoring deaths in state custody.

Joe Sim is Professor of Criminology in the School of Social Science, Liverpool John Moores University. He is the author of a number of texts including *Medical Power in Prisons, British Prisons* (with Mike Fitzgerald) and *Prisons Under Protest* (with Phil Scraton and Paula Skidmore) and co-editor of *Western European Penal Systems* (with Mick Ryan and Vincenzo Ruggiero).

Loïc Wacquant is Distinguished Professor of Sociology and Anthropology at the New School for Social Research, Professor of Sociology at the University of California-Berkeley, and Researcher at the Centre de sociologie européenne-Paris. His interests include comparative urban inequality and marginality, ethnoracial domination, penal institutions as instruments for the management of dis-possessed and dishonoured groups, the body and violence, and social theory. Among his recent books are *Body and Soul: Ethnographic Notebooks of an Apprentice Boxer* (2003), *Punir les pauvres* (2004), and *Deadly Symbiosis: Race and the Rise of Neoliberal Penality* (2005). He is co-founder and editor of the interdisciplinary journal *Ethnography*.

Introduction

Under the ominous banner 'Back to Basics in Georgia's Prisons', the Georgia Department of Corrections *Annual Report* (1996: 13) proudly boasts that it was 'one of the most responsive states' to enact 'tough on crime' legislation. As the following list reproduced from this report demonstrates, this was not a vain boast. What its 'new toughness' entailed was a regime that was determined to:

- 'Remove weights and non-athletic recreation equipment from prisons
- Cease all special leave programs. No holiday furloughs
- Require all inmates to walk 4½ miles per day
- Mark uniforms "state prisoner" or "state probationer"
- Toughen boot camp programs; cease graduation ceremonies
- Substitute a cold sandwich for lunch – no hot lunch
- Change its name from Correctional Institution to Prison'

What are we to make of such developments? Are they just another example of the eccentricities we have come to associate with the Deep South of the US that differentiate that region from the rest of the modern, civilized world? Or do they have more general significance than this, exemplifying the fierce drive towards mass incarceration in the United States that continues to take place (at the time of writing, the prison population there has reached 2.1 million and 1 in 75 of all men are in prison), with a new tolerance for brutalizing penal sanctions and prison conditions that some 30 years or so ago would surely have been quite unthinkable (the Georgia *Annual Report* of the State Board of Corrections, 1965: 5, had advertised the logo 'Rehabilitation Pays' and had referred to 'programs aimed at returning inmates to society as useful and productive citizens')? And then, if this new punitiveness, reflected in the values, strategies, language and practices embodied in the 1996 annual report is indeed embedded across the United States, and not just an aberration confined to the backward-looking South of that country, to what extent can it be seen as taking root in the other main English-speaking societies? And has it extended beyond them to be a phenomenon characteristic of modern society as a whole (Garland, 2001)? It is questions such as these that we are seeking to address and explain in this book.

What is the 'new punitiveness'?

First, though, let us try to identify the characteristics and contours of this 'new punitiveness' in more detail. The trend towards mass incarceration noted above has been accompanied not only by longer prison sentences but by penal laws that seem to abandon long-standing limits to punishment in modern societies. The advent, for example, of 'three-strikes' laws flagrantly breaches the principle that punishment should be proportionate to the harm caused, while additional powers of civil detention following completion of prison terms under the provisions of the various sexual predator laws in the USA would seem *prima facie* to breach the double-jeopardy principle. That the United States Supreme Court has upheld the constitutionality of such statutes in cases such as *Kansas* v *Hendricks* (1997) says much about the social milieu within which current penal developments are occurring. We are not, then, considering minor re-configurations to a penal landscape that remains otherwise benign. On the contrary, it would appear that what was once exceptional is now becoming far more central to the penal process as a whole.

Not only are prison sentences increasing, recent decades have also born witness, in varying degrees, to the emergence of penal sanctions that had previously been thought to be extinct and inappropriate in the modern civilized world. The United States, particularly, has overseen the return of shaming punishments that usually involve some form of public humiliation of the offender (Pratt, 2000), in addition to the resurrection of penal forms such as the chain gang and the death penalty. Decades of reform directed at ameliorating prison conditions have meanwhile been abandoned across a number of jurisdictions, in addition to Georgia above. Prisoners have had 'privileges' revoked while more austere and spartan prison regimes have been introduced. In the case of 'Supermax' prisons, another United States innovation, this has involved the introduction of 'lockdown' regimes wherein prisoners are routinely locked away for up to 23 hours per day; and where they are largely denied access to programmes, education, exercise and association with others.

What we have been charting here is a series of penal developments stretching over three decades affecting (and effecting) the shape and form of the penal terrain across the United States in particular, most of the other main English-speaking countries to a degree, and to a more limited extent in Europe. Such developments appear to go beyond the normal ebb and flow of penal policy that characterizes change over time in every jurisdiction. The idea of a new punitiveness also implicitly invites comparison to its referent: what was the 'old' punitiveness? In answer we might point to that cornerstone around which so much contemporary penal theory is formed, Michel Foucault's *Discipline and Punish: The Birth of the Prison* (1977). The central argument of *Discipline and Punish* was that the governance of modernizing European societies in the eighteenth and nineteenth centuries demanded new forms of power and control. Foucault used the penal sphere to illustrate how a sovereign form of power characterized by arbitrary, excessive, and destructive force gradually gave way to a form of disciplinary power that was fundamentally productive in character. Much of what is described here as the new punitiveness may therefore be understood as forms of punishment that seem to violate the productive, restrained, and rational tenets of modern disciplinary punishment and hark back, in different ways, to the emotive and destructive themes of sovereign punishment.

Taking this position a little further, if, as Foucault argued, the defining characteristic of modern penality was the tenacious way in which it developed the disciplinary machinery necessary for producing 'docile' and useful bodies, what is evident about the new punitiveness is that many of the punishments associated with it no longer appear motivated to achieve such ends. In sanctions such as indeterminate punishment and disproportionate punishment, the panopticon no longer appears as an organizing referent. From being a space wherein the reclamation of the evil and the fallen could be attempted, such punishments suggest interventions where no improvement is sought or expected from the inmate. From a social laboratory designed with the purpose of improvement, the prison has been reborn as a container for human goods now endlessly recycled through what has become a transcarceral system of control.

Penal strategies

That said, the question may yet be asked, precisely what sorts of measures are we referring to here? We have already noted disproportionate sentences, in the form of American-style three-strikes statutes and forms of indefinite detention both criminal and civil. The former build upon the tradition of life imprisonment sentences but are set apart by the much wider range of offences to which they are applied (traditionally life imprisonment has been restricted to the offences of murder or manslaughter) and the much greater frequency with which they are used. The latter – indefinite civil detention strategies – are best evidenced in the sexual predator statutes so widely adopted in the United States, that provide for post-prison detention of offenders labelled sexual or violent predators. Alongside these schemes have been a variety of measures that provide either radically disproportionate punishment (for example, in Australia's Northern Territory, although since repealed, a mandatory one-strike law applied to theft of such minor domestic items as pencils, towels, biscuits, and soft drinks) or seriously disproportionate punishment (for example, presumptions for cumulation on all counts of a serious offence) through what still remain as finite sentences. To this might be added schemes that curtail in important ways the civil liberties of ex-prisoners, such as sex offender registration and notification statutes, and schemes that provide for the public humiliation, degradation, or shaming of those under sentence (eg., in chain gangs) or ex-prisoners (eg., 'I am a sex offender'-style bumper stickers and house signs). The general prohibition against materially unproductive and psychologically destructive punishments so characteristic of modern disciplinary punishment is also violated in 'technical' innovations like the Supermax prison. Aside from long hours of lockdown, these prisons work actively to break the spirit and will of prisoners through sensory deprivation and psychic isolation in a kind of modern analogue to the Victorian-era treadwheel, crank and dietary regime (long since abandoned because of its pointless brutality). Again, on the one hand there is the re-emergence of the extinct sanctions; on the other, Supermax represents the most chilling indicator of the way in which futuristic technology makes possible the most encompassing form of prison control ever known. Indeed, as Mona Lynch vividly illustrates in her chapter in this book, the meeting of death row and Supermax in some American states represents a unique convergence of the old and the new: they come together to form a 'waste management' approach to penality. Lynch argues that 'states like Arizona are literally transforming those waiting to die from sociologically and psychologically rich human beings into a kind of untouchable toxic waste that need only be securely contained until its final disposal'. Such policy has become a new battleground for progressive and conservative penal forces in the United States and Lynch describes the astonishing ways in which two particular cases brought before the 9th Circuit Court of Appeals have played out.

The tension between technological possibilities and demands for an older, more viscerally punitive approach to crime has also been played out in the community punishment sector of some modern penal systems, particularly in relation to the growth of electronic monitoring. As Mike Nellis shows in his chapter, trends in this realm reflect considerable uncertainty: on the one hand, the risk-oriented managerialist approach to crime control that has featured strongly in the development of this strategy might be able to hold at bay some of the more emotive and ostentatious punishments (Pratt, 2001) noted above. On the other hand, there is also the inherent potential available to the state to harness efficient crime control strategies such as this to a more extensive and intrusive surveillance designed to keep deviant populations in check and under prolonged scrutiny.

Yet it might be wrong to conceive of punitiveness purely in terms of brutalizing or wasteful punishment, or the continual extension of punishment and control into the community. Certainly, this is the view of Moore and Hannah-Moffat, whose chapter in this volume seeks to push aside the 'liberal veil' of welfarist correctionalism in the Canadian penal system. They argue that while ostensibly progressive and moderate, particularly in comparison with the USA, and certainly continuous with earlier eras of Canadian welfarism, penal regimes in Canada have adopted increasingly oppressive undertones. Key among these is the trope of offender 'choice' around which most programming of rehabilitative services revolves. The so-called choices that an offender is expected to exercise are little more than a chimera, seeking to shift responsibility for behaviour change from the state to prisoners themselves. Viewed in this light, the Canadian penal-welfare system might well have taken a distinctly punitive turn, albeit by stealth and behind a veil of liberal progressivism.

The role of public opinion

Another recurrent feature of the emerging new punitiveness is the extent to which it has been promoted by appeals to a public who are now expected to perform a more active role in penal affairs. This often involves little more than populist appeals by political elites to insecure publics in order to promote a law-and-order agenda; however, it can extend much further. It can also involve the use of plebiscites, referenda, and other direct channels of dialogue between governments and the public, thereby radically reshaping the penal landscape: in other words, public opinion can become an inscribed part of the democratic process.

Zimring (1996), for example, has shown how this more active appeal to the public was used to legitimate the development of the Californian three-strikes law; Pratt and Clark (2005) show how, in New Zealand, a citizen's initiated referendum has had a direct impact on penal policy.

For commentators such as Ryan (this volume), this shift is part of a wider one wherein a penal policy agenda once monopolized by restricted professional elites has gradually given way to a more open policy field where voices once marginalized within penal welfarism are now heard – and listened to. Ryan characterizes penal policy until the 1970s as being a 'top-down' process characteristic of a 'deferential' political culture, which was destabilized first by the counter-culture (including prisoners' voices) and later by Thatcherite populism. He is far less hostile to the rise of popular punitiveness than many commentators, seeing it as part of a more general rise of the 'public voice', challenging elite penal policy formulation in a 'democratic' if often punitive way. Rather than deploring populism, Ryan suggests that a progressive approach to criminal justice strategy must engage with this 'public voice' in a process of 'lobbying outwards' beyond 'the academy'. A similarly radical re-reading of contemporary crime discourse is made by Franko Aas in her chapter in this volume. Looking to two modes of communication, the technical form and the political advertisement, she argues that penal communication is itself changing. These two modes of informational representation work to package and compress information, they shift the goals of communication from reflection toward action, and they also shift the traditional power alignments into which criminologists have inserted themselves as experts. Thus, criminologists' declining influence in debates on punishment reflects for Franko Aas much more than a failure of engagement or lobbying; it goes to the heart of changes in the structure and parameters of penal communications more generally.

The rise of the victims' movement and not least its contribution to growing punitiveness must also not be underestimated. In the USA, for example, victims and potential victims (i.e. the public at large) have accumulated new rights including notification of the release of ex-prisoners in their community. Victims have also accumulated a greater power to shape sentencing policy through being granted the right to have their voices heard at sentencing and parole hearings. At an informal level, there have been tendencies towards local 'naming and shaming campaigns' against particular criminals, troublemakers or ex-prisoners, often in the form of warning posters distributed around the immediate community. Public involvement in raising the punitive stakes, however, can also take a more immediate and potentially violent form, as expressed in the rise or return of vigilante activity. The public hounding of suspected paedophiles in Britain in 2000 following a vociferous naming and shaming campaign mounted by a tabloid newspaper is itself a potent symptom of what 'active' citizenship can be taken to mean in this context (Pratt, 2001).

Taken together, what these developments herald is the rise of a new punitiveness that, in a number of important ways, reverses long-standing traditions that had become hallmarks of modern democratic penal culture, while overseeing the introduction of sanctions that were, until recently, considered incommensurate with its values. Its rise also intimates that the penal developments documented above are obeying a different set of values and cultural expectations from those that had previously provided the frame of reference under conditions of welfare state/penal modernity.

A global phenomenon?

Nonetheless, there remains considerable debate about the extent and range of these changes and what they represent and how to explain them. At the interpretative level considerable differences also remain about the extent to which the new punitiveness has taken root and the effects it has produced. For example, though we commonly speak of penal trends in national terms – the United States, Britain, Canada – it is clear that trends evident at a national level often mask quite striking intra-national differences: as Lyn Hinds demonstrates in this volume with reference to the USA, the new punitiveness is unequally distributed across that country. There is much greater diversity now than 30 years ago and this points to different strategic and cultural responses to the demands of punishment emerging within American society. Similar trends can also be observed in Australia. In that country there is a national rate of imprisonment of 114 per 100,000 of population, but dramatic inter-state differences. Victoria, for example, has a rate of imprisonment of 62 per 100,000 of population. Its neighbour, New South Wales, markedly similar in population, demographics, wealth, and so on, has a rate of 120 per 100,000. Similar pictures emerge, both intra- and inter-nationally, when patterns of use of specific punitive measures are explored. Take the indefinite sentence of preventive detention. Since its enactment in 1993 just four offenders have been sentenced under Victoria's preventive detention legislation. In New South Wales, a form of *ad hominem* preventive detention was struck down as unconstitutional in *R. v Kable*. Looking internationally, New Zealand is geographically close and culturally quite similar to both Victoria and New South Wales. There, however, use of this punitive measure has been dramatically greater. Slightly smaller in total population than both Australian states, New Zealand has seen its population of preventive detainees rise from 10 in 1980 to around 150 in 2004.

This uneven scale of punitive development itself begets a number of important questions. Is the new punitiveness predominantly an issue of American exceptionalism and, if so, what explains North American readiness to embrace such a punitive culture? Or is the new punitiveness a wider issue pertinent to all English-speaking jurisdictions and the free-market principles around which they are now organized? If, as Van Swaningan (2004) argues, punitive cultures are also forming in continental Europe as well, what factors can be adduced to account for this development? Is it a matter of policy transfer or is an increasing degree of punitiveness a feature of all late-modern societies?

Baker and Roberts in their chapter see globalization as one explanation of increasing punitiveness, manifest in the creation of a populace that is anxious about crime trends and which lacks confidence in existing criminal justice systems to deal with them. In addition, the 'mediatization' of everyday life constantly draws attention to such problems. Public interest then looks to policies that seem to offer solutions from sources beyond traditional expertise and bureaucratic imperatives: populist solutions are perceived to be superior to evidence-based strategies and at the same time seem to offer an easy transfer from one jurisdiction to another.

Another way in which accounts of a rising and all-pervasive new punitiveness may be challenged is at the level of methodology. How are we to know if a punitive tendency is afoot? Where do we look, or what do we look for? David Brown's chapter stresses the importance of testing the extent to which some of the theoretical arguments for a 'punitive turn', resting largely on discourse analysis, fit empirical data derived from a specific analysis of penal practices in particular jurisdictions. He examines New South Wales' penal practice since the Nagle Royal Commission of 1978 and uses the results to identify tendencies which, he argues, 'result in minimising the extent of contestation in penal and criminal justice struggles; in over-reading the return of cultures and practices of cruelty and the pervasiveness of punitiveness; and in underplaying the resilience of penal welfarism and its social democratic heritage'. Yet it might also be argued that by looking just to the internal practices of nations we are missing important elements of punitiveness. This is just the argument raised by Morrison who, in his chapter in this volume, presents another level of analysis and adopts a self-conscious global context. The nation-state, the normal context for criminology, provides a constraining and false set of boundaries. We have a distinction between domestic civilized space and the chaotic space of the international area. Not only is this analytically wrong, for he argues that no state or society should be read as self-sustaining – all are part of global networks and have been for hundreds of years – but also the distinction provides a set of images that help persuade people that the measures taken by those in power are reasonable and necessary. Power elites can tell us that they are dealing rationally with the real threats to our civilized space and that wrongdoers are being justly punished, while massive harms and enormous crimes go unpunished. The 'international' arena is shown to be non-punitive, a realm of irrational interaction, where in contrast to the domestic space, politics is accepted as inherent to penality. A level of analysis that moves beyond the nation-state and traverses the great divide between the domestic and the international may show the reality of the new punitiveness and point the way to a more humane set of understandings and concepts.

Indicators of punitiveness

Punitive developments at play within a society, however, are not only confined to the way deviant populations are treated when they are caught and prosecuted. Any debate about the nature of the new punitiveness must also consider the ways in which the communities from which offenders derive are policed. Like punishment, policing varies considerably in the level of coercion and violence that can be applied and there are clear differences between societies that aspire to police with consent and those that delegate this function to imperative elements that rely upon naked coercion. In the case of the USA, for example, a key element in its punitive drift is evidenced in the way its ghettos are now routinely policed by paramilitary units such as SWAT teams. The degree to which a state militarizes its police or has recourse to paramilitary forms of policing might therefore also be considered another index of its punitive development (see Hinds, this volume).

Though notions of the punitive typically evoke ideas of visceral violence openly expressed, it is important to remember that occasioning direct pain or harm is not the only way in which punitive tendencies at play in state development may be mediated. Malign neglect may occasion as much harm as more direct attempts to punish cruelly, as the shocking rate of suicide in prisons in the UK or rape within the American prison system illustrate. Nor may such neglect be a feature of penal regimes alone. The way a society addresses the problems of its poorest citizens, or treats asylum seekers or refugees, may also say much about its punitive nature. There clearly remains a world of difference between the extensive forms of welfare provided in northern Scandinavian societies and that provided in the USA to its poor, who also constitute, as Wacquant argues in his chapter in this book, the vast majority of its prison population.

An old, new or non-punitiveness?

This collection thus marks an attempt to address the diverse issues that the new punitiveness poses. It does so not through attempting to resolve the complexities of the issues raised but rather by drawing together in one volume the work of commentators, using both empirical and theoretical research, to speak to the nature, extent, and causes of this phenomenon. Far from seeking to resolve the issues raised by recent punitive developments, this volume aspires instead to provide a discursive space in which a critical dialogue can occur. This means accepting from the outset the presence of different and often opposing interpretations of penal change as well as diverse and often competing theoretical standpoints and epistemologies. At the same time, to explain the socio-genesis of punitive development within a society not only requires that the structures and processes that facilitate such development be identified, it also means identifying why other societies do not embark on such trajectories of development. The issues at stake in explaining the absence of a punitive culture are as complex as explaining the emergence within a society that does aspire to punish more harshly. It requires both a comparative methodology as well as one that is sensitive to differences not only within accumulation regimes but political structures and cultural sensibilities. In this volume Meyer and O'Malley persuasively argue through a detailed case study of Canada that a punitive turn cannot be observed in its recent development. On the contrary, the changes that have characterized it represent a more benign and complex response in a world where distinctly modern penal principles still prevail. Far from following the lead taken by the United States, the very proximity of the two countries has provided the Canadian state with a clear view of the possibilities and consequences of the new punitiveness at work across the border. Having seen the future so close at hand, as it were, they argue that Canada has chosen not to follow the punitive turn.

A similarly strong resistance to punitiveness can be found in Italy, but it is manifested in quite different ways. David Nelken in his chapter argues that although the level of imprisonment and 'general level of harshness' of the Italian system is 'within the norm for Continental Europe', 'its approach to juvenile delinquency does stand out as relatively lenient'. He sees any perceived leniency in the Italian system not as being the result of 'economy in the use of the criminal law' but as connected with complex procedures and delays in trial processes together with the 'large variety of measures of mercy or conditional forgiveness'. He examines crucial juvenile reform legislation passed in 1989 and in particular the innovative system of pre-trial probation for juveniles, involving 'social intervention as an alternative to prison', available for all types of crime, even murder. Nelken examines some of the cultural conditions that sustain this 'leniency', the extent to which there is a growing 'bifurcation' of response between Italian juveniles and 'unaccompanied illegal immigrants and gypsy children', and the relationship between neoliberalism and leniency in Italian juvenile justice. Again, Bondeson in her chapter on Scandinavian developments suggests that the main reasons why the new punitiveness has had a limited impact in that region is because of the inclusive nature of its welfare state politics alongside a greater sense of national unity, trust, and reciprocity. But at the same time she notes the beginnings of a rupture in this fabric of tolerance. Young people, particularly, seem less inclined to follow the paths taken by their parents and so Bondeson asks whether indeed the time of low punitiveness in Scandinavia might well be passing – as it has in so many other modern societies.

Rupture or continuity?

A key and indeed decisive issue posed by any attempt to theorize a new punitiveness concerns the extent to which the developments that characterize it mark a break from or continuity with existing tendencies at play within distinctly modern penal regimes. Are we examining the emergence of a new and potentially divergent phase in penal development or are we looking at a less significant pattern of development in a penal landscape that is far more 'volatile and contradictory' than can be contained in models premised upon notions of 'break' or 'rupture'? To this extent, does the new punitiveness represent only one of a number of diverse penal trends in societies characterized by a proliferation of penal strategies, many of which also remain distinctly modern (Lutkin, 1998) as well as distinctly non-punitive in character (O'Malley, 1999)?

Hallsworth (in this volume) argues the case for seeing in the punitive excess characteristic of the new punitiveness a radical discontinuity with the penal trends characteristic of modernity and distinctly modern penal regimes. Challenging the reading of modernity offered by those who, like Bauman, see penal excess as intrinsic to modernity, Hallsworth argues instead that such transgressive violence cannot unproblematically be reconciled with distinctly modern projects. Using a framework influenced by Bataille's general economics, he argues in opposition to this that in the new punitiveness we are witnessing the re-emergence of heterogeneous forces into social life normally precluded by modern states in their homogeneous form. Using America's punitive turn as a case study, he argues that we are no longer looking at a modern state beholden to a distinctly modern economy characterized by limits. On the contrary, we are looking at the formation of what he terms a postmodern penal order organized around an economy characterized by excess.

Morrison's and Mark Brown's chapters in this volume proffer a different reading of the relationship between punitive development and modernity. As both highlight by reference to historical record, the self-same practices often identified as characteristic of the new punitiveness can also be identified in the penal repertoire of Western societies in their immediate past. Risk management and penal excess, for example, appear repeatedly in the penal repertoire of Western colonial states. Whether in the Congo of King Leopold or the brutal treatment of the rebels by the British following their suppression during the Indian Mutiny, penal excess has always featured prominently in the colonizing mission of otherwise 'civilized' societies. Could it therefore be that what the new punitiveness represents is less something new but more a movement towards a future already prefigured in the past; or indeed, as Coleman and Sim argue in this volume, a present defined not by notions of rupture but of tragic continuity?

Mark Brown develops such an argument by looking to liberal political doctrine itself as the source of contemporary tendencies toward penal severity and exclusion. Though there are manifest continuities in the techniques and practices of exclusion utilized by states over time, his emphasis on liberal thought and doctrine points to more fundamental drivers of the tendency toward severity and exclusion. He locates the origin of liberalism's exclusions in the defence of despotism and the elaboration of 'appropriate' forms of colonial government provided by liberal theorists like John Stuart Mill. Colonial subjects, he argues, were placed outside the realm of political citizenship enjoyed by the metropolitan subjects of an emerging British democracy during the nineteenth century. And so the techniques and strategies of civic and political exclusion developed in the colonial context can provide a useful lens through which contemporary strategies of exclusion, from civic commitment statutes to mass imprisonment, may be both viewed and understood. Coleman and Sim approach the same issue, of rupture or continuity, stability or change, but they utilize a much more localized analysis of social control processes in order to develop their argument. In their chapter they offer some critical reflections on the 'new penology' thesis of Feeley and Simon (1992; 1994), arguing that such analyses tend to overemphasize rupture at the expense of continuities, thereby foreclosing a consideration of developments in the state and processes surrounding 'the materialization of order'. They stress the importance of thinking of the state as a 'terrain of power relations', which then provides the discussion of morality and risk with a material foundation. These themes are pursued through a detailed analysis of the English city of Liverpool, demonstrating the ways in which neoliberal statecraft has been utilized in the building of an entrepreneurial city and associated forms of local crime control practice such as CCTV, with particular emphasis on political spatial dynamics and the struggles and resistances generated around attempts to exclude 'hindrances to entrepreneurial growth' such as 'youth, traders, homeless people, and unregulated thrill-seekers'.

As critical criminologists have demonstrated (again and again), crime is not something perpetrated by the poor alone. The crimes of the rich and powerful, for example, far outweigh in terms of material and social cost the damage occasioned by street robbers who derive predominantly from poor communities. Likewise, more people are routinely seriously injured or killed as a consequence of breaches of health and safety regulations in the workplace than are injured or die through being a victim of a street mugging. It is corporations, not the underclass, who are responsible for despoiling the environment; and it is corporations like Enron that perpetrate the most fraud and who have been able to do so with the complicit support of prominent firms of accountants and, not least, politicians. However, the sanctions emanating from the new punitiveness are unlikely to be directed against corrupt businessmen, accountants, and politicians. Nor are these communities subject to the level of surveillance and coercive regulation routinely applied to poorer sections of the community. When we consider the populations whose activities have been subject to visceral sentences, and disproportionate and cruel punishment, then they derive almost universally from populations that typically experience the most entrenched patterns of deprivation, poverty, and social exclusion. Any attempt to think through the implications of the new punitiveness must bear this point in mind. It is not a response to crime in general or indeed to the most serious crime; rather, it is a response directed at populations who in many respects are among society's most disadvantaged.

There remains a sharp ethnic dimension to the prison intake that also bears mention. As Wacquant illustrates in his chapter, visible ethnic minorities – in particular those who derive from black communities – appear disproportionately represented in the prison population as a whole – and this would appear to be the case in every English-speaking jurisdiction. In the USA it is now estimated that one in ten black adult men will at some point have been processed through its carceral system. In addition, 'one in nine of African-American males aged 20–29 is in prison at any one point and one in three is either in prison, on probation or parole' (Mauer, cited in Young, 1999: 147). Again, although rising imprisonment among males accounts for the vast majority of the carceral inflation of the last three decades, the rate at which women have been imprisoned has also increased dramatically. Other constituencies who, until recently, were able to avoid serious penal sanctions now appear more likely than before to find themselves subject to punitive disposition. In the case of the USA, for example, the death penalty is now applied both to young people and to those who have been certified as mentally ill. In the immediate past it would have been unthinkable to punish such populations in this way.

Explaining the new punitiveness

Though considerable theoretical differences exist in relation to grasping the nature of the causal forces at work in generating the punitive turn, most accept that its appearance is related to the social changes that have radically reshaped the cultural, political, and economic landscapes of Western societies from the 1970s onwards. Where commentators differ is in their interpretation of these changes and the causal significance they consequently ascribe to particular structures and processes at play within them.

For Garland (2001), the new punitiveness represents an irrational adaptation on the part of a state whose limits have been exposed by rising crime and by its failure to contain it. In terms of this narrative, the punitive response is not a sign of state strength and power but rather an expression of its weakness. What it represents, Garland argues, is nothing less than a symbolic attempt to reassert through violent means the sovereignty that rising crime in the post war period has challenged. Though a will to violence is certainly manifest in this response, Garland does not view such an adaptation as itself the only or indeed most significant response to the challenge posed by perennially high-crime societies. The culture of control is also expressed in other ways that represent a more rational and, he implicitly suggests, more proportionate response. The state responds to failure by seeking to delegate the business of crime management increasingly to local communities and individuals through strategies of responsibilization. It also embraces and drives a more rational form of crime prevention engineered through environmental modification. This tactic evident in the rise of situational crime prevention departs from the older and discredited welfare model of control, by not seeking to respond to the causes of crime, but by engineering incremental change that renders its commission more difficult. Considered through this theoretical lens, what the new punitiveness represents is only one of several adaptations on the part of a state whose response to crime remains highly volatile but also contradictory.

While, for Garland, the state's readiness to deploy violence is expressive of its weakness, this is not a standpoint that is generally found among those who write within a neo-Marxist framework of analysis. While accepting with Garland that the punitive shift is an adaptation to the failures of welfare state capitalism and the social mode of regulation with which it was associated, other critical penology scholars typically consider the new punitiveness to be indicative of the rise of a new and exceptional state form. Its appearance is particularly evident in societies that have become restructured around neoliberal states that promote free-market principles. Among writers such as Wacquant (this volume) we find the new punitiveness examined, not as an irrational expression of state weakness, nor as a rational response to rising crime, but as an integral aspect of control in post-welfare state societies. What is distinctive about the neoliberal state and what distinguishes it from its welfare state predecessor is that it no longer aspires to rid society of crime as the architects of the welfare state settlement had once dreamed. This is not a state, in other words, that is attached to older and distinctly modern norms of inclusion and homogenous reduction *vis-à-vis* its outside. The neoliberal state is a state form ideologically committed instead to a more exclusionary agenda. Like the welfare state, its functional role is certainly to manage the inevitable problems that capitalism generates, such as rising crime. Unlike the welfare state, the neoliberal state, however, is prepared to sanction more coercive measures to regulate the consequences.

In creating the preconditions for rising crime, ruling elites have exacted a functional payoff that operates at both a material and ideological level. On the one hand, the rising patterns of interpersonal violent crime that directly result from free market economics were used to justify swingeing cuts to the welfare state under the 'nothing works' mantra. Rising crime also provided law-and-order authorians with the legitimating rationale they required for (re)selling punitive 'solutions' to crime back to an ever more insecure and security-conscious public. On the other hand, by making the 'fight against crime' a number one public priority, the preconditions were established for the rapid growth and expansion of the penal industrial complex and in particular the private security industries to whom the state increasingly delegates the grim business of control.

Considered through this theoretical lens, the re-arrival of old punishments such as the death penalty and the chain gang and the advent of new forms of policing such as zero tolerance do not represent an irrational response to the exposure of the state's limits. On the contrary, the new punitiveness exemplifies a far more sinister expression of malevolence and design on the part of dominant elites who have benefited politically, culturally, and economically from the consequent formation of what Christie (2000) has termed 'gulags, western style'. Their gain, however, remains society's loss in so far as the resulting penal experiment entails what Wacquant identifies as a terrifying expansion in the number of poor people now subject to 'punitive tutelage'; in particular, the black population which appears over-represented at every level in the American carceral gulag. As his chapter indicates, what the punitive shift exemplifies is a new and deadly symbiosis between the ghetto and the prison in a state where poverty has become fully criminalised.

However, a key problem encountered among those who have sought to study the new punitiveness lies in attempting to explain how and why the violence that inheres to it has come to be considered socially acceptable. Modern societies, after all, not only defined themselves in terms that implied a profound distaste for violence and the punitive dispositions with which its use is associated but also have taken considerable effort to expel such tendencies from their penal repertoire. Consequently the re-arrival of punitive sensibilities within such societies needs to be explained and accounted for. How and why in societies that proclaim themselves humane and civilised, and which are organised around a core of rationality, could punishments be licensed that appear so contrary to their nature?

For Pratt, the answer to this question is found by studying the social processes at play within contemporary societies that now act to evoke punitive dispositions while also undermining those structures and processes which, in the modern period, had historically emerged to suppress their expression. In so doing, his aim is to account for the emergent culture of punishment that now underpins the contemporary will to violence evident in the new punitiveness. Methodologically this involves studying not only the forces at play that encourage punitive development but, as a precursor to this, identifying the articulation of social forces that had historically inhibited their expression in the development of the modern state.

Drawing upon the work of Elias, Pratt argues in this volume that the key to understanding how and why violence was eventually rescinded in the formation of the modern state lies in understanding how the civilizing process reconfigured its structure. Such reconfiguration during the nineteenth and twentieth centuries helped to provide the emerging self-image of the modern state as 'civilized': one of the signifiers came to be the way in which it punished its offenders – behind the scenes, avoiding punishments to the body, developed and monitored by bureaucratic expertise, in stark contrast to the punishment practices of the 'uncivilized world'. However, to account for the rise of punitive dispositions that would come to license the new punitiveness, Pratt develops the idea of a decivilizing process. This, he argues, does not entail a full reversal of the totality of processes constitutive of the civilizing process. Decivilizing trends can occur, he argues, alongside others that promote its development. With the advent of the neoliberal state, the authority of the central state is reconfigured in ways characterized by a process of fragmentation that would see many of the responsibilities it had accumulated delegated back towards communities now expected to manage them. These include, as Garland has identified, the responsibility for managing the risks and dangers inherent in modern life.

This trend occurs alongside a wider dislocating series of processes wherein the interdependencies that had traditionally stabilized social relations within the modern state become progressively undermined. Those subject to such dislocations consequently come to feel more insecure and more prone to emotional outbursts in a world where security and certainty are perceived as absent. Rising crime in the post-war period, coupled with the failure of established penal bureaucracies to manage it, feed this insecurity further and this is escalated by the sensational reporting of crime by the mass media. From being a problem the public were once prepared to delegate to professionals they trusted to manage it, crime comes instead to be perceived as a problem out of control, with liberal professionals unable to manage it. It is these factors, Pratt argues, that taken together create the preconditions for the rise of the punitive sensibilities that reveal themselves in the new punitiveness.

What the emerging culture of punishment then produces is a state formation organized around a new axis of penal power. If the state fragments in some areas in the field of crime control, it has responded instead by hardening itself further in others. Far from delegating the role of punishment to distant restricted professional elites, the business of crime is now mediated through a new and more active relationship between government and a public.

Organization of the book

The themes associated with the new punitiveness that we have raised in this introduction are variously addressed throughout the book. However, we have chosen to group the chapters around the following main subject areas in this sequence:

Punitive trends

In this section, the chapters by Wacquant, David Brown and Hinds address the varying dimensions and specifics of the new punitiveness, with particular reference to the United States and Australia. These are then followed by the chapter from Lynch, which focuses on the unique convergence in the United States of supermax and the death penalty; from Moore and Hannah-Moffat, who examine the implications of new penal trends on women offenders in Canada; and from Coleman and Sim who explore local tensions and dynamics around enhancements of penal control in the English city of Liverpool.

Globalization, technology and surveillance

Here the chapters by Baker and Roberts, Ryan, and Franko Aas variously explore the way in which the new punitiveness can be seen as the product of globalization, notwithstanding the local variations and manifestations of it. Not only this, but the technological advancements that are themselves a prerequisite for globalization also lead to new possibilities for the surveillance of individual offenders, as the chapter by Nellis illustrates. Importantly, then, the new punitiveness is not simply made up of intolerance, longer prison sentences, and a greater public involvement in the penal framework; it also equips this framework with an enhanced technological efficiency and pervasiveness.

Non-punitive societies

But international penal trends are not moving all in one direction. In this section we provide examples and varying explanations of why some modern societies are manifestly not following these trends. Specifically, the chapters from Bondeson, Meyer and O'Malley, and Nelken look successively at Scandinavia, Canada and Italy.

Explanations

Finally, what might have caused the new punitiveness to take the form that it undoubtedly has in other modern societies? And does this represent something 'new' as Hallsworth (postmodernism) and Pratt (decivilizing processes) maintain; or is it something which has much deeper roots within modernity itself, as the chapters by Mark Brown and Morrison argue?

References

Christie, N. (2000) 'Crime Control as Industry', London: Martin Robertson.

Feely, M. and Simon, J. (1992) 'The New Penology: Notes on the Emerging Strategy of Corrections and its Implications', *Criminology*, 30(4): 449–74.

Feely, M. and Simon, J. (1994) 'Actuarial Justice: The Emerging Criminal Law', in D. Nelken (ed.) *The Futures of Criminology*, London: Sage, 173–201.

Garland, D. (2001) *The Culture of Control*, Oxford: Oxford University Press.

Georgia Department of Corrections (1996) *Annual Report*, Atlanta: Department of Corrections.

Georgia State Board of Corrections (1965) *Annual Report*, Atlanta: Department of Corrections.

Kable v *DPP* (NSW) (1996) 189 CLR 51.

Kansas v *Hendricks* 1997 WL 338555 (US).

Foucault, M. (1977) *Discipline and Punish*, London: Allen Lane.

Lutkin, K. (1998) 'Contemporary Penal Trend: Modern or Postmodern', *British Journal of Criminology*, 38(1): 106–23.

O'Malley, P. (1999) 'Volatile and Contradictory Punishment', *Theoretical Criminology*, 3(2): 175–96.

Pratt, J. (2000) 'Emotive and Ostentatious Punishment: its decline and resurgence in modern society', *Punishment and Society*, 4: 417–440.

Pratt, J. (2001) 'Beyond "Gulags Western style"?', *Theoretical Criminology*, 5: 283–314.

Pratt, J. and Clark, M. (2005) 'Penal Populism in New Zealand', *Punishment and Society* (in press).

Van Swaningen, R. (2004) 'Crime Control and the Management of Fear', Joint BSC Manheim Lecture Series (unpublished paper).

Young, J. (1999) *The Exclusive Society: Social Exclusion, Crime and Difference in Late Modernity*, London: Sage.

Zimring, F. (1996) 'Populism, Democratic Government and the Decline of Expert Authority', *Pacific Law Journal*, 28: 243–256.

Part 1

Punitive Trends

1. The great penal leap backward: Incarceration in America from Nixon to Clinton

Loïc Wacquant

In 1967, as the Vietnam War and race riots were roiling the country, President Lyndon B. Johnson received a report on America's judicial and correctional institutions from a group of government experts. The Commission on Law Enforcement and Administration of Justice related that the inmate count in federal penitentiaries and state prisons was slowly diminishing, by about 1 per cent per annum (President's Commission on Law Enforcement and Administration of Justice, 1967). That year, America's penal establishments held some 426,000 inmates, projected to grow to 523,000 in 1975 as a by-product of national demographic trends. Neither prison overcrowding nor the inflation of the population behind bars was on the horizon, even as crime rates were steadily rising. Indeed, the federal government professed to accelerate this downward carceral drift through the expanded use of probation and parole and the generalization of community sanctions aimed at diverting offenders from confinement. Six years later, it was Richard Nixon's turn to receive a report on the evolution of the US carceral system. The National Advisory Commission on Criminal Justice Standards and Goals noted that the population under lock had stopped receding. But it nonetheless recommended a ten-year moratorium on the construction of large correctional facilities as well as the phasing out of establishments for the detention of juveniles. It counselled shifting away decisively from the country's 'pervasive overemphasis on custody' because it was proven that 'the prison, the reformatory, and the jail have achieved nothing but a shocking record of failure. There is overwhelming evidence that these institutions create crime rather than prevent it' (National Advisory Commission on Criminal Justice Standards and Goals, 1973: 597).

At about the same time, Alfred Blumstein and his associates put forth their so-called homeostatic theory of the level of incarceration in modern societies. According to the renowned criminologist, each country presents not a 'normal' level of crime, as Emile Durkheim had proposed a century before in his classic theory of deviance, but a constant level of punishment resulting in a roughly stable rate of penal confinement outside of 'severely disruptive periods like wars or depressions'. When this rate departs from its natural threshold, various stabilizing mechanisms are set into motion: the police, prosecutors, courts, and parole boards adjust their response to crime in a permissive or restrictive direction so as to redraw the boundary of deviant behaviours subjected to penal sanction, adjust sentences, and thereby reduce or increase the volume of people behind bars. The proof for this view was found in time-series analyses of the feeble oscillations of the imprisonment rates revealed by US statistics since the Great Depression and by Canadian and Norwegian statistics since the closing decades of the nineteenth century (see Blumstein and Cohen, 1973; Blumstein *et al.*, 1977; see also Zimring and Hawkins, 1991).

As for the revisionist historians of the penal institution, from David Rothman to Michael Ignatieff by way of Michel Foucault, they substituted a strategic narrative of power for the humanistic trope of enlightened reform and painted imprisonment not merely as a stagnant institution but as a practice in irreversible if gradual decline, destined to occupy a secondary place in the diversifying arsenal of contemporary instruments of punishment. Thus Rothman concluded his historiographic account of the concurrent invention of the penitentiary for criminals, the asylum for the insane, and the almshouse for the poor in the Jacksonian republic by sanguinely asserting that the United States was 'gradually escaping from institutional responses' so that 'one can foresee the period when incarceration will be used still more rarely than it is today' (Rothman, 1971: 295; see also Ignatieff, 1978). For Foucault, 'the carceral technique' played a pivotal part in the advent of the 'disciplinary society', but only inasmuch as it became diffused throughout the 'social body as a whole' and fostered the transition from 'inquisitory justice' to 'examinatory justice'. The prison turned out to be only one island among many in the vast 'carceral archipelago' of modernity that links into a seamless panoptic web the family, the school, the convent, the hospital, and the factory, and of which the human sciences unwittingly partake: 'In the midst of all these apparatuses of normalization which are becoming tighter, the specificity of the prison and its role as hinge lose something of their raison d'être' (Foucault, 1978: 306; my translation).

Spotlighting this tendency towards the dispersal of social control exercised by the state, the radical sociology of the prison hastened to denounce the anticipated perverse effects of 'decarceration'. Andrew Scull (1977) maintained that the movement to release inmates, from behind the walls of penitentiaries and mental hospitals alike, into the community worked against the interests of deviant and subordinate groups by giving the state licence to unload its responsibility to care for them. Conversely, Stanley Cohen (1979) warned against the dangers of the new ideology of the 'community control' of crime on grounds that diversion from prison at once blurs, widens, intensifies, and disguises social control under the benevolent mask of 'alternatives to imprisonment'. These academic critiques were echoed for the broader public by such journalistic exposés as Jessica Mitford's portrait of the horrors of America's 'prison business' and of the 'lawlessness of corrections', leading to the denunciation of further prison building as 'the establishment of a form of legal concentration camp to isolate and contain the rebellious and the politically militant' (Mitford, 1973: 291).

In short, by the mid-1970s a broad consensus had formed among state managers, social scientists, and radical critics according to which the future of the prison in America was anything but bright. The rise of a militant prisoners' rights movement patterned after the black insurgency that had brought down the Southern caste regime a decade earlier, including drives to create inmates' unions and to foster convict self-management, and the spread of full-scale carceral uprisings throughout the United States, followed by their diffusion to other Western societies (Canada, England, France, Spain, and Italy), powerfully reinforced this shared sense of an institution mired in unremitting and irretrievable crisis.[1]

The great American carceral boom

Yet nothing could have been further from the truth: the US prison was just about to enter an era not of final doom but of startling boom. Starting in 1973, American penal evolution abruptly reversed course and *the population behind bars underwent exponential growth*, on a scale without precedent in the history of democratic societies. On the morrow of the 1971 Attica revolt, acme of a wide and powerful internal movement of protest against the carceral order,[2] the United States sported a rate of incarceration of 176 per 100,000 inhabitants – two to three times the rate of the major European countries. By 1985, this rate had doubled to reach 310 before doubling again over the ensuing decade to pass the 700-mark in mid-2000 (see Table 1.1). To gauge how extreme this scale of confinement is, suffice it to note that it is about 40 per cent higher than South Africa's at the height of the armed struggle against apartheid and six to twelve times the rate of the countries of the European Union, even though the latter have also seen their imprisonment rate rise rapidly over the past two decades. During the period 1985–1995, the United States amassed nearly one million more inmates at a pace of an additional 1,631 bodies per week, equivalent to incorporating the confined population of France every six months. As of 30 June 2000, when runaway growth finally

Table 1.1 Growth of the carceral population of the United States, 1975–2000

	1975	1980	1985	1990	1995	2000
County jails	138,800	182,288	256,615	405,320	507,044	621,149
Federal and state prisons	240,593	315,974	480,568	739,980	1,078,357	1,310,710
Total	379,393	498,262	737,183	1,145,300	1,585,401	1,931,850
Growth index	100	131	194	302	418	509

Source: Bureau of Justice Statistics, *Historical Corrections Statistics in the United States, 1850–1984* (Washington, Government Printing Office, 1986); *ibid, Prison and Jail Inmates at Midyear 2000* (Washington, Government Printing Office, 2001).

There are three main types of carceral establishments in the United States. The 3,300 city and county *jails* house suspects brought in by the police, awaiting arraignment or trial, as well as convicts in transit between facilities or sanctioned by terms of confinement inferior to one year. The 1,450 *state prisons* of the 50 members of the Union hold felons sentenced to terms exceeding one year, while those convicted under the federal penal code are sent to one of the 125 *federal prisons*, irrespective of the length of their sentence. Each sector possesses its own enumeration system, which explains discrepancies in the data over time (including when they come from the same source). This census excludes establishments for juveniles, military prisons (which held 2,400 inmates at end of 2000), facilities run by the Immigration and Naturalization Service (8,900), prisons in US overseas territories (16,000), and jails in Indian reservations (1,800). It also omits police lock-ups, which are more numerous than jails (in 1993, 3,200 police departments operated one or more such facilities with an average capacity of ten detainees).[3]

seemed to taper off, the population held in county jails, state prisons, and federal penitentiaries had reached 1,931,000 and crossed the two-million milestone if one reckons juveniles in custody (109,000).

One might think that after 15 years of such frenetic growth American jails and prisons would reach saturation and that certain of the homeostatic mechanisms postulated by Blumstein would kick in. Indeed, by the early 1990s, federal penitentiaries were officially operating at 146 per cent of capacity and state prisons at 131 per cent, even though the number of establishments had tripled in 30 years and wardens had taken to systematically 'double-bunking' inmates. In 1992, 40 of 50 states and the District of Columbia were under court order to remedy overpopulation and stem the deterioration of conditions of detention on pain of heavy fines and prohibitions on further incarceration. Many jurisdictions took to hastily releasing thousands of nonviolent inmates to disgorge their facilities and over 50,000 convicts sentenced to terms exceeding one year were consigned to county facilities in 1995 for want of space in state prisons.

But America's carceral bulimia did not abate: at the end of the single year 1995, as Clinton prepared to campaign for re-election on a platform of 'community, responsibility, and opportunity' buttressed by the 'end of Big Government', an additional 107,300 found themselves behind bars, corresponding to an extra 2,064 inmates per week. Eight states had seen their carceral population grow by more than 50 per cent between 1990 and 1995: Arizona, Wisconsin, Georgia, Minnesota, Mississippi, Virginia, North Carolina, and Texas, which held the national record with a doubling in a short five years. As early as 1993, six states each counted more inmates than France (see Table 1.2). California, with 32 million inhabitants, confined nearly as many as the eleven largest continental countries of the European Union put together. Georgia, with a mere seven million residents, had more inmates than Italy with 50 million.

Table 1.2 The states leading carceral expansion in 1993

	State & federal prisons	County jails	Total incarcerated	Incarceration rate per 100,000 residents
California	119,951	69,298	189,249	607
Texas	71,103	55,395	126,498	700
New York	64,569	29,809	94,378	519
Florida	53,048	34,183	87,231	636
Ohio	40,641	11,695	52,336	473
Michigan	39,529	12,479	52,008	550
France	>	>	**51,457**	**84**
Georgia	27,783	22,663	50,446	730
Illinois	34,495	14,549	49,044	420
Pennsylvania	26,050	19,231	45,281	376
United States	**948,881**	**459,804**	**1,408,685**	**546**

Sources: For city and county jails, Bureau of Justice Statistics, *Jail and Jail Inmates 1993–94* (Washington, Bureau of Justice Statistics, 1996); for federal and state prisons, *idem*, *Prisoners in 1993* (Washington, Government Printing Office, 1994; Printing Office, 1995); for state populations, estimates by the U.S. Census Bureau, available on line.

And this is but the emerging point of the American penal iceberg. For these figures do not take account of offenders placed on probation or released on parole after having served the greater part of their sentence (typically 85 per cent by virtue of federal 'truth-in-sentencing' mandates). Now, their numbers far surpass the inmates count and they too increased steeply following the penal turnaround of the mid-1970s. Between 1980 and 2000, the total number of persons on probation leapt from 1.1 million to 3.8 million while those on parole shot from 220,000 to nearly 726,000. As a result, *the population placed under correctional supervision approached 6.5 million* at the end of this period, as against 4.3 million ten years earlier and under 1 million in 1975. These 6.5 million individuals represent 3 per cent of the country's adult population and one American male in 20 (Table 1.3).

Table 1.3 Population under correctional supervision in the United States in 2000 (in thousands).

	Probation	Jail	Prison	Parole	Total
1980	1,118	184	320	220	1,842
1985	1,969	257	488	300	3,013
1990	2,670	405	743	531	4,350
1995	3,078	507	1,078	679	5,343
2000	3,840	621	1,312	726	6,467
n blacks	1,306	255	604	319	2,484
% adult black males	12.2	2.4	5.6	3.0	23.2

Bureau of Justice Statistics, *Correctional Populations in the United States, 2000* (Washington: Government Printing Office, 2002), p. 2 and Census Bureau estimates of US population by race and age.

Breaking that figure down by ethnicity reveals that one black man in nine today is under criminal oversight. We will indeed see in this chapter that the massive and rapidly growing over-representation of African Americans at all levels of the penal system expresses the new role that the latter has assumed in the panoply of instruments of racial domination since the ghetto uprisings of the 1960s.

A correctional Marshall Plan

Another reliable indicator of the stupendous prosperity of the penal economy of the United States in the past two decades is that the 'corrections' rubric in the country's budget soared from $9 billion in 1982 to $54 billion in 1999. It now consumes a full third of direct public expenditures devoted to crime control of $160 billion, behind $70 billion for the police and well ahead of the $36 billion allotted to the courts. For the first time in modern American history, local governments spend more on criminal justice than they do on education, since 1977 in the case of cities and since 1982 as concerns counties. And this gap has been growing since crime control budgets at all levels have risen faster than other public expenditures: in 1995, in spite of several years of steadily declining crime rates, the states were set to augment their corrections outlays by an average of 8 per cent per year, as against a 4.3 per cent increase for schools and 2.1 per cent for the main assistance programmme for destitute households, Aid to Families with

Dependent Children (AFDC).[4] Between 1977 and 1999, total state and local government funds for all functions rose by 400 per cent; education budgets grew by only 370 per cent, hospitals and health care by 418 per cent, while corrections exploded by 946 per cent.

The result of this priority given to penal over social functions is that incarceration has overtaken the two main programmes of assistance to the poor in the nation's budget (see Table 1.4). In 1980, the United States spent three times more on Aid to Families with Dependent Children and food stamps taken together than it did on operating its jails and prisons ($11 billion plus $10 billion versus $7 billion); in 1985, these three programmes received each the same sum of about $13 billion; ten years later, on the eve of the abolition of 'welfare as we know it' on account of its excessive drain on the government's coffer, incarceration surpassed AFDC by 130 per cent and food stamps by 70 per cent. Yet there is scarcely any mention in the official debate on crime of the burden that an out-of-control correctional system places on taxpayers. Worse yet, on the heels of the most costly criminal justice package ever voted in world history, the Omnibus Crime Control Act of 1994, Congress passed the 1995 No Frills Prison Act, which compels states to apply 'truth-in-sentencing' provisions (on pain of losing federal funds earmarked for prison construction) requiring that all convicts serve at least 85 per cent of their sentence before being eligible for parole release, thereby guaranteeing massive across-the-board increases in correctional expenditures for years to come.

Table 1.4 Comparative evolution of correctional and public aid budgets, 1980–1995 (in billions of current dollars).

	1980	1982	1984	1986	1988	1990	1992	1993	1995
Corrections (state and federal)	6.9	9.0	11.8	15.8	20.3	26.1	31.5	31.9	46.2
Aid to Families with Dependent Children	10.9	12.1	13.4	14.3	15.5	17.1	20.4	20.3	19.9
Food Stamps	9.6	11.7	13.3	13.5	14.4	17.7	24.9	26.3	27.4

Source: Kathleen Maguire et Ann L. Pastore (dir.), *Sourcebook of Criminal Justice Statistics 1996* (Washington, Bureau of Justice Statistics, 1997), p.3; Lea Gifford, *Justice Expenditures and Employment in the United States, 1995*, Washington, Bureau of Justice Statistics, November 1999, p. 8; and Committee on Ways and Means, *1996 Green Book*, Washington, Government Printing Office, 1997, pp. 459, 861, 921.

The same disproportionate expansion in favour of penal functions has affected county and state employment: while the staff devoted to social services and education has stagnated or decreased over the past two decades, the American crime-fighting machine has doubled its personnel to 2.2 million in 1999, including 717,000 in correctional administrations, taking in an annual payroll of some $8 billion (Gifford, 2002). Fourteen states and the District of Columbia now have over 13 per cent of their employees in the justice system (in Florida, Nevada and the District of Columbia, this share approaches one in five). To say the least, the doctrine of 'small government' and the policy of downsizing public employment have not applied to penal confinement, whose unit cost has also risen steadily. In 1996, operating expenditures for state prisons came up to $20,142 per inmate after a 20 per cent increase in a decade in constant dollars,[5] with most large prison states of the East and Midwest falling in the 20,000- to 30,000-dollar range and Southern states lagging noticeably behind – seven of the eight states with annual costs inferior to $14,000 per inmate were located in the South, led by Alabama with a measly $7,987. Given that staff salaries and wages consume about half of total prison operating expenses, these regional disparities are explained primarily by lower pay and by the much higher inmate-to-staff ratio common in the South: in 1998, Alabama had one correctional employee for every 7 prisoners compared with one for 3.8 for California and one for 2.6 in Michigan and Minnesota.

'Government recognizes that it cannot allow the growth rate in its corrections budgets to continue at the pace of recent history. The private sector is the best way to constrain this growth. We save money on the front end, then hold increases to a minimum. At CCA, we understand the enormous opportunity this presents for our future'. (Corrections Corporation of America, 1997: 5). As this address to investors by the chief executive officer of Corrections Corporation of America indicates, the mad dash to mass imprisonment into which the United States has thrown itself has spawned *a new and thriving industry, private incarceration*, whose growth and profit rates rivalled those of the leading sectors of the national economy at the height of the mid-1990s' boom.[6] Two forces combined to foster the resurgence of for-profit imprisonment a half-century after the banning of the Southern convict-lease system, the one ideological and the other material.

The first is the ascendancy of the doctrine of privatization orchestrated by neoconservative think-tanks and widely relayed by the mainstream media and the established parties. Whether to care for orphans, to deliver health and social services, or to supply housing for the poor, successive governments since Ronald Reagan have consistently turned to firms and charitable organizations to carry out public missions. This 'new bipartisan consensus on market principles as the template for social policy' (Katz, 1996: 314) was extended to encompass corrections under the press of the second factor of material expediency. For counties and states simply did not have the capacity to contain the onrushing flood of inmates they unleashed: they possess neither the fiscal and human resources nor the bureaucratic agility to finance, design, build and staff the thousands of additional cells they have needed every year.[7] So they turned to specialized firms that promised to deliver facilities in short order while trimming the costs of confinement by 10 to 20 per cent per head, thanks to their ready access to the bond market, the low wages and paltry benefits they provide their guards (who, unlike their colleagues in the public sector, are not unionized), and their licence to circumvent cumbersome bureaucratic regulations. As a result, in just over a decade, privately built and operated facilities went from nonexistent to forming an integral and seemingly irreversible component of the US carceral system, extending across all security levels and present in two dozen states, where they contribute up to a quarter of total capacity: 'A critical mass has been reached in terms of prison and inmates numbers and percentages, custodial responsibilities as manifested by security ratings, participating states, and commercial maturity.

In addition, the financing arrangements tie governments in private sector participation in ways that would be difficult to unscramble' (Harding, 1999: 635).

Aside from supplying the gamut of goods and services required for operating a custodial facility (furniture, food, maintenance, health care, safety and surveillance, communication systems, etc.) as well as correctional services (such as education, drug treatment, and psychological counselling), which have long been largely contracted out to the commercial sector, by the late 1990s a dozen firms divided up the fast-growing market for the financing, construction, and management of private establishments of detention. In 1997, there were still only about 100 of them, distributed across 19 states, but they were spreading at vertiginous speed. From zero in 1983 at the founding of Correctional Corporation of America, the number of 'private beds' in the United States escalated to 15,000 in 1990 before surpassing 85,000 in 1997, corresponding to some 6 per cent of the country's carceral population (and equal to the inmate count of Spain and Italy put together). That year, one-quarter of the 100,000 new beds put 'on line' by the country's correctional system came from the private sector. With revenues doubling every two years and a seemingly infinite supply of new bodies to warehouse, it is no wonder that the top managers of the major corrections firms were unanimous in predicting in 1998 that their market share would at least triple over the ensuing decade.[8] The facilities director for the fourth largest enterprise in the industry commented thus:

> The era of prejudice against private prisons is behind us. More and more states are looking at privatization without that sort of prejudice, because it's been around long enough now, where there was a really big 'wait-and-see' attitude, and some states were very reluctant. But once privatization proved to be a viable alternative to the states, then more and more states are doing it too. And it's less expensive than the public sector to do it this way...
> Q: So this movement of opposition to the privatization of prisons is behind us?
> It's dying. And that's spilling over into the juvenile field too: more and more states and counties are looking into privatization in the juvenile area.

With 26 federal prisons and 96 state penitentiaries under construction in 1996, the financing of carceral building had become one of the most profitable sectors in the bonds market. This was not lost on the big Wall Street brokerage firms, such as Goldman Sachs, Smith Barney Shearson, Prudential-Bache, and Merrill Lynch, who sunk two to three billion dollars per year into it during the 1990s (Gragg, 1996: 50). The siting of penitentiaries has by the same token turned into a potent tool for regional economic development. Towns in declining monoindustrial regions and remote rural areas in particular spared no effort to attract them: 'Gone are the days when communities greeted the prospect of prisons with chants of "Not in my backyard!" Prisons do not use a lot of chemicals, do not create noise or atmospheric pollutants and do not lay off workers during recessions.' To the contrary, they promise to bring with them stable jobs, regular business and perennial tax receipts. Imprisonment is a thriving industry with a bright future, and with it all those who have an interest connected to American carceral hyperinflation (see Gibbons and Pierce, 1995; and the documentary movie by

Hurling, 1999). A large-scale market in the import–export of inmates has emerged, as correctional operators in areas with available beds court jurisdictions with a surplus of bodies desperate for room in which to lock them. As of 2000, some 15,000 inmates were kept in facilities outside their state of conviction. The deep crisis that shook up the private incarceration industry in the wake of the bursting of the stock-market and technology 'bubble' in 2000 has stopped its runaway growth but it has failed to significantly curtail its role in the penal economy of the country.

The crime–incarceration disconnection

How are we to explain this 'great leap forward' of the American carceral apparatus when all the observers of the penal scene agreed in forecasting its downturn – if not, for the boldest of them, its extinction – only a quarter of a century ago? The official doctrine on the matter, diffused conjointly by state managers, elected officials, and the media, is that it is a response to the relentless growth of crime, and especially violent crime (that is, offences against persons as distinct from offences against property). After the aborted 'War on Poverty' of the 1960s, the US government decided to wage a 'War on Crime' and devoted the necessary means to it (see Andreas, 1997). This endeavour was supported by a public that has been increasingly and intensely concerned about its safety as crime diffused throughout society. But there is a catch: this common-sense argument is directly contradicted by all the available data, provided that one examines it closely.

First, with few exceptions, well localized in time and space, crime rates have not increased but have *stagnated and then declined* over the past three decades. Next, the vast majority of new convicts thrown behind bars have not been dangerous and hardened criminals but small-time, non-violent offenders. And, finally, contrary to the obsessive drumbeat of the media, which have made commercial hay out of the daily spectacle of criminal violence, most Americans have had little reason to live in terror of anonymous physical aggression, for the latter remains strongly concentrated in social and physical space.[9]

As Figure 1.1 shows, the gross volume of crimes and misdemeanours committed in the United States remained roughly constant and then declined during the period corresponding to the steep take-off of the carceral population. From 1973 to 1982, in good years and bad, about 40 million Americans were victims of criminal offences. By 1992 this figure had fallen to about 35 million – and this decline has accelerated since to reach a low of 25 million in 2000. A close reading of the findings of the National Crime Victimization Survey confirms the drop in major criminal infractions and directly refutes the idea that the explosion of incarceration results from an upsurge in crime rates.[10] Thus, among offences against persons, the frequency of robberies declined between 1974 and 1978 before rising until 1981; it then headed down again from 1981 to 1985 before slowly increasing until 1994 – all without leaving a narrow range of between 200 and 250 incidents per 100,000 residents. The rate for aggravated assaults receded markedly from 1974 until the mid-1980s before stabilizing and then climbing back to its initial level from 1990 to 1993; it then fell sharply to reach its lowest

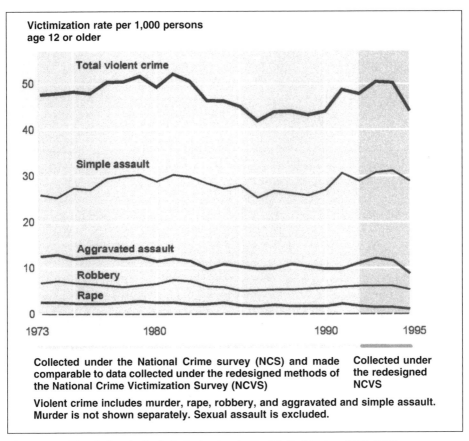

Figure 1.1   Trends in criminal victimization in the United States, 1973–1995.
Source: Bureau of Justice Statistics, *Criminal Victimization in the United States, 1975–1995* (Washington, US Department of Justice, 1997)

point in 23 years. Constant from 1977 to 1979 after a three-year rise, the probability of being a victim of assault has declined without interruption since; today it is at the same level as at the end of the 1960s.

According to the FBI's annual *Uniform Crime Reports*, the murder and non-negligent manslaughter rate fluctuated between 8 and 10 per 100,000 inhabitants between 1975 and 1995 without showing any particular trend in either direction. To be sure, the number of murders recorded by the Federal Bureau of Investigation exceeded 23,300 in 1994, as against 20,700 eight years earlier, but as a proportion of the country's population their occurrence was virtually unchanged. And, again, since 1995 the murder rate has declined markedly to close in on 5 per 100,000 in 2000 (corresponding to 12,943 victims). As for offences concerning property (burglary, simple theft, and auto theft), their frequency went down uniformly and continuously from 1974 to 1995, with the exception of the period 1985 to 1990 for motor vehicle theft. Overall, the victimization rate for property crime in the United States dropped steadily from 540 for 1,000 house-holds in 1974 to 385 for 1,000 in 1995, and it has continued to recede in the years since to below 200 in 1999 (US Department of Justice 1997; Blumstein and Wallman 2000).

Finally, during the 1980s the expression 'random violence' became a staple of public discourse about crime and served as blanket justification for the hardening of penal responses. A succession of media panics about 'drive-by shootings' and freeway violence, 'wilding' and stalking, kids and guns, carjackings, gang initiations and so-called sexual predators nourished the collective sense, cemented by the discourse of officials and official criminologists, that violent crime had become pandemic, predatory and unpredictable, and was spiralling out of control. In 1994, the Federal Bureau of Investigation accompanied the release of its latest instalment of the *Uniform Crime Report* with this alarming note: 'Every American now has a realistic chance of murder victimization in view of the random nature that crime has assumed' (cited by Best, 1999: 3). Yet the very data that the FBI compiled directly refutes this notion by displaying the obdurate social and geographic patterning of serious offences against persons. The perennial variables of race, class, and residence have never ceased to determine gaping disparities in chances of victimization. Thus, between 1975 and 1995, the murder rate of whites remained consistently one-sixth that of blacks (it fluctuated between a low of 4.8 and a high of 6.3 per 100,000 while the figures for blacks ranged from 27.7 to 39.3). Throughout that period, the incidence of homicide for white females over 25 years remained extremely low, oscillating between 2.6 and 3.3 per 100,000 – and in the large majority of cases they were killed by lovers and spouses (typically of the same ethnicity), not by strangers. In 1995, the frequency of robberies in the suburbs was one-third that in cities; the rate for suburban white females was 2.0 per 1,000 persons aged twelve and over compared with 24.6 for black men in urban centres. And, at the height of the fear of lethal violence from anonymous black men in public space, widely perceived as the modal crime risk, only 699 of 4,954 white victims had been killed by black assailants, representing a mere 3 per cent of the 22,434 homicides recorded that year (US Department of Justice, 2001: 313, 315; Federal Bureau of Investigation, 1995: 17).

Now, there was a spectacular and abrupt upsurge in murders between 1985 and 1993, but it was anything but 'random': it concerned essentially unemployed young black men in the poor neighbourhoods of big cities, both as perpetrators and as victims. In the dilapidated perimeter of the dark ghetto, the withdrawal of the wage-labour economy combined with the retrenchment of the welfare state to produce inordinately high rates of interpersonal violence fueled by the informalization of the economy, the homogenization of the social structure dominated by dispossessed households, and the waning of communal organizations liable to supply resources and stabilize life strategies. Where the booming crack trade became the leading employment sector for youth from the black subproletariat, violent crime became pandemic, tearing further at the local social and economic fabric (Wacquant, 1994; Wilson, 1996; Currie, 1998). But this lethal trend was well circumscribed within the racialized urban core and sharply divergent from the general tendency of criminality in the rest of the population and country, even as it dominated the media and public perception.

If the number of inmates grew fivefold since the mid-1970s even as crime rates failed to increase, and even curved sharply downward after 1993, it is because recourse to incarceration was vastly expanded and intensified. Over the years, the authorities have applied *penal confinement with growing frequency and severity to all* misdemeanants, petty or not, and felons, violent or not, and with a zeal inversely proportional to the seriousness of the offence. This can be seen in the fact that the share of convicts for violent crimes among admissions to state prisons dwindled from 50 per cent in 1980 to less than 27 per cent by 1990 while the weight of those sentenced for narcotics violations swelled from 7 to 31 per cent. Every year since 1989, convicts jailed for property and drug offences have been *twice as numerous as those confined for violent crimes* (see Figure 1.2). In 1997 for instance, 100,200 convicts entered the gates of state prisons to serve time for a felony against persons; but 102,600 new inmates were admitted for narcotics violations and an additional 94,700 joined them for having committed a property offence. The prison 'class of 1997' counted more burglars than robbers (39,300 versus 30,600), more thieves than criminals found guilty of aggravated assault (23,500 for larceny/theft plus 6,999 for vehicle theft versus 29,800), and nearly four times more convicts for public-order offences than murderers (35,700 versus 9,100) (Department of Justice, 2000: 11).

In 1992, at the acme of America's carceral boom, the typical inmate entering a state correctional facility was a man under 30 years of age (53 per cent of admissions) of African-American origin (nearly 54 per cent) who had not finished high school (for two-thirds of them), imprisoned for a *non-violent offence in over seven cases in ten*. Of the 27 per cent walking in through the gates for having committed a violent crime that year, 11 per cent had been convicted of aggravated assault and 7 per cent of simple assault, as against 5 per cent for sexual crimes and

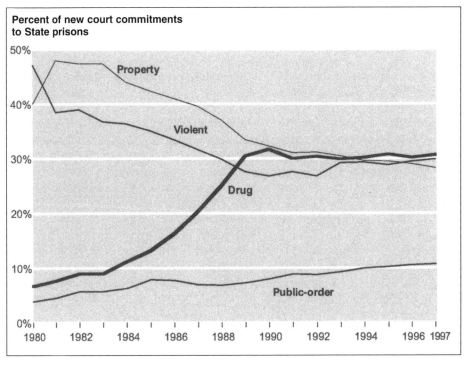

Figure 1.2   Most serious offence of convicts admitted to state prisons, 1980–1997
Source: Department of Justice, *Correctional Population of United States, 1997* (Washington: Government Printing Office, figure 5, p. 13).

only 3.5 per cent for homicide (Irwin and Austin, 1997: 23). These tendencies were particularly pronounced in the states that top the carceral charts. Of every 100 people sentenced to prison in Texas in the early 1990s, 77 were convicted of four lesser categories of infractions: possession and transport of drugs (22 and 15 per cent, respectively) and burglary and theft (20 per cent each). In addition, over half of those sentenced for narcotics offences had been caught for simple possession of *less than one gram* of drugs. California quadrupled its prison population between 1980 and 1993; 76 per cent of that growth was due to the incarceration of nonviolent offenders. This disproportion was even more glaring in federal penitentiaries, where 94 per cent of the 40,000 new inmates admitted in the course of a year during that period entered for nonviolent crimes.[11]

In short, American jails and prisons are overflowing with convicts who would not have been thrown behind bars 30 years ago and who, moreover, would not be rotting there if the public were better informed about the realities of the country's penal policy.[12] What changed during the intervening decades, then, is not the frequency and character of criminal activity but the *attitude of the society and the responses of the authorities toward street delinquency* and its principal source, urban poverty concentrated in the big cities. Since the about-turn of the mid-1970s, the carceral system of the United States serves not only to repress crime: it also has for mission to bolster the social, racial and economic order via the punitive regulation of the behaviours of the categories prone to visible and offensive deviance because they are relegated to the bottom of a polarizing class and caste structure. The prison has been called upon to contain the disorders generated by the rising tide of dispossessed families, street derelicts, unemployed and alienated youths, and the desperation and violence that have accumulated and intensified in the segregated urban core of the metropolis as the 'safety net' of the US semi-welfare state was torn, and desocialized wage labour in the low-wage service sectors was made the normal horizon of work for the deskilled fractions of the working class (see Wacquant, 2004).

The demise of rehabilitation and the politicization of crime

Three causal series have telescoped to make imprisonment America's punishment of choice and to produce the unparalleled carceral hyperinflation the country has witnessed from the Nixon presidency to the second Clinton administration. The first includes a string of *changes internal to the criminal justice system* tied to the demise of rehabilitation as the operant correctional philosophy and the correlative *de-autonomization of penal professionals* leading to a brutal hardening and acceleration in the mode of sentencing.

Hegemonic in America since the interwar period, the idea that imprisonment aims to reform the criminal with a view towards his eventual reintegration into society was abruptly discredited in the 1970s by the unexpected convergence of critiques from the right and the left.[13] Conservatives have at all times held that the primary mission of the prison is to punish and not to rehabilitate: believing that society is composed of two distinct types of individuals, honest citizens ('the innocent') and intrinsically bad deviants ('the wicked'), they contend that incarceration must first of all serve to protect the former by confining the latter within four walls as long as possible.[14] The novelty to come out of the 1960s was that this retrograde vision of the prison found powerful reinforcement in the progressive critique for which rehabilitation was but a sham and the modulation of punishment an illegitimate exercise in state power. The supporters of 'decarceration', sociologists and criminologists of self-professed radical persuasion, argued that educational measures and treatment programmes served mostly to legitimate a 'total institution' (to use Erving Goffman's characterization) that, by definition, corrodes those who are entrusted to it. And they attacked head-on the adjustment of penal sanctions to the individual characteristics of their perpetrators implemented under the regime of 'indeterminate sentencing' on grounds that it gravely disadvantaged convicts from the lower regions of social space, that is, poor people and African Americans.

Under the system of 'indeterminate sentencing' introduced in the 1920s and prevalent until the mid-1970s, the criminal courts condemned an offender to a term of confinement defined by broad parameters (e.g. between two and eight years) while the length of the sentence served was set later by a parole board in response to the inmate's behaviour and perceived advance toward 'rehabilitation'. The progressive reformers of the 1970s denounced the hypocrisy of such an offender-centred 'correctional' paradigm; to avoid rampant discrimination in the administration of justice, they recommended that the discretionary authority of judges be curtailed and that penalties be set *a priori* within strict brackets based essentially on the nature of offence. They were aware that their demand for such a system of 'determinate sentencing' risked lending credibility to the diametrically opposed proposals of the partisans of an extension of the carceral apparatus. But any reform seemed to them preferable to a penal *status quo* deemed intolerable by the libertarian yardstick of the 1960s and theories inspired by anti-psychiatry.[15] And they counted on politicians recoiling from the exorbitant cost of imprisonment to turn eventually towards 'intermediate' or community sanctions. It is an understatement to say that their expectations were cruelly disappointed. Historian David Rothman, who actively participated in this campaign of denigration of the rehabilitation model, draws up its miserable balance sheet in these terms:

> The reformers proved wrong on all counts. Determinate sentences were introduced in the 1980s, both in the federal system and in roughly one-third of the states. But, apart from a few jurisdictions (most notably Minnesota), sentencing guidelines have increased the time served, had relatively little impact on [social and racial] disparity in sentences, promoted prison overcrowding, and reduced the importance of judges in sentencing by enhancing the discretion of prosecutors. The distaste for rehabilitation has contributed as well to making prisons warehouses. If educational and training programs are mischievous and futile, why should the state spend 'money on them?' (Rothman 1995: 33)[16]

This shift of penal philosophy is well illustrated by the changing contents and tone of the run-of-the-mill teaching literature on the prison. A typical 'reader in penology' from the late 1960s portrays the prison as a 'complex organization' geared to the task of 'people-changing' and devotes its core chapters to 'the therapeutic function of prisons'. Even as it inadvertently recognizes that 'most of the "techniques" used in "correcting" criminals have not been shown to be either effective or ineffective and are only vaguely related to any reputable theory of behavior or criminality', *Prison Within Society* confidently asserts that 'the only means by which society can achieve its desired protection is a resocialization of the deviant which leads to his reintegration into society. Mere imprisonment can provide only a short-term protection at best and may in the long run compound the danger from which society seeks some relief' (Hazelrigg 1968: backcover text).[17] Thirty years later, a standard textbook on crime and punishment aimed at the booming market in criminal justice training centres on 'why prisons are built when they are, where they are, and administered as they are'. Its only discussion of offender treatment is to review the special management problems posed inside carceral facilities by 'specific inmate groups, from mentally ill offenders to those suffering from aids, to female inmates and gang members', not to mention the correctional staff. *Incarcerating Criminals* (the shift in title wording speaks volumes) addresses the question of offender employment, for instance, only *intra muros*, firstly as a means of 'reducing the strain that correctional expenditures have placed on state budgets' and second as way of reducing idleness and violence; the question of post-detention employment is never considered. This is because

> [v]ery few Americans today voice the inspiring, enriching motivations behind incarceration that our predecessors held. We approach prisons today with expectations that are minimal – we demand that these institutions keep them away from us, for as long as possible and as inexpensively as possible. Time in prison has become the metric through which effective response to crime is measured, and we demand more time for more offenders. We are impatient with the numerous community-based alternatives to prison that were pursued in previous decades, because anything that is an alternative to or in lieu of the 'real' penalty of incarceration represents a 'slap on the wrist' and an evasion of legitimate punishment. (Flanagan *et al.*, 1998: x)

The second engine of American carceral inflation is the *mutation of the political and media uses of criminality* in reaction to the protest movements of the 1960s and the ramifying social changes they ushered in. To curb the popular unrest provoked by the Vietnam War and the sweeping mobilization of blacks for civic equality that toppled Jim Crow in the South and overran the ghetto in the North, conservative politicians, Republicans and Democrats alike, pounced upon the 'problem' of urban turmoil and made the 'war on crime' their main bulwark against the (modest) expansion of the welfare state required to reduce both crushing poverty and abysmal racial inequality (Button, 1978). Introduced during the 1968 presidential campaign by Richard Nixon, who borrowed it from the political notables of the segregationist South, the repressive theme of 'law and order' offered a new proving ground for the restoration of government authority. It furnished an electoral leitmotiv that was all the more valued as it made it possible to express in an apparently civic idiom – ensuring the safety and tranquillity of the citizenry – the rejection of black demands and thereby to exorcise the menacing spectre of 'integration', which was accepted in principle but rejected in fact, as indicated by the mass migration of whites to the sheltered space of the suburbs and their abandonment of urban public institutions, from school and housing to hospitals and parks.

The success of this moral panic around criminality conflated with challenges to the racial order stems from the structural complicity that developed on this ground over the years between the political field, the journalistic field, and the field of penal institutions, whose autonomy was drastically curtailed and whose functioning was increasingly subjected to the rhythms and dictates of electoral and media competition. At first, fighting crime was the rallying cry of politicians anxious to reassure white, middle-class voters from suburban zones frightened by turmoil in the 'unheavenly city' (which they had just fled by the millions) and at the same time opposed to welfare policies and affirmative action, which they viewed as undue favours accorded to the blacks responsible for the urban riots that rocked the 1960s (Quadagno, 1994). But, under pressure from the media and its relentless logic of the 'soundbite' and constant search for spectacular news liable to boost ratings, the necessity of being 'tough on crime' swiftly came to be imposed on all politicians, as well as on prosecutors and judges whose positions are elective and for whom the suspicion of laxity soon amounted to an occupational death sentence (Anderson, 1995).[18]

For, in the meantime, crime had also become the darling subject of journalists. Crime allows the media to produce low-cost shows of morality that appeal to common sentiments and thus to preserve or conquer market shares by pandering to the morbid fascination of the public for violence. As a result, crime stories invaded the front page of newspapers and the television screen to saturation point, even as the incidence of violent offences was stagnating or declining in the country. Between 1989 and 1993, the number of such reports on the nightly news of the three major national networks (ABC, CBS, and NBC) quadrupled to reach 1,632, or nearly five per evening, despite the drop in offending rates – so much so that the Center for Media and Public Affairs wondered about the advent of 'drive-by journalism'. Crime rates continued to decrease rapidly for six years; yet in 1999 these three leading news outlet still broadcast an astounding 1,613 crime reports, keeping crime the first news topic (tied with the raging war in Kosovo at 1,615), with one-third of all stories devoted to murders (amounting to four times the score of Clinton's impeachment) (Lichter and Lichter, 1994, 2000).

In short, a crime wave did hit the United States after the 1980s, but it was a cultural wave generated by the media's increasing fascination with and use of criminal violence as cheap raw materials for 'infotainment' and even entertainment. By the mid-1990s, 'reality crime shows' had become a staple of television programming, with *America's Most Wanted* and *Unsolved Mysteries* vying for viewers with *Cops*, *Crimewatch Tonight*, and *Rescue 911*. These lurid shows consistently depicted crime as more frequent and more violent than it really is (Fishman and Cavender, 1998). The wide diffusion of footage of police operations and videos of live crime scenes, typically involving the forcible arrest of dark-skinned young men in poor neighbourhoods, cemented the association between dangerousness and blackness, and fueled a culture of vilification of criminals that harnessed underlying anti-black animus. It will come as no surprise that the shared obsession of the media and politicians with crime was met with the enthusiasm of those in charge of the country's penal institutions. Attorneys general, state correctional administrations, police departments, guards unions, and business lobbies connected to the prison sector: all concurred in seeing and portraying 'crime control' as a national priority that should brook no hesitation and no limitation. It is above all a priority tailor-made to justify the boundless expansion of their numbers, budgets, and prerogatives.

The de-autonomization of the penal field and the politicization-mediatization of the crime question stand in a dialectical relation of mutual reinforcement. The more the question of crime is posed in dichotomous moral terms geared to electoral games in the public sphere, the less relevant the empirical knowledge produced by experts and the technical constraints faced by correctional administrators become to the conduct of penal policy. Conversely, as the authority of penal professionals is eroded and disregarded, moral entrepreneurs in journalism and politics can shape the mission of the police, courts, and prisons to suit their own agendas and interests, thereby undercutting attempts to re-establish a prospective rationale for imprisonment going beyond retribution and neutralization (Zimring, 1996). The result of this collusive triangular relationship between the political, media, and penal fields has been the proliferation of repressive laws – California voted over a thousand in 15 years – that extend recourse to imprisonment, lengthen the duration of sentences inflicted and served, stipulate mandatory minimum sanctions for a wide range of offences, and go so far as to impose life imprisonment for the third violent crime or felony, a measure sold to the electorate with help of the baseball expression, 'Three Strikes and You're Out'.

The colour of punitiveness

Two deep-seated trends have struck observers of the contemporary penal scene in the United States. First, the percentage of prison inmates convicted for drugs-related offences has soared from 5 per cent in 1960 to 9 per cent in 1980 to nearly one-third in 1995. During the same period, the share of African Americans among admissions to federal and state penitentiaries has nearly doubled, with the result that for the first time in a century black convicts make up a majority of entering cohorts (55 per cent in 1995), even though black men compose under 7 per cent of the country's adult population. The concurrence of these two tendencies points to the third major cause of the quadrupling of the incarcerated population in America in 20 years: *the penal system has partly supplanted and partly supplemented the ghetto* as a mechanism of racial control, after the latter revealed itself unsuited to keeping the black urban (sub)proletariat consigned to the place assigned to it in the new American social space emerging from the upheavals of the 1960s and the accelerating restructuring of the metropolitan economy (Wacquant, 1997b).

It is true that blacks have been over-represented in America's penitentiaries throughout the twentieth century for two main reasons. The first is that they commit proportionately more crimes than whites owing to differences in class composition and socioeconomic stability between the two communities (one African American in three lived below the official poverty line in 1993 versus one European American in ten) and to the extreme levels of residential segregation inflicted upon them in the large cities. Douglas Massey has shown how the 'hypersegregation' of blacks combines with their high poverty rate to create a unique 'ecological niche' that is exceptionally conducive to the development of interpersonal violence and criminal activities (Massey, 1995; see also Morenoff and Sampson, 1997). This explains that urban blacks are the primary perpetrators but also the main victims of violent crime. But the share of African Americans among individuals arrested by the police for the four most serious offences against persons (murder, rape, robbery, aggravated assault) decreased from 51 per cent in 1973 to 43 per cent in 1996 (Tonry, 1999: 17). So if the ethnic composition of the prison population tracked trends in criminal violence, it should have *whitened* over the past quarter-century, and not blackened as it did.[19]

This points to the second reason for the astonishing rise of incarceration among black Americans, independent from rates of offending: the preferential enforcement of those laws most likely to lead to the arrest and prosecution of poor African Americans. True, discrimination in sentencing remains a reality at the final stage of the criminal justice process: controlling for prior record, seriousness of offence, and for indirect effects of race, blacks are more likely to receive a sanction of penal confinement than whites (Crutfield *et al.*, 1994). But such discrimination clearly has not increased since the mid-1970s and so it cannot account for the spectacular worsening of 'racial disproportionality' in prison admissions in the recent period. The latter suggests that a new relationship has been established between imprisonment and the caste division that underlies the structure of US society since the uprisings that shook the ghetto.

The black–white gap has deepened rapidly in the course of the last two decades, to the point where the incarceration rate of African Americans is nearly eight times that of their compatriots of European stock. This sudden and accelerating 'darkening' of the carceral population is directly connected to the onset of the 'War on Drugs' launched with fanfare by Ronald Reagan and amplified by his successors (Tonry, 1995). This policy has served as cover for a veritable police and penal guerrilla on sellers of narcotics and other street operators and, by extension, for the punitive containment of the residents of the dispossessed black urban neighbourhoods in which they congregate. Following the economic decay and collapse of public institutions in the inner city, ghetto dwellers have been suspected of deviating from national cultural norms and accused of adopting those 'antisocial behaviours' alleged by the pseudo-scientific discourse on the 'underclass' to be the cause of social dislocations in the metropolis.[20] Putting them under the tutelage of the penal apparatus at once extends and intensifies the paternalistic oversight already imposed on them by social services, first under the aegis of 'welfare' and later under the plank of 'workfare'. In addition it makes it possible to exploit – and to feed – the latent racial hostility of the electorate and its scorn for the poor for maximum media and political returns (Chambliss, 1994; Skogan, 1995; Gilens, 1995).

Far from hunting down the scourge wherever it strikes, starting with prosperous white suburbs and university campuses, the federal anti-drug campaign has concentrated squarely on the declining dark ghetto. As a result, the arrest rate of blacks for narcotics violation has shot up tenfold in ten years to peak at 1,800 per 100,000 by 1989, while the same rate for whites fluctuated between 220 and 250 per 100,000 (although the incidence of drug consumption is nearly identical in the two communities). As a result, the number of blacks caught in the snares of the penal apparatus has exploded, and with it the litany of deleterious consequences for their employment prospects and family life: if one adds those on probation and parole to jail detainees and prison inmates, nearly half of young African Americans in the big cities are currently under criminal justice supervision. The result is that a deep *structural and functional symbiosis has emerged between the ghetto and the prison*. The two institutions interpenetrate and complement each other in that both ensure the confinement of a population stigmatized by its ethnic origin and deemed superfluous both economically and politically (Wacquant, 2000). This symbiosis finds a striking expression in the lyrics and lifestyles flaunted by 'gangsta rap' musicians, as attested by the tragic fate of singer-songwriter Tupac Shakur.

Upon a painstaking examination of the relations between racial division, crime, and punishment in America, legal scholar Michael Tonry asserts that the architects of the War on Drugs were fully cognizant of what they were doing:

> They knew that drug use was falling among the vast majority of the population. They knew that drug use was not declining among the disadvantaged members of the urban underclass. They knew that the War on Drugs would be fought mainly in the minority areas of American cities and that those arrested and imprisoned would disproportionately be young blacks and Hispanics. (Tonry 1995: 104)

One is thus led to conclude that the 'War on Drugs' expresses the will to penalize poverty and to contain the assortment of 'pathologies' associated with it, either by hemming it at the core of the crumbling ghetto or, when these secondary effects spill over its scorned perimeter, by damming it inside the prisons to which the racialized urban core is now symbiotically joined. Beyond that, the functional coupling of the penal apparatus and the black ghetto fits with the onset of a 'new penology' whose objective is neither to prevent crime nor to reintegrate offenders into society once they have served their sentences, but merely to isolate groups perceived as dangerous and to neutralize their most disruptive members through the stochastic management of the risks they are believed to pose (Simon and Feeley, 1995).

All historical and comparative studies concur to demonstrate that the level of incarceration of a given society bears no relation to its crime rate: it is at bottom an expression of cultural and political choices (Christie, 1998). On this account, the carceral hyperinflation that the United States has experienced from Nixon to Clinton is revealing: it constitutes, as it were, the hidden face of the American 'social model', premised on the unfettered reign of the market, a categorical welfare state that buttresses labour discipline, and the continued socio-spatial isolation of African Americans. The grotesque overdevelopment of the penal sector over the past three decades is indeed the necessary counterpart to the shrivelling of the welfare sector, and the joining of the remnants of the dark ghetto with the penitentiary is the logical complement of the policy of criminalization of poverty pursued by the country's authorities (Wacquant, 1997a). Just as in other societies, the discourses that seek to connect crime and punishment in America have no value other than ideological. Far from accounting for America's great carceral leap backward, they partake of the social construction of a hypertrophic and hyperactive penal state that constitutes without contest one of the most unforeseen and most cruel historical experiments of the democratic era.

Notes

1 See Adams and Campling (1992). There is an intriguing parallel here with the trajectory of U.S. slavery in the Revolutionary era: with the gradual abolition of bondage in the North and its prohibition in the Northwest, the facilitation of manumission in the South, and the incipient termination of the foreign slave trade, opponents of the 'peculiar institution' in the 1780s had 'good grounds to be cautiously optimistic. Slavery appeared to be in full retreat, its end only a matter of time' (Kolchin, 1993: 80). Yet it would go on to endure and indeed expand for nearly another century and its demise would require a civil war leaving four million dead, much of the South shattered, and the country deeply divided.

2 For a detailed account of this movement and its impact, see Cummins (1994); for a linked series of case studies from an organizational perspective, see Useem and Kimball (1991).

3 See Frase (1999: 476). By Frase's computation, lock-ups could hold over 30,000 at any moment, a figure equal to twice the inmate population of the Netherlands that is erased from official correctional statistics.

4 Cf. Chambliss (1991), on city and county expenditures; and DiMascio (1999) on state budget planning.

5 The statistics on costs in this paragraph are drawn or computed from Stephan (1999). Note that these figures exclude capital outlays (purchase of land, facility construction and renovation, major repairs), as well as probation and parole services, juvenile corrections, and nonresidential community sanctions.

6 Corrections Corporations of America is the leader of this economic sector with nearly half the country's private beds. Founded in 1983, the Nashville firm was then in charge of 59 carceral establishments located in 19 states and abroad (Puerto Rico, Australia, and England), with gross sales of $300 million growing by 40 per cent per year.

7 By one estimate, to construct the prisons required to house these extra inmates would have required a veritable correctional Marshall plan of $6.6 billion per year (Thomas and Logan, 1993).

8 Based on interviews conducted by the author over the four days of the 127th Congress of Corrections, a bi-annual meeting of corrections professionals held under the auspices of the American Corrections Association (a professional organization founded in 1870 with over 24,000 members), in Orlando, Florida, in August 1998.

9 The criminological, sociological, legal, and policy literatures on criminal offending and victimization in the United States fill entire libraries. I limit myself here to pointing out those facts and figures that spotlight the consistent disconnection between trends in offences and trends in incarceration. For a panorama of normal research on the topic, typically limited to 'what the average person thinks of as predatory or street crime', see Wilson and Petersilia (1995).

10 The National Crime Victimization Survey (NCVS) is an annual questionnaire-based study conducted by the US Department of Justice with a representative sample of 45,000 households using a rotating panel design that tracks the evolution of major categories of criminal infractions. It is considered the most reliable source of data on criminal offending in the United States – more so than police statistics, which are known to conflate variations in police activity with changes in the incidence of criminal conduct.

11 On the profile of Texas prison convicts, see Fabello (1993); on the criminal profile of California and federal inmates, see Donziger (1996: 17–19).

12 Irwin and Austin (1997: 32–57) present a detailed qualitative analysis of the social and criminal careers of a random sample of 154 prisoners in three states (Washington, Nevada, and Illinois), from which it emerges that 'over half the persons being sent to prison are being sent for petty crimes, which are crimes without any aggravating features – that is, no significant amount of money, no injury, or any other feature that would cause ordinary citizens to view the crimes as particularly serious' (p. 34). The majority of inmates turn out to be mediocre criminals of opportunity (as opposed to proficient 'career criminals') who would not be incarcerated if the public knew their profile and the circumstances that led them to break the law.

13 The classic account of the collapse of the normalizing and therapeutic model that dominated US corrections from the interwar years until the mid-1970s is found in Allen (1981).

14 This moral fairy tale receives an impeccably academic treatment in Wilson (1975).

15 There is a striking parallel here with the 1996 'reform' of welfare passed in Congress with the willing consent of President Clinton – a 'reform' that amounts to abolishing the right of impoverished single-parent families and resident aliens to assistance and to making deskilled and precarious labour a civic obligation (Wacquant, 1997a). For, in this case too, it is the 'liberal' reformers (those on the left of the American political spectrum) who made possible the passage of this retrograde law by adopting themes dear to conservatives (starting with the idea that the welfare state is fundamentally dysfunctional) and by endorsing coercive and paternalistic measures (such as mandatory work at the end of two years and lifetime limits on the duration of assistance), on the pretext that their harmful effects would be compensated later by the adoption of other progressive measures (such as the creation of public jobs, which one could easily foresee would not see the light of day), and on grounds that any reform is better than no reform since the existing system mistreats the most dispossessed.

16 A germane diagnosis was offered earlier by Austin and Krisberg (1982).

17 The confession is by Cressey (1968: p. 371).

18 Chambliss (1994) offers a succinct and precise analysis of the fabrication of this moral panic that makes especially clear how opinion polls (on 'the main challenges facing the country') constituted as a national problem a question that the public was barely concerned about until politicians, the media, and pollsters thrust it upon them.

19 The proportion of blacks among arrests for property crimes remained roughly constant during that period, oscillating between 29 and 33 per cent.

20 A synoptic expression of this scholarly myth is Mincy (1994); a methodical critique of its tenets and bases is Wacquant (1996).

References

Adams, R. and Campling, J. (1992) *Prison Riots in Britain and the United States*, London: Macmillan.

Allen, F. A. (1981) *The Decline of the Rehabilitative Ideal: Penal Policy and Social Purpose*, New Haven: Yale University Press.

Anderson, D.C. (1995) *Crime and the Politics of Hysteria: How the Willie Horton Story Changed American Justice*, New York: Times Books.

Andreas, P. (1997) 'The Rise of the American Crimefare State', *World Policy Journal*, 14(3): 37–45.

Austin J. and Krisberg, B. (1982) 'The Unmet Promise of Alternatives to Incarceration', *Crime and Delinquency*, 28(3): 374–409.

Best, J. (1999) *Random Violence: How We Talk about New Crimes and New Victims*, Berkeley: University of California Press.

Blumstein, A. and Cohen, J. (1973) 'A Theory of the Stability of Punishment', *Journal of Criminal Law and Criminology*, 64(2): 198–207.

Blumstein, A., Cohen, J. and Nagin, D. (1977) 'The Dynamics of a Homeostatic Punishment Process', *Journal of Criminal Law and Criminology*, 67(3): 317–334.

Blumstein, A. and Wallman, J. (eds) (2000) *The Crime Drop in America*, Cambridge: Cambridge University Press.

Bureau of Justice Statistics (1996) *Prison and Jail Inmates, 1995*, Washington: Bureau of Justice Bulletin.

Button, J. (1978) *Black Violence: Political Impact of the 1960s Riots*, Princeton: Princeton University Press.

Chambliss, W. J. (1991) *Trading Textbooks for Prison Cells*. Alexandria, Virginia: National Center on Institutions and Alternatives.

Chambliss, W. J. (1994) 'Policing the Ghetto Underclass: The Politics of Law and Law Enforcement', *Social Problems*, 41(2): 177–194.

Christie, N. (1998) 'Essai de géographie pénale', *Actes de la Recherche en Sciences Sociales*, 124: 68–74.

Cohen, S. (1979) 'Community Control: A New Utopia', *New Society*, 858: 609–611.

Corrections Corporation of America (1997) *Annual Report 1996: Leaps and Bounds*.

Cressey, D. (1968) 'The Nature and Effectiveness of Correctional Techniques', in L. Hazelrigg (ed.), *Prison Within Society*, Garden City, NY: Doubleday.

Crutfield, R., Bridges, G. S. and Pitchford, S. (1994) 'Analytical and Aggregation Biases in Analyses of Imprisonment: Reconciling Discrepancies in Studies of Racial Disparity', *Journal of Research in Crime and Delinquency*, 31(2): 166–182.

Cummins, E. (1994) *The Rise and Fall of California's Radical Prison Movement*, Stanford: Stanford University Press.

Currie, E. (1998) 'Race, Violence, and Justice since Kerner', in F. R. Harris and L. A. Curtis (eds), *Locked in the Poorhouse: Cities, Race, and Poverty in the United States*, Lanham, MD: Rowman & Littlefield.

Department of Justice (2000) *Correctional Population of the United States, 1997*, Washington: Government Printing Office.

DiMascio, W. (1995) *Seeking Justice: Crime and Punishment in America*, New York: Edna McConnell Clark Foundation.

Donziger, S. R. (ed.) (1996) *The Real War on Crime: The Report of the National Criminal Justice Commission*, New York: Harper.

Fabello, T. (1993) *Sentencing Dynamics Study*, Austin: Criminal Justice Policy Council.

Federal Bureau of Investigation. (1995) *Uniform Crime Report 1995* [online], available from: http://www.fbi.gov/ucr/95cius.htm.

Fishman, M. and Cavender, G. (1998) *Entertaining Crime: Television Reality Programs*, New York: Aldine.

Flanagan, T. J., Marquart, J. W. and Adams, K. G. (1998) *Incarcerating Criminals: Prisons and Jails in Social and Organizational Context*, New York: Oxford University Press.

Foucault, M. [1975] (1978) *Discipline and Punish: The Birth of the Prison*, New York: Vintage.

Frase, R. (1999) 'Jails', in M. Tonry (ed.), *The Handbook of Crime and Punishment*, Oxford: Oxford University Press.

Gibbons, S. G. and Pierce, G. L. (1995) 'Politics and Prison Development in a Rural Area', *Prison Journal*, 75(3): 380–389.

Gifford, S. L. (2002) *Justice Expenditures and Employment in the United States, 1999*. Washington: Bureau of Justice Bulletin.

Gilens, M. (1995) 'Racial Attitudes and Opposition to Welfare', *Journal of Politics*, 57(4): 994–1014.

Gragg, R. (1996) 'A High Security, Low Risk Investment: Private Prisons Make Crime Pay,' *Harper's Magazine* August: 50.

Harding, R. W. (1999) 'Private Prisons' in M. Tonry (ed.), *The Handbook of Crime and Punishment*, Oxford: Oxford University Press.

Hazelrigg, L. (1968) *Prison Within Society*, Garden City, NY: Doubleday.

Hurling, T. (1999) *Yes, in my Backyard*, WSKG Public broadcasting. Galloping Girls Productions.

Ignatieff, M. (1978) *A Just Measure of Pain: The Penitentiary in the Industrial Revolution, 1750–1850*, New York: Pantheon Books.

Irwin, J. and Austin, J. (1997) *It's About Time: America's Imprisonment Binge*, Belmont, California: Wadsworth.

Katz, M. B. (1996) *In the Shadow of the Poorhouse: A History of Welfare in America*, New York: Basic Books.

Kolchin, P. (1993) *American Slavery: 1619–1877*, New York: Hill and Wang.

Lichter, R. S. and Lichter, L. S. (1994) *1993 – The Year in Review: TV's Leading News Topics Reporters, and Political Jokes*, Washington: Media Monitor.

Lichter, R. S. and Lichter, L. S. (2000) *1999 – The Year in Review: TV's Leading News Topics, Reporters, and Political Jokes*, Washington: Media Monitor.

Massey, D. (1995) 'Getting Away with Murder: Segregation and Violent Crime in Urban America', *University of Pennsylvania Law Review*, 143(5): 1203–1232.

Mincy, R. (1994) 'The Underclass: Concept, Controversy, and Evidence', in S. Danziger, G. Sandefur, and D. Weinberg (eds), *Confronting Poverty: Prescriptions for Change*, Cambridge: Harvard University Press.

Mitford, J. (1973) *Kind and Usual Punishment: The Prison Business*, New York: Random House.

Morenoff, J. D. and Sampson, R. J. (1997) 'Violent Crime and the Spatial Dynamics of Neighborhood Transition: Chicago, 1970–1990', *Social Forces*, 76(1): 31–64.

National Advisory Commission on Criminal Justice Standards and Goals (1973) *Task Force Report on Corrections*, Washington: Government Printing Office.

President's Commission on Law Enforcement and Administration of Justice (1967) *Task Force Report: Corrections*, Washington: Government Printing Office.

Quadagno, J. (1994) *The Color of Welfare: How Racism Undermined the War on Poverty*, New York: Oxford University Press.

Rothman, D. J. (1971) *The Discovery of the Asylum: Social Order and Disorder in the New Republic*, Boston: Little, Brown.

Rothman, D. J. (1995) 'American Criminal Justice Policies in the 1990s', in T. G. Blomberg and S. Cohen (eds), *Punishment and Social Control*, New York: Aldine de Gruyter.

Scull, A. T. (1977) *Decarceration: Community Treatment and the Deviant, a Radical View*, Englewood Cliffs: Prentice-Hall.

Simon, J. and Feeley, M. (1995) 'True Crime: The New Penology and Public Discourse on Crime', in T.G. Blomberg and S. Cohen (eds), *Punishment and Social Control*, New York: Aldine de Gruyter.

Skogan, W. G. (1995) 'Crime and the Racial Fears of White Americans', *Annals of the American Academy of Political and Social Science*, 539: 59–71.

Stephan, J. (1999) *State Prison Expenditures, 1996*, Washington: Bureau of Justice Statistics.

Thomas, C. and Logan, C. (1993) 'The Development, Present Status, and Future Potential of Correctional Privatization in America', in G. Bowman, S. Hakim, and P. Seidenstat (eds) *Privatizing Correctional Institutions*, New Brunswick: Transaction Press.

Tonry, M. (1995) *Malign Neglect: Race, Crime and Punishment in America*, New York: Oxford University Press.

Tonry, M. (1999) 'Crime and punishment in America', in M. Tonry (ed), *The Handbook of Crime and Punishment*, New York: Oxford University Press.

US Department of Justice (1997) *National Crime Victimization Survey: Criminal Victimization, 1973–1995*, Washington: Government Printing Office.

US Department of Justice (2001) *Sourcebook of Criminal Justice Statistics, 2000*, Washington: Government Printing Office.

Useem, B. and Kimball, P. (1991) *States of Siege: U.S. Prison Riots 1971–1986*, Oxford: Oxford University Press.

Wacquant, L. (1994) 'The New Urban Color Line: The State and Fate of the Ghetto in Postfordist America', in C. J. Calhoun (ed.), *Social Theory and the Politics of Identity*, Cambridge: Basil Blackwell.

Wacquant, L. (1996) 'L''*underclass*' urbaine dans l'imaginaire social et scientifique américain', in S. Paugam (ed.) *L'Exclusion: l'état des saviors*, Paris: Editions La Découverte.

Wacquant, L. (1997a) 'Les pauvres en pâture: la nouvelle politique de la misère en Amérique', *Hérodote*, 85: 21–33.

Wacquant, L. (1997b) 'Elias in the Dark Ghetto', *Amsterdam Sociologisch Tidjschrift*, 24(3–4): 340–348.

Wacquant, L. (2000) 'The New 'Peculiar Institution': On the Prison as Surrogate Ghetto', *Theoretical Criminology*, 4(3): 377–389.

Wacquant, L. (2004) *Punir les pauvres. Le nouveau gouvernement de l'insécurité sociale*, Paris: Editions Dupuytren.

Wilson, J. Q. (1975) *Thinking About Crime*, New York: Vintage.

Wilson, J. Q. and Petersilia, J. (eds) (1995) *Crime: Public Policies for Crime Control*. San Francisco: ICS Press.

Wilson, W. J. (1996) *When Work Disappears: The World of the New Urban Poor*, New York: Knopf.

Zimring, F. (1996) 'Populism, Democratic Government, and the Decline of Expert Authority: Some Reflections on "Three Strikes" in California', *Pacific Law Journal*, 28: 243–256.

Zimring, F. and Hawkins, G. (1991) *The Scale of Imprisonment*, Chicago: University of Chicago Press.

2. Continuity, rupture, or just more of the 'volatile and contradictory'? Glimpses of New South Wales' penal practice behind and through the discursive

David Brown

In 1970 all prisoners in Bathurst gaol, New South Wales (NSW), Australia, were subjected to a cell-by-cell bashing led by the prison superintendent, as a reprisal for taking part in a peaceful protest. Four years later Bathurst gaol was nearly razed in a major riot and fire, followed again by reprisal bashings. After a delay during which prisoners were charged with riot offences, a Royal Commission headed by Nagle J of the NSW Supreme Court was established in 1976 and handed down its influential *Report* in 1978 (see Vinson, 1982; Zdenkowski and Brown, 1982; Findlay, 1982). In the *Report* Nagle called for 'a building plan to be drawn up until the year 2000', the aim of which 'should be to replace old gaols which cannot immediately be satisfactorily altered by new facilities' before expressing the hope that 'the prison population will not necessarily continue to increase proportionately to any population increase because of, inter alia, the adoption of alternative modes of punishment and improvements in the organisation of society' (Nagle, 1978: 25).

This hope was unrealized, as imprisonment rates have doubled in NSW and in Australia[1] nationally in the 26 years since the release of the *Nagle Report* and the proportion of indigenous prisoners has trebled in NSW. One answer to why Nagle's prediction that the prison population would not continue to increase proportionately to any population increase failed to materialize is that in the late 1970s what is now often referred to as 'the punitive turn' was not widely foreseen. There *has* been an expansion in available sentencing alternatives since 1978, but for a whole range of reasons an institution under significant challenge in the 1960s and 1970s, regarded by some as deeply obsolete and likely to be consigned to a marginal status or even abolished, has undergone a revival across a number of jurisdictions internationally, particularly in the US where leading criminologists now talk of 'mass imprisonment' (Garland, 2001b: 5–6).

The most theoretically sophisticated explanations for this punitive turn and the rapid increase in imprisonment rates across the West have increasingly looked to more general changes in social, political, economic, and cultural organization rather than to any specific forces confined to the criminal justice sphere, in short to the conditions of life in 'late modernity'. They have sought to understand how a 'popular punitiveness' (Bottoms, 1995) has been constructed across a number of jurisdictions starting in the 1980s and have sought to delineate the conditions which sustained it. Different analyses have focused on:

- an increasingly virulent, politicized and 'uncivil' (Hogg and Brown, 1998) politics of law and order;

- an increasing recognition of the inability of the 'sovereign' state to protect citizens from rising crime rates and consequent strategies of either adapting to or attempting to deny the limits of the sovereign state, through 'criminologies of the self' or 'criminologies of the other' (Garland, 1996);

- rapid economic and social restructuring in late modernity, involving the weakening or 'hollowing out' out of the welfare state, the rise of neoliberalism as the dominant political force and the ascendancy of market society and market culture, including a market in social control (Taylor, 1999);

- a 'volatile and contradictory' penality stemming from conflict between neo-liberalism and neoconservatism (O'Malley, 1999);

- the rise of 'governmentality' (Rose, 1999; Garland, 1997);

- the emergence of a 'risk society' (Feeley and Simon, 1992) and the development of a 'new penology' operating through actuarial and statistical techniques (Feeley and Simon, 1994);

- the emergence of postmodernity (Simon, 1995; Pratt, 2000; Hallsworth, 2002);

- the emergence of a cultural politics of exclusion (Young, 1999);

- the emergence of a new cultural formation, 'the crime complex' (Garland, 2001a: xi);

- a highly racialized criminalization of minorities and immigrants (Wacquant, 2001, 2002);

- shifts in cultural sensibilities towards punishment in the direction of Elias's 'decivilization' (Pratt, 2000b, 2002; Vaughan, 2000);

- a populist, 'anti-elites' backlash, characterized in the criminal justice realm by the rise of a less deferential public voice critical of judges and experts as out of touch with popular sentiment, demanding heavier penalties, truth in sentencing, the winding back of judicial discretion, diminution of defendants' rights, and a greater role for victims (Ryan, 2003).

These various accounts have enriched and revitalized penology, reconnecting it with broader social theory (Garland and Sparks, 2000).

But inasmuch as some of the accounts tend to be a little sweeping and generalized, are weighted towards US exceptionalism, gloss over local, regional and national differences, focus on the discursive and the cultural, and tend towards what O'Malley calls 'criminologies of catastrophe' (2000: 164) and Zedner 'a dystopic future' (2002: 364), it may be a useful exercise to engage in a more detailed and specific, empirically based assessment of both transformations and continuities in the penal practices of particular jurisdictions over recent decades. This chapter will attempt such an assessment in relation to NSW penal practice over a 30-year period, from the Nagle inquiry to the present (for a similar empirically based analysis of trends in sentencing and penal policy in New Zealand, see Brown and Young, 2000). The first half of the chapter is an empirical look at post-Nagle changes (for a fuller and more referenced account, see Brown, 2004) and the second half examines how a number of theoretical arguments resting on discourse analysis fit with the empirical data. The aim will be to show a disposition towards the empirical, on the hypothesis that some of the increasingly culturalist emphasis on shifting public sensibilities to punishment in the direction of 'emotive and ostentatious' punishment (Pratt, 2000b: 417) is more in evidence at the discursive level and has had less impact 'on the ground'. The chapter thus presents a three-way analysis: first, empirical data on NSW penal practices post-Nagle; second, reflections on that data at both discursive and non-discursive levels; and third, testing theory against the data: the 'punitive turn', the 'demise' of penal welfarism and the rise of 'popular punitiveness' measured against recent NSW penal history at both discursive and non-discursive levels.

New South Wales penal practice since 1978

1. Increasing imprisonment rates and cost, new prisons, better conditions

The increases in imprisonment rates noted above have led both to levels of significant overcrowding (Steering Committee (hereafter SC), 2004: 7.26–7) and a massive prison-building programme, providing ammunition for arguments about a prison-industrial complex as rural communities in particular vie to be the site of the next prison as a source of jobs, revenue and services. The operating expenditure of the NSW Department of Corrective Services for 1975–76 was $A30 million (Nagle, 1978: 16) and for 2001–02, $A560 million (SC, 2004: 7.21–3). The average daily cost per prisoner in 1975–76 was $A28.12 across all institutions (Nagle, 1978: 161) and in 2002–03 total cost per prisoner per day in NSW was $A221 (SC, ibid.). Total annual expenses for the Department of Corrective Services has increased by 37 per cent in real terms between 1994 and 2001, an additional $A45 million a year in current terms (NSWLC, 2001: 73). The expansion in the number of new prisons (at least eight since Nagle) has meant, with significant exceptions like the Goulburn 'Supermax', that the quality of buildings and facilities has improved.

2. Sentencing changes

Nagle recommended in 1978 that remissions apply to the non-parole period rather than just the head sentence (Nagle, 1978: 305), a change introduced in 1983, reducing the length of sentences actually served. The 'early release' of prisoners became a source of public and media disquiet following the conviction and imprisonment of former State Australian Labor Party (ALP) Corrections Minister, Rex Jackson, in 1987 for conspiracy in relation to a short-term licence release scheme (Chan, 1992). Remissions were then abolished as part of the 'truth in sentencing' package of changes introduced by the conservative Coalition State government in 1989, a move which significantly increased sentence lengths and contributed to a 30 per cent increase in the prison population within two years. The 1989 legislation introduced a ¾ formula between the minimum term and the head sentence, together with so called 'natural life' sentences. In the 1990s guideline sentences increased sentence lengths in specific offence areas such as culpable driving causing death and armed robbery and maximum sentences for a range of offences were increased. In 2003 'standard minimum terms' were introduced for a range of serious offences. These sentences can be reduced or increased by reference to a range of mitigating or aggravating circumstances already operative within the common law, retaining judicial discretion (Brown, 2002a). Attempts have been made to prevent access to parole to a small number of former life sentence prisoners convicted of notorious crimes, or in the current ALP premier's words, to 'cement them in'.

3. Deaths in custody

There is no separate entry for deaths in custody in the *Nagle Report*, although there is reference to the fact that 'several prisoners committed suicide while at Grafton' (1978: 143). Deaths in custody, police stations and prisons became an issue in the mid-1980s after an escalating number of specifically Aboriginal deaths in custody and the Hawke federal ALP government set up a Royal Commission in 1988. The Reports of the Commission suggested that the high indigenous death rates were a consequence of the disproportionately high indigenous imprisonment rates and made a range of recommendations (RCIADC, 1991). Critics have suggested that implementation has been tardy and partial (Cunneen and Behrendt, 1994; Cunneen and McDonald, 1997). The disproportion in indigenous people imprisoned has increased, from 7 per cent of the NSW prison population when Nagle reported to 20 per cent in 2003. Hogg suggests that the reasons for increasingly disproportionate indigenous imprisonment rates since the early 1970s lie in 'the legacy of segregationist policies, especially the wholesale removal of children and attempts to annihilate the means of reproduction of Aboriginal culture' (2001: 355). Nationally in 2003 indigenous people were imprisoned at 16 times the non-indigenous rate (ABS, 2003:5). In the decade before the Royal Commission 12 per cent of deaths in prison were of indigenous people, rising to 17 per cent in 1998 (Dalton, 1999). While deaths in police custody decreased during the 1990s, all prison deaths doubled nationally and in NSW, from the 1980s to a high point in 1997 (Dalton, 1998).

4. Bashings

The practice and culture of systematic bashings of prisoners in NSW, evidenced in the 43-year Grafton 'reception biff' regime and the Bathurst bashings of October 1970 and February 1974, were laid out in gory detail in the *Nagle Report* (chapters 4–7). Nagle's argument was that once the brutality had been revealed for all to see it was unlikely to reappear (p. 119; cf. Zdenkowski and Brown, 1982:180–1). Shortly after the release of the *Nagle Report* a group of old guard officers, some formerly from Grafton, engaged in violent behaviour at Goulburn but an inquiry was quickly called by Commissioner Vinson and some Public Service Act charges laid (Henry, 1979; Zdenkowski and Brown, 1982: 197–206). Since this time little evidence has emerged or complaint been made about systematic bashing. A significant culture change away from the use and legitimacy of direct physical violence seems to have been achieved in the last three decades, a not insignificant achievement, especially given that some of the individual officers named as bashers at Grafton and Bathurst are still, 25 years later, in the Department, at senior levels.

5. Prisoner-to-prisoner assaults and sexual assaults

The rate of assaults (number of assaults per 100 prisoners) by prisoners on other prisoners and prison officers was introduced as a performance indicator in the *Review of Government Service Provision 1998*. On official figures in 2002–3 NSW had the highest rate of 'assaults by prisoners on other prisoners per 100 prisoners of any Australian jurisdiction at 16.86' (SC, 2004:7.13–4) but comparison with the Nagle period is not possible. While it might appear that prisoner-to-prisoner assaults are increasing, whether this is an artefact of the recording practices, refinement of categories and shifting sensibilities, is difficult to determine given the low rate of reporting of assault and sexual assault within an overall culture of prison hyper-masculinity. Older prisoners talk in terms of 'blue on green' being replaced by 'green on green', meaning that the former culture of mutual prison officer/prisoner hostility and violence has changed to one of prisoner against prisoner, exacerbated by the grouping or prisoners' along ethnic/racial lines at particular prisons such as Goulburn, heightening divisions and tensions and leading to increased levels of violence among the various groups.

David Heilpern's (1998) study suggested that 1 in 4 male prisoners were sexually assaulted during their term of imprisonment. The Department claims such figures are exaggerated and point to the 0.11 reported rate of serious assaults of prisoner on prisoner, which includes sexual assaults, per 100 NSW prisoners in 2002–3 (SC, 2004:7.13–14). Then Prisons Minister Michael Yabsley infamously remarked in 1991 that rape was 'inevitable' in prison and indeed that fear of prison rape might be a useful 'deterrent factor' to those thinking of offending (*Sydney Morning Herald*, 22/2/1991). It seems likely that levels of reporting of sexual assault in prison are significantly lower than in the outside community and thus it is difficult to determine whether sexual assault and the preparedness to report it have increased and whether tolerance of sexual assault in prisons (both on the part of the administration and prisoners) has diminished.

6. Riots, 'lockdowns', time out of cell and escapes

The level of riots and major disturbances such as those which gave rise to the Nagle Royal Commission and were common in prisons across Australia in the 1960s and 1970s has diminished significantly. This has not been a linear process: there were numerous major disturbances during the reign of Michael Yabsley as Prisons Minister in the late 1980s and early 1990s (Brown, 1990, 1991). Nagle noted the practice of what we now call 'lockdowns', resulting from industrial action by prison officers, saying they caused 'great hardship to the prisoners' (1978: 228–9). Their use, which effects a form of collective punishment in a particular gaol or section and might be seen as an indicator of an intensification of penal discipline, seems to have become a more common practice since Nagle. Whatever the official reasons for lockdowns (security, drug searches, staffing, industrial), collective punishment and deprivation of prisoner access to amenities are clear effects.

Nagle was critical of the Department of Corrective Services, for not introducing more time out of cells (ibid: 201–2). He noted that time confined to cells varied and in secured institutions was up to 15 hours per day (i.e. nine hours out of cells) and in Grafton more than 17 hours a day (ibid: 330–1). He recommended that prisoners should not be locked in their cells overnight for longer than ten hours (ibid: 471). Hours out of cell was introduced as a performance measure for inmate care in the 1995 *Report on Government Service Provision*. In the 2004 *Report* for the year 2002–03 the average hours out of cells across all institutions were 10.6 total; 12.3 for open and 9.2 for secure prisons (SC, 2004:7.16–7), indicating little movement since Nagle. Preventing escapes has taken on a high priority in terms of expenditure on security and Departmental priorities. The rate of escapes in NSW is currently at its lowest level since 1980, 0.47 per 100 prisoners in open security and 0 in secure custody (SC, 2004: 7.16).

7. From bashings to sensory deprivation to Supermax

In a bold move Nagle recommended that the state's then newest high-security prison, Katingal, be abandoned, its cost being 'too high in human terms'. He added: 'it was ill-conceived in the first place, was surrounded by secrecy and defensiveness at a time when public discussion should have been encouraged. Its inmates are now suffering the consequences' (1978: 165). The exact rationale for Katingal is obscure given the secrecy surrounding its planning, but in part at least it was a replacement for the bash regime at Grafton, replacing physical brutality to so-called 'tracs' ('intractables') with sensory deprivation. Its closure was a victory for the prison movement and a testimony to Foucault's argument that prison revolts were: 'revolts, at the level of the body, against the very body of the prison. What was at issue was not whether the prison environment was too harsh or too aseptic, too primitive or too efficient, but its very materiality as an instrument and vector of power' (1978: 30).

Nagle favoured a policy of dispersal rather than concentration but the discussion was ill-developed (1978: 263–8). The Goulburn High Risk Management Unit (HRMU) opened in June 2001, appears to be the replacement for Katingal, for 'high-profile-crime' offenders and more recently anyone charged with alleged terrorist-related offences. Complaints about a lack of natural light and air, isolation, deprivation of association, lack of access to law books, limited and enclosed exercise, self mutilation and a generally harsh environment and regime, similar to complaints at Katingal, have recently been made. It has been alleged in parliament that the unit and its inhabitants have been subject to strategic media access at crucial junctures to suit 'tough on crime' political electioneering.

8. Prison discipline

Nagle reported in the shadow of the *Fraser* [1977] 2 NSWLR 867 decision which found that internal disciplinary courts presided over by visiting magistrates (VJ's) were 'courts' administering a 'punishment' within the meaning of the *Justices Act* 1902 and thus a right of appeal lay to the District Court. The *Fraser* decision had major repercussions, such as the requirement for a proper transcript of proceedings, and effectively ended what had widely been viewed as 'kangaroo courts', illustrated by one case in which prison activist Brett Collins was charged and convicted of an internal disciplinary offence for writing to the Legal Aid Manager of the NSW Law Society seeking assistance with a pending High Court appeal. VJ courts could no longer convict without some consideration of the evidence; legal representation was introduced and the conviction rates dropped significantly (Brown, 1986). Since then a substantial overhaul of prison disciplinary offences has occurred, retaining the VJ hearing for only a few specified more serious offences at which the prisoner is represented by the Prisoners Legal Service, while the vast bulk of offences are heard by the prison governor, whose power to increase the sentence length has been removed and from whom there is no right of appeal.

9. The legal status of prisoners and prisoners' rights

Nagle made a number of recommendations which were aimed at the legal status of prisoners in an attempt to remove elements of forfeiture and restrictions on legal subjectivity and citizenship. For example, he recommended the abolition of all restrictions on prisoners' right to sue, to vote, and to serve on juries (1978: 474). While the first was partly remedied by legislation to overturn the effect of the *Dugan* (1979) 53 ALJR 166 decision which upheld the antiquated notion of civil death of capital felons, neither clear rights to vote nor to serve on juries have come to fruition and in certain respects prisoners' rights to legal and political subjectivity are being eroded (Brown, 2002b). Prisoners in NSW serving more than 12-month sentences are not entitled to vote in NSW State elections. In federal elections where until recently prisoners serving less than five years retain the vote, the Howard government attempted in 1998 and again in 2004 to remove the franchise altogether but were defeated by the ALP, Democrats, Greens and Independents in the Senate (Ridley-Smith and Redman, 2002). In June 2004 following a compromise by the ALP the vote was restricted to prisoners serving three years or less.

Nagle recommended 'prisoners should have full access to legal advisers and to the Courts' (1978: 474). An overview by Edney (2001) suggests that there has been a movement away from the 'hands off' doctrine articulated most clearly by Dixon CJ in *Flynn v King* (1949) 79 CLR 1 at 8 that: 'prison regulations ... are directed to discipline and administration and not to the legal rights of prisoners...'. Edney argues that in the 1970s following prison riots and disturbances and the Nagle and other inquiries, courts 'became more cognisant of the rights of prisoners and demonstrated a greater willingness to intervene into the administration of prisons than had hitherto been the case' (2001: 113). However, he goes on to suggest that this willingness has transmuted into a form of 'hands off by stealth' achieved through deference to the judgment and 'expertise' of correctional administrators. Edney argues that such an approach ignores the particular vulnerability of prisoners and is empirically suspect, treating prison administration as a science rather than a matter of practical policy which is highly variable and as open to judicial inquiry as to its reasonableness as any other area of expertise or administration under established heads such as 'legitimate expectation'. Australian developments compare poorly with developments in the UK under the spur of the European Court of Human Rights and the Human

Rights Act 1998 (UK). International human rights law relevant to prisoners has had little direct effect in Australia (Minogue, 2002).

10. Drug use, culture, and security

There are only six entries on drugs in the index to the *Nagle Report*, with the longest discussion constituting one paragraph. Drug and particularly heroin use has now become a major feature of the criminalization of an identifiable 'delinquent' population, a 'delinquent cataloguing', either through drug use and dealing or through the commission of property offences such as theft, fraud, break and enter and armed robbery. Illegal drug use does not stop in prison as drugs are brought in on visits, through staff or in other ways. It might be possible to make an estimate of whether drug use in prison is now decreasing after a major upward trend since Nagle, through figures of drug seizures in prisons, although seizure levels may only be an effect of the level of resources devoted to drug searches and security, which have been stepped up in NSW.

Whatever the exact levels and whether increasing, levelling out or decreasing, drug dependency and use are now a major feature of the lives of many of those coming to prisons. The NSW Legislative Council *Final Report* put the figure of prisoners with 'a history of drug use' at 60 per cent of males and 70 per cent of females (2001: xv). Drug use, dealing and attempts at regulation have significantly affected prison life and culture in all sorts of ways, including the violent enforcement of drug debts incurred in prison, informing, and in breaking down older 'crim' solidarities and oppositional cultures (Brown, 1993). Drugs are now the major official justification for a battery of new technological identification and surveillance devices, urine testing, dog squads, strip searching, cell ramps, lockdowns, harassment of visitors, and increases in powers of search outside the confines of the prison. [2]

11. Access to programmes

There has been a significant expansion in prison programmes post-Nagle although availability is often limited both in numbers and location and their effectiveness in reducing recidivism remains unclear or unevaluated. Individual case management was introduced in the early 1990s and despite some criticism (ICAC, 1999) has promoted a shift in the roles of prison officers involved away from the purely custodial to a more welfarist, probation and parole type orientation. A multitude of smallish programme units (for example, for anger management, drug and alcohol use, violence prevention, sex offenders) are in operation, utilizing a variety of methodologies and aimed at specific categories of prisoners. Increasingly, completion of these programmes is required as a condition of a grant of parole or reclassification. Assessments of risk are clearly a key factor in the allocation of programme resources to particular prisoners. A part of the newly amended mission statement of the Department is to 'reduce re-offending through secure, safe, humane management of offenders' (NSWLC, 2001: 8).

12. Summary

To summarize, post-Nagle there have been major increases in the prison population as a rate, and of indigenous and remand populations in particular.

Sentencing changes include 'truth in sentencing', loss of remission, and restrictions on bail, all resulting in longer sentences. Prisoner-on-prisoner violence, some engendered by racial and ethnic streaming, seems more prevalent and deaths in custody have increased. Drug use has had a huge impact as a factor in increases in property crime, and on prison culture, security and health issues. However, there is less *official* physical violence, systematic bashings have stopped and animosities between prisoners and prison officers have diminished; riots, major disturbances and escapes are down; physical conditions have improved; the prison officer's role is being restructured in a welfare direction through case management; and there is a proliferation of programmes oriented around education and rehabilitation, although largely unevaluated in their effects, uneven in their reach and often subject to risk-based assessments and classification decisions. There has been little change in time out of cells. A new 'Supermax' section has concentrated a slightly different group of prisoners as a replacement for previous 'intractable' regimes based on sensory deprivation (Katingal) and bashings (Grafton). The legal status of prisoners and their partial status as citizens have shown elements of both continuity and regression as practices of forfeiture are continued and refurbished. The prison disciplinary system was legalized in the Nagle era and then more recently changed to internal administrative governance. Limited privatization (one prison) has taken place in NSW (cf. more extensive privatization in Victoria and Queensland) and some prison services have been privatized. Performance indicators on a range of criteria have been introduced as a form of monitoring at a national level while at the same time NSW prison watchdog agencies such as the Ombudsman have increasingly been muzzled and the Inspector-General's position was abolished in 2003.

The 'punitive turn' and late modernity

How might this overview of trends in aspects of penal practice in NSW over the last 26 years be explained in the more general analyses of the conditions of life in late modernity underpinning the punitive turn? The empirical (already in part theoretically framed) does not 'speak for itself' and particular developments might be pointed to as illustrations of any or all of the various accounts of the 'punitive turn' outlined at the start of this chapter, or indeed of accounts which challenge the existence or extent of such a turn. Individual practices and developments might be read as signifying continuity rather than change, others as signifying rupture; bringing us back to the realm of 'volatile and contradictory' penality (O'Malley, 1999). Probably the strongest indicator of shifts in political and public sensibilities in the direction of a 'punitive turn' or 'decivilization' can be found in the mandatory detention and shocking treatment of asylum seekers, including children, but significantly this has taken place in privatised detention centres under the political auspices of the federal government, outside the State-based penal welfare complex (HREOC, 2004).

It is probably true that at a more general cultural level there is a trend of decreasing interest in and sympathy for prisoners, a hardened public sensibility against offenders and a lack of concern over the treatment of prisoners, although this is more evident in relation to selected notorious offenders and offences of violence and is far more ambiguous in relation to juveniles and less serious offenders. It is undoubtedly the case that there has been a substantial increase in demands for recognition of victims' interests, sometimes in terms of an increased participation in the criminal justice system (including various restorative justice schemes like juvenile and family group conferencing and circle sentencing) and sometimes at a more abstract and rhetorical level as a code for diminution of suspects' rights, longer sentences and hostility to rehabilitative programmes. But what this survey of penal practices since Nagle tends to show, however sketchily and impressionistically, is that such changes in cultural sensibilities have not necessarily been translated on the ground into more punitive practices, at least in any uniform way, within the sphere of the actual delivery of punishment in a prison context, despite the significant increase in the use of imprisonment.

Apart from yet another demonstration of complexity, the discussion shows the importance of leavening the often brilliant and insightful results of discourse analysis with more mundane reference to the empirical, and not just the empirical as selected 'iconic' examples. In a replication of the 'bad news is good news'/ 'Hannibal Lector is coming to your suburb' format of the tabloids, the apocalyptic tendency noted by O'Malley tends to focus on the exceptional and the excessive, in the process passing over other tendencies which might conceivably provide a counterweight to the perceived inevitability of the 'eclipse of the solidarity project' (Garland, 1996: 463). One such tendency is a certain resilience in a battered and reconfigured penal welfarism, defined by Garland as a 'hybrid structure, combining the liberal legalism of due process and proportionate punishment with a correctionalist commitment to rehabilitation, welfare and criminological expertise' (2001a: 27). In what remains of this chapter I would like to sketch out a number of linked approaches which may contribute to under-estimating that resilience. These include a tendency to nostalgia in portraying the post-war settlement, overplaying its 'inclusive' character and underplaying earlier critiques of penal welfarism; a tendency to treat 'adaptive' responses to Garland's 'myth of sovereign crime control' as wholly neoliberal in character, minimizing some of their penal welfare continuities; a tendency to invoke Stan Cohen's net-widening critique against 'alternatives' in inappropriate contexts and in ways which distract from the paucity of, for example, post-release services; and a general tendency to focus on discourse rather than practice.

A critical defence of penal welfarism, its links to a 'broader politics of social change and a certain vision of social justice' (Garland, 1996: 466) and its social democratic heritage, might be assisted by less dystopic analyses which stress contestation rather than hegemony and thus open up rather than close off resistant spaces, politics and passions. It might be assisted also by an attempt to rethink a unitary and hostile view of 'popular punitiveness' in the direction of a more nuanced understanding which recognises the ambiguous nature of emotional responses, the legitimacy of popular demands for victim recognition and services, and the importance of social movement involvement in a range of penal and criminal justice campaigns contesting punitiveness.

Overplaying the 'inclusive' society and minimizing problems in penal welfarism

Some of the accounts which accentuate rupture and change overplay the dominance or hegemony of penal welfarism at its peak in the period of post-war reconstruction. Programmes of treatment and rehabilitation, aspirations of perfectibility and amelioration through social and economic reform, claims of equality, a cradle-to-the-grave welfare net, universal education and health care, redistribution through the tax system and the social wage, were always partial, contested, grafted on to earlier practices and traditions, subject to limits and less than ideal in their implementation (Garland, 1985: 257–60). Notions of an inclusive society which are now used as a point of reference and contrast for the shift to an 'exclusive society', omit significant sections of the populace, most obviously in Australia, Aborigines, non-whites and in various ways women. The implementation of treatment programmes frequently involved problematic features such as the suspension of important due process and proportionality protections, as critiques of the rehabilitative ideal made clear. Finnane notes that numerous Australian prison disturbances in the inter-war years provoked little concern and generated no public inquiries, and 'the prisoner's voice was little noticed and certainly rarely publicised', in contrast to the post-convict era. 'A political consensus on progressive penal reform largely distracted attention from any potential review of conditions within institutions' (1997: 143). The Grafton 'regime of terror' for 'intractables' (Nagle, 1978: 134) which ran for 33 years from 1943 was being planned 'at about the same time … that rehabilitation was being promoted as official policy in the NSW prison system and prisons were being called "moral hospitals"', leading Hogg to comment that 'a high price in hidden violence, brutality and discrimination was paid for social democratic solidarity and the passive political consensus that supported it' (2002: 240). As significant as the achievements of the post-war reconstruction carried out in the name of social democracy, the welfare state and the penal welfarism were, it is undesirable to romanticize and overplay their effects and reach so as to construct sharper accounts of the ruptures and cataclysmic changes wrought under neoliberalism or late modernity.

Underplaying the penal welfare roots of 'adaptive' responses

Many of the 'adaptive' measures attributed to the 'logics' and 'programmes' of neoliberalism and governmentality have a more hybrid genesis in earlier welfarist and social democratic concerns. One might be forgiven for thinking from some of the 'risk society' literature that the origins of insurance lay in neo-liberalism rather than in the formation of the 'social'. A commercial technique transposed to 'the vast domains of poverty' in an attempt to control the 'hazards' and social dislocations of the nineteenth century through mechanisms such as the unemployment benefit, it results in both a 'dedramatisation of social conflicts by eluding the question of assigning responsibility for the origin of "social evils"' and the creation of a 'passive social solidarity' (Donzelot, 1979a: 81; Hogg, 1988: 112–15). Or to take another more recent example such as 'early childhood intervention' programmes, there are elements of social work and welfare, discipline, epidemiology, medical care and employment training, parenting and health education, information provision, sanctions in the form of removal of the child in cases of neglect or abuse; redolent of Donzelot's 'tutelary complex' (1979b) through which the family, far from being a discreet 'private' institution in civil society was rendered permeable and open to a variety of state policies and interventions. Certainly on much closer analysis of the detail of specific programmes it is possible to trace the extent to which, as Garland (2001a: 175) suggests, notions of risk, culpability, personal responsibility and desert have increasingly permeated specific welfarist interventions and rehabilitative programmes. But such notions were often operative in earlier penal welfare formats of these programmes. In the prison context one of the most significant shifts in the trajectory from Nagle to the present is the reconstitution of prison officers away from a purely custodial role (from a prisoner's point of view locking and unlocking gates) to a more welfarist probation officer type role involving engagement with individual prisoners under the rubric of case management.

Looking behind the 'net-widening' mantra

A reading of the appeals by the NSW Legislative Council Committee in 2000 for the creation of bail hostels, probation hostels, halfway houses, drug rehabilitation units and transitional centres for women reveals that Stan Cohen's nightmare vision of a 'net-widening' extension of social control into the community through diversion into a network of halfway houses, ¼ and ¾ way houses and 'Community Correctional Facilities' (Cohen, 1979: 351) did not materialize, at least in NSW. It is true that since the 1970s new sentencing alternatives such as community service orders (CSOs), suspended sentences and home detention have been introduced and the number of people on community corrections orders has increased and involves at any one time three times as many people as are in prison, although evidence before the Legislative Council Committee noted that 'in the period 1994–1999 when NSW imprisonment rates increased dramatically, there was a corresponding decrease in community-based correctional orders' (2001: 113). But in terms of post-release halfway houses there is little change since Nagle, who recommended that the Department 'should in appropriate cases provide funding for halfway houses' (1978: 477). The whole thrust of the recent Legislative Council Report was that post-release services were woefully inadequate and that even for established community corrections orders such as CSOs, periodic detention or home detention they were often unavailable in rural areas or were difficult to access or unsuitable for women and for particular categories of offender such as indigenous people, people with mental illness, the homeless and drug dependent.

Rather than net-widening, the situation is closer to John Pratt's nightmare vision (Pratt, 2002a) in his review of Cohen's *Visions of Social Control* (1985), namely a lack of social control as the state vacates or offloads its responsibilities and services are insufficient and inadequate, leaving the way open for varieties of extreme neglect or vigilante action. The manager of Guthrie House (the only halfway house for women in NSW, with eight beds) in evidence before the NSW Legislative Council Committee on the Increase in the NSW Prison Population, recounted how one of the 90 women turned away from the house in that year was found in a park, 'lying in the grass just waking up from her night's sleep. She had been pretty stoned, drug affected.' When asked how she was going, she 'replied that she was not going very well, she thought she would be dead very soon and she was pretty desperate and did not know what to do' (NSWLC, 2000: 147–8). While Stan Cohen's net-widening thesis served a useful purpose in challenging the taken-for-granted benefits of community corrections and diversionary schemes, it is now time to consider the extent to which constant repetition of the 'net-widening' mantra tends to operate in tandem with neoliberal undermining of penal welfare provision. There is nothing particularly desirable about a form of freedom which can indeed mean 'nothing left to lose', as the disproportionate death rates of people serving community corrections orders (often on parole after release from prison) compared with those in prison show (Biles *et al.*, 1999). Further, automatic deployment of the 'net-widening' argument ignores the degree of commitment and political struggle necessary to establish and run a halfway house and the possibilities presented of their being sites of training in community-based activism and advocacy.

Differing fields and habitus: the discourse and practice of punishment

The continuities of penal welfarism in contemporary penality are indicative of certain underlying material issues and problems which cannot just be deconstructed, re-interpreted or 'spun' away. The backgrounds of social and economic disadvantage so depressingly familiar, recited in the NSW Legislative Council Report (e.g. '60% of NSW inmates are not functionally literate or numerate; 60% did not complete year 10 schooling; 64% have no stable family; 21% have attempted suicide; and 60% of males and 70% of females had a history of illicit drug use'; 2001: xiv–xv) will not disappear just because mentalities of choice, freedom, the market, incentive, personal responsibility, 'mutual obligation', risk calculation, and so on, are invoked, especially when such invocations are so often attended by a lessening of concern and provision for a more egalitarian distribution of wealth and life chances and a hardening of attitudes towards those who can be characterized as *in essence* unproductive, feckless, deviant, criminal, or 'other', and thus deserving of more and harsher punishment.

However appealing at a general rhetorical level the language of punitive denunciation, desert and forfeit may be, and however powerfully it may resonate within media flows and loops increasingly focused on affect, emotion and image, there are very real limits to the effectivity of such language when it comes to concrete practical issues of how to attribute culpability, judge, sentence and implement that sentence. That is part of the reason why many of the institutional sites and agents in the criminal justice system are still bearers of legal due process and penal welfare values while politicians, media columnists, talk-back radio personalities and many of their citizen callers are not: because the symbolic politics of law and order feeds on the abstract, the emotive and the discursive but falters at the specific and the practical. It is also why research suggests that public attitudes to sentencing and punishment become less punitive the more extensive the information provided about the circumstances of the offence and the background to the offender (Roberts *et al.*, 2003). Some of the appeal of popular punitiveness is precisely because it is part of a more general anti-elites attack which portrays the often defensive and sometimes arrogant responses of key criminal justice agents such as judges and lawyers and commentators such as academics, as out of touch with popular sentiment over penalty lengths, as operating a professional closed shop to which specific groups such as victims and more generally the tabloid-consuming public are excluded, and thus as undemocratic.

Some of this criticism is ill-informed, highly opportunistic and hypocritical, part of a more general political repertoire employed by multi-millionaire dema-gogues who claim to be the voice of the people or the 'battler', and who far from being marginalized are sufficiently powerful to increasingly influence the direction of criminal justice policy through media campaigns which are constantly monitored and appeased by governments; indeed sufficiently powerful in the NSW context to secure the dismissal or resignation of police commissioners and cabinet ministers. But as Ryan points out (2002; this volume) the public mobilized by such campaigns are engaging in a broader trend, a 'rise of the public voice' outside the formal and traditionally more deferential political structures, utilizing talk-back radio and the internet to 'operate on politicians through the media' as part of a 'democratic' anti-elites politics. At a more complex level such a politics is powerful because it connects with the tendency in late modernity for senses of community to be increasingly constructed, not through bonds of commonality, trust, sharing, equality, and recognition of difference, but through the risk of victimisation. It is as (supposedly equally) at risk individuals that community is increasingly constructed, in media loops saturated with images of violence, fear and insecurity, which acts of terrorism such as 11 September, the Bali bombings, and the 'war against terror' serve to accentuate. As Alison Young argues, a community founded on victimization is 'a simulacrum of a community; a phantasm that speaks of a nostalgic desire for oneness and unity, while at the same time structuring itself around its dependence upon fear, alienation and separateness for its elements to make sense' (Young, 1996: 10).

Rethinking and contesting popular punitiveness

But while some of the leading media exponents of popular punitiveness are demagogic and some of the 'uncivil' law and order policies generated are exceedingly dangerous in terms of the integrity of established institutions and traditions (Hogg and Brown, 1998), it is important to respond in ways that acknowledge the strength and legitimacy (even desirability) of emotive feelings and responses to violent crime in particular and avoid responses located solely on the terrain of the rational, the instrumental or the utilitarian. As Richard Sparks points out:

our engagement with crime and punishment is inherently ambiguous. It catches us as much in and through our attempts to express our better (more moral, more sympathetic, more civically responsible) selves as through the hatreds, enmities, prejudices and distortions so much beloved of media scholars, radical criminologists and moral panic theorists (2001: 210).

Precisely one of the strengths of new forms of increased victim and community involvement in various schemes under the rubric of restorative justice, such as juvenile and family group conferencing and circle sentencing, is the recognition that very strong, conflicting and ambiguous emotions are engendered, even in relation to what might be seen as minor crimes. The expression and channelling of that emotion is what often gives participants, from all positions and associations, a potential sense of involvement in and satisfaction with the process far greater than that derived from the seemingly impersonal, bureaucratic and exclusive everyday professional routines of the criminal court, hedged about as they are by the increasing pressures towards efficiency, cost effectiveness and 'clearing the lists'; although in some jurisdictions commentators suggest there is disenchantment and a declining victim interest in restorative justice schemes (Stenning, 2004).

While the disposition of criminal justice agencies forced to confront the practical problems of how to respond to specific cases is often tempered by a knowledge that judgment is not possible without understanding the specific actions in context and such understanding tends to generate and validate responses in terms of penal welfarism, the difficulty is how to articulate that response with the more legitimate features of popular punitiveness. Two of those features are the increasingly powerful emotive sentiments engendered by certain crimes, and the extent to which current criminal justice practices *do* exclude forms of victim participation which might give fuller expression to the passions and emotions so engendered and provide a greater sense of participation, resolution and justice. This is far from easy given that one of the key elements of a fair trial and a striving for justice in particular cases is precisely that emotions do not circulate in such a way or in such terms as to become prejudicial to a fair trial, productive of both miscarriages and yet further crimes committed in the name of populist justice.

But it is debilitating politically to cede or consign emotion, anger, and visceral passions only to penal campaigns waged around revenge and punitiveness. Anger and emotion over the disproportionate, unjust and racially inflected Northern Territory (NT) mandatory sentencing regime helped remove its architects from office in 2001 and led to its repeal by the incoming ALP NT government. Repealed at the same time was the 'punitive work order' introduced in 1996 and often cited as emblematic of the return of stigmatizing punishments in Australia (e.g. Pratt, 2000a: 129; 2002b: 176; Hallsworth, 2002: 156). In the four years they were in operation only 20 punitive work orders were made, illustrating a familiar pattern that was also apparent in the operation of the NT mandatory detention provisions, namely that legislation which is contrary to the habitus (cultural dispositions) of police, prosecutors, lawyers, magistrates, judges and in some cases juries, is mitigated, read down, avoided or under-utilized in various ways (Johnson and Zdenkowski, 2000; Freiberg, 2001). 'Punitive work orders' are another illustration of the danger of focusing on the discursive rhetoric ('stigmatizing clothing', 'a shameful experience') of its proponents and neglecting the practical empirical operation of particular provisions and, in this case, their eventual repeal through popular campaigns utilizing emotion and anger against punitiveness. A further complexity is that one of the reasons cited for the repeal of punitive work orders was that they were, according to the new Attorney General 'both ineffective and extremely expensive to maintain', as they required a detailed suitability assessment and one-on-one supervision; in practice then, some distance from a Georgia 'chain gang'.

As I write, a wave of international anger over violent and abusive treatment (including at least 39 deaths in custody) of prisoners in Iraq, Afghanistan, and Guantanamo Bay is threatening the electoral futures of individuals and governments in the 'coalition of the willing' unwilling to comply with the Geneva Conventions on the treatment of prisoners. At a local, state and national level, many individual citizens, volunteers, community groups, and social movements are currently engaged in Australia in a range of 'popular' involvements in various aspects of the criminal justice system: as mentors, victim support workers, community mediators, participants in family group and youth justice conferencing panels, indigenous circle-sentencing programmes and so on, not to mention ex-prisoner and community justice organizations campaigning, for example against the expansion of prisons, violence against women, deaths in custody and conditions in the HRMU 'Supermax', to mention only a few. Such involvements, actions and campaigns, utilizing the internet and 'lobbying outwards' (Ryan, this volume) are as much contestations within the 'popular' as are NIMBY ('Not in My Backyard') meetings called to oppose the opening of a women prisoners' transitional centre in inner-city Sydney or the public hounding of released sexual offenders and paedophiles (Lumby, 2002).

While all of the more general analyses of penality in late modernity listed at the beginning of this chapter have significantly enhanced understanding of transformations over the last three decades, there are tendencies in some of them which result in minimizing the extent of contestation in penal and criminal justice struggles; in over-reading the return of cultures and practices of cruelty and the pervasiveness of punitiveness; and in underplaying the resilience of penal welfarism and its social democratic heritage. Foremost among these tendencies perhaps is the neglect of the empirical, the nondiscursive, the particular to time and place, lost in the exciting generalities and transportability of discourse analysis. Theory is not its own justification and requires testing against an empirical or non-discursive dimension particular to time and place, or face rejection or modification. The project of linking penal transformations with major changes in the conditions of life in late modernity has revitalized the intellectual life of penology. But care needs to be taken to ensure that the desire to account theoretically for such transformations does not lead to investing their manifestations with such a coherence and inevitability as to consign citizens of late modernity to the position of hapless passengers on an express train to dystopia, from the windows of which other stations, lines and destinations flash past as mere blurs.

Notes

1   It should be noted that prisons in Australia are a State responsibility and that there is no federal prison system. Imprisonment rates have varied considerably across the States and across time, with high imprisonment rates historically in those States and territories with higher Aboriginal populations, namely the Northern Territory and Western Australia. Queensland has generally been above the national average, NSW on it, South Australia and Tasmania below it and Victoria and the Australian Capital Territory well below it. Imprisonment rates per 100,000 adult population on 30 June 2004 across States and territories were: NT 512.6; WA 212.6; Qld 177; NSW 179.7; Tas 122.9; SA 125.3; Vic 93.6; ACT 112.6; Aust av 157.1 which is a national increase of 43% since 1994 (from 127) (ABS, *Prisoners in Australia*, 2004, 12).

2   A letter from NSW Commissioner of Corrective Services, Ron Woodham, to the *Sydney Morning Herald*, reveals the considerable resources devoted to drug detection operations: 'Tough on drug detection' *SMH*, 3 November 2003. Commissioner Woodham argues that 'NSW has one of the most stringent drug-detection practices in the world'. Methods include:

   joint drug-interdiction operations with police; drug detector dog-unit deployment; visitor searches; comprehensive centre searches; daily searches in accommodation units; inmate strip searches before and after visits; a urine analysis programme randomly targeting all inmates and those suspected of drug usage.

   In the first six months this year there were 164,143 cell searches, 231 searches of the entire centre, 19,000 visitor searches and 150 vehicles were searched. As a result, 294 inmates were found with drugs or contraband resulting in visit restrictions and police charges.

References

ABS (2004) *Prisoners in Australia 2004*, Canberra: AGPS.

Beck, U. (1992) *Risk Society: Towards a New Modernity*, Newbury Park: Sage.

Biles, D. and McDonald, D. (eds) (1992) *Deaths in Custody Australia, 1980–1989 Research Papers of the Criminology Unit of the Royal Commission into Aboriginal Deaths in Custody*, Canberra: Australian Government Printer.

Biles, D., Harding, R. and Walker, J. (1999) 'The Deaths of Offenders Serving Community Corrections Orders', *Trends and Issues* No 107, Canberra: AIC.

Bottoms, A. E. (1995) 'The Philosophy and Politics of Punishment and Sentencing', in C. Clarkson and R. Morgan (eds) *The Politics of Sentencing Reform*, Oxford: Clarendon Press.

Brown, D. (1986) 'Prison Discipline, Legal Representation and the NSW VJ Courts', in R. Tomasic and R. Lucas (eds) *Power, Regulation and Resistance*, Canberra: School of Administrative Studies, Canberra CAE.

Brown, D. (1990) 'Putting the Value Back into Punishment', *Legal Service Bulletin*, 15(6): 177–185.

Brown, D. (1991) 'The State of Play in the Prisons under the Greiner Government: Definitions of Value', *Journal of Studies in Justice*, 4: 27–60.

Brown, D. (1993) 'Notes on the Culture of Prison Informing', *Current Issues in Criminal Justice*, 5(1): 54–71.

Brown, D. (2002a) 'The Politics of Law and Order', *Law Society Journal* (2002) October, 69–72.

Brown, D. (2002b) 'Prisoners as Citizens', in D. Brown and M. Wilkie (eds) *Prisoners as Citizens*, Sydney: The Federation Press.

Brown, D. (2004) 'The Nagle Royal Commission 25 years on', *Alternative Law Journal*, 29(3), 135–141.

Brown, D. and Wilkie, M. (2002) *Prisoners as Citizens*, Sydney: The Federation Press.

Brown, M. and Young, W. (2000) 'Recent Trends in Sentencing and Penal Policy in New Zealand', *International Criminal Justice Review*, 10: 1–31.

Chan, J. (1992) *Doing Less Time: Penal Reform in Crisis*, Sydney: Sydney Institute of Criminology.

Cohen, S. (1979) 'The Punitive City', *Contemporary Crises*, 3: 339–363.

Cohen, S. (1985) *Visions of Social Control*, London: Polity Press.

Cunneen, C. and Behrendt, J. (1994) 'Report to the National Committee to Defend Black Rights: Aboriginal and Torres Strait Islander Custodial Deaths Between May 1989 and January 1994', *Aboriginal Law Bulletin*, 68: 4.

Cunneen, C. and McDonald, D. (1997) *Keeping Aboriginal and Torres Strait Islander People Out of Custody*, Canberra: ATSIC.

Dalton, V. (1998) 'Prison Deaths 1980–97: National Overview and State Trends', *Trends and Issues* No 81, Canberra: AIC.

Dalton, V. (1999) 'Aboriginal Deaths in Prison 1980 to 1998: National Overview', *Trends and Issues* No 131, Canberra: AIC.

Donzelot, J. (1979a) 'The Poverty of Political Culture', *Ideology and Consciousness*, 5: 73–86.

Donzelot, J. (1979b) *The Policing of Families*, London: Hutchinson.

Edney, R. (2001) 'Judicial Deference to the Expertise of Correctional Administrators: The Implications for Prisoners' Rights', *Australian Journal of Human Rights*, 7(1): 91–133.

Feeley, M. and Simon, J. (1992) 'The New Penology: Notes on the Emerging Strategy of Corrections and its Implications', *Criminology*, 30(4): 449–74.

Feeley, M. and Simon, J. (1994) 'Actuarial Justice: The Emerging New Criminal Law', in D. Nelken (ed.) *The Futures of Criminology*, London: Sage.

Findlay, M. (2001) *The State of the Prison*, Bathurst: Mitchellsearch.

Finnane, M. (1997) *Punishment in Australian Society*, Melbourne: Oxford University Press.

Foucault, M. (1978) *Discipline and Punish*, New York: Pantheon.

Freiberg, A. (2001) 'Three strikes and you're out – it's not cricket: Colonisation and resistance in Australian sentencing', in M. Tonry and R. Frase (eds) *Sentencing and Sanctions in Western Countries*, New York: Oxford University Press.

Garland, D. (1985) *Punishment and Welfare*, Aldershot: Gower.

Garland, D. (1996) 'The Limits of the Sovereign State: Strategies of Crime Control in Contemporary Society', *British Journal of Criminology*, 36(4): 445–471.

Garland, D. (1997) '"Governmentality" and the problem of crime', *Theoretical Criminology*, 1(2): 173–214.

Garland, D. (2001a) *The Culture of Control*, Oxford: Oxford University Press.

Garland, D. (2001b) 'Introduction: The meaning of mass imprisonment', in D. Garland (ed.) *Mass Imprisonment*, Sage: London.

Garland, D. and Sparks, R. (2000) *Criminology and Social Theory*, Oxford: Oxford University Press.

Hallsworth, S. (2002) 'The Case for a Postmodern Penality', *Theoretical Criminology*, 6:2, 145–64.

Heilpern, D. (1998) *Fear or Favour: sexual assault of young prisoners*, Lismore: Southern Cross University Press.

Henry, R. W. (S.M.) (1979) *Report of Inquiry into Allegations of Misconduct by Prison Officers at Goulburn Gaol*, Sydney: NSWGP.

Hogg, R. (1988) 'Criminal Justice and Social Control: Contemporary Developments in Australia', *Journal of Studies in Justice*, 2: 89–122.

Hogg, R. (2001) 'Penality and Modes of Regulating Indigenous Peoples in Australia', *Punishment and Society*, 3(3): 355–79.

Hogg, R. (2002) 'Crime Control in Late Modernity', *Current Issues in Criminal Justice*, 14:2, 224–241.

Hogg, R, and Brown, D. (1998) *Rethinking Law and Order*, Sydney: Pluto Press.

Human Rights and Equal Opportunity Commission (HREOC) (2004) *A Last Resort?, The Report of the National Inquiry into Children in Immigration Detention*, Canberra: AGPS.

ICAC (1999) *Case Management in NSW Correctional Centres* Sydney: NSW GPS.

Johnson, D. and Zdenkowski, G. (2000) *Mandatory Injustice: Compulsory Imprisonment in the Northern Territory*, Sydney: Centre for Independent Journalism, UTS.

Lumby, C. (2002) 'Televising the Invisible: Prisoners, Prison Reform and the Media', in D. Brown and M. Wilkie (eds) *Prisoners as Citizens*, Sydney: The Federation Press.

Minogue, C. (2002) 'An Insider's View: Human Rights and Excursions from the Flat Lands', in Brown and Wilkie (eds) *Prisoners as Citizens*, Sydney: The Federation Press.

Nagle, J. (1978) *Report of the Royal Commission into NSW Prisons*, Sydney: NSW GPS.

NSW Legislative Council Select Committee on the Increase in Prisoner Population (2000) *Interim Report: Issues Relating to Women*, Sydney, NSW GPS.

NSW Legislative Council Select Committee on the Increase in Prisoner Population (2001) *Final Report*, Sydney: NSW GPS.

O'Malley, P. (1999) 'Volatile and contradictory punishment', *Theoretical Criminology*, 3(2): 175–196.

O'Malley, P. (2000) 'Criminologies of Catastrophe? Understanding Criminal Justice on the Edge of the New Millennium', *Australian and New Zealand Journal of Criminology*, 33(2): 153–167.

Pratt, J. (2000) 'The Return of the Wheelbarrow Men; or The Arrival of Postmodern Penality', *British Journal of Criminology*, 40(1): 127–45.

Pratt, J. (2000a) 'Emotive and Ostentatious Punishment: its decline and resurgence in modern society' *Punishment and Society*, 2(4): 417–40.

Pratt, J. (2002a) *Punishment and Civilisation*, London: Sage.

Pratt, J. (2002b) 'Critical Criminology and the Punitive Society: Some New "Visions of Social Control"', in K. Carrington and R. Hogg (eds) *Critical Criminology*, Cullompton: Willan.

Ridley-Smith, M. and Redman, R. (2002) 'Prisoners and the Right to Vote', in D. Brown and M. Wilkie (eds) *Prisoners as Citizens*, Sydney: The Federation Press.

Roberts, J., Stalans, L., Indermauer, D. and Hough, M. (2003) *Penal Populism and Public Opinion*, New York: Oxford University Press.

Rose, N. (1999) *Powers of Freedom: Reframing Political Thought*, Cambridge: Cambridge University Press.

Royal Commission into Aboriginal Deaths in Custody (RCIADC) (1991) *Final Report*, Canberra: AGPS.

Ryan, M. (2003) *Penal Policy and Political Culture in England and Wales*, Waterside Press: London.

Simon, J. (1995) 'They Died with Their Boots On, The Boot Camp and the Limits of Modern Penality', *Social Justice*, 22: 25–48.

Sparks, R. (2001) '"Bringing it all back home": Populism, Media Coverage and the Dynamics of Locality and Globality in the Politics of Crime Control', in K. Stenson and R. Sullivan (eds) *Crime, Risk and Justice*, Cullompton: Willan.

Stenning, P. (2004) 'Two Modes of Governance – Is There a Viable Third Way?' Opening Plenary Address, British Criminology Conference, University of Portsmouth, 6 July 2004.

Steering Committee for the Review of Commonwealth/State Service Provision (2004) *Report on Government Services* 2003, Canberra: AGPS.

Taylor, I. (1999) *Crime in Context*, Cambridge: Polity Press.

Vaughan, B. (2000) 'The Civilizing Process and the Janus-Face of Modern Punishment' *Theoretical Criminology*, 4(1): 71–91.

Vinson, A. (1982) *Wilful Obstruction*, Sydney: Methuen.

Wacquant, L. (2001) 'Deadly Symbiosis: When Ghetto and Prison Meet and Merge', *Punishment and Society*, 3(1): 95–133.

Wacquant, L. (2002) 'From Slavery to Mass Incarceration', *New Left Review*, January/February, 41–60.

Young, A. (1996) *Imagining Crime*, London: Sage.

Young, J. (1999) *The Exclusive Society*, London: Sage.

Zdenkowski, G. and Brown, D. (1982) *The Prison Struggle*, Melbourne: Penguin Books.

Zedner, L. (2002) 'Dangers of Dystopias in Penal Theory', *Oxford Journal of Legal Studies*, 22(2): 341–366.

3. Crime control in Western countries, 1970 to 2000

Lyn Hinds

This chapter explores variation among states in the United States, Europe, and Australia in crime control from 1970 to 2000 using two measures: the number of people incarcerated per 100,000 population and the number of police (sworn and non-sworn) per 100,000 population. Custody rates are a back-end measure of developments in crime control, whereas police employee rates are a measure of activities at the front end of the criminal justice system.

Custody rates are a familiar measure of crime control. Contrary to an assumed uniformity in increases in punitiveness in crime control over the last three decades, which has been most prominently measured by increasing rates of imprisonment, findings reveal great diversity among states within the United States, and between the United States, Europe, and Australia. Analysis of police rates reveals greater homogeneity and stability among Western states and over time. These findings suggest two things. First, there is limited utility in thinking about crime control developments using a singular framework of punitiveness and increases in national custody rates as its measure. Second, a clearer but more complex picture emerges of what is happening in states by analysing both front- and back-end measures of crime control over time. The understanding of US exceptionalism compared to other Western nations is challenged by distinctive regional signatures in custody and police rates in states within the United States, and homogeneity and stability in police rates among Western nations. Differences in the nature of policing are linked to variation in levels of imprisonment in Western nations.

Comparing criminal justice systems

Comparative research on crime control in Western nations is a quixotic enterprise. While offering the promise of simplifying complexity or enlarging singularity, comparative research abounds with selection decisions that challenge the usefulness of research findings. Comparisons of the level and type of crime and changes over time are limited by data availability, data compatibility caused by definitional problems, and procedural practices in the offences recorded, cleared, and prosecuted (see Parks, 1975; Collier and Tarling, 1987; Lynch, 2002).

Comparisons of state variation in the level of punishment based on a single measure, such as imprisonment rates, are limited by not considering other custodial policies, including prison admissions, the length of prison sentences, the numbers of confined but unconvicted offenders, the numbers sentenced to custody rather than community-based sanctions and fines, and parole practices (see Wilkins and Pease, 1987; Young and Brown, 1993; Pease, 1994; Lynch, 2002).

Other factors relevant to crime control policy decision-making are crime rates, sentencing practices, conviction rates, and resource allocations (see Kommer, 1994; Langan and Farrington, 1998; Spelman, 2000; Kuhn, 2003). Structural differences in criminal justice systems between common law and civil law and legal traditions significantly challenge comparative research, as do the broader political, social, economic, cultural, and historical contexts of criminal justice policies and practices within and between nations (see Garland, 1990; von Hofer, 2003). As Garland (1990) has noted, punishment levels are not dictated solely by the instrumental goal of crime control. A range of symbolic values and norms are expressed in a society's response to crime, including the extent to which punishment is viewed as the right response to crime, and the level of punitiveness considered to be tolerable in a civilized society (Pratt, 1995).

Methodological approaches also affect the utility of research (see Lynch, 2002; Nelken, 2002). Research that uses a larger number of variables in a few selected jurisdictions, or a few variables in a larger number of jurisdictions, is limited by problems of small sample size and data aggregation at the national level (see Biles, 1983; Doleschal, 1977; Kommer, 1994; Lynch, 1988, 2002; Savelsberg, 1994; Young and Brown, 1993).

In acknowledging these difficulties, it is important to not lose sight of the commonalities shared by Western criminal justice systems. For example, Tonry (1999: 50) reminds us that Western countries share similar concepts of justice (such as the presumption of innocence, right to counsel, and judicial independence), and investigative and adjudicative institutions of police, prosecutors, and judges.

Measuring crime control

Custody is the primary measure of a more punitive direction of crime control policies during the last three decades. It is also the most readily available penal measure and represents the most severe sanction generally in Western nations. While increases in imprisonment rates have been experienced by most Western nations,[1] it is the United States that has gone further than other nations. Garland (2001: 5) characterizes the fivefold increase in US imprisonment rates over the last three decades as a 'pathological phenomenon' that differentiates the United States from other Western nations. In 1972 the United States recorded its lowest imprisonment rate in almost half a century; but by mid-2002 over two million people were incarcerated in US prisons and jails (US Dept of Justice, 2002).

Western nations vary widely in the level of prison use. For example, in the year 2000, imprisonment rates among European Union countries varied from a low of 58 people per 100,000 population in Denmark to a high of 124 people per 100,000 population in the United Kingdom (Walmsley, 2003). In the same year, there were

113 people per 100,000 population in prison in Australia and six times that rate, a massive 685 people, in prisons and jails in the United States (Walmsley, 2003).

In federal countries like the United States and Australia, aggregated national data mask large differences in prison use across states. In 2000, imprisonment rates varied among US states from a low of 127 people per 100,000 population in Maine to a high of 800 in Louisiana (US Dept of Justice, 2002). In Australia in 2000, Victoria recorded the lowest imprisonment rate of 62 people per 100,000 population compared with a high of 321 in the Northern Territory (Australian Bureau of Statistics, 2001).

Explanatory accounts of increased punitiveness in Western nations focus on a number of factors, including rising crime rates, economic and social disruption, postmodernist angst, cultural factors and popular punitivism (see Bottoms, 1995; Caplow and Simon, 1999; Garland, 1996; Mauer, 2001; Savelsberg, 1994; Tonry, 1999, 2001; Tyler and Boeckmann, 1997). Accounts of US exceptionalism in increased punitiveness, particularly the disproportionately higher rates of imprisonment of African Americans, centre on the interconnection between race, crime, and drugs (see Beckett, 1997; Blumstein and Beck, 1999; Edsall and Edsall, 1991; Sampson and Lauritsen, 1997; Tonry, 1995).

While increases in the use of imprisonment are the most prominent measure of a more punitive crime control over the last three decades, it is an inadequate measure because imprisonment rates are not a uniform phenomenon within or among Western states. It is inadequate to uncritically accept an understanding of what is happening in crime control based on a singular measure of the extent of custodial control at the back end of the criminal justice system. Moreover, a focus on prison use skews our understanding towards acceptance of an assumption of increased punitiveness in crime control, not only at the back end of the criminal justice system, but throughout the entire system. For example, and consistent with the contemporary understanding of increased punitiveness in crime control, a range of policies over the last three decades emphasize increased punitiveness in law enforcement: zero-tolerance policing (Grabosky, 1999), political rhetoric that emphasises *law and order* themes of more police and wider police powers (Hogg and Brown, 1998), and technologies such as electronic surveillance, private security companies, and gated communities that increasingly exclude targeted groups and behaviours from public spaces (see Davis, 1992).

Is this correct? Does increased punitiveness adequately characterize crime control developments in the criminal justice systems of Western nations over time? In this study, police rates are analysed to explore developments at the front end of the criminal justice system, as an alternative to the use of custody at its back end.

Policing activities have been measured using a number of variables, including arrest rates, expenditure on policing, and the number of police employees (see Bayley, 1985). In this study the preferred measure of policing activities at the front end of the criminal justice system, for both conceptual and methodological reasons, is the number of police employees. Conceptually, the number of police employees captures differences in policing activities among states and over time independent of variation in police organization and the scope and nature of policing practices and objectives (see Bayley, 1985). The number of police employees was identified as significant in three separate factor analyses of over

30 variables (including expenditure on policing) that differentiated crime control developments in US states in three time periods between the early 1970s and late 1990s (see Hinds, 2002).

Research has linked police numbers to economic inequality (Jacobs, 1979; Jacobs and Helms, 1997), and the size of the black or non-white population (Liska *et al.*, 1981; Greenberg *et al.*, 1985). Stern (1998: 34) argues that lower imprisonment rates in some countries may be related to the use of lethal force in street-level law enforcement. Using national level data, Neopolitan (2001) found a negative relationship between use of imprisonment and street-level law enforcement (defined as use of excessive and lethal extra-legal force), use of corporal punishment, and informal family and tribal responses to crime.

Data measures and method

This study analyses state-level data. The United States and Australia are federal countries: statistics aggregated at the national level do not adequately quantify diversity across state jurisdictions. In the United States, corrections and courts are primarily administered at the state level, while policing is primarily a municipal/ local government responsibility. In Australia, policing, corrections, and courts are primarily the responsibility of states. Europe is a fictional creation comprising the 17 European Union states.[2] In European countries criminal justice decision-making is centralized: Germany's federal system is an exception.

My analysis of United States data also uses regions to identify and examine patterns. Imprisonment rates in the United States are strongly and positively related to jurisdictions in the South and to large percentages of African Americans (Blumstein, 1982; Liska, 1987; Tonry, 1995). US states are grouped using the well-established four regions of South, West, Midwest, and Northeast. These are used in many US data sources, including the *Statistical Abstract of the United States* and the *Sourcebook of Criminal Justice Statistics*.

Data for 50 US states are analysed; the District of Columbia (DC) is excluded due to the extremity of its data. Australian data include six states; the Northern Territory is excluded due to extreme data and the Australian Capital Territory (ACT) is excluded for methodological reasons.[3] Data for the United Kingdom are not aggregated: England and Wales, Scotland, and Northern Ireland are analysed separately as distinct European countries.

This comparative study of state variation in crime control uses two measures. The *custody rate* is the number of people incarcerated per 100,000 population. The *police employee rate* is the number of sworn and non-sworn police per 100,000 population. Both variables were identified from three factor analyses of over 30 variables that differentiated crime control policies in the 50 US states at three points in time: the early 1970s, the mid-1980s and the late 1990s (Hinds, 2002).

For the United States, the custody rate combines both prison and jail rates.[4] Combined US imprisonment and jail rates are compared with state imprisonment rates in states in Australia and European Union member countries. Custody rates include sentenced and unsentenced persons. Police employee rates include sworn and non-sworn police employees. US data were calculated as full-time equivalent (FTE) employment.

Analyses cross four decades: 1970, 1980, 1990, and 2000.[5] Analysis of 1970 data should capture state characteristics prior to the influence of the get-tough movement and increases in custody use. Data for each year were examined to ensure the year selected was not an outlier. The significance of relationships between variables is analysed using difference of means tests. Analyses are of entire state populations, not sample populations.

Findings

Study 1: Custody rates

Table 3.1 presents changes in custody rates per 1,000 population[6] in the United States, Australia, and Europe across four decades, in 1970, 1980, 1990, and 2000. There are significant differences between jurisdictions over time. The use of custody is consistently higher across time in states in the United States compared with states in Australia and Europe. For example, in 1970 custody rates in the United States were 1.3 people per 1,000 population, compared with .81 in Australia and .65 in Europe. By 2000, in the United States there were 6.15 people in custody per 1,000 population, compared with 1.1 in Australia and .87 in Europe. Increases in custody rates in the United States were significant in each decade. In both Australia and Europe increases were significant between 1990 and 2000 only. Between 1970 and 2000, custody use in the United States increased by 473 per cent, compared with increases of 136 per cent in both Australia and Europe.

Table 3.2 explores custody use within the 50 US states grouped into four regions of South, West, Midwest, and Northeast, and finds significant regional differences in custody rates over time. In 1970, 1980, 1990, and 2000, the use of custody was consistently higher in the South and lower in the Northeast and Midwest compared with other regions. For example, in 1970 the custody rate in the South was 1.78 people per 1,000 population, compared with 1.01 in the Midwest and .81 in the Northeast. By 2000 the custody rate in the South was 8.34 people per 1,000 population, compared with 4.86 in the Midwest and 4.09 in the Northeast. Custody rates are average in the West over time.

The data from Tables 3.1 and 3.2 are shown graphically in Figure 3.1. The higher use of custody in states in the United States, and the dramatic increases between 1970 and 2000, are clear and pronounced in comparison with states in Australia and Europe, which are similar in custody use across the three decades of the study.

States in the southern United States use custody significantly more than states in other US regions or states in Australia and Europe over time. In 1970, the custody rate in the South was 1.78 people per 1,000 population, compared with 1.3 in the West, 1.01 in the Midwest, and .81 in both the Northeast and Australia and .64 in Europe. By 2000 the South's custody rate of 8.34 people per 1,000 population was higher than 6.08 in the West, 4.86 in the Midwest, and 4.09 in the Northeast, 1.1 in Australia, and .87 in Europe.

The South's higher custody rate compared with other US states, and states in Australia and Europe, is evident before the impact of the get-tough movement in

Table 3.1 Custody rates per 1,000 population in the United States, Australia and Europe by time period

		Number	Mean	Std dev	t	df	Sig. (2-tailed)*
1970/80	US1970	50	1.3	.57			
	US1980	50	1.78	.83	8.43	49	.000
	Aust1970	6	.81	.24			
	Aust1980	6	.72	.22	−1.61	5	.168
	Eur1970	15	.65	.31			
	Eur1980	15	.72	.36	.95	14	.36
1980/90	US1980	50	1.78	.83			
	US1990	50	3.5	1.43	16.23	49	.000
	Aust1980	6	.72	.22			
	Aust1990	6	.73	.2	.27	5	.799
	Eur1980	16	.72	.35			
	Eur1990	16	.75	.2	.48	15	.637
1990/2000	US1990	50	3.5	1.43			
	US2000	50	6.15	2.35	17.62	49	.000
	Aust1990	6	.73	.2			
	Aust2000	6	1.1	.4	4.42	5	.007
	Eur1990	17	.75	.19			
	Eur2000	17	.87	.22	2.06	16	.056
1970/2000	US1970	50	1.3	.57			
	US2000	50	6.15	2.35	17.5	49	.000
	Aust1970	6	.81	.24			
	Aust2000	6	1.1	.4	2.09	5	.091
	Eur1970	16	.64	.3			
	Eur2000	16	.87	.23	2.41	15	.029

The number of European states varies: $n=15$ in 1970/80; $n=16$ in 1980/90; $n=17$ in 1990/2000; $n=16$ in 1970/2000.

the mid–late 1970s. The extremity of the South's use of custody over time differentiates it from other US states and those in Europe and Australia.

In 1970 custody use in the Northeast was the same as that in Australia. The custody rate in Australia decreased between 1970 and 1980, from .81 to .72 people per 1,000 population, compared with an increase from .81 to 1.00 in the Northeast. By 1990 the use of custody is significantly higher in the Northeast and all US regions compared with Australia and Europe. Australia and Europe are most alike in custody use. In 1970, 1980, 1990, and 2000 custody rates in Australia and Europe are similar.

Study 2: Police rates

Table 3.3 presents police rates per 1,000 population in the United States, Australia, and Europe across four decades. In 1970 there were 2.93 police per 1,000 population in Europe and 1.97 in both the United States and Australia. By 2000, there were 3.39 police per 1,000 population in the United States, 3.05 in Europe, and 2.29 in Australia. Increases in police rates in the United States were significant in each decade, while increases in police rates in Europe were

Table 3.2 Independent sample means and t-tests for custody use, by US region and time period

	1970			1980			1990			2000		
	Mean	Std. dev.	t-value	Mean	Std. dev.	t-value	Mean	Std. dev.	t-value	Mean	Std. dev.	t-value
South												
Sth = 16	1.78	.42	5.34***	2.55	.69	5.54***	4.55	1.26	4.07***	8.34	2.29	5.11***
Rest = 34	1.07	.48		1.42	.62		3.00	1.24		5.12	1.54	
West												
West = 13	1.3	.6	.029	1.76	.72	-.13	3.54	1.36	.11	6.08	1.3	-.18
Rest = 37	1.3	.56		1.79	.87		3.48	1.47		6.18	2.63	
Midwest												
MW = 12	1.01	.33	-2.74***	1.38	.45	-2.75***	2.79	1.04	-2.43***	4.86	1.39	-3.02***
Rest = 38	1.39	.6		1.91	.88		3.72	1.48		6.56	2.45	
Northeast												
NE = 9	.81	.28	-4.67***	1.00	.39	-5.26***	2.52	1.14	-2.7***	4.09	1.36	-4.36***
Rest = 41	1.41	.56		1.95	.8		3.71	1.41		6.61	2.29	

Equal variances not assumed
***p = <.001; **p = <.05; *p <1.0.

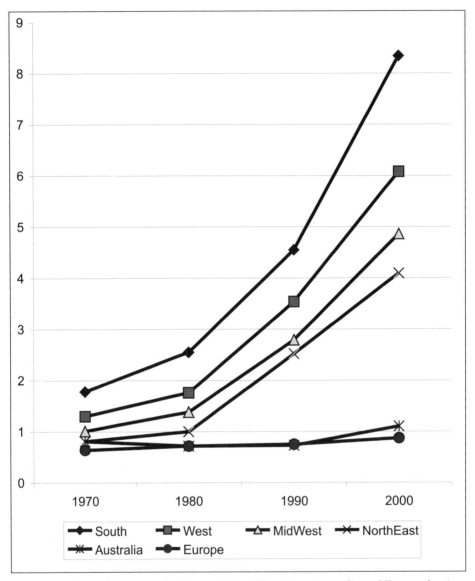

Figure 3.1 Custody rates per 1000 population, US regions, Australia and Europe, by time period

significant between 1980 and 1990. Police rates are consistently lower in Australia compared with other countries from 1980 onwards. Between 1970 and 2000, police rates in the United States increased by 172 per cent, compared with increases of 116 per cent in Australia and 110 per cent in Europe.

Table 3.4 presents findings for police rates by region in the United States in three time periods. The South had lower police rates in 1970 and 1980 compared with other regions, and the Midwest had lower police rates in 1990 compared with other regions. The Northeast and West had consistently average police rates over time. By 2000 police rates were average in all four regions: in the South there

Table 3.3 Police rates per 1,000 population in the United States, Australia and Europe by time period

		Number	Mean	Std dev	t	df	Sig. (2-tailed)*
1970/80	US1970	50	1.97	.51			
	US1980	50	2.45	.45	−14.08	49	.000
	Aust1970	6	1.97	.21			
	Aust1980	6	2.1	.28	−1.4	5	.222
	Eur1970	10	2.93	.87			
	Eur1980	10	3.03	.85	.4	9	.695
1980/90	US1980	50	2.45	.46			
	US1990	50	2.67	.5	−6.92	49	.000
	Aust1980	6	2.1	.28			
	Aust1990	6	2.23	.16	−1.2	5	.284
	Eur1980	12	2.72	.99			
	Eur1990	12	3.4	.76	−2.79	11	.018
1990/2000	US1990	50	2.67	.5			
	US2000	50	3.39	.65	−12.18	49	.000
	Aust1990	6	2.23	.16			
	Aust2000	6	2.29	.21	−.9	5	.408
	Eur1990	16	3.21	.75			
	Eur2000	16	3.22	1.1	−.094	15	.926
1970/2000	US1970	50	1.97	.51			
	US2000	50	3.39	.65	−14.08	49	.000
	Aust1970	6	1.97	.21			
	Aust2000	6	2.29	.21	−4.07	5	.010
	Eur1970	12	2.94	.8			
	Eur2000	12	3.05	.82	−.413	11	.687

The number of European states varies: $n=10$ in 1970/80; $n=12$ in 1980/90; $n=16$ in 1990/2000; $n=12$ in 1970/2000.

were 3.53 police per 1,000 population, compared with 3.45 in the West, 3.19 in the Midwest, and 3.33 in the Northeast. Between 1970 and 2000, police rates increased by 151 per cent in the Northeast, 159 per cent in the West, 171 per cent in the Midwest, and 197 per cent in the South.

The graphic presentation of police data from Tables 3.3 and 3.4 (see Figure 3.2) reveals a distinctly different pattern in police rates compared with that for custody rates. In contrast to large increases in custody rates, increases in police rates are smaller and comparatively homogeneous among states in the United States, Europe, and Australia over time.

In 1970 police rates are higher in Europe than in states in the United States and Australia. By 2000, police rates are average in all states except Australia, which are lower than in the United States and Europe. Increases in police rates were larger in US states between 1970 and 2000 compared with states in Europe and Australia.

States in Europe and the Northeast of the US were most alike in police rates over time. In 1970, there were 2.94 police per 1,000 population in Europe and 2.21 in the Northeast. In 1980, police rates were 2.76 in Europe and 2.66 in Europe. In

Table 3.4 Independent sample means and t-tests for police rates, by US region and time period

	1970			1980			1990			2000		
	Mean	Std. dev.	t-value	Mean	Std. dev.	t-value	Mean	Std. dev.	t-value	Mean	Std. dev.	t value
South												
$n = 16$	1.79	.38	−2.00**	2.3	.34	−1.92**	2.59	.42	−.81	3.53	.71	.98
Rest = 34	2.05	.54		2.53	.49		2.71	.54		3.33	.63	
West												
$n = 13$	2.17	.53	1.65	2.64	.48	1.63	2.79	.49	1.05	3.45	.52	.43
Rest = 37	1.9	.48		2.39	.43		2.63	.5		3.37	.7	
Midwest												
$n = 12$	1.8	.37	−1.57	2.31	.37	−1.46	2.43	.37	−2.33**	3.19	.52	−1.44
Rest = 38	2.02	.53		2.5	.47		2.75	.52		3.46	.68	
Northeast												
$n = 9$	2.21	.66	1.31	2.66	.58	1.24	2.59	.68	1.43	3.33	.88	−.23
Rest = 41	1.91	.46		2.41	.42		2.61	.44		3.41	.61	

Equal variances not assumed
***$p = <.001$; **$p = <.05$; *$p <1.0$.

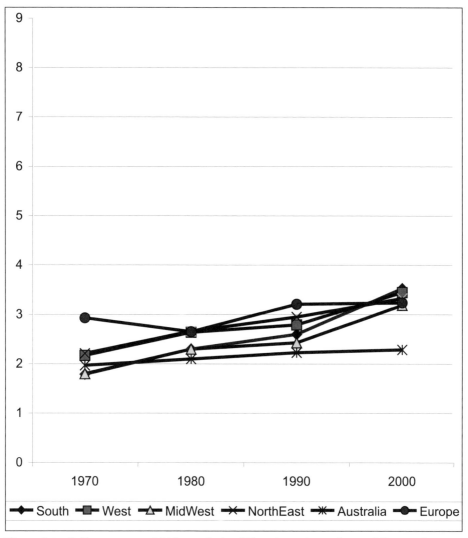

Figure 3.2 Police rates per 1,000 population US regions, Australia, and Europe, by time period

1990 Europe's police rate was 3.21 compared with 2.95 in the Northeast. By 2000, the police rate in Europe was 3.22 compared with 3.33 in the Northeast. Between 1970 and 2000, police rates increased by 110 per cent in Europe and 151 per cent in the Northeast.

Discussion

Analyses of crime control at the state level in the United States, Australia and Europe show two contrasting trends. First, there is increasing variation and diversity over time in the use of custody. Second, there is greater homogeneity and stability in police rates over time. While increases in custody rates at the back end of the criminal justice system are consistent with the contemporary understanding of increased punitiveness in crime control, stability in front-end policy outcomes, as measured by police rates, suggests different forces.

Consistent with the literature, custody rates are significantly and consistently higher in the United States over time compared with states in Australia and Europe. Custody data show that 'getting tougher' by imprisoning more people has not been pursued by states in Australia and Europe as strongly as it has been in the United States. Just as the appeal of punitiveness is stronger in some US regions than others, some Western countries are less reliant on imprisonment than others.

Police rates tell a different story about crime control. Police rates show greater homogeneity and stability in the United States, Europe, and Australia over time. While there is greater diversity among US states in custody rates in 2000 than there was in 1970, US states are more alike in police rates in 2000 than three decades earlier. Police rates suggest that states in Europe and Australia continue to focus, and have over time focused, on the front end of the criminal justice system and policing more than custody use. States in these countries exhibit similar national signatures in a focus on policing activities at the front end of the criminal justice system.

These findings suggest that states can be characterized by their place on a *crime control continuum*:[7] at one end are policing activities of social control at the front end of the criminal justice system and, at the other, policies focused on custodial control at the back end of the criminal justice system. States in Europe and Australia are closest to the social control end. States in the United States are towards the custodial control end, with states in the South at the extreme of custodial control. US states in the Northeast, Midwest and West lie midway.

The concept of a continuum gives a more accurate picture of states' crime control directions over the last few decades. It shows that some states have got tougher than others. As well as the *push* towards increased punitiveness and higher custody rates, it is also valid to discuss the *pull* of maintaining social order at the front end of the criminal justice system, or what constrains states' greater custody use.

In the remainder of this chapter, I suggest three ways that these findings add to our understanding of crime control in Western countries between 1970 and 2000. First, while increases in incarceration have been prominently emphasized in the contemporary literature, my study shows that the more important story is *variation*. Increases in custody rates in US states over time are an inadequate measure of crime control because it is to be expected that there will be smaller increases when base rates are high, and larger increases when base rates are smaller. Increasing disparity over time shows important regional differences within the United States in the appeal of getting tougher on offenders. While there have been increases in custody rates in all US states, the South stands out from the rest. The data shown in Figure 3.1 dramatically reveal the extent to which the South is tougher at the back end of the criminal justice system compared with other states. The South has higher custody use across three decades, but lower police rates between 1970 and 1990; police rates are average in the South in 2000. States in the Northeast, in contrast, have lower custody use and average police rates over time.

The consistently higher use of custody in the South during the last four decades is consistent with long-term patterns: since 1940 imprisonment rates are consistently higher in the South, which is typically viewed as more conservative, compared with lower rates in the Northeast and Midwest states, which are generally viewed as more liberal (Blumstein, 1982; Cahalan, 1986; Wright *et al.*, 1987; Zimring and Hawkins, 1991). Over the last three decades the disparity in custody use between the South and other states has expanded dramatically.

These findings support a view that themes used in the get-tough movement found a more receptive audience in southern states. According to Beckett (1997), race was initially used by politicians in the South to oppose the civil rights movement. Race, and the war on drugs in particular, were politicized at a national level as part of the crime problem by Republican Presidents Nixon, Reagan, and Bush (see Musto, 1987; Simon, 2001; Tonry, 1995). While imprisonment rates increased in all US states, rates are higher in the South due to its history of race relations, and increased anxiety due to larger percentages of African Americans in the populations of southern states.

A second implication drawn from this study is the challenge to explanations of increased punitiveness that draw on broad 'Western' cultural factors (see Garland, 1996, 2000). Findings challenge the notion that cultural factors centred on punitiveness alone are the main determinant of larger increases in custody use and more diversity among Western states at the back end of the criminal justice system, but smaller increases in police and greater homogeneity among states at the front end of the criminal justice system.

According to Garland (1996), state failure to control crime effectively has weakened the authority of the state. The state's response has been, first, to retreat from responsibility as sole or principal provider of protection for a range of social ills, including crime; and second, to reassert its power to punish (Garland, 1996). Reasserting the power to punish is a back-end strategy that this study shows has been differentially pursued by Western states. The reclamation of state sovereignty via the power to punish has been pursued much more strongly in some states than others: there is greater variation in custody rates between Europe, Australia, and the United States by the year 2000 than three decades earlier.

The third implication from this study centres on challenges to the responsibilization strategy, which is linked to policing activities at the front end of the criminal justice system. Garland (1996) argues that states have stepped back from ownership of the crime problem and made individuals, communities, and organizations primarily responsible for their own safety and welfare. Findings from this study reveal that there is little variation among states and over time in police rates, a measure of front-end crime control activity. Contrary to what might be expected if the responsibilization strategy adequately characterizes developments in crime control at the front end of the criminal justice system, states have maintained their sovereign investment in policing.

Findings from this analysis of changes in police rates in the United States, Australia, and Europe between 1970 and 2000 suggest support for a distinction between *policing for public order* and *policing for crime control*. Policing activities in states in Australia and Europe that aim to maintain public order do not necessarily feed states' back-end punishment systems, which is reflected in lower custody rates at the back end of the criminal justice system. Policing for crime control is related to law-enforcement activities aimed at the detection and apprehension of street criminals, particularly in the United States, which is linked to higher custody rates in US states, particularly in the South.

Such a distinction in the focus of policing among Western nations may be related to differences in institutions of social control other than the criminal justice system (see Bayley, 1985; Lynch, 2002; Nelken, 2002). The contemporary governance literature, particularly from the United States, draws attention to developments in crime control over the last three decades that are characterized as increasingly part of the management of problem populations due to the loss of other mechanisms of social control (see Simon, 1997). Compared with the United States, the broader social welfare systems in Australia and Europe suggest retention of stronger institutions of informal social control other than the criminal justice system (see Downes, 2001; Nelken, 2002).

The concept of policing for crime control is also supported by the more intense politicization of crime control evident in the United States in comparison with Australia and Europe. For example, research on the 'war on drugs' in the United States shows that the number of offenders available for criminal justice processing was largely determined by the level of proactive police enforcement (see Tonry, 1995; Daly and Tonry, 1997; Caplow and Simon, 1999).

The number of police alone can say little about whether policing is experienced as exclusionary and restrictive, or whether socially disadvantaged communities experience policing in similar ways to middle-class and affluent communities. The decarceration movement of the 1970s, where the formal system of control in the prison was added to, not replaced, by less formal control in the community, provides a salutary example of the reluctance of the state to lessen levels of social control (see Scull, 1977; Cohen, 1979, 1985). Research by Neopolitan (2001) suggests that low incarceration rates in some states are associated with extra-legal, street-level responses to crime by law-enforcement officials.

While developments in policing over the last three decades have been characterized as tougher and more exclusionary, the data show that police rates have remained relatively stable. Homogeneity in police rates exists alongside state diversity in increases in custody rates. Crime control is not a uniform or singular development in Western states. Drawing a distinction between policing for public order and policing for crime control, while speculative, offers an account of contemporary variation and increasing disparity among states in the level of custody use over time, while also providing a plausible framework for further research.

Conclusion

This study shows that analysing both custody and police rates reveals distinctly different crime control patterns over time in the United States, Australia, and Europe that provide a more accurate and complex picture than that available from custody rates alone. Findings show that punitiveness, as measured by increasing custody rates, does not adequately account for crime control variations across states over the last few decades. The data also show that contemporary understanding of US exceptionalism in the use of custody is inadequate because it fails to take into account variation among US states: in addition to increases in imprisonment rates, data show states have become more diverse between 1970 and 2000. Variation within the United States and between the United States, Australia, and Europe in the extent to which some states have got tougher than others raises questions such as why some states have resisted getting tougher, or why getting tougher has been more vigorously pursued in some states than others.

Empirical analyses of police rates in the United States, Europe, and Australia show more stability and greater homogeneity compared with custody use. Findings suggest tentative support for differentiating two approaches to policing at the front end of criminal justice systems. First, policing for public order characterizes a focus on the front end of the criminal justice system and smaller increases in custody use in states in Europe and Australia. Second, policing for crime control is associated with increasing custody use in the United States and a focus on the back end of the criminal justice system.

Notes

1   Not all states have increased imprisonment use. For example, von Hofer's (2003) study of changes in imprisonment rates in Finland, Holland, and Sweden between 1950 and 2000 reveals three different trends: there have been increases, decreases, and stability in imprisonment rates in these three northern European neighbours over time.

2   States are: Austria, Belgium, Denmark, England and Wales, Finland, France, Germany, Greece, Ireland, Italy, Luxembourg, Netherlands, Northern Ireland, Portugal, Scotland, Spain, and Sweden.

3   The Australian Capital Territory (ACT) was excluded because: (i) persons convicted in ACT courts serve their custodial sentences in New South Wales (NSW) prisons; separate data on ACT prisoners in NSW prisons have been published since the early 1980s; and (ii) the police employee rate was problematic due to the role of the Australian Federal Police (AFP), which provides a general police function within the ACT although it is not under the control of the ACT government. Until the 1990s, the number of AFP personnel dedicated to policing in the ACT was not separately identified.

4   Persons sentenced to jail serve terms usually less than 12 months, while prison sentences are usually of more than one year's duration. Substantial proportions of US jail populations comprise persons awaiting trial. Ouimet and Tremblay (1996) exclude jail rates from their recent study of states' punishment levels because the large number of persons awaiting trial are 'not technically being punished' (p. 111). I include jail rates in my analysis because, convicted or not, jail populations are a measure of the extent of states' custodial control of their population.

5   Prison and police data for Europe in 1970 and 1980 were obtained from the First and Second United Nations Crime Surveys and supplemented with data published by the Council of Europe, and the *Annual Abstract of Statistics*, British Home Office for England and Wales, Scotland and Northern Ireland (various years). Prison data for all years for Denmark, Finland and Sweden are from Falck *et al.* (2003). European prison data for 1990 and 2000 were sourced from Walmsley (2003). US data for all years were sourced from the *Dept of Justice: Sourcebook of Criminal Justice Statistics* (various years).

Australian data for 1970 and 1980 were sourced from Mukherjee *et al.* (1989). Data in 1990 and 2000 were sourced from publications by the Australian Bureau of Statistics and Australian Institute of Criminology (various years).

6 Values re-scaled to 1,000 in lieu of 100,000 population for ease of data presentation.

7 The term 'continuum' is borrowed from Young and Brown (1993: 41); which the author conceptualize as rewards provided for success (e.g. higher incomes and social status) at one end and at the other end as punishments for breaking social rules.

References

Australian Bureau of Statistics (2000) *Corrective Services.* 4512.0. March Quarter 2000. Canberra.

Australian Bureau of Statistics (2001) *Prisoners in Australia.* 4517.0. 30 June, 2001. Canberra.

Australian Institute of Criminology (1995) *Australian Prisoners 1982–93.* Canberra.

Bayley, D. (1985) *Patterns of Policing: A Comparative International Analysis*, New Brunswick, NJ: Rutgers University Press.

Beckett, K. (1997) *Making Crime Pay: Law and Order in Contemporary American Politics*, New York: Oxford University Press.

Biles, D. (1983) 'Crime and Imprisonment'. *British Journal of Criminology*, 23: 166–172.

Blumstein, A. (1982) 'On the Racial Disproportionality of United States' Prison Populations', *Journal of Criminal Law and Criminology*, 73(3): 1259–81.

Blumstein, A. (1988) 'Prison Populations: A System Out of Control?', in M. Tonry and N. Morris (eds), *Crime and Justice: A Review of Research*, 10: 231–266. Chicago: University of Chicago Press.

Blumstein, A. and Beck, A. J. (1999) 'Population growth in the US Prisons, 1980–1996', in M. Tonry and J. Petersilia (eds), *Prisons: Crime and Justice, A Review of Research*, 26: 17–61. Chicago: University of Chicago Press.

Bottoms, A. E. (1995) 'The Philosophy and Politics of Punishment and Sentencing', in C. Clarkson and R. Morgan (eds), *The Politics of Sentencing Reform*, Oxford: Clarendon Press.

Cahalan, M. W. (1986) *Historical Corrections Statistics in the United States, 1850–1984.* NCJ-102529. Bureau of Justice Statistics, Rockville, MD: Westat Inc.

Caplow, T. and J. Simon (1999) 'Understanding Prison Policy and Population Trends', in M. Tonry and J. Petersilia (eds), *Prisons: Crime and Justice: A Review of Research*, 26: 63–120, Chicago: University of Chicago Press.

Chambliss, W. J. (1994) 'Policing the Ghetto Underclass: The politics of law and order enforcement', *Social Problems*, 41(2): 177–194.

Chiricos, T. (1987) 'Rates of Crime and Unemployment: An Analysis of Aggregate Research Evidence', *Social Problems*, 34: 187–211.

Chiricos, T. (1991) 'Unemployment and Punishment: An Empirical Assessment', *Criminology*, 29: 701–724.

Cohen, S. (1979) 'The Punitive City: Notes on the Dispersal of Social Control', *Contemporary Crises*, 3: 339–363.

Cohen, S. (1985) *Visions of Social Control: Crime, Punishment and Classification*, Cambridge: Polity Press.

Collier, P. and Tarling, R. (1987) 'International Comparisons of Prison Populations', *Home Office Research Bulletin* 23: 48–54. London: Home Office Research and Planning Unit.

Daly, K. and Tonry, M. (1997) 'Gender, Race and Sentencing', in M. Tonry (ed.), *Crime and Justice: A Review of Research*, 22: 210–252. Chicago: Chicago University Press.

Davis, M. (1992) *The City of Quartz: Excavating the future in Los Angeles*, London: Vintage.

DeFina, R. H. and Arvanites, T. M. (2002) 'The Weak Effect of Imprisonment on Crime: 1971–1998', *Social Science Quarterly*, 83(3): 635–653.

Doleschal, E. (1977) 'Rate and Length of Imprisonment: How Does the United States Compare with The Netherlands, Denmark, and Sweden?', *Crime and Delinquency*, 23: 51–56.

Downes, D. (2001) 'The Macho Penal Economy: Mass Incarceration in the United States – A European Perspective', *Punishment and Society*, 3(1): 61–80.

Edsall, T. B. and Edsall, M. D. (1991) *Chain Reaction: The Impact of Race, Rights and Taxes on American Politics*. New York: Norton.

Erikson, R. S., Wright, G. C. and McIver, J. P. (1989) 'Political Parties, Public Opinion and State Policy in the United States', *American Political Science Review*, 83(3): 729–750.

Falck, S., von Hofer, H. and Storgaard, A. (eds) (2003) *Nordic Criminal Statistics 1950–2000*. Report 2003: 3. Stockholm: Dept of Criminology, Stockholm University.

Freiberg, A. (1998) 'Prison Population Up, Sentencing Policy Harsher in Australia', *Overcrowded Times*, 9(1): 1–11.

Garland, D. (1990) *Punishment and Modern Society: A Study in Social Theory*, Oxford: Clarendon Press.

Garland, D. (1996) 'The Limits of the Sovereign State: Strategies of Crime Control in Contemporary Society', *British Journal of Criminology*, 36(4): 445–471.

Garland, D. (2000) 'The Culture of High Crime Societies: Some Preconditions of Recent "Law and Order" Policies', *British Journal of Criminology*, 40: 347–375.

Garland, D. (2001) 'Introduction: The Meaning of Mass Imprisonment'. *Punishment and Society*, 3(1): 5–7.

Grabosky, P (1999) 'Zero Tolerance Policing', in *Trends And Issues In Crime And Criminal Justice* No 102. Canberra: Australian Institute of Criminology.

Greenberg, D. F., Kessler, R. C. and Loftin, C. (1985) 'Social Inequality and Crime Control', *Journal of Criminal Law and Criminology*, 76(3): 684–704.

Hinds, L. (2002) 'Law and Order: The Politics of Get Tough Crime Control', unpublished PhD research, School of Criminology and Criminal Justice, Griffith University, Australia.

Hogg, R. and Brown, D. (1998) *Rethinking Law and Order*, Annandale, NSW: Pluto Press.

Jacobs, D. (1979) 'Inequality and Police Strength: Conflict Theory and Coercive Control in Metropolitan Areas', *American Sociological Review*, 44: 913–925.

Jacobs, D. and Helms, R. E. (1997) 'Testing Coercive Explanations for Order: The Determinants of Law Enforcement Strength Over Time', *Social Forces*, 75(4): 1361–1383.

Kommer, M. (1994) 'Punitiveness in Europe', *European Journal on Criminal Policy and Research*, 2: 29–43.

Kuhn, A. (2001) 'Incarceration Rates Across the World', in M. Tonry (ed), *Penal Reform in Overcrowded Times*. New York: Oxford University Press.

Kuhn, A. (2003) 'Prison Population Trends in Western Europe', *Criminology in Europe*, 2(1): 1, 12–16.

Langan, P. A. and Farrington, D. P. (1998) *Crime in the United States and in England and Wales, 1981–96*. US Dept of Justice NCJ 169284. Washington DC: Bureau of Justice Statistics.

Liska, A. E. (1987) 'A Critical Examination of Macro Perspectives on Crime Control', *Annual Review of Sociology*, 13: 771–92.

Liska, A. E., Lawrence, J. J. and Benson, M. (1981) 'Perspectives on the Legal Order: The Capacity for Social Control', *American Journal of Sociology*, 87: 412–426.

Lynch, J. P. (1988) 'A Comparison of Prison Use in England, Canada, West Germany, and the United States: A Limited Test of the Punitive Hypothesis', *The Journal of Criminal Law and Criminology*, 79(1): 180–217.

Lynch, J. (2002) 'Crime in International Perspective', in J. Q. Wilson and J. Petersilia (eds), *Crime: Public Policies for Crime Control*. Oakland, CA: ICS Press.

Marshall, I. H. (1996) 'How Exceptional is the United States?', *European Journal of Criminal Policy and Research*, 4(2): 7–35.

Mauer, M. (2001) 'The Causes and Consequences of Prison Growth in the US', *Punishment and Society*, 3(1): 9–20.

Mukherjee, S. K., Scandia, A., Dagger, D. and Matthews, W. (1989) *Sourcebook of Australian Criminal and Social Statistics, 1804–1988,* Canberra: Australian Institute of Criminology.

Musto, D. (1987) *The American Disease: Origins of Narcotics Control*, New York: Oxford University Press.

Nelken, D. (2002) 'Comparing Criminal Justice', in M. Maguire, R. Morgan and R. Reiner (eds), *The Oxford Handbook of Criminology* (3rd edn), Oxford: Oxford University Press.

Neopolitan, J. L. (2001) 'An Examination of Cross–National Variation in Punitiveness', *International Journal of Offender Therapy and Comparative Criminology*, 45(6): 691–710.

Ouimet, M. and Tremblay, P. (1996) 'A Normative Theory of the Relationship Between Crime Rates and Imprisonment Rates: An Analysis of the Penal Behaviour of US States from 1972 to 1992', *Journal of Research in Crime and Delinquency*, 33(1): 109–125.

Parks, R. B. (1975) 'Sources and Limitations of Data in Criminal Justice Research', in J. A. Gardiner and M. A. Mulkey (eds), *Crime and Criminal Justice: Issues in Public Policy Analysis*. Lexington, MA: D C Heath and Co.

Pease, K. (1994) 'Cross-National Imprisonment Rates: Limitations of Method and Possible Conclusions', *British Journal of Criminology*, Special Issue, 34: 116–130.

Pratt, J. (1995) 'Dangerousness, Risk and Technologies of Power', *Australian and New Zealand Journal of Criminology,* 29(1): 3–30.

Reiner, R. (2000) *The Politics of the Police* (3rd edn), New York: Oxford University Press.

Rusche, G. and Kirchheimer, O. (1939, reprint 1968) *Punishment and Social Structure*. New York: Russell and Russell.

Sampson, R. J. and Lauritsen, J. L. (1997) 'Racial and Ethnic Disparities in Crime and Criminal Justice in the United States', in M. Tonry (ed.), *Crime and Justice: A Review of Research*, 21: 311–374.Chicago: University of Chicago Press.

Savelsberg, J. J. (1994) 'Knowledge, Domination and Criminal Punishment', *American Journal of Sociology*, 99(4): 911–943.

Scheingold, S. A. (1984*) The Politics of Law and Order: Street Crime and Public Policy*, New York: Longman.

Scull, A. T. (1977) *Decarceration: Community Treatment and the Deviant: A Radical View*, New Jersey: Prentice-Hall.

Simon, J. (1997) 'Governing through Crime', in L. M. Friedman and G. Fisher (eds), *The Crime Conundrum: Essays on Criminal Justice*. Boulder, CO: Westview Press.

Simon, J. (2001) 'Fear and Loathing in Late Modernity: Reflections on the Cultural Sources of Mass Imprisonment in the US', *Punishment and Society*, 3(1): 21–33.

Softley, P. (1983) 'The Use of Custody: Some European Comparisons', *Research Bulletin*, 16: 49–50, London: Home Office Research and Planning Unit.

Spelman, W. (2000) 'What Recent Studies do (and don't) Tell Us about Imprisonment and Crime', in M. Tonry (ed.), *Crime and Justice: A Review of Research*, 27: 419–494. Chicago: University of Chicago Press.

Stern, V. (1998) *A Sin Against the Future: Imprisonment in the World*, Boston: Northeastern University Press.

Tham, H. (2001) 'Law and Order as a Leftist Project? The Case of Sweden', *Punishment and Society*, 3(3): 409–426.

Tonry, M. (1995) *Sentencing Matters*, Oxford: Oxford University Press.

Tonry, M. (1998) 'Crime and Punishment in America, 1971–1996', *Overcrowded Times*, 9(2): 1,12–20.

Tonry, M. (1999) 'Parochialism in U.S. Sentencing Policy', *Crime and Delinquency*, 45(1): 48–65.

Tonry, M. (2001) 'Symbol, Substance and Severity in Western Penal Policies', *Punishment and Society*, 3(4): 517–536.

Tyler, T. R. and Boeckmann, R. J. (1997) 'Three Strikes and You're Out, but Why: The Psychology of Public Support for Punishing Rule Breakers', *Law and Society Review*, 17(1): 21–45.

US Dept of Justice (1973) *Sourcebook of Criminal Justice Statistics 1972*, Washington DC: Bureau of Justice Statistics.

US Dept of Justice (1987) *Sourcebook of Criminal Justice Statistics 1986*. NCJ 105287, Washington DC: Bureau of Justice Statistics.

US Dept of Justice (2002) *Sourcebook of Criminal Justice Statistics, 2001*. NCJ 196438, Washington DC: Bureau of Justice Statistics.

von Hofer, H. (2003) 'Prison Populations as Political Constructs: The Case of Finland, Holland and Sweden'. *Journal of Scandinavian Studies in Criminology and Crime Prevention*, 4(1): 21–38.

Walmsley, R. (2003) *World Prison Population List* (5th edn), London: Home Office.

Wilkins, L. T. and Pease, K. (1987) 'Public Demand for Punishment', *The International Journal of Sociology and Social Policy*, 7(3): 16–29.

Windlesham, L. (1998) *Politics, Punishment and Populism*, New York: Oxford University Press.

Wright, G. C., Erikson, R. S. and McIver, J. P. (1987) 'Public Opinion and Policy Liberalism in the American States', *American Journal of Political Science*, 31(4): 980–1001.

Young, W. and Brown, M. (1993) 'Cross-National Comparisons of Imprisonment', in M. Tonry (ed.), *Crime and Justice: A Review of Research*, 17: 1–49. Chicago: University of Chicago Press.

Zimring, F. E. and Hawkins, G. (1991) *The Scale of Imprisonment*, Chicago: University of Chicago Press.

4. Supermax meets death row: legal struggles around the new punitiveness in the US[1]

Mona Lynch

In two recent cases, the 9th Circuit Court of Appeals – the federal intermediary court for the western United States – raised a question about whether the conditions of confinement in Arizona's supermaximum security housing unit for those awaiting death in Arizona may be so oppressive that they were in essence compelling some inmates to 'volunteer' to die in order to escape death row (*Comer* v. *Stewart*, 2000; *Miller* v. *Stewart*, 2000). The written decisions, which sent the cases back to the lower court for evidentiary hearings on the issues, open an interesting line of inquiry into the contemporary state of penality in the US. In this chapter, I examine these two cases and the subsequent proceedings in order to explore the contemporary meaning of punishment and penal subjectivity, as it is reflected in the practice of putting the condemned on 'cold storage' (Human Rights Watch, 1997) in Supermax units and the judicial interpretation of its potential penal harm.[2] This intersection of harsh penal practices, and its ultimate acceptance by the courts, represents a vivid example of the new punitiveness at work in the US where disturbing consequences of penal extremism are normalized and ratified.

I will begin by describing in detail the practices at issue and their recent development in US penal policy. While the underlying policies – the use of capital punishment in a modern democracy and the use of long-term solitary confinement within penal institutions – are not unusual within the US, both are relatively extreme and anachronistic from a more global perspective. And, as Hallsworth (2000) has argued, these practices stand as prime examples of the 'punitive turn' that has occurred in recent decades. Further, their intersection seems to extend the boundaries of acceptable punishment in a democratic state, ultimately, perhaps, begetting a unique penal consequence: the state-produced death-row volunteer.

I will move on to outline my argument by briefly describing theoretical understandings of contemporary penality in order to analyse the competing conceptions of the punishment and its subjects reflected in these cases. I suggest that this hallmark example of the irrationality of the new punitive turn (Hallsworth, 2000) is first made salient through the 9th Circuit's invocation of 'modern' principles of punishment and penal subjectivity, but is ultimately made rational in the subsequent proceedings through an elision of those principles and the construction of a competing penal subject: the rational 'other'. Through the use of this construction, I suggest, the dichotomies and contradictions in contemporary punishment that have been described by several scholars (Garland, 1996; Hallsworth, 2000) are amalgamated: in such a way that the irrational becomes rational and the extreme punishments at issue are made nearly irrelevant to the legal inquiry.

To flesh out my argument, I examine the language of the cases themselves and the legal events that follow in order to illustrate the meaning of punishment in this central arena of the American justice system – the federal courts. In the US, these courts have been major arbiters in the new punitiveness over the past three to four decades, especially in defining the boundaries of constitutional capital punishment and articulating standards for conditions of confinement. And as numerous commentators have pointed out, there has been a marked path of devolution in how they define the 'standards of decency' that dictate constitutional punishment, the legal limits of penal pain, and, more broadly, acceptable criminal legal procedure over that period (see, e.g., Haney, 1997, 1998, for detailed accounts). Thus many federal courts have been instrumental, in concert with state and federal lawmakers and the public, in furthering an extreme penal regime in the US since the 1980s.

In recent years, the 9th Circuit Court has in some key instances, however, countered the broader trend, and has pointedly challenged some of the punitive policies that have flourished across the nation, including, more recently, the inflexible and punitive federal sentencing guidelines (*U.S.* v. *Parish*, 2002), California's far-reaching three-strikes law (*Andrade* v. *Lockyer*, 2002), and the constitutionality of death sentencing procedures (e.g. *Summerlin* v. *Stewart*, 2001).[3] In the *Miller* and *Comer* cases, which are the subject of this chapter, the 9th Circuit also bucked the trend of its sister courts and raised new questions about penal extremism that transcend the legal, while the District Court, in a lengthy narrative, and the US Supreme Court – with virtually no words – worked to close that line of inquiry and maintain the current *status quo* of penal harshness. Thus the competing rhetoric about punishment and the punished in these cases offers a telling illustration of how such extreme practices are legally and ideologically constructed by judicial actors in the new punitive era.

The rise of Supermax death row

One of the features of the contemporary era of capital punishment in the United States is that those who receive death sentences reside on death rows for significantly longer periods of time than they have at any time prior to the *Furman* v. *Georgia* (1972) decision.[4] The national average of time spent on death row from sentence imposition to execution is now over a decade, and is significantly longer in most non-Southern states (Bonczar and Snell, 2003). Consequently, inmates on state death rows constitute a significant and distinct population that is treated as a special management issue by penal authorities and death row overcrowding seems to be as big a concern for penal administrators as carrying out executions.

In a number of states, this population is now being managed through the use of high-security facilities like the distinctly American penal phenomenon, the 'Supermax' housing unit. While death row inmates have historically been subject to relatively high-security conditions of confinement and have been treated as a distinct class of inmate, the ratcheting up of security level to 'Supermax' has developed just over the last decade or so, and has brought with it a major change in the quality of life for those on such death rows.

'Supermax' or 'SHU' units, which have grown hugely popular with corrections officials across the nation over the past decade, are a form of highly restrictive housing where inmates are generally subjected to solitary lockdown for approximately 23 hours a day in windowless cells that allow for very little visual stimuli, where possessions are restricted and activities nearly completely eliminated, and where, by design, contact with other human beings is almost made nonexistent (King, 1999). Penal administrators justify the use of Supermax as necessary to maintain internal security, in that inmates who are defined as 'the worst of the worst' can be isolated and contained within these units. Thus, they are said to provide the state corrections machinery with the tool to manage unruly populations within the system (Hermann, 1996; King, 1999; Leary, 1994), and have been credited by corrections managers as accomplishing that goal (Hermann, 1996; Leary, 1994; *Madrid* v. *Gomez*, 1995), while the harshly punitive nature of these settings is generally downplayed or denied. Indeed, the extreme deprivation to which inmates are subjected in such housing units is said to arise only out of security and management needs, rather than out of punitive urges (Leary, 1994; Steckner, 1998).

The use of Supermax for prolonged confinement of inmates has been con-troversial, for the most part due to the effect of the harsh conditions on inmates' mental and physical health. SHUs are routinely used for indefinite periods of confinement, and some inmates may spend years upon years in this housing. This feature in particular causes psychological harm to inmates (Haney, 1993, 2003; Haney and Lynch, 1997; Rhodes, 2004). The kinds of documented effects that isolated SHU prisoners experience include attempted and completed suicides, self-mutilation, psychotic breaks, extreme feelings of anger, rage, and hopeless-ness, eating and sleeping disturbances, and physical ailments, among others (Haney and Lynch, 1997). The risk of psychological damage is even greater for inmates who come to such units with pre-existing psychological conditions, who, ironically, are often disproportionately represented in the SHU due to their propensity to be management 'problems' in the general population (Rhodes, 2004). 'SHU Syndrome' is the label, coined by psychiatrist Stuart Grassian, often used to describe this constellation of psychological symptoms suffered by some of those subjected to the living conditions inherent in SHU units (Lehmann, 1999).

Several have argued that the use of Supermax for death row inmates also furthers the psychological damage wrought by such confinement, due to the already vulnerable state of condemned inmates' psychological health (see, e.g., Ferrier, 2004). Those who are sentenced to death are uniquely burdened with the specific knowledge of their own fate, thus their thoughts about their own death 'must necessarily be focused more precisely than other people's' (Ferrier, 2004,

301). Furthermore, the use of Supermax for death row is for the duration of those inmates' lives – there is no hope of returning to less restrictive housing before execution; rather it can be considered a form of indeterminate life sentence. Finally, condemned inmates tend to arrive on death row with extremely high rates of pre-existing psychological problems – much greater than the general prison population rates – including psychoses, major depression, and post-traumatic stress disorder, and such inmates tend to deteriorate even further on death row (Cunningham and Vigen, 2002). Thus, it may be that the harsh living conditions combined with the particularly vulnerable psychological state and the unique status of those condemned to die works to create a disproportionate number of 'volunteers' in states that have Supermax death rows.[5]

And as I have argued before, the use of Supermax isolation for death row inmates, at least in Arizona, may consequently work to 'prime' the condemned inmates for death (Lynch, 2000a). Non-condemned inmates who have been subjected to these kinds of units have characterized the experience as analogous to living in a sort of purgatory, somewhere between life and death (Haney, 1993), or like living in a tomb (Hentoff, 1993). Thus, those waiting to be executed may well be 'readied' for the process by the absence of a life experience in their final months, making them less resistant to the final step, and prompting some to simply give up and give in. One indicator consistent with this possibility is the demonstrated increased risk of attempted and completed suicide among inmates subjected to confinement conditions analogous to those on death row SHUs (Benjamin and Lux, 1977; Grassian, 1983; Haney, 1993; Jackson, 1983).[6] In the case of death row inmates, the decision to give up appeals and volunteer for execution is potentially the product of such suicidal urges brought on by the living conditions.

New punitiveness and the rational man

Clearly, a longstanding assumption in modern Anglo-American law is that those subject to the law are (with a few specified exceptions) rational actors who make choices as a product of their own free will (Connolly, 1999). Yet in recent decades, this 'rational choice actor' has become a dominant figure across a broader swathe of criminal justice domains, from academic scholarship to policy-making in many Western democracies. The more sociologically (and psychologically) informed understanding of criminality and deviant behaviour that dominated mid-20th-century criminological scholarship and criminal justice policy gave way by the 1980s to the simpler rational choice theory (or rational action theory), especially in the policy arena (De Haan and Vos, 2003; Garland, 2001).

This transformation has not only influenced how policing and crime control are practised, but has also had a major impact on penal policy. The reformative goals of the rehabilitative era became largely irrelevant, and punishment, at best, now ideally serves as a deterrent and/or incapacitator to redirect or block the choice to commit crime by offenders (Garland, 2001; Lynch, 2001). Furthermore, inherent in the rational choice conceptualization is the notion that offenders have chosen their fate by exercising their free will in choosing to commit crime, thus the pains of punishment they must endure as a consequence are by their own doing. Indeed, as I have illustrated previously, criminal justice personnel and political figures are increasingly casting the punishment experience itself as a choice made by offenders, rather than something imposed on them (Lynch, 2000b, 2001).

And while theorists such as Garland (1996, 2001) have dichotomized the contemporary criminal/penal subject as falling into one of two polar categories that lead to very different state responses: either the normal, rational, opportunistic actor described above (i.e. common burglars, thieves, drug dealers, etc.) or the alien 'other' (such as murderers, sex offenders, and other such violent or dangerous offenders), such a division does not capture how these two distinct subjects are actually integrated in much contemporary penal discourse. So while in the first case, deviance is defined downward and sanctions are lightened, and in the second case, punitive response is generally ratcheted upward, the underlying psychological being in both cases is relatively simple, rational, and freewilled in making his behavioural choices.

To illustrate, as I have found in my work with Craig Haney (Lynch and Haney, 1998) examining how attorneys characterize capital defendants in their closing arguments at trial, prosecutors uniformly construct this hybrid rational 'other' criminal subject: a cold, calculating, free-willed actor who chooses evil in killing and harming others. This characterization allows prosecutors to argue for the most extreme penal response – capital punishment – since the defendant himself chose to do evil, he thus chose his own fate. The resulting punishment imperative is that offenders have made the choices that have exposed themselves to penal intervention, and the prudent response is maximum containment through death or long-term, highly secure confinement (see also Simon, 1998, for his discussion of sex offenders).

A strict adherence to the rational action/actor perspective allows legal and policy decision-makers to eschew any complex inquiry into the nature of human behaviour; it assumes that behaviour is simply a product of individual rational choices 'disembodied from all social context' (Cohen, 1996: 5). Thus structural forces, situational influences, and even individual psychodynamic factors underlying the 'crime problem' have little bearing on the assessments that shape official responses to deal with it.

This transformation can be detected in American case law that defines the limits of constitutional state punishment. Again, although the assumption of free will and rationality has permeated the law for centuries, there was, particularly during the 1960s and 1970s, a more psychologically and sociologically nuanced conceptualization of the penal subject that was articulated in a number of US 8th Amendment cases.[7] This trend was turned back by the 1980s, however, and with it came a shift back to a hands-off approach to state penal practices, contributing to the proliferation of penal extremism that we have witnessed ever since. And, as I will illustrate below, it is that rational actor who is set against the more psychologically rich, multiply influenced subject constructed in the 9th Circuit decisions to shut down the questions raised about the use of the SHU as death row.

The Arizona cases

Arizona's Supermax death row

Arizona Department of Corrections, which was home to the first state-level new construction Supermax prison (it opened in 1987), began to use one of their two SHUs – the Eyman SMU II (Special Management Unit II) – as the state's death row in the summer of 1997 after an escape attempt by several death row inmates who were on chain-gang agricultural duty on the old death row prison grounds.[8] Approximately 120 men are currently housed in this unit awaiting execution, making it one of the larger Supermax death rows in operation today (Arizona Department of Corrections, 2004).

Shortly after the relocation, Arizona Department of Corrections' officials justified the change in terms of the threat to internal security posed by the condemned 'class' of inmates, and denied any punitive element to subjecting the condemned to this kind of final living existence (Steckner, 1998). Yet the move to the SMU unit represented a fundamental change in the quality of life for death row inmates, who had previously been allowed, under some circumstances, limited contact visits with loved ones as well as work opportunities, albeit on a condemned row chain gang (Dayan, 1997). Since the move to the Supermax death row, the state has proceeded with executions of at least two 'volunteers' – Arthur Ross in 1998[9] and Don Jay Miller, the most recently executed inmate in the state, in 2000 – and has been involved in the litigation surrounding one other volunteer – Robert Comer.

Procedural background

Comer's case was the first to move through the federal courts on the issues surrounding his decision to volunteer. In June 2000, the Arizona Attorney General's office asked the 9th Circuit to dismiss the pending appeals in that case because Comer had indicated his desire to cease his appellate efforts (*Comer v. Stewart*, 2000).[10] Comer himself filed a motion in the 9th Circuit as well, claiming that he never authorized his court appointed attorneys to file appeals on his behalf. Despite Comer's apparent wishes, his appointed counsel opposed the motions. Because the law requires that a condemned inmate must not only be competent to be executed, but also must be competent to waive his rights to appeal, and that such a waiver must be voluntarily made, the court ruled that: (1) Comer's competence to waive his rights had to be determined before the merits of the motion could be decided; and (2) a determination must be made as to whether Comer had *voluntarily* waived his rights or whether, conversely, the conditions of confinement in Arizona's SMU II had compelled his decision. The case was remanded back down to the federal district court in Arizona for an evidentiary hearing on those two issues.

The evidentiary hearing took place in March 2002 in Judge Roslyn Silver's court. Comer himself testified, as well as two psychiatric experts. The Judge visited the death row SHU unit and Comer's cell to evaluate those conditions of confinement, and she read an array of written materials in assessing the issues (see *Comer* v. *Stewart*, 2002a). In the end, Judge Silver concluded that Comer was competent to waive his rights and had waived those rights voluntarily. The case returned to the 9th Circuit for resolution on the State's motion to dismiss. That court declined to take any action until the applicability of a further-reaching case – *Ring* v. *Arizona* (2002), which had declared Arizona's death penalty sentencing statute unconstitutional – to other Arizona death row prisoners was determined (*Comer* v. *Stewart*, 2002b).[11]

In Miller's case, which reached the 9th Circuit on this issue in November 2000, a Pima County public defender appealed a district court decision denying her 'next friend' status in her effort to intervene in Miller's decision to volunteer for his execution (*Miller* v. *Stewart*, 2000). She offered evidence that Miller might not be competent in regard to waiving his rights, so sought legal standing to act in his best interests. Miller's execution was scheduled for the next day, so she also requested a stay of execution while the court considered the case. The State argued that Miller should be presumed competent, since he had been determined to be competent for a different purpose two years earlier.[12] The 9th Circuit panel reviewed the record and found that the earlier competency finding was not only irrelevant since the issues were different, but it was no longer timely. As in *Comer*, the court determined that it was not in the position to decide on the motion (in this case the 'next friend' standing issue) without first ordering an evidentiary hearing to determine his competence to choose to die and the quality of his decision to volunteer. Thus, the court granted the stay of execution and remanded the case back to the District Court for a hearing on Miller's competency and on the voluntariness of his decision to waive his rights (*Miller* v. *Stewart*, 2000). Again, the court raised specific concerns that the conditions of confinement on Arizona's death row may have compelled the decision to 'volunteer' for execution. No evidentiary hearing was ever conducted, however. Instead the State appealed the 9th Circuit ruling to the US Supreme Court, asking them to vacate the stay. That court complied with the state's request, and Miller was executed that afternoon, a day after these appellate proceedings began (*Stewart* v. *Miller*, 2000).

Conceptions of penality in Comer and Miller

In several ways, the 9th Circuit's inquiry seemed to evoke the more sociologically and psychologically attuned understandings of criminality and penality that prevailed in the mid-20th century. First, in constructing the penal subject at issue – the Supermax death row volunteer – they raise a question about the limits of free will and suggest the possibility that the situational context of the condemned, rather than simply his rational choices, might at least in part account for his decision to waive his rights and volunteer for execution. While this penal subject is by legal necessity constructed in terms of traditional psycho-legal conceptions (i.e., is he incompetent due to a mental disease or defect?), the second prong of the court's inquiry regarding voluntariness extends to allow for an examination of the effects of a particularly powerful setting on individual behaviour (see Ross and Nisbett, 1991, for a discussion of this social psychological line of inquiry).

In *Comer* (2000), the court begins with a relatively conventional approach to these questions, by painting a picture of the man in question as suffering from long-term mental instability. They describe how Mr Comer had refused to even attend his own death penalty trial, and was brought to his sentencing hearing at the end of it all, unwillingly. They imply an underlying mental condition that calls into question his current competency in describing that scene of his sentencing:

> He was shackled to a wheelchair and, except for a cloth draped over his genitals, he was naked. His body was slumped to one side and his head drooped toward his shoulder. He had visible abrasions on his body. After asking both the court deputy and a prison psychiatrist whether Mr. Comer was conscious, the state trial judge sentenced him to death. (*Comer v. Stewart*, 2000, 912)

In this recounting of how Comer came to death row, the court also appears to be raising questions about the very nature of the American capital punishment enterprise, which is supposed to target the 'worst of the worst', cold-blooded murderers, and spare all others, including those with mental problems. The man being sentenced in this portrayal is not the prototypical (in legal terms) free-willed, rational, evil-doing actor, but rather a shell of a human being who had to be checked for mere consciousness before judgment was imposed.

The court continues to make the case that Comer is not sound of mind by citing his letters to various legal actors in which he expressed his wishes to cease all appeals. These letters were submitted by the State in support of their position that he was competent; however, the court uses them to insinuate the opposite. In those letters, Comer denies that he ever authorized anyone to pursue appeals for him despite the fact that he has signed legal documents confirming otherwise, he asserts that a vast 'ZOG' (Zionist Occupation Government) conspiracy was working to thwart his efforts to be executed, and he admits to not being '100% sane'. The court concludes that 'the letters the State characterizes as merely "colorful", instead demonstrate the need for a hearing' (*Comer v. Stewart*, 2000, 916).

After establishing a pattern and history of 'irrational behavior' by Comer, the court expands outward in its analysis of his behaviour by discussing the effect of the SMU living conditions on his mental state. They assert that 'we and other courts have recognized that prison conditions remarkably similar to Mr. Comer's descriptions of his current confinement can adversely affect a person's mental health' (*Comer v. Stewart*, 2000: 916), and cite several prior cases on those grounds. They refer to Comer's own admissions that living in the SHU can cause inmates to 'wig out' (p. 916) and cite documentation that he engaged in bizarre and delusional behaviour on previous occasions while living in similar isolated conditions. In ordering a hearing on his competency, the court expressed 'grave concerns that a mentally disabled man may be seeking this court's assistance in ending his life' (p. 916) that resulted from the interplay of his pre-existing mental problems with the effects of the SHU housing conditions on his mental state.

Finally, they raise the separate issue of the voluntariness of his waivers, and in doing so propose a fully situational rather than dispositional potential explanation for his behaviour. In this inquiry, the court maintains that even if Comer is found mentally competent, the waiver of his appellate rights cannot be accepted if it was not voluntarily made. Although again constrained by legal (rather than social scientific) parameters for analyzing human behaviour, they ask if 'coercion', which would negate the legality of his waiver, may have played a part in his decision. While coercion is usually thought of as a product of one or more person's influence over another, in this analysis, it is the power of the setting in Arizona's SMU that was accused of being coercive. Comer's counsel had argued to the court that the conditions of confinement had 'extinguished his desire or will to live, thus rendering his apparent decision to withdraw this appeal involuntary' (p. 917) and the court accepted this as a possibility in ordering an evidentiary hearing on the issue. There is limited precedent for courts to examine the effect of conditions of confinement on waiver decisions, which is cited here, yet in this case the court narrates a rather detailed and plausible scenario of how such coercion may be at issue, and even in its early telling implies a belief that this is indeed what has happened to Comer:

> Mr. Comer describes the conditions of his confinement in nothing short of Orwellian terms. He tells us that he is in 'sensory deprivation,' has no access to legal materials, is permitted nothing in his cell, and must walk continuously for fear of becoming a 'veggie'. Mr. Comer's choice between execution at the State's hands and remaining in the particular conditions of his confinement may be the type of 'Hobson's choice' that renders his supposed decision to withdraw his appeal involuntary ... The issue is whether Mr. Comer's conditions of confinement constitute punishment so harsh that he has been forced to abandon a natural desire to live. (*Comer* v. *Stewart*, 2000: 918)

In the *Miller* case, the court similarly begins its analysis by describing a man with long-term psychological problems, stemming back to his childhood maltreatment. Saying it is necessary to look at his entire record before making a decision on the legal issues, the court describes Miller as follows:

> Mr. Miller's history of depression and abuse are well-documented. The record shows that Mr. Miller was physically, sexually, and psychologically abused as a child. He grew up in an environment of abuse and neglect. His mother, who at times ran a 'massage parlor' and at other times was a stripper, once chased him with a butcher knife and put out cigarettes on the body of one of his siblings. He has a documented history of suicidal impulses, depression, alcohol abuse, and physical injuries. Significantly, in 1982, as a juvenile offender, he threatened suicide should he not be released from confinement. (*Miller* v. *Stewart*, 2000: 1251–1252)

The decision further cites evidence that Miller is depressed and has on several occasions suffered from auditory hallucinations, calling into question the State's assertion that Miller is competent. Next, as in *Comer*, the court introduces the SHU as a potential contributing factor to Miller's mental state. They cite the psychiatric declarations submitted in the case which assert 'that it is well accepted that conditions such as those present in the SMU II where Miller is housed can cause psychological decompensation to the point that individuals may become incompetent' (p. 1252). Those experts further suggest that due to Mr Miller's background and history, he is particularly susceptible to psychological damage from the harsh housing conditions on Arizona's death row.

Finally, the court again raises the possibility that these extremely harsh conditions in Arizona's SHU have had a coercive effect on Miller. They cite a declaration from an attorney stating that Miller told her he was willing to 'pay with his life to escape the conditions of SMU II' (p. 1252). Then the court cites its own decision in *Comer* to bolster its argument here, that the harsh conditions of confinement on Arizona's death row could have such a coercive effect.[13]

Response to Miller and Comer

In Miller's case, as noted above, the US Supreme Court immediately closed down the 9th Circuit's inquiry by lifting the stay of execution one day after that decision. The Supreme Court decision consisted of one sentence which in no way addressed the concerns raised by the 9th Circuit: 'The application to vacate the stay of execution of sentence of death entered by the United States Court of Appeals for the Ninth Circuit on November 7, 2000, presented to Justice O'Connor and by her referred to the Court, is granted' (*Stewart* v. *Miller*, 2000: 986). Miller was executed in Arizona that day, which ensured that at least in this case, there would be no further inquiry about the effects of SHU housing on death row inmates.

Comer's case, though, lived on. Of particular interest is the district court's decision, following the evidentiary hearing, in which the presiding judge rhetorically worked to deny the validity of the 9th Circuit's concerns in 56 published pages of narrative. After providing a detailed procedural history of the case, Judge Silver offered a lengthy biographical portrait of the man in question, a task she deemed necessary to determine his present state of mind, which she concluded to be both sound and free of coercion. In doing so, she strove to make it clear that she had done her job as thoroughly as possible, with seriousness and care, even if she was not comfortable with the inevitable legal conclusion of that assessment. By providing this biographical portrait, she was also able to highlight the extreme risk Comer posed to prison personnel, which served to implicitly justify the use of the Supermax in his case.[14]

From this set-up, under a section entitled, 'Conditions in Soledad, DVI and Folsom Security Housing Units' (*Comer* v. *Stewart*, 2002a: 1028), Judge Silver wrote five full pages of description of the grotesque conditions that Comer was subjected to in California prisons between 1979 and 1984, even though these were not the conditions of confinement at issue here.[15] In her narrative, she pointed out that several of the units in which Comer had been housed in California were subject to court orders to improve the unconstitutionally harsh living conditions, and asserted that, '[i]t is undisputed that Mr. Comer endured most, if not all and possibly worse, of these deplorable conditions while he was confined in [those California] SHUs' (*Comer* v. *Stewart*, 2002a: 1032). Implied by this historical telling is that Comer has endured horrible living conditions far longer than his confinement on death row (without, presumably, being suicidal). It also set up the contrast to the conditions in question on Arizona's death row.

Again, because of his disciplinary problems, Comer was moved (along with his troublemaking death row friend) to a Supermax unit in Arizona just a few months after arriving on Arizona's old death row in 1988. So he started living in the same conditions as the current death row fully nine years before the rest of the condemned population was moved to the SMU II. Yet despite the fact that the conditions in Arizona's SMU were a key issue in this case, and even though Comer had endured them for almost three times the period he had spent in California isolation units (14 years vs. 5 years), Judge Silver devoted only one short paragraph of description to those conditions.[16] In doing so, she never referred to them as 'deplorable' or 'abhorrent' or any other such adjective, as she had when describing the conditions in California; rather, she presented, in very neutral language, an image of confinement that while clearly secure was neither cruel nor intolerable.

She first described the SMU unit's physical layout and structure, then moved on to describe the standard cell interior and furnishings, making note of their size, which is significantly larger than that of the SHU units Comer was confined to in the California prisons (77 square feet vs. 45–49 square feet). She concludes the section with a list of the 'privileges' afforded Comer within that unit:

> Mr. Comer receives between an hour and an hour and a half of individual recreation three times a week. He also has the opportunity to shower three times a week. In addition, Mr. Comer has access to cleaning materials. Pursuant to ADOC policy, he and other death row inmates are not permitted 'contact' visits absent court order, but he is permitted non-contact visits. (*Comer* v. *Stewart*, 2002a: 1034; internal citations omitted)

Much later in the decision, when justifying her conclusions on specific questions of fact, Judge Silver engages in further discussion of the conditions in Arizona's SMU II. She even relies on Comer's own words to make explicit the contrast between the conditions in the California prisons and those in Arizona's SMU:

> Mr. Comer described his conditions at SMU II as heaven compared to Folsom, which was hell, and the staff at SMU II as humane. He did not unrealistically paint a 'rosy picture of SMU II,' but compared to other units 'it's better' because it is 'less dangerous,' 'less assaultive,' 'cleaner' and 'smells' better. Mr. Comer observed that by the time ADOC officers 'stripped [him] out' of the Rec Pen in 1999, there was not a bruise on him, whereas the guards at Folsom beat inmates because, he surmised, they thought the more they beat inmates the better persons they would become. Mr. Comer's cell is also much larger and cleaner now than the ones at Folsom and the Lexan on the cell fronts keep the prisoners from 'getting stuck' with a shank or darted. The temperature in the cell is comfortable. All of these features are important to Mr. Comer on a day-to-day basis. (*Comer* v. *Stewart*, 2002a: 1059; internal citations omitted)

Judge Silver confirms Comer's assessment of the conditions, which he also described in his oral testimony as 'harsh' but not enough to drive him crazy, by sharing her own impressions after visiting his cell in SMU II. She admits that it is, 'not the place a non-imprisoned person would voluntarily choose as a home'

(*Comer* v. *Stewart*, 2002a: 1060), but asserts that it has adequate lighting and temperature, and that the bed was comfortable enough. She further points out the amenities available to Mr Comer, including a mirror, a Walkman, and a television set for his entertainment, and concludes that his cell was 'not intolerable'. Thus, by using the demonstrably unconstitutionally horrible conditions of the California prisons which Comer endured more than two decades earlier as a point of contrast, Judge Silver negated the pains of imprisonment – and their potential consequences – inflicted within the SMU. Clearly, she could have referenced human rights standards for imprisonment conditions in order to grade the SMU, but did not do so, as such a contrast may well have led to a very different conclusion.

After thus setting the stage for her analysis, Judge Silver moves to the question of Comer's competency. In her reading of the evidence (which is much more voluminous than what the 9th Circuit had before it) Comer's psychological health is quite robust. Indeed, what seemed troubling to the 9th Circuit was evidence of healthy adaptation for Judge Silver. For instance, Comer's letters, which the 9th Circuit found indicated a need for the competency hearing, were for Judge Silver indicative of his strategic abilities to get what he wanted. Indeed, she pointed out in her decision that, '[she] was also a recipient of one of Mr. Comer's bold and flashy letters designed to capture the Court's interest' (*Comer* v. *Stewart*, 2002a: 1048). She went on to describe the second letter she received from Comer, which was also, 'straight forward, passionate, bold and flashy … convey[ing] that Mr. Comer is a resolute man with the courage to express his opinions his way to anyone and everyone sometimes without considering the long-term consequences' (*Comer* v. *Stewart*, 2002a: 1049).

In her reconstruction of Comer as a rational, psychologically healthy man, Judge Silver essentially contrasted the psychiatric evaluation and testimony presented by Comer's appellate attorneys with that of the court-appointed psychiatrist and Comer himself. The psychiatrist for the appellate attorneys – Dr Kupers – concluded that Mr. Comer suffered from a major depressive disorder, post-traumatic stress disorder, and 'SHU syndrome', and the court psychiatrist concluded he suffered from no mental disease or defect. The court psychiatrist – Dr Johnson – expressed her scepticism about the existence of SHU syndrome as a credible diagnosis, referring to it instead as a 'concept', and interpreted all the other indications of Comer's mental illness as appropriate and/or rational responses to his circumstances. The judge fully accepted the interpretation of this psychiatrist, therefore ruling that Comer suffered none of the mental illnesses diagnosed by Dr Kupers and was competent to waive his rights.

In so doing, the judge put forth a micro-analytic construction of Mr Comer as a man whose actions are simply the work of his own free will and exercise of rational choice. Her method for constructing this portrayal of Mr Comer begins by offering alternative interpretations of the individual items of evidence that led Dr Kupers to his diagnosis of mental illness. By parsing the totality of evidence in such a way, the analysis, by design, denies the cumulative effects of the various and long-term impacts of his confinement. Let me illustrate with several notable examples.

In his diagnosis of the major depressive episode after his death row friend was executed, Dr Kupers reported that for several months Comer:

had no interest in anything. He had no pleasure in anything. He spent most of the time in his bunk. Contrary to his usual pattern of walking 14 to 20 hours a day in his cell or in any recreation area [that he had access to], he didn't walk much at all. He expressed great sadness and he was in deep depression. (p. 1042)

The judge discounted that interpretation in favour of Dr Johnson's that he was simply 'bereaved' over the death of his friend, a normal and healthy human response. Two years later, Comer had another major episode in which he lost significant amounts of weight over a period of about six months, spent most of his time in bed, stopped communicating with others, and had no interest in anything. The judge suggested that Comer's symptoms may have merely mimicked those of depression, but were really the response to his 'semistarvation during this period when he voluntarily chose not to eat' (*Comer* v. *Stewart*, 2002a: 1044). Finally, she concluded that if he was so depressed he would have been suicidal, and there is no indication that he had tried to kill himself in all of the years of his confinement, referring to Comer's own 'coherent and rational' testimony that he knew how to commit suicide if he had wanted to.

In reference to the SHU syndrome diagnosis, Judge Silver again frames Comer's behaviour as rational choices made by him. Dr Kupers referred to two of his behaviours: his incessant pacing in his cell, which he does for 14–20 hours a day (except when immobilized as described above) and his legendary shank-making[17] as compulsive behaviour indicative of SHU syndrome. Yet rather than accept this psychiatric assessment, the judge relied on and put forth Comer's own assessments of this behaviour to deny the presence of SHU syndrome: his walking was a healthy outlet for exercise and meditation, and his shank-making was purposeful, rational behaviour for self-protection. His memory lapses (another symptom of SHU syndrome) were also discounted by Judge Silver, again by citing Comer's own words that support a rational choice interpretation of this symptom: 'He testified that he remembers only "what [he] wants to remember". It is beyond peradventure that people generally remember what is important to them' (*Comer* v. *Stewart*, 2002a: 1058).[18]

Finally, she pointed out that his living conditions had improved in recent months, in that he was allowed the use of a Walkman, a television, and was given more selection in his meals. Nonetheless, he still stood by his decision to volunteer for execution. This led her to her conclusion that Mr Comer did not suffer from SHU syndrome. Rather, her overall interpretation of Mr Comer's mental status, which was heavily influenced by Dr Johnson's assessment, implied that he was mentally healthy by choice, by taking advantage of the simple pleasures of such a life in the SHU:

Mr. Comer … has developed the means to cope with the conditions, and he exercises the initiative to ensure that he maintains his mental health while housed in them. According to Dr. Johnson, Mr. Comer is successful and functional in prison because he lives 'it to the fullest of his capacity in the environment that he is in'; by learning to 'value smaller increments of things' and to 'gain pleasure on a day-to-day basis with the little things in his existence'. (*Comer* v. *Stewart*, 2002a: 1059–60)

This construction then led Judge Silver straight to the answer to the second question at issue: whether Comer had waived his rights voluntarily. She did not have to say much to justify her conclusion that he had, given her preceding interpretation of his behaviour as the product of his free and voluntary choices. In opening her discussion of the facts in Comer's case, she begins with her conclusion:

> that Mr. Comer's decision to waive his right to habeas appeal and to accept execution is voluntary. In particular, it is the product of a rational intellect and an unconstrained will; it is not the result of an overborne will or the product of an impaired self-determination brought on by the exertion of any improper influences. (*Comer* v. *Stewart*, 2002a: 1071)

She then reiterates her earlier point that even though his conditions have improved, Comer had not chosen to 'forgo the decision he has consistently asserted and pursued acceptance of for over two years' (*Comer* v. *Stewart*, 2002a: 1071). Again minimizing the scope of her inquiry, Judge Silver turned to Dr Johnson's testimony indicating she had found no coercive forces influencing Mr Comer. This testimony clearly indicates that Dr Johnson's investigation of any potential coercion was limited to looking for coercive force exerted by another person (rather than by the setting itself), in that she claimed to find no one pushing Comer toward his decision, and if anything she found the opposite – his lawyers pushing him to fight for his life. Consequently, virtually no analysis of coercive power of the place – the very issues raised by the 9th Circuit about the potential of the SHU conditions to compel behaviour – was needed to arrive at her decision. The elision of this inquiry thus allowed the judge to avoid confrontation with the meaning, impact, and consequences of such extreme penal practices, which the 9th Circuit seemed to be prompting in its original order for an evidentiary hearing.

Conclusion

I have made the argument before that this development in penality – the Supermax death row – can be seen as a furthering of the transcending post-rehabilitative, 'waste management' new penological regime that has been described by Feeley and Simon (1992) as well as many others. My observations of the Arizona execution process, beginning with the death row experience in SMU II, in some ways is best described as the ultimate iteration of the new penology: 'waste disposal' (Lynch, 2000a). By using SHU units for the condemned to finish out their lives, states like Arizona are literally transforming those waiting to die from sociologically and psychologically rich human beings into a kind of untouchable toxic waste that need only be securely contained until its final disposal (Lynch, 2000a: 15). In just the way that the 9th Circuit imagined, those subject to this end-of-life experience may well be made more pliable and willing to die as a result.

In these cases, the rhetorical process in the law that works to first challenge, but ultimately sanction the post-rehabilitative waste-management style of punishment is revealed. As I suggested earlier, it is through the construction of the penal subject as a rational choice 'other', denuded from his history, social place, and psychological self that propels the normalization of extreme punishments here. First, though, the 9th Circuit forces such a machination by reconstituting the penal subject as a rehabilitative era throwback, and in doing so, that court's decisions can be seen as not only questioning the actual practices and their impact on these two men, but at a deeper level, questioning the entire contemporary penal enterprise. Thus, their framing of the issues in these cases suggests their attempt to break from the new punitive trend by reinstating a sociologically (or social psychologically) richer view of penality and penal subjectivity. Their vision of the potential consequences of harsh punishment on its recipients necessitates an investigation into the practices themselves, which in turn calls into question their value, utility, and humaneness as penal policy. Thus, their inquiry in some ways revives the 'modern' penal paradigm that views penal subjects as individuals who are shaped by myriad forces and influences outside of their control, including by the punishment to which they are subjected by the state. While the court was neither addressing the constitutionality of the death penalty nor of the long-term use of Supermax on 8th amendment grounds, it was still able to raise questions about the cruelty of those practices. By presenting the scenario in these cases as a 'Hobson's choice' they imply that any noble, philosophically sound goals of punishment have been lost by the state's adoption of such extreme practices.

That break from the new punitiveness was aborted in these cases, though, by the courts above and below the 9th Circuit. Structurally, the US Supreme Court has the prerogative simply to ignore the specific directives issued by the 9th Circuit, and it did just that to shut down the inquiry in *Miller*. The District Court in *Comer*, on the other hand, had no choice but to deal with the higher court's orders. Yet even here, Judge Silver was able to evade direct confrontation with the implications of the painful penal regime at work in Arizona. And it is likely that Comer's case will eventually go the way of Miller's once back on the court dockets. Even if the 9th Circuit rules in that case in a way to impede Mr Comer's execution, the US Supreme Court is not likely to let that stand, given its response to *Miller*.

By rhetorically relying on the contemporary construction of the criminal as a rational actor brimming with free will to choose to die, Judge Silver was able to reframe the very disturbing evidence about Comer's hellish existence in the SMU II and its impact on him as a series of rational choices. She did not deny his 'otherness', and indeed simultaneously painted him as an extreme danger to others, in that she offered detailed accounts of his violent and troublesome behaviour within prison throughout her opinion, but constructed him as a rational 'other' who not only can and perhaps should be eliminated by the state process, but chooses to be as well. In the process, she avoided addressing the elephants in the room that highlight the irrationality of the broader penal scene in question. For instance, Comer's 'normal, healthy' bereavement over his comrade's execution was in fact a direct consequence of deliberate state action – execution – against his friend, an action that is eventually to be imposed on Comer himself. And what she characterized as a healthy exercise outlet is literally analogous to a desperate caged animal at the zoo pacing around and around its confined space during all of its waking hours (see *Madrid* v. *Gomez*, 1995, for the judge's description of this phenomenon in California's SHU), and is a direct consequence of the painful punishment itself. In the end, by so eliding engagement with the central issue raised by the 9th Circuit about the impact of the state's imposition of one punishment – SHU confinement – on the state's ultimate punishment – execution – both harsh practices remain unquestioned as penal policy.

Notes

1 This material is based upon work supported by the National Science Foundation under Grant No. 0112585. Any opinions, findings, and conclusions or recom-mendations expressed in this material are those of the author(s) and do not necessarily reflect the views of the National Science Foundation.

2 This will not be a traditional doctrinal analysis where I critique the use of precedent and/or the application of constitutional principles in these cases, but rather an examination of the underlying conceptualizations of penality reflected in the narratives of the decisions.

3 As a result of its 'ultra-liberal' maverick reputation, this court's decisions are disproportionately likely to be taken up for review by the conservative dominated US Supreme Court (Chorney, 2004; Herald, 1998). See *Vasquez* v. *Harris* (1992), Leff (1994), and Noonan (1993) for a discussion of one of the most famous and troubling battles over capital punishment between these two courts.

4 This was the landmark US Supreme Court decision that deemed capital punishment, as then being administered, unconstitutional in the US. The holding left open the possibility for a return of the death penalty so long as the decision-making pro-cedures for how sentence was determined were altered. By 1976, the court approved several new models for a constitutional death penalty (*Gregg* v. *Georgia*, 1976), by which time the majority of states had new capital punishment laws in effect.

5 It should be noted that there is little empirical evidence to support the policy of using SHU housing for death row inmates, and more evidence to suggest it is not necessary or advisable. See Ferrier (2004) for a full discussion on this. Indeed, the state of Missouri has moved in the opposite direction, mainstreaming their death row inmates into the general prison population, resulting in substantial cost savings, social and psychological benefits for condemned and non-condemned inmates alike, and easier management of the condemned prisoners for institutional staff (Lombardi *et al.*, 1996).

6 Consistent with this body of research, completed suicides and serious attempts occur with some regularity at Arizona's Supermax unit, Eyman SMU II.

7 This is the US constitutional amendment that bans the infliction of 'cruel and unusual' punishments.

8 This is not the first or only state to move death row to such facilities: Delaware, Arkansas, Maryland, Pennsylvania, and Texas are among a number of others that now use Supermax units as death rows. Maryland has since had second thoughts about the Supermax as a correctional facility in general. They are now considering moving death row out of that facility and indeed are entertaining the possibility of shutting down the whole SHU unit due to its detrimental effects on those incarcerated there.

9 I have previously written about Ross, whose execution I personally witnessed (Lynch, 2000a). His voluntary execution generated no litigation as no one sought

to intervene. This chapter focuses on the other two volunteers mentioned here.

10 In the US, state convicts generally have two routes of appeal – through their own state courts and through the three-tiered federal system, and can either directly challenge the trial record (a direct appeal) or allege a violation outside of the record (usually a habeas corpus). The twelve Circuit Courts are the intermediary appellate courts, and generally function as the federal court of last resort since the US Supreme Court only takes up a tiny fraction of the cases that seek consideration there. Comer's federal case began as a habeas corpus petition challenging the constitutionality of his conviction and sentence. By 2000, he and the State lawyers attempted to withdraw his appeal to allow his execution to proceed. In Miller's case, he declined to pursue federal habeas corpus relief, so his former attorney filed the appeal at issue here.

11 The US Supreme Court has since ruled that the *Ring* decision cannot be applied retroactively (*Schriro* v. *Summerlin*, 2004) so Comer's sentence will not automatically be overturned by that case. At the time of this writing, though, no further decisions have been made in this case and Comer continues to await execution on Supermax death row in Arizona.

12 In that case, the question was whether Miller was competent to represent himself in his appeals, which he was pursuing at the time.

13 In both cases, 9th Circuit Judge Rymer wrote a dissent that took her colleagues to task for the content of their analysis. She actually concurred with the decision in Comer, but dissented from the 15 pages of 'dicta' that preceded it. She suggested that almost the entire opinion, besides its conclusion, was both unnecessary and unfounded, and accused the majority of overstepping their role by making comments about Comer's mental state. In *Miller*, she dissented in full, and described the evidence presented that Miller may not currently be competent and that his waiver may not be voluntary as speculative at best.

14 Several times, she even highlighted the extreme dangerousness of his deceased death row best friend, which was completely irrelevant to this case.

15 Comer has a long history of being a discipline problem while incarcerated and so spent significant portions of his sentences throughout his prison career in punitive isolation units.

16 There is about a full page of narrative under the heading, 'Mr. Comer's Conditions of Confinement While Incarcerated in Arizona' (*Comer* v. *Stewart*, 2002a: 1033), but most of it is devoted to describing his disciplinary problems while confined in Arizona.

17 A hand-made knife used as a weapon in prison. Comer was notorious for making shanks out of anything he could, including the metal on his allegedly indestructible metal cell desk and chair. Prison officials thus removed this furniture from his cell, leaving only his bunk and toilet.

18 She didn't even try to rationalize away evidence that Comer suffered from auditory hallucinations and paranoia; rather she just didn't address it.

References

Andrade v. *Lockyer*, 308 F.3d 1025 (9th Cir. 2002).

Arizona Department of Corrections (2004) *ADC Inmates on Death Row*. Available at http://www.adc.state.az.us/DeathRow/DeathRow.htm#Number. Last accessed 2 August 2004.

Benjamin, T. and K. Lux (1977) 'Solitary Confinement as Psychological Punishment', *California Western Law Review*, 13: 265–290.

Bonczar, T. B. and T. L. Snell (2003) *Capital Punishment, 2002*. Bureau of Justice Statistics Bulletin. Washington DC: U.S Department of Justice (November).

Chorney, J. (2004) '9th Circuit Stays Under Microscope', *The Legal Intelligencer*, 231: 4 (1 July).

Cohen, S. (1996) 'Crime and Politics: Spot the Difference', *British Journal of Sociology*, 47: 1–21.

Comer v. Stewart, 215 F.3d 910 (9th Cir. 2000).

Comer v. Stewart, 230 F. Supp. 2d 1016 (2002a).

Comer v. Stewart, 312 F.3d 1157 (9th Cir. 2002b).

Connolly, W. (1999) 'The Will, Capital Punishment, and Cultural War', in A. Sarat (ed.) *The Killing State*, New York: Oxford University Press.

Cunningham, M. and M. Vigen (2002) 'Death Row Inmate Characteristics, Adjustment, and Confinement: A Critical Review of the Literature', *Behavioral Sciences and the Law*, 20: 191–210.

Dayan, J. (1997) 'The Blue Room in Florence', *Yale Review*, 85: 27–46.

De Haan, W. and J. Vos (2003) 'A Crying Shame: The Over-rationalized Conception of Man in the Rational Choice Perspective', *Theoretical Criminology*, 7: 29–54.

Feeley, M. and J. Simon (1992) 'The New Penology: Notes on the Emerging Strategy of Corrections and its Implications', *Criminology*, 30: 449–474.

Ferrier, R. M. (2004) 'Note: "An Atypical and Significant Hardship": The Supermax confinement of death row prisoners based purely on status – A plea for procedural due process', *Arizona Law Review*, 46: 291–315.

Furman v. Georgia, 408 US 238 (1972).

Garland, D. (1996) 'The Limits of the Sovereign State', *British Journal of Criminology*, 36: 445–471.

Garland, D. (2001) *The Culture of Control*, New York: Oxford University Press.

Grassian, S. (1983) 'Psychopathological Effects of Solitary Confinement', *American Journal of Psychiatry*, 140: 1450–1454.

Gregg v. Georgia, 428 US 153 (1976).

Hallsworth, S. (2000) 'Rethinking the Punitive Turn', *Punishment and Society*, 2: 145–160.

Haney, C. (1993) 'Infamous Punishment: The Psychological Effects of Isolation', *The National Prison Project Journal*, 8: 3–21.

Haney, C. (1997) 'Psychology and the Limits to Prison Pain: Confronting the Coming Crisis in Eighth Amendment law', *Psychology, Public Policy and Law*, 3: 499–588.

Haney, C. (1998) 'Riding the Punishment Wave: On the Origins of our Devolving Standards of Decency', *Hastings Women's Law Journal*, 9: 27–78.

Haney, C. (2003) 'Mental Health Issues in Long-term Solitary and "Supermax" Confinement', *Crime & Delinquency*, 49: 124–156.

Haney, C. and M. Lynch (1997) 'Regulating Prisons of the Future: A Psychological Analysis of Supermax and Solitary Confinement', *New York University Review of Law and Social Change*, 23: 477–570.

Hentoff, N. (1993) 'Buried Alive in American Prisons: Charles Dickens's Report to Zoe Baird', *Washington Post*, A21 (9 January).

Herald, M. (1998) 'Reversed, Vacated, and Split: The Supreme Court, the Ninth Circuit, and the Congress', *Oregon Law Review*, 77: 405–496.

Hermann, W. (1996) 'Escape Unlikely at New High-security Unit; Best Prison for Worst Inmates', *Arizona Republic*, A1 (22 June).

Human Rights Watch (1997) *Cold Storage: Supermaximum Security Confinement in Indiana*. Available at http://hrw.org/reports/1997/usind/. Last accessed 30 July 2004.

Jackson, M. (1983) *Prisoners of Isolation: Solitary Confinement in Canada*, Toronto: University of Toronto Press.

King, R. (1999) 'The Rise and Rise of Supermax: An American Solution in Search of a Problem?', *Punishment and Society*, 1: 163–186.

Leary, K. (1994) 'Pelican Bay as Prison of the Future', *San Francisco Chronicle*, A7 (18 April).

Leff, L. (1994) 'Reflecting Law's Violence: Press Coverage of an Execution', *Studies in Law, Politics, and Society*, 14: 213–243.

Lehmann, C. (1999) 'Putting Prisoners in Isolation Units Causes More Problems Than It Attempts to Correct', *Psychiatric News* (9 February). Available at http://www.psych.org/pnews/99-02-05/prison.html

Lombardi, G., R. D. Sluder and D. Wallace (1996) 'The Management of Death-Sentenced Inmates: Issues, Realities, and Innovative Strategies', paper presented at the Annual Meeting of the Academy of Criminal Justice Sciences, Las Vegas, Nevada, March, 1996.

Lynch, M. (2000a) 'The Disposal of Inmate #85271: Notes on a Routine Execution', *Studies in Law, Politics, and Society*, 20: 3–34.

Lynch, M. (2000b) 'Rehabilitation as Rhetoric: The Reformable Individual in Contemporary Parole Discourse and Practices', *Punishment and Society*, 2: 41–65.

Lynch, M. (2001) 'From the Punitive City to the Gated Community: Security and Segregation across the Social and Penal Landscape', *Miami Law Review*, 56: 601–623.

Lynch, M. and Haney, C. (1998) 'Impelling/Impeding the Momentum Toward Death: A Contextual Analysis of Attorneys' Final Arguments in California Capital Penalty Phase Trials'. Unpublished manuscript.

Madrid v. *Gomez*, 889 F. Supp. 1146, 1265 (N.D. Cal. 1995).

Miller v. *Stewart*, 231 F.3d 1248 (9th Cir. 2000)

Noonan, J. (1993) 'Horses of the Night: Harris v. Vasquez', *Stanford Law Review*, 45: 1011–1025.

Rhodes, L. (2004) *Total Confinement: Madness and Reason in the Maximum Security Prison*, Berkeley, CA: University of California Press.

Ross, L. and R. E. Nisbett (1991) *The Person and the Situation: Perspectives of Social Psychology*, New York: McGraw-Hill Publishing.

Schriro v. *Summerlin* US Supreme Court Case No. 03–526, decided 24 June (2004).

Simon, J. (1998) 'Managing the Monstrous: Sex Offenders and the New Penology', *Psychology, Public Policy and Law*, 4: 452–467.

Steckner, S. (1998) 'Killer of 17 is Executed for 2 deaths; Inmate Waited 25 years in Florence to Die', *Arizona Republic*, B1 (4 June).

Stewart v. *Miller*, 531 US 986 (2000).

Summerlin v. *Stewart*, 267 F.3d 926 (9th Cir. 2001).

U.S. v. *Parish*, 308 F.3d 1025, 1032 (9th Cir. 2002).

Vasquez v. *Harris*, 503 US 1000 (1992).

5. The liberal veil: revisiting Canadian penality

Dawn Moore and Kelly Hannah-Moffat

Punitiveness in Western penal systems has gained increased attention over the last ten years. Some (e.g. Garland, 2001) suggest that we have entered a new age of punitiveness characterized by the rise of boot camps, use of the death penalty, austere and overcrowded prison conditions, and chain gangs. Others (e.g O'Malley, 1999: Pratt, 2002) see a more complicated turn of events whereby the rise of punitiveness is concomitant with the introduction of neoliberal strategies that mandate efficiency and effectiveness. Although there is contention about the degree to which the 'punitive turn' has taken place, there appears to be a degree of accord on the notion that rehabilitation has abated and been replaced (in some instances) by more punitive mentalities.

To date, the changes in penality and penal practice in Canada have not been taken into account in attempts to theorize changes in punishment. Exploring the terrain of punishment in Canada is important for two reasons. First, Canada's incarceration rates, while among the highest in the Western world, are closer to those of other Western nations than those of the US. The Correctional Service of Canada's (CSC) most recent statistics place Canada's prison population as the fourth highest per capita of all European and North American countries, placing it only marginally behind England and Scotland.[1] Second, the practices and rationales of punishment in Canada are exported through the Western world. The 'Canadian model' of punishment operates under a liberal veil and is increasingly popular and far removed from the kind of punishment described through the punitive turn thesis.

This chapter explores the punitive turn thesis in relation to punishment in Canada, offering two central observations. First, the notion of a punitive turn fails to capture the complexity and diversity of Canadian penality. It implies that more liberal welfare penal practices have been replaced and that those which existed previously were preferable to more punitive developments. Second, the definition of punitiveness as it exists within the penal-turn literature is too narrow. What remains understudied is how welfare practices, which continue to exist, have evolved and are central to Canadian penality. The initiatives currently aimed at 'changing' prisoners in Canada are consistent with the age-old goals of rehabilitation and reform of prisoners but the practices through which these transformations are meant to take place are different. On the surface, many of the current practices (emphasis on therapeutic interventions, programming which is gender and culturally sensitive) appear preferable to the corporeal punitiveness of countries like the United States. Canadian punishment appears liberal and progressive. However, our analysis of these initiatives reveals that therapy is not the antithesis of punitiveness. Therapeutic discourses and practices are also punitive. The Canadian criminal justice system operates under the liberal veil of the free subject who makes her or his own choices. Prisoners are not, however, by their very definition, free subjects. They are not at liberty to make personal choices and are made to participate in programming designed to change them as part of their punishment. The following will outline some of the recent developments in federal and provincial (Ontario) regimes[2] and show how these changes in penality mark wider shifts in punishment that are not explained by the punitive turn thesis.

Contradictions and changes: thinking beyond eras

Historical accounts of practices of punishment in North America typically cite four eras: rehabilitation (or reform or change), retribution, deterrence, and incapacitation. These eras are often talked about as universal trends in the practice of punishment. Both pedagogically and theoretically, punishment is often described in terms of the waxing and waning of 'eras'. The majority of attempts to explain changing practices of punishment in the twentieth century centre on the rise, fall, and rise again of penal welfarism. Garland (2001: 27) defines the modern penal welfare structure as a hybrid that combines:

> ... The liberal legalism of due process and proportionate punishment with a correctionalist commitment to rehabilitation, welfare and criminological expertise.

Specifically here, Garland sees practices like treatment programmes, criminological research, and indeterminate sentences all as features of penal welfarist practice, the rehabilitative era. These practices have, in the eyes of many, evaporated from the landscape of punishment in the Western world. We are said to have entered a new era of punishment – the punitive era. And though there has been much contestation about its naming and specific nature, this new time is seen by all as having disavowed rehabilitation.

In Canada, if we take the practices of rehabilitation as they were established during the 'welfarist era' as the defining characteristics of the period, then the thesis proposed by Garland is accurate. Punishment through the 1950s and 1960s in Canada (more so in the 1960s) was increasingly informed by social and psychological expertise. Social workers and psychologists held directive positions in Canadian institutions as well as working on the front line in prisons. Much of the political and governmental rhetoric about punishment at the time was focused on the betterment of the individual as part of a broader project of the betterment of society (see Moore, 2005).

These sentiments are reflected in the report of the Fauteaux Committee of Inquiry. The Committee, established in 1953 to study remission of federal prisoners, strongly recommended that the penal system take up a decidedly more rehabilitation-oriented agenda at both the federal and provincial levels. Fauteaux (1956) called for an increased system of probation and parole, the establishment of treatment prisons and treatment programmes within mainstream prisons, increased use of minimum-security institutions, and the professionalization of staff. The adoption of the medical model also influenced Fauteaux's report. Following on Fauteaux's report, the federal government did instigate some changes in its penal practices. A treatment prison aimed at responding to drug and alcohol use was opened in British Columbia and other kinds of therapeutic initiatives (e.g. psychotherapy) were established at prisons across the country. These initiatives, however, appeared to be largely piecemeal and lacked any coherent vision. Their implementation appears to have depended more on the personnel found in specific locales rather than on a system-wide plan.

The landscape of punishment in Canada today is markedly different from that of the 1960s and 1970s. It is also, however, markedly different from the kind of punishment imagined and theorized in current academic writings. Canada has not experienced the punitive turn chronicled by Garland and others. While some jurisdictions, most notably Ontario, have embraced some aspects of the new punitiveness through the establishment of boot camps, mega-jails, and the demise of parole, all of which rest on a mantra of 'get-tough efficiency' (see Moore and Hannah-Moffat, 2002), all jurisdictions, including Ontario, have also implemented a wide array of initiatives aimed at changing and responsibilizing individual offenders.

In 1991, the Correctional Service of Canada (CSC) underwent a system-wide overhaul which altered practices at every level. Largely as a result of the vision of the new Commissioner, Ole Ingstrup, the CSC fully embraced a therapeutic position regarding punishment. In *Our Story*, CSC's own reflection on its 'rebirth', Vantour (1991: 7) describes the purpose of federal punishment in Canada:

> We have part of the responsibility to deal with one of society's most fundamental values – its collective security. But we must do much more. Corrections is not just confinement – keeping people in cells until they have reached the end of their sentences. We must also deal with the freedom of individual members of our society, including the offenders under our jurisdiction. As the name of the organization implies, we are an agency devoted to bringing about a change for the better in those legally committed to our care so that they may eventually return to their communities as law-abiding citizens.

In practice, these changes meant the adoption of the same, standardized, 'core' programmes across the country. These programmes are said to be based on empirical evidence that supports a broader understanding of criminal activity, which, in turn, prescribes the need for specific, targeted interventions. CSC's commitment to this new vision also includes an extensive research branch that is intended to contribute to broader criminological knowledge, mainly about the psychology of the prisoners themselves, in order to further the 'what works' agenda of offering the most 'effective' and empirically proven penal programming in addition to establishing a set of best practices. CSC's research branch has offices across the country (including a specific research unit for substance abuse in Prince Edward Island), and produces its own research periodical (*Forum on Correctional Research*). The correctional vision imagined by the network of psychologists central to CSC is marketed throughout the world and some of their work has become canonized reading in criminal psychology (cf. Andrews and Bonta, 1998).

Comparable changes occurred in provincial institutions.[3] However, at the same time the correctional narratives in some provincial penal systems such as Ontario de-emphasized treatment in favour of a more punitive rhetoric while continuing to deliver therapeutic programmes in many institutions. In 1996, the Conservative provincial government of Mike Harris introduced its plan for correctional renewal. This plan, which was followed through by the subsequent Conservative government of Ernie Eves and, most recently, Dalton McGuinty's Liberal government, has now been almost fully implemented province wide. The plan operates on the mantra of 'get-tough efficiency' and includes the creation of mega-jails, boot camps, private prisons, and work gangs. The system in the province is, by all accounts, decidedly more austere and brutal than at the federal level. Indeed, people facing a prison sentence will often vie for a longer sentence, which places them in federal custody, rather than have to serve time in the provincial system. Conditions in the detention centres in Ontario are often deplorable as prisoners are forced to triple-bunk, face vermin infestations, and risk contracting tuberculosis. Those held in detention are often locked down for 23 hours a day and have almost no programming or services available to them. For those held in correctional centres, conditions are marginally better. Many prisoners are now housed in one of four new mega-jails across the province, each of which holds approximately 1,200 prisoners in specially designed and self-contained 'pods'. They wear uniforms, have little chance of gaining parole and some are made to participate in work crews. Still, within this system there are also strong elements of therapeutic programming. Like CSC, criminogenic programmes are available to provincial prisoners and those on probation have access to a variety of programmes and services. Unlike the federal system, little attention is devoted to women's or ethno-cultural concerns.

Alongside this austerity there is a boom in standardized psychological programming throughout both the community and institutional components of the system. The programming draws extensively on the precedent set by CSC, using similar assessment schemes and designing initiatives intended to respond to offenders' criminogenic factors (the same factors as those identified at the federal level). As of the summer of 2004, programmes in anger management, substance abuse, and anti-criminal thinking are underway in most of the province's prisons. Like CSC, the provincial system has developed its own research branch, is employing psychologists in unprecedented numbers and uses standardized risk/need assessment techniques.

Explaining changes

Given these contradictory changes, how can we characterize and understand the penal practices currently underway in Canada? If the punitive turn thesis does not hold true either when we look at the nation as a whole or when we focus specifically on different jurisdictions within the country, then what patterns are emerging and how can they be understood? That CSC has not adopted an overt punitive mentality is, perhaps, obvious. Nowhere in the organization is there any hint of interest in adopting the practices that have come to characterize the punitive model of punishment. CSC is moving toward smaller, not larger prisons. It patently refuses to engage in privatization and regularly defends its use of programming and parole opportunities as integral to the overall goal of reducing recidivism. CSC is, in fact, so far removed from the notion of punitiveness – at least in its own rhetoric – within popular thinking that its prisons are often referred to as luxurious 'club feds' and are criticized for coddling prisoners and lacking any sort of punitive features.

Punishment in Ontario is often juxtaposed with the federal system and held up as the most harsh, brutal, and punitive system in the country. The rhetoric of penality in Ontario bears this out to a certain extent. The province has adopted more punitive practices if we take the American model of punishment as the basis of the definition of punitiveness. Alongside privatization, boot camps, mega-jails, and work gangs Ontario is also committed to therapeutic programming which closely follows the model set out by CSC. As with the federal system, the commitment to a project of change in Ontario is formidable and does not fit easily into the punitive turn thesis. The situation in Canada is 'volatile and contradictory' (O'Malley, 1999). On the one hand it is punitive and the other therapeutic. The seemingly schizophrenic nature of the province's penal vision is well understood through a careful consideration of the nature of the bureaucracy through which penal policy and practices are established. Penal policy is best thought of as consisting of two components, rhetoric and practice. The rhetoric often comes from the political side of policy-making. Ontario politicians in the mid-1990s were claiming that Ontario was going to 'get tough on crime' and establish 'truth in sentencing'. This rhetoric does not, however, translate automatically into practice. Instead, it is interpreted by a buffer zone of high-level bureaucrats (i.e. deputy ministers, directors[4]) whose job it is to turn rhetoric into practice. In Ontario, many of these bureaucrats who were responsible for implementing the government's rhetorical changes and translating them into practices were the same people who had participated in the changes towards rehabilitation in the 1970s. As such, many of these individuals continued to have a strong commitment to the idea of rehabilitation and worked hard to implement changes which would both satisfy the government's rhetorical needs while maintaining, on the level of practice, a system committed to working with and changing individual prisoners (for a more detailed discussion see Moore, 2005). Thus, while at the level of rhetoric Ontario's penality clearly adopts a more punitive argot, the practices are not best understood as punitive.

Neither can we understand the changes wrought in Canadian punishment as indicative of a move towards rehabilitation as previously conceptualized. The notion of rehabilitation, if we take as its hallmark the welfarist era Garland describes, is marked by psycho- and pharmaco-therapies, humanization, and the rise of medical and psychotherapeutic practitioners holding positions of influence within the institutions. The practices and ideas currently implemented in Canadian punishment – actuarial assessments, targeted programming and criminogenic factors – were not features of the penal welfarist terrain of the post-World War 2 period.

There are, however, notable similarities between the penality of the welfarist era and the contemporary penality of Canadian punishment. Most notably, in each of these schemes, there is a commitment to the notion that individuals can, and should be changed. Change brought about in the right way will have a positive impact not only on the individual but also on the broader society through protection of public safety and the creation of a more socially productive individual. These practices, which were the hallmarks of the welfarist era, are also characteristic of Canadian punishment in 2004. While there are notable differences between the practices of the post-World War 2 time and contemporary practices, this basic sensibility, that people can and should be changed, remains constant. Following this, we suggest a different way of thinking about practices of punishment. There is a difference, as we noted above, between penality and penal practice. Theorizing about punishment tends to overemphasize the directive importance of penality and often ignores the very crucial importance of the actual practices of punishment within a jurisdiction or an 'era'. The effect here is a skewed view of both penal history and contemporary penal trends which sees a shift in penalities as coterminous with a shift in practices and vice versa. The penality of punishment in Canada is not all that notably different from that of 30 years before, largely because there is still a strong commitment to the project of changing prisoners. What has shifted are the practices through which this change project is meant to be carried out. If the penal practices of the welfare era were understood as liberal practices then today's practices are well characterized as neoliberal.

The neoliberal face of Canadian punishment

Targeted governance

Theorists argue that the ascendance of neoliberal regimes has given rise to new forms of 'targeted' governance (Valverde and Mopas, 2004). Valverde (2003), in her study of pharmaceutical drugs designed to 'target' alcoholism, and Rose (2003), in his study of pharmaceuticals which target the action of certain brain chemicals, both show the emergence of 'magic bullets' that are designed not to address the classic binary between normal and pathological, but rather to constitute specific targets in a bid to constantly correct and manage certain behaviours. Rose uses the example of Prozac – a drug developed to target very specific neurochemical activity – in order to show how forms of governance are concerned with acute and precise strategies. Valverde (2003) argues that the emergence of targeted governance, be it in relation to alcoholism, policing of specific communities, immigration profiling, or brain chemicals, signifies a bid to govern more 'modestly and specifically'. The notion of targeted governance is helpful in further understanding current practices of punishment in Canada, specifically focusing on the programmes established by CSC. Maurutto and Hannah-Moffat's (2005) recent analysis of the hybridization of actuarial and welfare strategies argues that targeted treatment is achieved by matching the level and type of intervention to the risk and need posed by an offender. Given the cost of treatment services, universal access for all offenders to all available programmes is no longer deemed tenable, and hence only 'essential services' are delivered and only to those deemed most in need. New strategies are developed to calculate and categorize who will most benefit from a particular service (Maurutto and Hannah-Moffat, 2005: 18).

There is a new legitimization of treatment and a shift in how correctional treatment is delivered. In essence, correctional interventions are now *targeted*. Correctional programme narratives speak of interventions that 'target criminogenic needs' and stratify service delivery. CSC is committed to finding and intervening with these 'magic bullets' of criminality – criminogenic factors. Correctional treatment narratives claim to target those dynamic (changeable) attributes of an offender that are related to criminal behaviour: a criminogenic need (Hannah-Moffat, 2005). A fundamental goal of national correctional assessment classification is to identify needs that can be targeted for intervention to reduce the risk of recidivism. Offenders are placed in a variety of generic programmes designed to target the need area, enhance their ability to self-govern, and prudently manage their risks of recidivism. A central aspect of the new rehabilitative programming is the provision of core programmes that target relevant need areas, which include cognitive skills, substance abuse, living skills, abuse and trauma, and employment and education programmes.

Through the promise of empirical evidence, CSC suggests that it has, through its network of psychologists, found the way to zero in on the factors that are not only most likely to cause criminality within an individual but also most easily intervened upon from the perspective of penal authorities. Andrews (1989: 9) argues, 'if correctional treatment services are to reduce recidivism, which is the established Canadian federal correctional logic, then the criminogenic needs of offenders must be targeted ... Some promising targets of rehabilitative service include drug and alcohol use, relationships, choice of friends, and thinking patterns.' For example, drug testing and medical examinations provide 'concrete' evidence of substance abuse. It is allegedly[5] possible to prove that an individual uses marijuana. Once subjects have been through substance abuse programming, it is also possible to retest them in order to 'see' if they have stopped using substances. Although more subjective, CSC deploys other measures in order to assess the effectiveness of targeting. Beyond paying attention to recidivism rates (which are the main factors used in illustrating the effectiveness of these programmes) the same battery of psychological tests and assessments can be used repeatedly on individuals in order to judge whether or not their cognitive skills have improved or their anger is better managed. Targeted, needs-focused treatments provide the skills necessary for managing needs (and risk) and helps the offender gain insight into patterns of offending so 'pro-social choices' can be made. Correctional programmes enjoy an elevated and renewed status, as vehicles for teaching risk/need management, by having offenders assume responsibility for their situations and take responsibility for changing their circumstances.[6]

Targeted governance also lends economic accountability to practices of punishment. One of the major failings of the kinds of interventions mobilized throughout the 1960s and 1970s was that it was next to impossible to 'prove' whether or not they 'worked'. This, of course, was one of the central concerns originally raised by Martinson (1974) at the beginning of the 'what works' debate. The targeting of criminogenic factors means that it appears to be much easier to isolate a certain practice (e.g. intervening with someone's ability to manage anger) and measure how effective that practice is (i.e. through recidivism rates). Targeted governance thus makes it much easier to justify the continuation of certain kinds of interventions on the grounds that they are empirically proven to work.

Personal choice/personal responsibility

Neoliberalism is perhaps best described through its emphasis on individuality. Both the federal and provincial penal systems place a good deal of emphasis on the centrality of the individual within the context of individual choice-making. This emphasis draws on two central themes: that individuals can and should be able to make rational choices and that individuals must take personal responsibility for the choices they make.

The notion of choice is present in just about every facet of penal programming in Canada. Those incarcerated in the federal system in Canada are supposed to be taught how to make 'pro-social' choices that are personally resonant, largely around the ways in which they will conduct themselves while in prison. Likewise, the substance abuse programmes at both the federal and provincial levels take the word 'choice' as part of their titles. Ontario's newly devised substance abuse programme is called 'Change is a Choice'. The training manual for the programme directs programme facilitators to act as guides rather than judges and assist offenders in making 'good choices' around their substance use and other lifestyle habits. CSC's guiding document on women prisoners, *Creating Choices*, and subsequent policy documents outline five central principles around which the new women's system is meant to operate (Hannah-Moffat, 2000). One of these principles is the ability to make meaningful choices. The offender's poor decisions were a consequence of an absence of or deficiencies in requisite skills, abilities, and attitudes necessary for proper informed decision-making; or more aptly stated, 'Crime was the outcome of insufficiently or unevenly developed rational or cognitive capacities. Criminals did not know how!' (Duguid, 2000: 183). Techniques like cognitive therapy or other programmes are vehicles through which offenders can learn how to manage their criminogenic needs and reduce their risk of recidivism by acquiring the requisite skills, abilities, and attitudes needed to lead pro-social lives. In 1991, this logic resulted in CSC designating 'cognitive skills' a compulsory core programme for most prisoners.

This notion of choice-making also translates into notions of personal responsibility. Central to the therapeutic ethos currently at play in Canada is the idea that individual offenders must take responsibility for their past actions as well as their future changes. The wedding of individual choice and responsibility is a common feature of neoliberal practice, especially within the realm of psychology and therapeutic interventions (see O'Malley, 1999). Born largely out of the work of a network of criminal psychologists, CSC organizes its new correctional vision around the logic that individuals engage in criminal behaviour because they suffer from cognitive distortions and poorly managed lifestyles. These deficits are categorized into seven criminogenic factors: personal/ emotional issues, substance abuse, employment, education, family/marital, friends, and associates. While the theory put forward by these psychologists acknowledges that there are other factors that may contribute to criminal behaviour (e.g. poverty), social explanations for criminality are specifically disavowed in favour of a focus on individual characteristics. This focus is derived from the 'what works' debate and is justified on the basis that there is empirical evidence supporting the view that intervening with individuals around these 'core' factors is a proven way to reduce recidivism. As such, an individual incarcerated in a federal penitentiary (and increasingly in provincial correctional centres) undergoes a series of actuarial assessments designed to identify the kinds of interventions which will be most effective on the individual (see Maurutto and Hannah-Moffat, 2005; Hannah-Moffat, 2004). Based on the outcome of this assessment process, an individual is recommended to participate in 'core programmes' intended to 'target' their individual criminogenic needs. Thus, an individual who is assessed as having problems with anger will be recommended to participate in the anger management programme, an individual with an addiction might be recommended to participate in a substance abuse programme.

In particular, since the early 1980s there has been a marked increase in the use of cognitive behavioural therapy (CBT) in all realms of intervention, including the penal system. CBT is rooted in many different psychological and psychiatric traditions including the structuralist and cognition-based Adlerian and Freudian schools and Skinner's behaviourism. It was shaped in the 1970s primarily by Aaron Beck,[7] who first used it to address depression. CBT was quickly taken up as the choice therapy in dealing with everything from anxiety to body image issues to schizophrenia (cf. Dobson, 2001). In clinical initiatives, the draw of CBT is that it can be designed to meet very specific needs of the client, targeting identified problematic behaviours instead of having to engage in long-term, more holistic interventions as in the case of psychoanalysis. CBT focuses on cognition or thought and begins with the assumption that a problematic behaviour (violent outbursts, depression, smoking) is directly linked to errors and distortions in thinking. The therapeutic process is designed to give clients tools through which they can correct flawed thought processes. Often this involves a blend of therapy sessions with a psychologist and 'homework' the client is given to practise new thought skills. In Beck's (1988: 1541) own words:

> [t]he techniques [of CBT] are designed to help the patient to identify, to test the reality of, and to correct distorted conceptualizations and dysfunctional beliefs underlying these cognitions. By thinking and acting more realistically and adaptively with regard to here-and-now psychological situations and problems, the patient is expected to experience improvement in symptoms and behaviour.

CBT is set up as a progression from the widespread popularity of psychoanalysis in the 1950s and 1960s. When CBT arose in the 1970s it was with the offer of scientifically provable interventions that were rooted in observable behaviours rather than what the early CBT champions thought of as somatic and psychic vagaries (Hoffman, 1984). Individual choice and individual responsibility are also core aspects of CBT. The 'client' is reminded again and again that he or she can choose how he or she acts and reacts within any situation and, consequently, must take responsibility for those actions and reactions. CBT is the basis for most of the penal interventions found in Canadian punishment. The prisoner is imagined as the free and responsible subject with no apparent attention paid to the rather obvious irony of this characterization.

The centralizing of notions of freedom and choice are crucial to constituting a liberal veil because they help to create the illusion that crime is an individual phenomenon and that individuals in conflict with the law are free to choose whether or not they will commit more crimes. Of course, this sort of mentality works to completely erase any chance to see crime as a social phenomenon. Rather than allowing space for structural issues such as poverty and racism to play a role in the explanation and subsequent arresting of criminal behaviour, responsibility rests solely on the individual offender. Thus the logic tells individuals that they chose to commit a crime. This choice, following the popular psychological logic, indicates that they suffer from thinking errors that can and should be corrected – but only if the individual chooses to do so. Therapeutic interventions offered in the penal system are thus not said to be coercive as no prisoner is forced to participate. They make *choices*.

Punitive therapy

Here the veil of liberalism starts to thin on several counts. First, there is a systemic thinking error that assigns responsibility for criminality solely to the individual and thus makes the individual the only actor subject to punishment. Even the psychologists responsible for designing the targeted programmes and the rhetoric of choice admit that there are social factors implicated in criminal behaviour. These they classify as 'static factors', meaning that they may be taken into consideration but they are unchangeable (Andrews and Bonta, 1998). A prisoner's impoverished history, repeated experiences of marginalization and past traumas might contribute to criminal acts but there is nothing that can be done to rectify these systemic and historic factors in order to reduce this individual's future chances of recidivism. The focus is placed instead on those 'dynamic' or individual factors that can be worked with or intervened upon. The result is the imagining of crime as a strictly individual phenomenon which can be solved only if the individual chooses to do so. Of course, despite the fact that systemic factors are understood as contributing to crime, there is no acknowledgement that it is precisely with regard to these social factors that individuals are denied choice and made to feel unempowered in the first place. The logic is faulty. If we acknowledge that crime is a product of some combination of social and individual factors, then how can we assume that crime will be solved through addressing only these individual factors?

Second, an argument that proposes that Canadian punishment is neoliberal and non-punitive ignores the instances of brutality and human rights abuses that occur in Canadian prisons, albeit typically far from the gaze of media and politicians. The liberal veil conjured through the rhetoric of criminogenic factors creates the illusion that intervening with criminogenic factors means Canadian penal institutions operate humanely. Abuses of human rights are notable in all Canadian penal institutions (Canadian Human Rights Commission, 2004). Elsewhere (Moore and Hannah-Moffat, 2001), we chronicled human rights abuses emerging from the newly renovated penal system in Ontario. Here, alongside the systemic problems we noted above, reports indicate that prisoners have been denied adequate winter clothing, access to the telephone, books, and programmes. There are reports of prisoners held in detention centres – meant to serve only as transitory, short-term accommodations – for years. Escapes and deaths in custody have raised the ire of human rights activists.

The federal system is not exempt from such transgressions. Far from the image of 'club fed', the federal prisons have been the sites of human rights abuses and several governmental inquiries that challenge CSC's practices and call for greater accountability and humanity. The sharply criticized women's branch of the federal system was the subject of a Commission of Inquiry headed by Justice Louise Arbour. Arbour's (1996) final report returned a scathing commentary on the entire system of federal punishment, finding a 'culture of lawlessness' which pervaded the entire system. The office of the Correctional Investigator routinely finds that correctional staff and the entire penal system routinely transgress boundaries of acceptable and humane treatment of prisoners.[8] While programme initiatives are being expanded, so too are the powers of correctional officers. Recent use of force/restraint policies were amended to permit all federal Correctional Officers in direct contact with inmates in maximum, medium, and multi-level security institutions to carry handcuffs.[9]

The use of solitary confinement within the federal prisons has also come under scrutiny. The Task Force on Administrative Segregation was born out of Arbour's (1996) observations that the use of solitary confinement in Canadian prisons was unlawful and inhumane. The Task Force found that prisoners were being held in solitary confinement for indeterminate periods of time for questionable reasons. The punitiveness of the practice of segregation was amplified by the fact that those held in segregation were routinely denied the basic rights afforded to prisoners housed in the general population. Specifically, the Task Force found that when in segregation, prisoners did not have the same access to health care, spiritual guidance, and recreational time and activities as did their general population counterparts.

We cannot assume that liberal practices are antithetical to practices of punishment. Contemporary attempts to define punitiveness tend to focus on abuses of the body and overt abuses and injustices inflicted on the mind. The recent images from Iraq of American military personnel torturing and humiliating Iraqi prisoners are a case in point. Punitiveness must be clearly harsh and cruel. We wish to challenge that narrow definition of punitiveness with the assertion that liberal initiatives within a penal system – in particular, therapeutic initiatives such as those found in Canadian prisons – are also punitive and sometimes cruel.

Often discussions about penal reform initiatives juxtapose therapy and punitiveness. There is an assumption that if a penal system is offering individuals therapeutic programming then somehow this same system is not acting punitively toward its prisoners or, at the very least, it is far less punitive than a system which offers little or no programming. This, we argue, is perhaps the most dangerous of assumptions made regarding punishment. The current definitions of punitiveness are far too narrow. Typically, the model of punishment character-ized largely by the United States is held up as typifying punitiveness. Torture, the denial of basic human rights, living in austere conditions, the death penalty, being made to pay for one's own incarceration, physical brutality, chain and work gangs, and elongated sentences are all held up as examples of punitiveness. We do not disagree. Certainly all these practices are egregious and need to be monitored. But this does not mean that replacing these practices with more therapeutic ones removes the punitiveness from the system.

Foucault (1977), in *Discipline and Punish*, suggests that punishment in the eighteenth century moved from a focus on the body to one on the mind of the condemned. This, he argued, was the entire purpose of establishing prisons in the first place. Instead of the corporeality which characterized punishment in much of the eighteenth century, interest was in the mind of the condemned, with making lawbreakers penitent and remorseful. Looking back on the practices of Auburn and Cherry Hill, few would be quick to say that the move from the body to the mind made punishment less punitive or more humane for lawbreakers. By today's standards, hooding prisoners, mandating silence and isolation, forcing prisoners to participate in religious ceremonies and subjecting them to religious teaching are all well understood as abusive of the basic standards of human rights established by the United Nations and generally accepted throughout the world.[10] To the reformers, however, these practices were extremely humane and were guaranteed to bring prisoners closer to redemption, lower recidivism rates, and increase the protection of public safety. They also appeared notably less punitive than the practices that had come before. It is not difficult to present forced silence as more humane than the thumb screws or the Iron Maiden. In comparison with physically cruel and torturous practices, it is understandable that the focus on the mind and the soul was far more palatable to reformers.

The ways in which punitiveness is imagined and described in current dis-courses sets up a similar juxtaposition. Those who call for reforms of the current systems of punishment focus mostly on what happens to the bodies of the prisoners. Do they have adequate food and shelter? Are they physically safe? Are they made to work too much or for the wrong reasons? Organizations such as the Sentencing Project in the United States and the less politicized John Howard Societies in Canada focus much of their advocacy and reform initiatives around these kinds of questions. What is held up as favourable about the Canadian penal systems is that the bodies of prisoners are treated, relatively speaking, reasonably well.[11] The question must be raised, however, of just how humane it is to focus on the minds and behaviours of prisoners when they are held in such a coercive setting.

Prisoners in Canada have little choice with regards to their participation in treatment programmes. Should they opt not to participate they invariably significantly weaken their chances of attaining parole. The content of the programmes and the ethos behind them ensure and demand that prisoners understand their criminal activity as a product of their own actions and choice-making without consideration for the broader social context in which they find themselves. Crime is entirely their fault. In order to rectify this faulty thinking, they must actively participate in programming. In the course of this active participation, an individual may well find herself facing the fact that she was sexually abused as a child, that her parents were neglectful or that she suffers from a mental illness. The prisoner is expected to continue to address and deal with these issues during the course of her imprisonment where she has little privacy, is locked away by the same people who play an active role in her therapeutic process, and does not have the option of calling a crisis line, seeing a therapist of her choosing on demand, or seeking the support of friends and family. In addition, once she is released from prison, the same social factors that played a role in her original incarceration (poverty, racism, etc.) have not disappeared, increasing the chances she will reoffend. This, we argue, is punitive.

Conclusion

Punishment in Canada operates under different practices and policies than those suggested through the punitive turn thesis. Where Garland suggests that punishment in the Western world is increasingly harsh and austere, emphasizing incapacitation and deterrence over rehabilitation, the Canadian experience indicates that the inverse is, in fact, a more accurate depiction of penal trends. While some jurisdictions in Canada have experienced a turn towards increasingly incapacitative and deterrence-oriented practices and mentalities, these do nothing to displace the mandate of any Canadian penal system to attempt to change lawbreakers. Correctional programming in Canada appears to have taken a step towards a liberalized notion of punishment where individual offenders are themselves responsibilized and given the 'choice' to participate in their own change processes. Explicit attention is given to the needs of women and minorities, and, at least at the federal level, entire institutions are established to meet their specific needs.

Appearances, however, can be deceiving. The liberalism of Canadian punishment is a veil underneath which remains an extremely punitive system. It is dangerous to fall into the juxtaposition of punitiveness and therapeutic initiatives. The endurance of the project of change in Canada offers a different kind of punitiveness to those incarcerated here, one in which the object of punishment is very much the mind and behaviour of the condemned person. This punishment mandates that individuals with varying histories of trauma, violence and marginalization must attempt to heal themselves while in prison, a space which offers the antithesis of the support and empowerment the Canadian penal systems imagine they provide.

Notes

1   www.csc-scc.gc.ca 14 July 2004. Canada's overall incarceration rate (both federal and provincial) is 116 per 100,000 (cf. www.prisonstudies.org). The rate of incarceration in the United States is 686.
2   In Canada, responsibility for punishment is divided between the federal, provincial, and territorial governments. Those serving sentences of two years less a day fall under the jurisdiction of their provincial or territorial governments whereas those serving longer sentences are the responsibility of the federal government's penal institution, the Correctional Service of Canada.
3   For example, the province of Ontario opened its first therapeutic community prison in 1964 in order to offer specialized interventions for alcoholics, addicts, and, later, paedophiles. During the 1970s, the corrections branch of the provincial government adopted a heavy community focus which included the extensive use of temporary absence passes, community corrections and the use of community-based social services within provincial prisons. The role of the prison guard was revamped to become far more social-service oriented and all manner of therapeutic practices were introduced within the prisons themselves (see Moore, forthcoming).
4   All ministries, regardless of whether they are provincial or federal, have several deputy ministers who serve as bureaucrats and usually continue their work with the ministry through one or more changes in government. Deputy ministers typically oversee more specific parts of a minister's portfolio. Thus, in Ontario's Ministry of Community Safety and Correctional Services there are different deputy ministers for corrections, policing, youth corrections and public safety.
5   Of course, the fallibility of current drug-testing technologies must be taken into account here. For a broader discussion see Moore and Haggerty (2001).
6   Advocates of cognitive training also argue that programmes, such as anger management, life skills, and critical thinking, could be administered by correctional staff (Duguid, 2000), thus deskilling treatment provision.
7   Despite the fact that Beck (1969) has emerged as the paramount 'father' of CBT, Ellis (1962) and Frankl (1973) are also typically cited as having significant generative roles in the movement.
8   See Annual reports of the Office of the Correctional Investigator http://www.oci-bec.gc.ca/
9   See the news release, 9 July 2004 'Csc Policy On The Use Of Restraint Equipment Amended' http://www.csc-scc.gc.ca/text/releases/04-07-12_e.shtml
10 The global outcry in response to the treatment of prisoners in Iraq by American guards who hooded and tortured POWs is testament to how widely acknowledged these basic standards are.
11 We do not want to suggest that physical abuse of prisoners does not happen in Canada.

References

Andrews, D. (1989) 'Recidivism is Predictable and Can be Influenced: Using Risk Assessments to Reduce Recidivism', *Forum on Corrections Research*, 1(2): 11–17.

Andrews, D. and J. Bonta (1998) *The Psychology of Criminal Conduct*, Cincinnati: Anderson.

Arbour, Madame Justice L. (1996) *Commission of Inquiry into Certain Events at the Prison for Women in Kingston* (Arbour Report), Ottawa: Public Works and Government Services of Canada.

Beck, A. (1969) *Cognitive Therapy and the Emotional Disorders*, New York: International University Press.

Canadian Human Rights Commission (2003) *Protecting their rights: A systemic review of human rights in correctional services for federally sentenced women*, Ottawa: The Canadian Human Rights Commission. www.chrc-ccdp.ca

Correctional Investigator (2001, 2002, 2003, 2004) *Annual Report of the Correctional Investigator 1999–2000*, Ottawa: Ministry of Public Works Canada.

Dobson, E. (2001) *Handbook of Cognitive Behavioural Therapy* (2nd edn), New York: Guilford.

Duguid, S. (2000) *Can Prisons Work? The Prisoner as Object and Subject in Modern Corrections*, Toronto: University of Toronto Press.

Fauteaux, G. (1956) *Report of the Committee Appointed to Inquire into the Principles and Procedures Followed in the Remission Service of the Department of Justice of Canada*, Ottawa: Queen's Printer.

Foucault, M. (1977) *Discipline and Punish: The Birth of the Prison*, London: Allen Lane.

Garland, D. (2001) *The Culture of Control*, Chicago: University of Chicago Press.

Hannah-Moffat, K. (2000) 'Prisons that empower: neoliberal governance in Canadian women's prisons', *British Journal of Criminology*, 40: 510–551.

Hannah-Moffat, K. (2005) 'Criminogenic Need and the Transformative Risk Subject: Hybridizations of Risk/Need in Penality', *Punishment and Society*, 7(1).

Hoffman, V. (1984) 'The Relationship of Psychology to Delinquency: A Comprehensive Approach', *Adolescence*, 19(73). 55–62.

Jackson, M. (2002) *Justice Behind the Walls*, Vancouver/Toronto: Douglas and McIntyre.

Martinson, R. (1974) 'What Works? Questions and Answers About Prison Reform', in *Public Interest New York*, 35: 22–54.

Maurutto, P. and K. Hannah-Moffat (2005) 'Retrofitting Risk and Restructuring of Penal Control'. Submitted to *BJC*.

Moore, D. (2005) 'To Cure the Offender: Drugs, Users and the Canadian Criminal Justice System'. PhD dissertation: University of Toronto.

Moore, D. and K. Hannah-Moffat (2002) 'Get Tough Efficiency: The Politics of Correctional "Renewal" in Ontario', in J. Hermer and J. Mosher (eds) *Disorderly People: Law and the Politics of Exclusion in Ontario*, Halifax: Fernwood.

Moore, D. and K. Haggerty (2001) 'Bring it on Home: Home Drug Testing and the Relocation of the War on Drugs', *Social and Legal Studies*, 10(3).

O'Malley, P. (1999) 'Volatile and Contradictory Punishments', *Theoretical Criminology*, 3(2): 252–75.

Pratt, J. (2002) *Punishment and Civilization: Penal Tolerance and Intolerance in Modern Society*, London: Sage.

Rose, N. (2003) 'The Neurochemical Self and itsAnomalies', in R. Ericson and A. Doyle (eds) *Risk and Morality*, Toronto: University of Toronto Press.

Task Force on Federally Sentenced Women (1990) *Creating Choices – Report of the Task Force on Federally Sentenced Women*, Ottawa: Ministry of the Solicitor General.

Valverde, M. (2003) 'Targeted Governance and the Problem of Desire', in R. Ericson and A. Doyle (eds) *Risk and Morality*, Toronto: University of Toronto Press.

Valverde, M. and M. Mopas (2004) 'Insecurity and the dream of targeted governance', in W. Larner and W. Walters (eds) *Global Governmentality*, London: Routledge.

Vantour, J. (1991) *Our Story: Organizational Renewal in Federal Corrections*, Ottawa: Correctional Service of Canada.

6. Contemporary statecraft and the 'punitive obsession'[1]: a critique of the new penology thesis

Roy Coleman and Joe Sim

A hard core of prolific offenders – just 5,000 people – commit around 1 million crimes each year, nearly 10 per cent of all crime. *That's only 15 or 20 people* for each of our Crime and Disorder Reduction Partnerships. Yet they are wreaking havoc. The financial loss is estimated to be at least £2 billion a year … This hard core of offenders may include local gang leaders, drug dealers, vandals, car thieves and others whose prolific anti-social behaviour is causing most harm to local neighbourhoods. We will use the National Intelligence Model to help identification. *Once targeted, it will be possible for all of the Agencies concerned to focus, and bear down on, the same key group of offenders.* (Blair, 2004: 3; emphasis added)

In the key speech from which the above quote is taken, British Prime Minister Tony Blair articulates and reinforces a view of crime, criminality, and punishment that pre-dates New Labour thinking on crime control by over a century. After identifying a core group of offenders, Blair goes on to detail the strategy to be mobilized to target these offenders including the deployment of 'modern surveillance techniques and intensive intelligence gathering – including *individually targeted CCTV* – to collect evidence to support more successful prosecutions' (*ibid.* 3–4; emphasis added). In the contemporary context of a febrile and often excruciatingly anxious concern around law and order, his view resonates with and reimposes an understanding of crime and punishment held within policy and political circles, some definers of 'public opinion' and elements within academic criminology. Furthermore, Blair highlights the evolving nature of twenty-first century statecraft, which may be characterized by some as a 'baffling constellation' (Sparks, 2003: 157), but nevertheless is central for carrying this strategy forward in the cities of the UK. For Blair, local partnerships backed by 'central government' and supported by 'the right legal framework' are the vehicles for mobilizing 'tough action' against contemporary urban degenerates through the channels of contemporary statecraft (Blair, 2004: 1).

Blair's comments lead us to a more general consideration of some interrelated questions concerning the interpretation of contemporary crime control and in particular its governing rationale and effectivity. On these questions, theoretical criminology has been considerably influenced by the debates around the new penology (Feeley and Simon, 1992, 1994), the 'amoral assessments of the other' associated with risk indicators, and 'dangerization' (Lianos and Douglas, 2000: 104), and the question of governmentality (Garland, 1997). Without wishing to oversimplify or conflate the work of scholars in these fields, we intend to build upon and critique some of the lines of argument found in this work and develop arguments contained in our earlier work (Coleman and Sim, 2000; Coleman *et al.*, 2002). We do so through utilizing data from a case study concerning the strategies of punishment and social control currently being deployed in Liverpool in the early twenty-first century. Focusing on the city also puts empirical flesh on a set of theoretical bones that has been missing in much of the literature around the new penology (Coleman, 2004).

The chapter is organized into three main sections. First, it offers critical reflections on contemporary crime control and punishment that have been influenced by, or are aligned with, the new penology thesis. Second, it uses developments in the processes of city rule in Liverpool to argue for a more materialist analysis of contemporary mechanisms of crime control. Finally, the chapter concludes by considering the theoretical and political implications of the analysis for understanding the future contours of crime control.

Critical reflections on the new penology

Richard Sparks has recently pointed to a number of important and interrelated themes concerning 'punishment, populism and contemporary political culture' which are deeply embedded within contemporary concerns with 'states of insecurity' (Sparks, 2003: 149). For Sparks, this is underpinned by the seeping prevalence of the discourse of risk into the criminal justice system alongside a media and politically inspired penal populism in which the language of punitive discipline has ideologically cemented the political elite with the wider population into an often grim and emotional desire for inflicting vengeful retribution on the 'lesser breeds outside of the law' (Gilroy, 1987: 72).

In criminology, the explanatory framework within which these developments have been understood has been generated by the work of Feeley and Simon. In their early work Feeley and Simon (1992, 1994) identified an emerging scepticism towards liberal interventionist and welfare based strategies of rehabilitation. Such strategies emphasized individual redemption and the proportioning of responsibility through 'making the guilty "pay for their crime" or changing them' (Feeley and Simon, 1994: 173). A new penology was under development which was 'actuarial', and was constructed around 'techniques for identifying, classifying and managing groups assorted by dangerousness' (ibid.). For Shearing and Stenning, these disciplinary techniques could assume various forms without being moral in orientation. Thus the growth of private policing and mass private property has generated and facilitated a 'reconstruction in the social world' towards 'instrumental' ordering practices, which have replaced questions of right and wrong (Shearing and Stenning, 1996: 416). This has led to a 'restructuring of our institutions for the maintenance of order and a substantial erosion by the private sector of the state's assumed monopoly over policing and, by implication, justice' (Shearing and Stenning, 1985: 496). For these authors, the rise of large commercial complexes – such as Disneyland – has undermined the unitary order of a sovereign state. The 'new instrumentalism' has sought the maximization of profit and brought with it 'not one conception of order but many' (Shearing and Stenning, 1996: 417). In a similar vein, Rose and Miller (1992: 173) have talked about 'political power beyond the state', while Rose (1996: 58) has pointed to a range of technologies or 'plethora of indirect mechanisms' which are central to strategies of governance but which 'do not have their origin or principle of intelligibility in "the State"'.

However, important though this work has been, we take issue with a number of theoretical premises on which it is based and briefly sketch them out here. Firstly, following Sparks we wish to broaden the debate around the significance of risk discourses by placing these discourses within an analysis of power relations and struggles that exist within a reconstituted state form. We wish to construct an analysis that asks 'how ... do penal practices intersect with other spheres of the culture, politics or economic structures of the social formations in which they arise?' (Sparks, 2003: 150). In doing this, we seek to challenge the ethnocentrism in much of the literature on risk, its lack of empirical exploration, and its insensitivity to local variations in crime control (Ferret, 2004).

Secondly, one of the central arguments developed in the new penological literature is that the drive towards a neoliberal, globalized social order has been underpinned and legitimated by an emphasis on 'governing through crime' (Simon, cited in Hudson, 2001: 158). This is a particularly important insight picked up and developed by a number of writers (Stenson, 2001; Sparks, 2003) and is clearly an issue that deserves to be the focus for sociological inquiry. However, we want to make what might appear to be a banal point but an important one nonetheless, which is that the images of crime that are being mobilized to consolidate the governance project are not only precise and particular but have a long history that precedes the emergence of the current strategy. These images are built on the activities of the powerless, not the powerful, and are indelibly and inevitably racialized. Therefore if we are to accept the argument about 'governing through crime' the debate needs to be much more specific with respect to what crimes are being mobilized to achieve this governance and conversely what crimes and socially harmful activities are *not* being mobilized in the drive to construct a respectable and a contract-based social order more generally.

Thirdly, far from there being a rupture from a positivist emphasis on individual criminals existing on the margins of the society to one that implies that all citizens are potential criminals, we concur with Crawford's view (2003: 54) that the actuarial approach *overemphasizes* the discontinuity between different historical moments and time periods and *underestimates* the continuities and material and ideological connections between these periods. Notions of clean breaks with past practice, found in what O'Malley calls 'catastrophic theorisations', assume rather than demonstrate the existence of a 'mass risk consciousness' (2004: 185) that supposedly infiltrates and guides the contemporary crime control matrix. Oversimplifying processes of change has had the effect of marginalizing an analysis of politics and history and crucially, as in the case of new penological arguments, has foreclosed a consideration of developments in the state and processes surrounding – what Mitchell (2003: 235) calls in another context – 'the materialisation of order'. Furthermore, the deployment of risk discourse masks a resurgent positivism based on individual offender profiling that is increasingly being legitimated by research built around theories and methods deriving from crime 'science' including forensic podiatry, optimal foraging behaviour, and anomaly surveillance systems. As Kendall has noted, 'by insisting that the problem of crime inheres in cognitive deficits, the focus of intervention remains at the level of the individual. Thus social inequalities and oppressions need not be addressed' (Kendall, 2003: 197).

Fourthly, the notion of a limited capacity of the sovereign state to reduce the crime rate has led to a proposed shift in criminal justice policy so that responsibility for preventing crime has been devolved into the social body and onto the individual. In exploring these changes, Garland argues that it is the contemporary 'state's task ... to augment and support ... multiple actors and informal processes' in a manner that disperses and pluralizes social control, rather than engage in a project of 'establishing a sovereign state monopoly' (Garland, 2001: 126).

Contrary to this position, and following the work of others (Stenson, 1999; Coleman, 2003), we would argue that the state does not use or merely support other players (private authorities, etc.) and form partnerships with them; rather the state exists and is constituted through alliances and partnerships that – however momentarily and with contradictory tendencies – define its boundaries and scope of action. Neither 'sovereignty' nor state power is on the decline, but these categories are *both* processual *and* dialectical and are subject to rescaling and relegitimation. Indeed the capacity and ideological fervour of local state actors to govern through *particular forms of crime* has been neglected in risk-orientated analysis.

Governmentalized views of the state (Barry *et al.*, 1996: 12) have depicted the latter as melting away into the social body to become no more than the combined effect of 'micro powers'. In thinking about power relations and statecraft in the city, we do not propose a reductionist or homogenized view of state institutions. The state is not a 'thing' reducible to fixed, static boundaries but an active and creative process of institution-building and intervention. We are not arguing for a zero-sum conceptualization that stresses an either/or demarcation in the analysis of state power, but we are drawing attention to the process of state building itself with a recognition that the state may have 'multiple identities' and 'multiple boundaries' (Cooper, 1995: 63). Focusing attention on the state-building process aids an understanding of the actors and ideologies now operating in the field of crime control. We wish to focus on the organizational powers of the state as a terrain subject to restructuring through the discourse and practice of partnership. Moreover, the discourses of morality, risk, and strategies of intervention are entwined, organized, and rendered socially meaningful through the organizing force of state institutions. Thinking of the state as a terrain of power relations provides the discussion of morality and risk with a material foundation, which is still lacking in the literature to date (Coleman, 2004; Hudson, 2003).

Finally, it is important to understand the limitations inherent in, and imposed on, those powerful individuals and organizations involved in this process. These limitations and restrictions surrounding the exercise of power and the imposition of social control arise not only as a result of internal contradictions, conflicts, and inconsistencies between the individuals and organizations involved – 'turf wars'[2]

– but also arise from below in the attitudes, articulations, and actions of individuals and groups resistant to becoming 'docile bodies', living like ghosts, in spaces designated by the mercantile planners of the twenty-first-century entrepreneurial city.

Entrepreneurialism, statecraft, and the city

We now turn to Liverpool as an example of a contemporary city where 'the deeply dysfunctional yet extraordinarily malleable character of neoliberal statecraft' (Brenner and Theodore, 2002: 345) has been a particularly influential, though rarely analysed component in the building of an entrepreneurial city and associated forms of local crime control practice. Thinking about the institutional forms, justificatory rhetorics, and political spatial dynamics of contemporary city space aids an understanding of the dynamics of punitiveness sketched above and the role of these dynamics in reproducing the landscapes of power we describe below.

Our argument begins with the recognition of a convergence in the city, particularly in North America and the UK, of private-sector business and property interests with public-sector local authorities that constitutes a localized neoliberal statecraft. From the Urban Development Corporations in the Thatcher era and the sprouting of BIDS (Business Improvement Districts) in the Reagan/ Bush years, to the Third Way of the Clinton/Blair successions, partnerships have assumed the guise of technical and neutral players in the urban scene, dispensing with red tape (i.e., earlier and 'outmoded' democratic forms of decision-making) and delivering the goods (the 'goods' usually being gentrified spaces and spectacular, headline-grabbing architectural gestures). This form of statecraft remains central in local urban regeneration strategies. The neoliberal state, following Peck's argument, is not an 'absentee state' (Peck, 2003: 226). Rather it operates between national and local levels 'as [an] *organiser* of new forms of investment, market regulation, new forms of control and policing and as [a] *disorganiser* of old forms of welfare and social collectivity' (Savage *et al.*, 2003: 197, emphasis in original). One effect of the forms of statecraft and institutional settlements that now constitute city rule is the heightening of control of the polity by bourgeois and property interests.

Crucially, these developments in statecraft represent a form of *politics-through-partnership* in the process of urban rule that selectively engages in a rehabilitation of space through the generation of discourses and practices that reflect the interests of new primary definers at the centre of urban statecraft. Crime control discourses and practices in the city have become increasingly merged with entrepreneurialized forms of rule that stress marketing, quality-of-life indicators, and other promotional discourses that cities have adopted in the competition to attract and retain investment. The marketing of particular places with 'desirable qualities' has placed crime and disorder and their management at the heart of entrepreneurial rule and, at the same time, reconfigured crime control practices as well as the punitive discourses that justify such practices. We want to stress the *creative* and *productive* character of state formation involved here (through, for example, visionary and marketing-based institutions) and its impact upon local primary definers, both old and new, whose power to effect change on the urban landscape gives this social group a 'homogeneity and ... awareness of its own function', for example as 'an organiser of the "confidence" of investors in their business, of the customers for their product ...' and as 'the organisers of a new culture, of a new legal system ... (Gramsci, 1971: 5). As participants in the building of a particular social bloc, itself always contradictory and discordant, primary definers can be understood as engaged in local political struggles designed to forge a 'hegemonic project' (Jessop, 1990: 260) that has relevance in relation to the meaning and trajectory of urban crime control, particularly with respect to who is targeted for punishment when this project is challenged, by-passed, or simply ignored.

Thus within Liverpool – particularly in the consumption and service-driven areas of the city – the promotion of social contracts and normative prescriptions have proceeded apace in relation to the regulation of conduct in the public sphere. These normative-contractual impositions on the use of space are not only illustrated in place marketing strategies themselves but also in the use of local by-laws (Coleman, 2003), and the introduction of banning orders through legislative powers such as those in the Anti-Social Behaviour Act of 2003. A prominent New Labour architect in this area is Frank Field, who sees anti-social behaviour legislation as part of a wider move towards a 'contract based citizenship' that would work through 'a series of contracts which cover the behaviour of all of us as we negotiate the public realm' (Field, cited in Grier and Thomas, 2004). The socio-moral regulation of the kind Field endorses has a complex relationship to aggressive place marketing. In addition, the wider commitment to 'civilize cities' is central to the rationale found within partnership rule (Ward, 2003: 117), with the implications this brings for social control.

Under the Crime and Disorder Act (1998), business organizations are expected to participate more fully in the funding, planning, and delivery of crime control agendas via auxiliary criminal justice mechanisms. The Act consolidates political changes already underway in cities since the middle of the 1980s. State identity and morphology since this time have been channelled into the power and resources of city centre managers, marketing agencies, and developmental and speculative property organizations. As new primary definers of the public good, the actors within this local political class have entered into the administration and distribution of crime control and delivered it via public–private sector partnerships. A range of phenomena exists in this spatial ordering strategy: business watch schemes; pro-prosecution and exclusion policies to deal with small traders, shoplifters, beggars, and protestors; CCTV and electronic surveillance systems coordinated across the city centre; security guard communication networks; and themed anti-crime campaigns. This rehabilitation of space has a central strategic position within the organs of partnership rule and has a strong punitive element. As a strategically selective endeavour, the strategy casts its gaze firmly upon the spaces of the poor and/or those spaces of spectacle where anti-social con-taminants from the former may overspill. In the case of key investment sites, neoliberalized space is over-surveilled and carefully managed by private security agencies and CCTV. Thus, in the poorer outer estates in East Manchester, 'heavy ... in-your-face policing' is underpinned by a re-civilizing urge under an 'entrepreneurial urbanism' that 'demands more, not less, state intervention' (Ward, 2003: 112, 117).

In Liverpool as elsewhere, CCTV is an exemplary creative act of neoliberal statecraft. The development of mass street camera surveillance in the city has its roots in a particular document: the *Action Plan – Regeneration Agenda for Liverpool: To Develop a Safer City*. This plan came out of meetings between old and new primary definers – senior police, private security, local developers, the Chamber of Commerce, the City Council, and Liverpool Vision. It placed safety at the centre of the city's renaissance. Particular definitions of 'safety' were positioned as 'quality of life' indicators in the process of rehabilitating space:

> Developing a Safer City is an essential element of the holistic approach to promoting Liverpool as a safe, vibrant, regenerating city, which is attractive to inward investors and supports a high quality of life for residents and visitors. (Liverpool City Council, 1997: 1)

Hegemony and governing through deviance

Entrepreneurial rule is also having implications for what kinds of activities and behaviours are subject to penal control and which are not. The punitive gaze, in focusing upon activities and behaviours in the aestheticized public realm, is not only reinforcing some long-established punitive practices but is also diverting attention and resources from other harmful activities that are of concern in any city.

Excavating a material understanding of contemporary forms of crime control such as the development of street cameras requires looking into wider political relations in the city. Indeed, the notion of 'governing through crime' does not capture the wider picture of what is happening on the ground, where developments in policing and social control targeting strategies in entrepreneurialized spaces are opening up the development of punitive risk projects which are not necessarily directed at 'crime' in the legal sense of the word. An expansive targeting of 'suspiciousness' is bringing people within penal control with or without legal suspicion being established. We would argue that the interpretative basis for suspicion is 'made in the context of underlying features of the social order', which also contain 'locally dominant ideologies' pertaining to the nature of that order (Lacey, 1994: 30–1). The preferred meanings of an orderly city centre translate into techniques of control underpinned by a persistence and reworking of long-standing moralizing discourses of censure aimed at problematic categories. The power to carry out surveillance and inflict punishment is being enhanced in the context of the material and political redevelopment of city space. For example, a scheme to privatize up to 35 city centre streets, at a cost of £800 million, with no public right of way is underway in Liverpool and is one of a series of national experiments in US-style Business Improvement Districts. Although officially dubbed a 'public realm', this area is to cater for high-end consumption, tourism, and leisure. The 42-acre site is to be 'ring-fenced' by cameras and patrolled by 'US-style quartermasters' whose role, as described by one council official involved in the scheme, is to 'control and exclude the riff-raff element' (Indymedia, 2003). The logic behind this first step towards constructing a Business Improvement District in the city was articulated by a spokesperson for the developers involved:

> People [sic] tell us they don't come shopping to Liverpool because it's dirty, there is chewing gum all over the place and pavements are cracked. We are developing a series of quarters for the area which will have security staff making sure that people maintain reasonable standards of behaviour. (ibid.)

By operating within the discourses of 'reasonableness' and 'responsibility', the architects of the entrepreneurial city are able to articulate a version of the public interest in a language of civility that mystifies the roots of these rehabilitated spaces within capitalist social relations; relations that, under neoliberal conditions, are diminishing the meaning and scope of 'the public' as well as the contours of 'freedom' in public space. Within this context, the camera network itself is ideologically positioned by its proponents as a 'people's system' and the city centre as a 'people's place' (Coleman, 2004). In Liverpool the camera network monitors a range of behaviours that are deemed incongruous with a notion of rehabilitated space. In doing so they legitimate a series of punitive interventions and sanctions for those who fail to 'perform' in these spaces. With the application of by-laws these behaviours include the monitoring and fining of skateboarders, beggars, rag sellers, and out-of-pitch *Big Issue* sellers. As this spatial ordering strategy unfolds, the right to decide who walks through a city's streets will not only impact on the 'usual suspects' mentioned above but also upon the right to protest and publicly campaign in the city against, for example, shops dealing in sweatshop goods or those encouraging environmental destruction. The arrival of entrepreneurial spaces means that those who engage in such forms of protest are likely to be labelled as trespassers in the feudal-like fiefdoms of those who manage and control these spaces. The logic is that they should be punished by being removed from the view of the public and excluded. We would argue that private agencies involved in these processes are not solely directed by an over-rationalized risk mentality but draw upon a language of moral condemnation as a routine aspect of their work through, for example, the operation and management of CCTV schemes (Norris and Armstrong, 1998).

This highly selective and targeted governance through crime/deviance intensifies the punitive gaze through its focus upon visibly designated social problems that are not necessarily criminal in the legal sense. At the same time this governance reinforces a long-standing and partial prioritization of public over private order (Stanko, 1990). This process intensifies the creation of 'unseen' spaces (Bauman, 2000: 103) where the victimization of women, ethnic minorities, and the homeless goes relatively unacknowledged and unpunished. This is illustrated in Liverpool where a telephone help line for domestic violence set up at the end of 2003 showed a 130 per cent increase in reported assaults upon women from partners over the previous year. Figures for 2003 showed that 25 per cent of all violent crime reported to the police was accounted for by domestic violence. While the Assistant Chief Constable stated that these figures 'show a definite increase in victims' confidence ... that the police and our partners are getting it right' (*Liverpool Echo*, 2 February 2004), this has to be set against a national report published in 2004 which indicated that police forces only recorded half of all crimes of domestic violence reported to them while only 11 per cent of cases led to a conviction (*The Guardian*, 19 February 2004).

Furthermore, the easy availability of funds to market cities and develop law-and-order strategies can be contrasted with the abject funding for social policy and welfare orientated work. According to NACRO, the amount of funding made available for CCTV in the UK up to 2003 was more than 50 times the amount given to programmes tackling domestic violence (cited in Erzan-Essien, 2003: 12). Thus the reconfiguration of local political priorities impacts directly on the quality of life for local people and indeed redistributes the risks people may have to negotiate. Moreover resources for staff in youth work have been cut back to the point where the number of youth workers is now 40 per cent below stipulated government targets for Liverpool (*Liverpool Echo*, 27 November, 2003). In addition, the Racial Harassment Unit has been downgraded and merged with a council services help line (*Liverpool Echo*, 3 May 2004). This can be contrasted with the financial and ideological support for street policing activities.

Older and newer discourses are developing and combining in complex ways to construct those groups and individuals 'deserving' of protection and/or exclusion in entrepreneurial landscapes. However, the idea that there is a 'new' punitiveness in operation for city dwellers is misplaced. The punitive landscape for black people has changed little in relation to police practice and their freedom of movement around the city since the late nineteenth century (Fryer, 1984). The continuation, and indeed intensification, in the containment and harassment of the black population in Liverpool is indicated by the fact that one in three black people were stopped and searched in 2002/03 – a rise of 112 per cent (*Liverpool Echo*, 2 July 2004). In addition, black people lodge 40 per cent of complaints against the police in relation to stop-and-search practices and are nearly ten times more likely than whites to be stopped and searched in the city (*Liverpool Echo*, 29 March 2004).

Responsibilization and irresponsibilization

At the same time as 'business friendliness' in city management has led to a redistribution of resources from public projects to private investment initiatives (Katz, 2001; Mitchell, 2003; Peck, 2003), an increase in financial leverage has occurred for the provision of 'community policing' initiatives accompanied by a general ideological investment in appeals to communities that mobilize support for street-focused governing through crime schemes. As part of the rehabilitation of space, the resources and political will to tackle forms of crime and victimization are skewed in favour of the 'public' over the 'private' sphere.

For example, a mile to the east of Liverpool city centre lies Kensington, an area which since 1998 has been recognized as an area of high social exclusion and has been designated a Home Office 'crime hot spot'. Between 1998 and 2003 in an attempt to 'bridge the gap' between this area and the city centre, £61.9 million was spent with £643,000 allocated to CCTV and community wardens from the New Deal for Communities programme. In Knowsley – the most deprived local authority area for 2004 as measured by the government's Indices of Deprivation (*The Guardian*, 29 April 2004) – a total of £2.6 million was provided to fund 100 Neighbourhood Wardens (*Liverpool Echo*, 1 June 2004). In the west of the city a pilot scheme has started where 'public spirited people have taken to the streets to become the eyes and ears of the police' mainly to target nuisance youths (*Daily Post*, 5 June 2004). These initiatives, along with trends in police intelligence gathering, point to a responsibilization process in which 'local residents have been implicated in their own regulation' in and around the public spaces of the entrepreneurial urban core (Ward, 2003: 122). To use the phraseology of the 2003 White Paper – *Respect and Responsibility: Taking a Stand Against Anti-Social Behaviour* – 'accredited community safety schemes' should be used to bolster 'the extended police family' who can draw on a range of 'powers to designate areas to disperse groups and use the child curfew' laws (Home Office, 2003: 54). This 'extended police family' – as numerous Home Office guidelines make clear – involves not only local residents but business consortia, developers, private police, and local authorities who are involved in a re-moralization of city streets which, although not entirely coordinated, is indicative of the attempted orchestration of a popular punitiveness through an entrepreneurialized statecraft. As Sparks has noted, 'public sensibilities … are plainly not politicians' modelling clay' (Sparks, 2003: 169) and punitive rhetoric and practice, such as those articulated above, do not always succeed in shaping and directing public thought and action.

In Liverpool the discourse and practices of re-moralization have focused particularly on the policing of young people in and around the city. While punitiveness aimed at the young is 'not exactly new' (Goldson, 2002: 386), 'experiments' in the policing of youth in Liverpool have culminated in the recruitment of a 'Yob Tsar' who is to work with police, landlords, and community groups to 'speed up' the process of bringing anti-social youths to justice (*Liverpool Echo*, 13 April 2004). The management of troublesome behaviour in city space has been formalized under the Anti-Social Behaviour Act (2003). The Act enables Community Safety Officers to work with police in issuing tickets and fines to control graffiti, fly-posting, truanting, and begging. Moreover, it has been used in Liverpool to enforce a number of 'no-go zones for yobs' where 'police can banish youths congregating' in particular areas. Up to April 2004, this policy had been enforced in four areas and involved the dispersal, arrest, or fining of over 200 young people (*Liverpool Echo*, 2 April 2004). In the run-up to becoming European Capital of Culture in 2008, the City Council is placing entrepreneurialism at the heart of its Acceptable Behaviour Contracts (ABCs) that deal with young offenders. These contracts attach educational training as a component of their issue. On being asked if tourism and the drive to 2008 were having any impact upon anti-social behaviour strategies in the city, the executive member of the city's Community Safety Department replied:

> Yes, yes, absolutely, that is why we are expanding to have more wardens on the streets. We're determined to have a safer city and actually one of the things we are going to do is provide language training. [As part of an ABC] youngsters can learn French and Spanish … so they'll be able to respond to

other people, so when foreigners come into the city, they will be less scared to come. (Interview, May 2004)[3]

Developments in penal discipline are irresponsibilizing certain activities and, where possible, responsibilizing those targeted towards a 'moral way of life' in the city. Furthermore, camera networks not only exclude but also cultivate responsibilizing messages as to what is and what is not acceptable behaviour in the public realm and reinforce Foucault's original idea of disciplinary power and its integral moral component of 'soul training' (Foucault, 1979: 294–5).

In Liverpool, orchestrated campaigns that oscillate between expulsion and responsibility are aimed at the homeless. Those who sell the *Big Issue* magazine have been banned from the main indoor shopping mall and the stores of the larger retailers, and are subject to a 'curfew' on selling after 8pm (*Daily Post*, 11 May 2002). 'Operation Change', launched in Liverpool in 2003, aimed to reduce 'anti-social behaviour' among beggars and, in the words of a Chamber of Commerce spokesperson, was designed to target 'people who allegedly can't speak English, using their children to ask for money' (*Daily Post*, 13 March 2003). Publicity posters, entitled: 'Fact: Nobody needs to beg for a bed', were used which showed a picture of a homeless person crouched on a city street, whose face was covered by a cardboard sign which read: 'Help them make the change, keep your change'. A process of silencing the experiences of homeless people and *irresponsibilizing* their presence in the city was thus reflected in the poster campaigns, which discouraged local people from talking to and handing over loose change to street people. This was coupled with the use of undercover policing and targeted surveillance resulting in the arrest, caution, or charging of over 800 people in 2002 for begging offences. All beggars are now routinely fingerprinted and placed on the Police National Computer (ibid.). Oppressive monitoring of the homeless is leading to their outright removal as court injunctions are set to lead the way to a national ban on begging on city streets (*The Independent*, 22 August 2003).

Camera networks, and the official discourse that surrounds them, provide an indication of the increasing importance of 'fear' in the governing process. This is not to deny the reality of the fear of crime, but it is to point to how fears can be spoken to, exaggerated, and articulated for particular political ends. The manner in which campaigns of censure aimed at the homeless, street traders, and other low- or no-income categories reminds us of the continuing importance of authoritarian populism (Hall, 1988) that, when orchestrated by the primary definers of city renaissance, link the themes of crime, discipline, and social order to produce, not always successfully, a new common sense. In the regenerating city the rise of street camera surveillance, and the fear this feeds off and reinforces in relation to certain forms of crime, has instigated a process of governance through street crime as a means to manage the non-entrepreneurial degenerate. As part of the drive for a particular, entrepreneurial civic order, the role of the local press in this drive has been rarely analysed yet ties into this governing process with campaigns in Liverpool to 'Shop a Yob' along with crusading slogans such as 'Justice for All' that more often than not are aimed at the poorest sections of the population. Thus these discourses have targeted the least powerful inhabitants of the city and can be understood as components of a broader landscape of risk propagated and given prominence in times of social, political, and economic upheaval.

Continuity, discontinuity, and resistance to the punitive obsession

Brogden (1991: 1) used the phrase 'uniformed garbage men' to describe the role of the police in nineteenth-century Liverpool as they swept up the objects of mercantile discomfort in the city – the poor, destitute, 'street Arab' children, and casualized labour. As enhanced surveillance and a contract-based citizenship increasingly come to oversee and define the streets of the twenty-first-century city, they reinforce the moral codes, intolerances, and normative prescriptions of their entrepreneurial creators. Nineteenth-century discourses on the city created an urban landscape in which the slum, the unclean, the poor, and the wayward were effectively separated from the idealized cityscape. Furthermore, 'this separation enabled the social reformer, as part of a process of validation of the bourgeois imagery, to survey and classify its *own antithesis*' (Marriott, 1999: 83; emphasis in original). The complex structure of entrepreneurialism and moral scriptures in the city is not an exact copy of Victorian governance and morality, but the loathed antithesis of the contemporary cityscape has remained remarkably similar. The reinvention of the city centre goes hand in hand with the perception and labelling of multiple threats posed in terms of contagion across a range of redrawn urban boundaries between centre/periphery, clean/filth, and rough/respectable.

If these binary opposites remain salient for thinking about the relations between power, morality, and risk, then this also points to an incredible myopia displayed by risk practitioners and, more surprisingly, risk theorists. The contemporary morality and punitiveness increasingly incorporated in the form of contracts for behaviour in public spaces has had the effect of denying and marginalizing the risks posed from the activities of the powerful (Tombs and Whyte, 2003). These non-risks, or unseen risks, are less likely to be rendered visible and subject to intellectual and public challenge if those criminologists who claim knowledge of risk fail to explore the material dimensions that give rise to and guide risk discourses and practices.

We would argue that the attempts to cultivate a punitive public consciousness around hindrances to entrepreneurial growth around youth, traders, homeless people, and unregulated thrill-seekers (for example, skateboarders) have not been entirely successful. It is in the contemporary city that 'the policing of image and perception matters precisely *because* politics and economy have not drifted off into free floating abstractions, but have instead remained practices grounded in everyday life, contested in the domain of street corners, sidewalks, radio stations, and abandoned buildings' (Ferrell, 2001: 227; emphasis in original). The 'political spaces of resistance' are an important dimension of city life (MacLeod *et al.*, 2003: 1657) where the possibilities for contestation regarding the criminalization and punitive dimensions of urban rule should not be overlooked. Popular punitive projects through media-inspired campaigns in Liverpool are contested at different spatial scales and for various reasons. The attempted removal of homeless *Big Issue* vendors from the streets of Liverpool accompanied by a vicious council and police discourse of unsuitability and criminalization failed in 2003 thanks to a public outcry in letters pages in the local press and the threat of legal action by the *Big Issue in the North* against the council and police under human rights legislation. There have also been 'sleep-outs' by community groups to raise awareness of rough sleeping in the city along with challenges to the punitive rhetoric and criminalization of asylum seekers by groups such as 'People Not Profit'.

Conclusion

In conclusion, we have sought to provide an empirical illustration of the theoretical position we outlined at the start of the chapter. In doing so we have developed an analytical framework that recognizes the theoretical contribution that has come out of the new penology thesis. At the same time we have also illustrated the weaknesses in the thesis, particularly in its reliance on a dichotomous, ideal typical model of social change and the ahistorical generalizations that underpin this ideal typicality. More fundamentally, we have also sought to provide a *materialist analysis* of the strategies of crime control that are being developed and deployed, thereby challenging the often theoretically abstruse, and conceptually nit-picking debates that underpin much of the literature around risk, governmentality, and social control.

In 'bringing the state back in' (Jessop, 2001) – antediluvian and unfashionable though this might be in many criminological circles – albeit in seemingly unfamiliar territory, we have sought to place its institutions and personnel at the centre of contemporary punitiveness without constructing either an homo-genized, non-contingent analysis of its institutions or a conspiratorial view of its personnel. Rather in the early twenty-first century, the state under New Labour can be conceptualized as an 'enabler', allowing individuals to become:

> reflexive ... possessing a kind of permanently revisionist self; an em-powered and mobile subject (geographically, economically and psychically) who is his/her own entrepreneur of selfhood ... In New Labour's discourse of community, questions of moralisation, individualism, citizenship responsibility and adaptability all find a presumed answer. (Finlayson, 2003: 194)

For Finlayson, 'culture as a strategy of governance' plays a key role in New Labour's world of entrepreneurial subjects (ibid.: 193).

Within this discourse, the individual's rights are recognized by a social contract that transcends the dirty world of politics and activism while a sense of acquiescent responsibility is branded onto and into their conscious and subconscious mind. Many of those who subscribe to the new penology thesis would find little to disagree with here. However, there is another side to this argument which has remained neglected and pushed aside in the attempt to theorize the various nuances in the demarcated governance of advanced capitalism.

At the time of writing (July 2004) inequality in the UK was at its highest level for 40 years. Between 1991 and 2001 the gap between rich and poor rose by 40 per cent, the fastest rise of any developed state. And while New Labour has attempted some redistribution of resources particularly towards lone parents and single pensioners, single and disabled people and unemployed couples without children have been 'left behind', surviving 'on price-indexed rather than earnings-related benefits' (Dean, 2004: 5). Those left behind – the 'rabble' whose 'essential characteristics' are 'detachment and disrepute' (Irwin, 1980: 2) – pose individual and collective problems for maintaining order either in a proactive sense through engaging in deviant activities, or in an ideological sense because of their corrosive presence in the antiseptic, urban spaces populated by a citizenry caught in the dyad of panoptic and synoptic social control (Mathiesen, 1997). For the 'rabble' – the materially deprived, the socially degenerate, the irresponsible, the non-adapter, the non-citizen – the 'new' punitiveness can be understood as a criminology of intolerance. Regulating their immoral and amoral activities in an urban environment in which cities compete for government funds via regeneration programmes and for celebrity status via city of culture competitions is the coercive, dialectical flip-side of 'culture as a strategy of governance'. If they refuse to be 'hailed' in an Althusserian sense as decent citizens then they will be coerced into respectable subjectivity via harsh policing methods, disciplinary welfare programmes, and corrective institutional regimes where old and new 'judges of normality' (Foucault, 1979: 304) monitor their behaviour, ideas, and needs in order to construct the normalized, compliant subject. In this context, according to Pat Carlen, what is emerging is a hybrid model of penal control and intervention where the official, postmodern discourse which targets 'individual (criminogenic) need' is being mobilized through 'multiple programming'. Crucially, however, this programming is being:

> implemented alongside all the old modernist disciplinarities of placing, normalising and timetabling, and against a backcloth of the even older premodern controls such as lock-ups, body searches and physical restraints ... the *postmodernist* emphasis on the reconfigurability of all disciplines ... manages to convert even primarily material needs such as homelessness, sexual abuse and unemployment into the *criminogenic* needs of people defined by their crimes rather than by their citizenship. (Carlen, 2004: 10; emphasis in original)

Carlen's argument points to the need to think in dialectical rather than in ideal typical terms with respect to the punitive trajectory of social control in the twenty-first century. Thus, we have sought to place this trajectory within the complex forces and political alignments shaping an entrepreneurial urbanism and the statecraft that accompanies it in order to explore the unleashing of the latent powers of punitive politics in capitalist social formations. The political and material configurations we have examined have given rise to powerful political visions and a 'backlash' mentality turned against progressive political forces (Katz, 2001: 108) expressed by the business classes and new-right revisionists (Smith, 1996). In putting forward a dialectical argument we seek to aid the creation of a theoretical and political space to challenge this punitive trajectory, thereby offering an alternative vision for responding to crime and deviance in the twenty-first-century city and beyond.

Notes

1   This phrase is taken from Giles Playfair (Playfair, 1971).
2   Thanks to Pete Gill for pointing this out.
3   We would like to thank our undergraduate students Bushra Arshad, Alan Cunningham, Pauline Smith, and Stephanie Yau in the School of Social Science, Liverpool John Moores University. This quotation is taken from their project on anti-social behaviour in Liverpool.

References

Bauman, Z. (2000) *Liquid Modernity*, London: Polity Press.

Barry, A., Osborne, T. and Rose, N. (1996) 'Introduction', in Barry, A., Osborne, T. and Rose, N. (eds) *Foucault and Political Reason*. London: UCL Press.

Blair, T. (2004) *PM's Speech on Crime Reduction, 30 March 2004* www.number-10.gov.uk/output/Page 5603.asp

Brenner, T. and Theodore, N. (2002) 'Cities and Geographies of "Actually Existing Neoliberalism"', *Antipode*, 24(3): 349–379.

Brogden, M. (1991) *On the Mersey Beat: Policing Liverpool Between the Wars*, New York: Oxford University Press.

Carlen, P. (2004) 'Imprisonment and the Penal Body Politic: The Cancer of Disciplinary Governance'. Paper presented at The Effects of Imprisonment: An International Symposium, University of Cambridge, April.

Coleman, R. (2003) 'Images from a Neoliberal City: The state, surveillance and social control', *Critical Criminology: An International Journal*, 12(1): 21–42.

Coleman, R. (2004) *Reclaiming the Streets: Surveillance, Social Control and the City*, Cullompton: Willan.

Coleman, R. and Sim, J. (1998) 'From the Dockyards to the Disney Store: Surveillance, Risk and Security in Liverpool City Centre', *International Review of Law, Computers and Technology*, 12(1): 27–45.

Coleman, R. and Sim, J. (2000) 'You'll Never walk Alone: CCTV Surveillance, Order and Neo-Liberal Rule in Liverpool City Centre', *British Journal of Sociology*, 51(4), December: 623–639.

Coleman, R., Sim, J. and Whyte, D. (2002) 'Power, Politics and Partnerships: the state of crime prevention on Merseyside', in A. Edwards and G. Hughes (eds) *Crime Control and Community: the new politics of public safety*, Cullompton: Willan.

Cooper, D. (1995) *Power in Struggle: Feminism, Sexuality and the State*, Buckingham: Open University Press.

Crawford, A. (2003) 'Contracted Governance of Deviant Behaviour', *Journal of Law and Society*, 30(4): 479–505.

Daily Post (2002) 'City Shops Ban Big Issue Sales', 11 May.

Daily Post (2003) 'Crackdown on Street Beggars', 13 March.

Daily Post (2004) 'Volunteers Helping Police in the Fight Against Crime', 5 June.

Dean, M. (2004) 'Opinion', *The Guardian*, 1 July 2004, p. 5.

Erzan-Essien, A (2003) 'Private Misery', *The Big Issue in the North*, March 1–7, No. 455.

Feeley, M. and Simon, J. (1992) 'The New Penology: Notes on the Emerging Strategy of Corrections and its Implications', *Criminology*, 30(4): 449–474.

Feeley, M. and Simon, J. (1994) 'Actuarial Justice: The Emerging Criminal Law', in D. Nelken (ed.) *The Futures of Criminology*, London: Sage: 173–201.

Ferrell, J. (2001) *Tearing Down the Streets: Adventures in Urban Anarchy*, New York: Palgrave.

Ferret, J. (2004) 'The State, Policing and "Old Continental Europe": Managing the Local/ National Tension' in *Policing and Society*, 14, 1 March: 49–65.

Finlayson, A. (2002) *Making Sense of New Labour*, London: Lawrence and Wishart.

Foucault, M. (1979) *Discipline and Punish*, Harmondsworth: Peregrine.

Fryer, P. (1984) *Staying Power: The History of Black People in Britain*, London: Pluto Press.

Garland, D. (1997) '"Governmentality' and the problem of crime: Foucault, criminology, sociology', *Theoretical Criminology*, 1(2), May: 173–214.

Garland, D. (2001) *The Culture Of Control: Crime And Social Order In Contemporary Societies*, Oxford: Oxford University Press.

Gilroy, P. (1987) *There Ain't No Black In The Union Jack*, London: Hutchinson.

Goldson, B. (2002) 'New Punitiveness: The politics of child incarceration', in J. Muncie, G. Hughes and E. McLaughlin (eds) *Youth Justice: Critical Readings*, London: Sage Publications in association with the Open University: 386–400.

Gramsci, A. (1971) *Selections from the Prison Notebooks*, London: Lawrence and Wishart.

Grier, A. and Thomas, T. (2003) 'A War For Civilisation As We Know It: Some observations on tackling anti-social behaviour', *Youth and Policy: A Critical Analysis*, Issue No. 82, Winter 2003/04: 1–15.

The Guardian (2004) 'Knowsley Heads Most Needy List', 29 April.

The Guardian (2004) 'Police Failing to Tackle Domestic Violence', 19 February.

Hall, S. (1988) *The Hard Road to Renewal: Thatcherism and the Crisis of the Left*, London: Verso.

Hall, T. and Hubbard, P. (1996) 'The Entrepreneurial City: new urban politics, new urban geographies', *Progress in Human Geography*, 20(2): 153–174.

Home Office (2003) *Respect and Responsibility: Taking a Stand Against Anti-Social Behaviour*. CM5778.

Hudson, B. (1996) *Understanding Justice*, Buckingham: Open University Press.

Hudson, B. (2001) 'Punishment, Rights and Difference: Defending justice in the risk society', in K. Stenson and R. Sullivan (eds) *Crime, Risk and Justice*, Cullompton: Willan.

Hudson, B. (2003) *Justice in the Risk Society*, London: Sage.

Hudson, B. (2004) 'Book Review of Ericson, R. V. and Doyle, Aaron, D. (eds.) Risk and Morality', *Theoretical Criminology*, 8(2): 239–243.

The Independent (2003) 'Court Ruling May Lead to National Ban on Beggars', 22 August.

Indymedia (2003) 'The Duke and Chums turn the Screws on the Working Class'. www.indymedia.org.uk/en/regions/liverpool/20/03/12/282695.html.

Irwin, J. (1980) *The Jail*, Berkeley: University of California Press.

Jessop, B. (1990) *State Theory*, Cambridge: Polity.

Jessop, B. (2001) 'Bringing the State Back In (Yet Again): Reviews, Revisions, Rejections and Redirections', *International Review of Sociology*, 11(2): 149–173.

Katz, C. (2001) 'Hiding the Target: Social Reproduction in Privatised Urban Environment', in C. Minca (ed.) *Postmodern Geography: Theory and Praxis*, Oxford: Blackwell Publishers: 93–110.

Kendall, K. (2003) 'Time to Think Again About Cognitive Behavioural Programmes', in P. Carlen (ed.) *Women and Punishment*, Cullompton: Willan.

Lacey, N. (1994) 'Introduction: Making Sense of Criminal Justice', in N. Lacey (ed.) *A Reader in Criminal Justice*, Oxford: Oxford University Press.

Lianos, M. and Douglas, M. (2000) 'Dangerization and the End of Deviance: the Institutional Environment' in D. Garland and R. Sparks (eds) *Criminology* and *Social Theory*, Oxford: Oxford University Press.

Liverpool City Council (1997) *Action Plan – Regeneration Agenda for Liverpool: To Develop a Safer City*, Liverpool: Liverpool City Council, Officer Partnership Group.

Liverpool Echo (2003) 'Youth Fears', 27 November.

Liverpool Echo (2004) 'Shock Increase in Domestic Violence', 2 February.

Liverpool Echo (2004) 'No-Go Zones for Yobs', 2 April.

Liverpool Echo (2004) 'Hunt for City Yob Catcher', 13 April.

Liverpool Echo (2004) 'City Race Helpline is Saved' 3 May.

Liverpool Echo (2004) 'More Wardens on the Streets', 1 June.

Liverpool Echo (2004) 'Police Launch Race Inquiry', 29 March.

Liverpool Echo (2004) 'Stop and Search Scandal', 2 July.

MacLeod, G., Raco, M. and Ward, K. (2003) 'Negotiating the Contemporary City: Introduction', *Urban Studies*, 40(9), August: 1655–1671.

Marriott, J. (1999) 'In Darkest England: the Poor, the Crowd and Race in the Nineteenth century metropolis', in P. Cohen (ed,) *New Ethnicities, Old Racisms*, London: Zed Books.

Mathiesen, T. (1997) 'The Viewer Society: Michel Foucault's "Panopticon" revisited', *Theoretical Criminology* 1(2), May: 215–234.

Mitchell, D. (2003) *The Right to the City: Social Justice and the Fight for Public Space*, New York: The Guilford Press.

Norris, C. and Armstrong, G. (1998) 'The Suspicious Eye', *Criminal Justice Matters*, No. 33, Autumn: 10–11.

O'Malley, P. (2004) 'Penal Policies and Contemporary Politics', in C. Sumner (ed.) *The Blackwell Companion to Criminology*, Oxford: Blackwell.

Peck, J. (2003) 'Geography and Public Policy: Mapping the Penal State', *Progress in Human Geography*, 27(2): 222–232.

Playfair, G. (1971) *The Punitive Obsession*, London: Victor Gollancz.

Rose, N. (1996) 'Governing "advanced" liberal democracies', in A. Barry, T. Osborne and N. Rose (eds) *Foucault and Political Reason*, London: UCL Press.

Rose, N. and Miller, P (1992) 'Political Power Beyond the State: Problematics of Government', *British Journal of Sociology*, 43(2): 173–205.

Savage, M., Warde, A. and Ward, K. (2003) *Urban Sociology, Capitalism and Modernity*, London: Macmillan.

Shearing, C.D. and Stenning, P.C. (1985) 'Private Security: Implications for Social Control', *Social Problems*, 30(5): 493–506.

Shearing, C. D. and Stenning, P. C. (1996) 'From the Panopticon to Disney World: The Development of Discipline', in J. Muncie, E. McLaughlin and M. Langan (eds) *Criminological Perspectives: A Reader*, London: Sage.

Sim, J. (2000) 'Against the Punitive Wind: Stuart Hall, the State and the Great Moving Right Show', in P. Gilroy, L. Grossberg and A. McRobbie (eds) *Without Guarantees: Essays in Honour of Stuart Hall*, London: Verso.

Sim, J. (forthcoming) 'At the Centre of the New Professional Gaze: Women, Medicine and Confinement', in W. Chan, D. Chunn and R. Menzies (eds) *Women, Mental Disorder and the Law: A Feminist Reader*, London: Cavendish.

Smith, N. (1996) 'After Tompkins Park Square: Degentrification and the Revanchist City', in A. D. King (ed.) *Re-Representing the City: Ethnicity, Capital and Culture in the 21st Century Metropolis*, London: Macmillan, 93–107.

Sparks, R. (2003) 'States of Insecurity: Punishment, Populism and Contemporary Political Culture', in S. McConville (ed.) *The Use of Imprisonment,* Cullompton: Willan.

Stanko, E. (1990) *Everyday Violence: How Men and Women Experience Sexual and Physical Danger*, London: Pandora.

Stenson, K. (1999) 'Crime Control, Governmentality and Sovereignty', in R. Smandych (ed.) *Governable Places: Readings on Governmentality and Crime Control*, Dartmouth: Ashgate.

Stenson, K. (2001) 'The New Politics of Crime Control', in K. Stenson and R. R. Sullivan (eds.) *Crime, Risk and Justice: The politics of crime control in liberal democracies*, Cullompton: Willan.

Tombs, S. and Whyte, D. (2003) 'Scrutinising the Powerful? Crime, contemporary political economy and critical social research', in S. Tombs and D. Whyte (eds) *Researching the Crimes of the Powerful: Scrutinising States and Corporations*, New York: Peter Lang.

Ward, K. (2003) 'Entrepreneurial Urbanism, State Restructuring and Civilising "New" East Manchester', *Area*, 35(2), June: 116–127.

Part 2

Globalization, Technology, and Surveillance

7. Globalization and the new punitiveness[1]

Estella Baker[2] and Julian V. Roberts

It has been suggested that: 'globalisation may be *the* concept, the key idea by which we understand the transition of human society into the third millennium' (Waters, 2001: 1; emphasis in original). Reflecting that assertion, globalization has become 'a central topic of debate across the social science disciplines' (Waters, 2001: 210; see also Giddens, 2002: 7), including those concerned with matters of criminal law and justice (see, for example, Findlay, 1999; Loader and Sparks, 2002; Nelken, 1997). This chapter aims to contribute to the latter, specialized discussion by offering a critical examination of the relationship between globalization and what has been described as the new punitiveness. In so doing, it does not focus on developments in any specific jurisdiction, but rather seeks to draw some general conclusions about the role that globalization forces have played across a diversity of Western nations.

Western penal policies over the past decade have been largely, but not exclusively, punitive. Specific examples of the criminal law reforms that have been adopted during this time include mandatory sentencing legislation, sex offender registries, and community notification laws. Besides these statutory developments, punitiveness has manifested itself in criminal justice practices; for example, in the rise of shaming penalties (e.g. Pratt, 2003; see Roberts *et al.*, 2003) and the movement towards 'penal austerity'. There are at least four reasons for thinking that the recent propensity for penal policies to assume this newly punitive cast may be caused by factors related to globalization. They are:

1. Timing: the trends in penal policy that have earned the label the 'new punitiveness' began to appear during the 1990s, just as the pace of globalization began to accelerate.

2. These trends are not restricted to a single jurisdiction, but have emerged to a degree across the principal English-speaking societies where a similar set of penal policies has been pursued during the last decade or so.[3] A tendency towards the development of this type of cross-border homogeneity and integration is consistent with globalization processes (Nelken, 1997: 260–266).

3. The coincidental adoption of these policies was not fortuitous. On the contrary, the emergence of newly punitive policies in one jurisdiction facilitated their appearance in others, notwithstanding the considerable

geographical distance that separates the jurisdictions concerned. Again, 'the intensification of worldwide social relations which link distant localities in such a way that local happenings are shaped by events occurring many miles away and vice versa' is compatible with a globalization explanation (Giddens, 1990: 64).

4. The particular brand of oppressive penological thinking that is represented in the policies themselves: without pre-empting the discussion that follows, there are resonances with globalization here too; a preoccupation with risk as a dominant structural factor in decision-making, for example.

Taken together, these considerations amount to a reasonable prima facie case for concluding that the development of the new punitiveness is indeed linked to globalization trends. But if that deduction is correct, why is the new punitiveness not surfacing as a universal phenomenon, even among English-speaking jurisdictions (see, for example, Meyer and O'Malley, this volume)? Does its selective appearance mean that the globalization account is misconceived, or at least insufficient to explain its development?

The answer is, not necessarily. Globalization is a complex phenomenon with an inherent capacity to generate paradoxical effects (Giddens, 2004; Twining, 2000: 5). Therefore, while it may create tendencies towards greater transnational homogeneity and integration in some circumstances, it can equally well spark diverse, jurisdiction-specific responses in others (Nelken, 1997: 260–266). Taking this confounding quality into account, there is nothing intrinsically contradictory in enquiring whether globalization might play a role in accounting for why certain jurisdictions have *not* taken up the new punitiveness while simultaneously proposing that it is useful in understanding the decisions of those that have. Similarly, there is as much potential in examining whether the forces of globalization might be generating processes with the capacity to arrest the further intensification and transmission of the new punitiveness as there is in investigating whether these same forces are encouraging the crystallization of policies through which it is being spread.

Most of the discussion in this chapter will consider the extent to which the new punitiveness is a product of, or can be explained by, globalization. However, it will conclude by briefly addressing the latter, superficially contradictory questions concerning the relationship between the two phenomena. First, though, the opening section will provide an introduction to the concept of globalization itself.

Definition

The literature offers a variety of definitions of globalization (for discussions see, among others, Loader and Sparks, 2002: 96; Waters, 2001). At heart, they all suggest that the central tenets of the concept concern the construction and intensification of relationships across the planet, and the processes through which these relationships occur. Given this quintessential core, globalization cannot be a new phenomenon even though its relatively recent rise to prominence might imply the opposite.[4] In fact, commentators have demonstrated that globalizing forces had already emerged by the sixteenth century, and some have argued that they have existed throughout human history (Twining, 2000: 7; Waters, 2001: 4–7). Accordingly, what accounts for the privileged attention that globalization is currently receiving is not the novelty of its arrival on the international scene, but rather the way in which the so-called 'communications revolution' that occurred towards the end of the twentieth century led to a sudden increase in the momentum of these forces to the extent that it can be described as having propelled globalization into a new era (Giddens, 2002; Loader and Sparks, 2002; Waters, 2001).

The critical catalyst that prompted the new era was the invention of technology that enabled instantaneous trans-global communication to occur (Giddens, 2004; Twining, 2000: 7f; Waters, 2001). Its availability means that it has become possible to exchange information across the planet under conditions in which the constraints of geographical space and time have been compressed almost to vanishing point (Waters, 1995: 55f). Thus, the two fundamental obstacles to the construction of genuinely global relationships have been rendered all but redundant and a new environment has been forged in which it is no longer necessary for social and cultural exchange to be linked to territoriality (Waters, 2001). Coupled with the extraordinary rapidity with which the technology has become accessible to a critical mass of intercontinental consumers,[5] there has been a sudden shift in the pace and scope of global interaction – individuals have becoming empowered to conduct relationships across an arena that is truly global in nature and scale.

Communications and the significance of the cultural sphere

Extraordinary opportunities for 'symbolic exchange' (exchanges of signs such as data and information) have been generated by the new technology, and this is crucial in understanding why the pace and penetration of global forces into all aspects of society have suddenly intensified. For, as Waters points out, symbolic exchanges 'release social arrangements from spatial referents. Symbols can be proliferated rapidly and in any locality … Moreover, they are easily transportable and communicable. Importantly, because symbols frequently seek to appeal to human fundamentals they can often claim universal significance' (2001: 19–20).

These generic remarks appear to be highly relevant in the context of the new punitiveness because its adoption has been promoted through the use of its own distinctive language of punishment. Slogans such as 'three strikes and you're out', 'life means life', and 'zero tolerance' have become familiar features of the penal landscape across those societies where the new punitiveness has taken off, and the explanation is not hard to identify. Faced with electorates who are both highly sophisticated consumers of the advertising industry and lacking in time and attention to digest communications of any length, political proponents of the new punitiveness have attempted to tailor their message to their audience by reducing relevant policies to shorthand form. Moreover, in doing so, they have tended to draw directly on imagery from popular culture ('three strikes') or to tap into instinctive beliefs about punishment ('life means life') in order to target the hearts and minds of a mass public. Cast in Waters' terms, they have thus invented a language of 'penal symbols' and there is ample evidence that it has proved ripe for rapid transmission and proliferation between localities in just the way that he describes.

Global consciousness

A second important effect of the new communications environment is that it has provided the impetus for so-called 'global consciousness' to emerge (Robertson, 1992: 8). This is the idea that globalization encourages a conceptual appreciation that the world is a unified whole in which individuals are interdependent in myriad ways (Robertson, 1992; Waters, 2001). Like others that are associated with globalization, this cognitive habit is reflexive in character in that the very fact that individuals display an increasing tendency to situate their thinking in the global context itself promotes the global processes that stimulated that thinking in the first place.

Arguably, global consciousness is cultivated by at least two mutually re-inforcing processes. One derives directly from the unprecedented access to information about what is going on in the world that is now available for mass public consumption. By heightening the likelihood that connections between ostensibly independent events will become exposed, it ensures that individuals are becoming progressively more insightful as to how they might actually be interlinked (Giddens, 2004). Hence, global consciousness arises through the mechanism of a growing awareness of factual interdependence. But strongly allied to this primary process is a second that arises from the intrinsic correlation between access to knowledge and expansion in choice.

Thanks again to the new communications technology, people no longer have to be content with the range of ideas that happens to be available in their immediate locality, because they are increasingly well placed to access a potentially rich and diverse further repertoire that is internationally sourced. This is not simply because the global traffic in information is becoming impervious to the physical barriers that were formerly presented by territorial borders, but also because the technology that supports its transmission is inherently resistant to effective legal control and/or regulation and is, therefore, correspondingly problematic to censor. The net effect is that individuals are acquiring what might be described as a consciousness of the global sum content of knowledge, thoughts, and beliefs that exist around the world. Those relating to the realm of punishment are, of course, no exception. Not least because of the way that the distinctive language of punishment that is associated with the new punitiveness complies with the requirements for effective symbolic exchange. This includes an evolving awareness of the global wealth of penal ideas.

Democratization and the rise of global consumer culture

From a globalization perspective, the trend towards unrestricted information flow is interesting for another reason too. As the new technology comes within reach of a progressively greater proportion of the global population, so connotations of equality, universality, and free, informed choice with respect to the receipt of information increasingly attach to the means by which symbolic exchange occurs. That being so, there are grounds for labelling the process that is underway the 'democratization' of access to information.

Democratization is another key theme in the globalization debate. However, the consequences of its emergence here merit special mention because of its particularly potent cultural impact. This comes about because, in popular perception, the democratic attributes that properly belong to the means by which information is circulated seem to be being projected onto the information itself so that it is presumed to be invested with equivalent characteristics. As a result, all pieces of information that enter currency are coming to be regarded:

1. as having equal worth, regardless of the credibility of their source;

2. as equally susceptible to evaluation by everybody, regardless of the knowledge, insights or qualifications with which their recipients are equipped to perform that task; and

3. as equally disposable as, and/or freely interchangeable with, all others because of the parity of value that is attached to each.

One source of enlightenment regarding this phenomenon is the literature on communications. It suggests that its manifestation can be explained in terms of twin failures on the part of recipients of relevant information. First, to separate its content ('the message') from the means by which it is delivered ('the messenger') and, second, to differentiate the 'factual' from the 'inferential' components of each of these variables. In other words, individuals are failing to distinguish matters such as identity, content, and source from the conclusions that are based on them (Renn, 1991; Renn and Levine, 1991). Cast in these more technical terms then, inferences that might plausibly be drawn about the democratizing potential of the new communications technology as the messenger are being mistaken for inferences that can be made about the messages that are delivered by it.

This basic confusion is proving to have consequences that are deeply inimical to established social and political power structures because it drives a logical dynamic whereby the only determining factor as to whether any particular idea is adopted at any particular time is the exercise of free choice by the individual to whom it is presented. For fairly transparent reasons, globalization theorists have dubbed this phenomenon 'global consumer culture' and have recognized that it has very considerable potential to undermine notions of expertise and professionalism, and thus to bring about the triumph of 'popular' over the 'high' culture with which experts and professionals are associated. Moreover, there are already signs that these effects are being felt.

Globalization, democratization, and the nation-state

It is necessary to highlight a further important theme in the globalization debate: the pernicious effects of globalizing forces on the sovereign nation-state. Just about all of the processes described so far pose a serious challenge to the fundamental tenets upon which this key political concept is built. Credibility in the assertion of sovereign power, for example, is hard to maintain when individuals have unfettered access to information that tells them that the root causes of many social and political problems lie outside the state's borders and, consequently, beyond its capacity to address. A similar logic applies to the claim to statehood. At the heart of the concept lies the notion of the territorially bounded community, but in a globalizing world evidence of the permeable nature of international borders, and thus of their ineffectiveness in separating the internal from the external community, accrues daily. And then there is nationhood, an idea predicated on common identity and culture. Global forces undermine that too. Modern communications technology ensures that what were once alien beliefs and customs can be imported within the state's borders to intermingle with those of domestic origin, thereby threatening to dilute the indigenous cultural fabric upon which the sense of nationhood thrives.[6] Together, these factors amount to a testing backdrop against which the pressures of global consumer culture must also be contended with.

Politicians, civil servants, and others involved in governance are certainly not immune from the corrosive effects of global consumer culture with respect to expertise and professionalism. On the contrary, the fact that their work is so intimately bound up with factors that are serving to undermine confidence in the nation-state appears to be resulting in the growth of a serious 'trust deficit' that is affecting government in all its guises, including the way that policy is fashioned and implemented. Those charged with persuading the public to accept government decisions and intervention are increasingly unable to take it for granted that their motives and judgments will be regarded as above suspicion. Instead, a state of affairs has arisen in which what Gros terms 'the new sovereignty' (to exercise governmental decisions, implement policies, and so on) must be earned; not claimed as a 'divine right' (Gros, 2003: 78). If it is not, policies that are soundly planted in evidence, or otherwise represent the accumulated wisdom of professional experience, may be rejected in favour of alternatives that appear to the lay public to be more congruent with (so-called) 'common sense'.

The relationship between global consumer culture and Gros' concept of earned sovereignty also raises further points concerning the significance of democratization as a theme in the globalization debate. Whatever the substantive merits of decisions that place a greater premium on (perceived) expressions of public opinion than the views of experts, the trend towards this type of broader-based decision-making is consistent with the view that global processes are enlarging the concept of democracy. Whereas until recently it has been taken to denote a form of political organization in which power is exercised by an elected government against the backdrop of a constitutional separation of powers, it is starting to have salience as a form of social and cultural organization as well.[7] Coming from a stance of their presumed right of equal participation, people are demanding a say in many aspects of life in a way that would previously have been unimaginable. Consequently, there seems to be a growing thirst for moving towards a new style of democracy in which the power of decision-making is vested more universally than at present, instead of lying almost exclusively in the hands of formal state institutions. While this quest for 'deeper democracy' may spark healthy reforms in the conduct of political affairs in due course, for the present its manifestation reinforces the conclusion of some commentators that globalization is propelling the nation-state into a condition of crisis.

That perspective, though, is not shared by all scholars. Pointing out that the number of nation-states has actually multiplied in recent years, Giddens, for example, has argued that it is in fact becoming the universally preferred form of political organization (Giddens, 2004). He acknowledges, though, that states are making conscious manipulations to their structural form that he interprets as attempts to ward off the destructive forces that globalization pressures are exerting upon them. They include transferring competences to sub-national level, as has occurred recently within the United Kingdom (devolution) and/or entering into cooperation with other nation-states (intergovernmentalism), or actually sharing sovereignty with others (supranationalism); the power-sharing mechanisms that underpin the European Union, for example (Giddens, 2004). In addition, there are signs that governments are seeking to address the demands of global consumer culture by incorporating elements of popular participation into decision-making processes within the public sphere.

Not all supporters of the sovereign nation-state interpret such moves as being in the interests of its self-preservation, however. For those who continue to adhere to the nineteenth-century model of the nation-state as an independent entity that constitutes the highest aggregate unit of political authority, these modifications represent a surrender to global pressures, not a means of protection from them. Instead of embracing globalization to the extent that is necessary to devise effective adaptations to the new environment, what is required in their eyes is an emphatic reiteration of the continuing validity of the nation-state as that concept has hitherto been understood.

Responses to globalization: cosmopolitanism versus fundamentalism

The coexistence of these contradictory responses is consistent with another theme in the globalization literature. On the one hand, there are the 'global cosmopolitans' – those who are receptive to the diversity of ideas now accessible by virtue of the new communications technology and who are excited by the potential of cross-fertilization and fusion. On the other, there are those to whom this prospect represents an extraordinary threat to the established social and cultural infrastructure and who seek refuge in a return to traditional and/or fundamentalist doctrines.[8] The differing reactions of observers to the constitutional adaptations that are being made by states in the face of global pressures provide a nice reflection of these opposing perspectives. Their manifestation can also be detected in relation to matters of criminal law and justice and, arguably, in ways that are relevant to the emergence of the new punitiveness.

Starting with changing patterns of governance, the criminal justice sphere has clearly been affected. In the European Union (EU), for example, constitutional control is now a complex patchwork of national, intergovernmental, and supranational elements, and the ongoing evolution of much of this infrastructure can be explained in terms of the operation of, and need to respond to, globalization pressures.[9] There is recognition on the part of EU member states that they are increasingly unable to exercise sovereignty over the problem of crime because it too is taking on characteristics associated with globalization (Garland, 1996). But it is instructive in the context of the current discussion to note that while the EU's initiatives have been subject to well-placed criticism for privileging crime control over civil liberties (Asp, 2002), they cannot be described as fitting into the new punitiveness mould. Accordingly, they bear out the opening remarks of this chapter that suggested that production of the new punitiveness was only one among a range of effects that might be caused by the operation of global forces on the institution of punishment.

On the other hand, however, there appears to be a symbiosis between the promotion of policies that are newly punitive in hue and a concern to shore up the nation-state. Pared down to its core, the new punitiveness combines a moral stance that criminals should suffer through enduring 'hard treatment' and being afforded lesser rights than their victims, with a 'common sense' conviction that harsh punishment deters crime. Translated into practice, these beliefs have sparked a vigorous resurgence of the sorts of draconian, and sometimes humiliating, penalties and spartan correctional regimes that were phased out during the twentieth century as being incompatible with maturing notions of civilized society. There is, therefore, a clear sense in which their reappearance can be depicted as a return to 'penal fundamentalism'.

But that is not all. Implicitly at the very least, when modern politicians advocate a return to measures of this nature, they seek to stimulate an under-standing in the electorate that, were the state to intervene in the ways that they suggest, the result would be effective crime control. In other words, they imply that the state remains capable of exercising sovereignty with respect to delivering internal security for the benefit of its citizens (contrary to the impression that may be gleaned from other sources such as the global mass media) and, therefore, that it retains relevance and value. Unfortunately, however, at the same time, they are betraying their increasing impotence to combat crime problems by themselves by engaging in a variety of forms of international cooperation, such as those within the EU. Furthermore, as many of the politicians concerned surely know, the claim that highly punitive 'get tough' measures do much of worth to dissuade potential offenders from committing crimes in and of themselves is refuted by well-grounded research (see especially von Hirsch *et al.*, 1999). Accordingly, their persistence in maintaining a newly punitive line has been the subject of trenchant academic criticism (see, for example, Ashworth, 2004).

Globalization and the 'risk society'

Most of the background that is necessary to discuss the extent to which globalization might be the cause of, or provide an explanation for, the new punitiveness has now been sketched out. However, there is one more issue that must be touched on before turning to look specifically at these questions: that is, the interaction between globalization and another important theme in contemporary debate – risk and the risk society (Beck, 1992). Like globalization, a great deal has been written on the latter subject over recent years. This is not the occasion to review that literature, but it is appropriate to make a few brief points about its relevance to the current discussion.

The reasons why risk has become such a dominant focus of attention are complex and cannot properly be explained here, but for present purposes they can be summarized in terms of a three-stage process. First, the nature of the risks to which society is exposed has undergone a material change. Giddens explains the shift in terms of a contrast between 'external' and 'manufactured' risk. External risk has always been there, it 'com[es] from the outside, from the fixities of tradition or nature' and provokes worry 'about what nature can do to us'. By contrast, manufactured risk is new, 'created by the impact of our developing knowledge upon the world' and leads us to worry instead 'about what we have done to nature' (Giddens, 2002: 26). What this means in effect is that a price has had to be paid for technological innovation in the form of the creation of previously undreamt-of risks. Second, driven partly by the logical inference that what we can do to nature, we ought also to be able *not* to do, a keen interest has grown up in risk management and control. Because these tasks involve the interaction between technology and people, the social sciences have been drawn into the study of risk and have had to develop a dialogue with those engaged on the scientific side (see Royal Society, 1992). Third, the fruits of this work have proliferated so that a broader pool of social scientists have become aware of the value of risk as a conceptual frame through which to analyse a wide range of social problems that have little, if anything, to do with technological change. As a result, risk has become embedded in the intellectual infrastructure of the social science disciplines as well as those of the natural sciences.

This brief outline is of relevance to two aspects of what has been said about globalization. The first concerns the contribution of our growing preoccupation with manufactured risks to the emergence of global consciousness. Compared with the hazardous consequences of external risks that tend to be relatively localized, the effects of manufactured risks are more likely to be universally felt. Consequently, the latter play a greater role in producing global consciousness because, unlike the former, geographical distance does not confer immunity from their impact and so their existence serves to emphasize global interdependence.

In the present context, it is worth pausing briefly to consider the application of these remarks to the risk represented by crime. As a social construct, it does not seem natural to label it as either 'external' or 'manufactured'. However, classified in terms of the geographical impact of its effects, the bulk of conventional crime has characteristics that ally it more closely to the first than to the second type of risk. There is already detectable political and public concern, though, that the forces of globalization are disturbing this equilibrium. Advancing technology combined with the increasing permeability of geographical and political borders is multiplying the opportunities to commit transnational crimes such as international fraud or internet crime, and the effects are sometimes felt globally (Edwards and Gill, 2003). In other words, globalization seems to be generating new forms of crime with a profile resembling that of a manufactured rather than an external risk. Hunting for a link between globalization and the new punitiveness, this might seem fertile territory to examine. But while the changing nature of crime is generating a rich array of criminal justice responses, those associated with the new punitiveness are not among them.

The second link between risk and what has been said about globalization relates to the impact of global consumer culture on governance and the nation-state. One contributory explanation as to why risk has become such a prominent structuring factor of contemporary life concerns the transformations that have occurred in the pattern of social organization over time, many of which are themselves strongly related to entrenched patterns of globalization in the economic and political spheres. Rather than living in small, enclosed communities that are based on extended family ties as they once used to, especially in the developed world, people tend these days to move away from the immediate locations in which they grew up to live, instead in the company of strangers. Meanwhile, the structure of society has taken on increasingly complex forms so that it is in any event necessary to rely on the labour and services of strangers, who may well also be geographically remote, in order to conduct ordinary activities of everyday life. Together, these factors ensure that individuals have little option but to take the risk of placing trust in the integrity of often anonymous others; notably, of course, experts and professionals, including those involved in governance. The trust deficit that is arising as a result of the spread of global consumer culture sits in obvious tension with that need and, somewhat paradoxically, may also be partly fuelled by the psychological anxieties that it provokes.

Globalization as a cause of, or explanation for, the new punitiveness

International crisis of confidence in criminal justice

The new punitiveness to which the title of this volume refers is a consequence of many influences that researchers are only now beginning to understand. One clear cause of punitive policies is the current crisis of confidence in criminal justice in most Western nations. This crisis itself has origins in the forces of globalization that promote a 'consumer culture' with respect to public services such as criminal justice. The public repose little faith in the professionals who administer the criminal justice system. With the exception of the police, most criminal justice professionals receive poor ratings from the public. However, even the police have attracted declining performance ratings from the public in recent years (Roberts and Hough, 2005). A principal cause of this disaffection is the perception held by many people that the system fails to respond adequately to crime. The public is also sceptical of experts and populist solutions perceived to be superior to evidence-based policies. This popular response to crime is consistent with the consumerist culture to which reference has already been made. To paraphrase an old saying, 'the public may not know much about criminal policy, but they know what they like'. Growing disenchantment with government, a sceptical attitude towards 'experts', and increasing expectations about the performance of public services – these trends are all fuelled by, or consistent with, globalization forces.

Criminal justice systems vary considerably from country to country, notwithstanding the common elements that have just been described. Yet the low levels of public confidence in justice (relative to other public institutions) appear to characterize all Western jurisdictions (see Hough and Roberts, 2004, for a review of international trends). This shared reaction is therefore attributable to factors other than a close consideration of the merits of each system. In the absence of comparative public opinion research conducted 30 years apart, it is hard to be definitive about changes over time. However, a plausible argument can be made that globalization forces have created a homogenization of criminal justice problems and policies. With respect to the problems, the public in all Western nations believes that crime rates are increasing, regardless of actual trends (Roberts *et al.*, 2003). Issues in criminal justice such as the excessive use of force by the police, teenage gangs, sex offenders, and random kidnappings rapidly become international problems of concern to people around the world.

The crisis in public confidence creates fertile ground for the new punitiveness. A survey conducted in the US in 1998 found that over 80 per cent of respondents favoured 'totally revamping the way that the criminal justice system works' (Sherman, 2002). The public is likely to support new responses to crime that are readily comprehensible and offer a 'quick fix'. Programmes and policies that aim to address the roots of crime, or prevent crime through better social development, will carry as much appeal as the often-derided 'five-year' economic plans beloved of Soviet economists in the 1960s.[10] The public will gravitate to specific reforms that target a problem and guarantee a result – life imprisonment for a third serious felony being the most obvious example. Public impatience with crime as a social problem has been encouraged and exploited by politicians and political parties in most Western jurisdictions.

Another pervasive attitude also has consequences for the nature of emerging penal policies. The public believes that the justice system is skewed in favour of protecting the rights of suspects and defendants. According to most members of the public, 'criminals' are treated better and have more rights than crime victims. For example, 70 per cent of Americans polled on the issue agreed that the criminal justice system is more concerned with protecting the rights of criminals than with protecting the rights of victims (Cole, 1991). Similarly, almost three-quarters of respondents to a MORI poll in Britain agreed that 'the law works to the advantage of the criminal and not victims' (MORI, 2003). Any reform that 'redresses' this imbalance will prove popular; hence the support for increased police powers and for re-trying defendants that have been acquitted. Thus a poll conducted in Britain in 2003 found that four out of five respondents were in favour of permitting the state to re-try defendants (*Observer*, 2003). Surveys conducted over the past 40 years in many countries have revealed that people often want a simple solution to the complex problem of offending, and they frequently see little merit in a justice system that goes to some lengths to protect the rights of defendants.

New punitiveness affects more than sentencing

The new punitiveness is usually defined to include reforms that directly affect the punishment of offenders, but it permeates other areas of criminal justice. The evolution of the role of the victim in adversarial systems of justice offers a useful illustration of this tendency. Victims' rights have generally been construed within a punitive rather than a restorative or non-punitive framework (Roach, 1999). Victims have many needs throughout the criminal process, including information about the case, access to services, and the right to make representation at various stages of the criminal process – all 'non-punitive' in nature. However, the emphasis of the most popular victim reforms has been upon promoting victim interests at the expense of the offender, or what Rock (2002) describes as the 'estranging moral contrasts of the adversarial system' (p. 22). This tendency results in a punitive zero-sum game in which victims benefit when offenders' procedural rights are curtailed[11] (see also Tonry, 2004).

Impacts of globalization pressures

Globalization pressures result in the emergence and proliferation of simplistic penal policies that have considerable mass appeal and great 'portability' from one jurisdiction to another. These meretricious policies tend to displace more sophisticated responses to crime that carry less media appeal. Making sentencing practices harsher through mandatory sentencing laws is an example of a simplistic and ineffective solution that is nevertheless preferred over longer-term responses. We regard this as the penal version of Gresham's law: 'bad crime policies drive out good ones'. Policies consistent with a particular profile are more likely to emerge, and to proliferate across jurisdictions. Globalization forces work in a number of ways: directly, in terms of political initiatives resulting in statutory reforms; and indirectly, by fostering a climate conducive to the passage of particular policies.

Globalization has accelerated the proliferation of specific penal reforms, such as electronic monitoring and home confinement. Jones and Newburn (2004) note that the adaptability of particular policies will determine the extent and speed of transfer from one country to another. They cite the example of zero-tolerance policing, but there are many others. Mandatory sentencing incarnates most of the characteristics of a portable penal policy, and this helps to explain its pro-liferation. Many punitive reforms carry a recognizable 'tag' (e.g. 'three strikes'); a readily comprehensible logic (of rapidly escalating penalties); an appeal to populist punitiveness; and a logic that can readily be adapted to different local requirements. In fact, the 'three strikes' statutes vary considerably across the US, the UK, and Australia, and this helps to explain the appeal of the idea.

Many examples exist of the way in which globalization privileges certain penal policies; for example, the promotion of 'penal austerity' – the attempt to reduce reoffending by making prison conditions more austere. Penal austerity policies have been promoted in part to respond to a perception – shared by the public around the world – that prison life is too easy (see Roberts and Hough, 2005, for a review). In order to understand how globalization pressures may help to explain the emergence of these policies, we need first to understand what the policies that have proliferated have in common.

Table 7.1 summarizes some of the features common to the most popular punitive penal policies in recent years. Policies and programmes that carry these characteristics are likely to proliferate to the greatest extent.

In addition, globalization pressures undermine 'evidence-based' crime prevention strategies, and promote reforms based more on symbolic politics. Evidence-based policies develop relatively slowly, in response to the steady accretion of empirical research. This feature of these policies makes them hard to pass rapidly from one jurisdiction to another.

Globalization and counter-trends

Although the focus of this chapter has been to examine the extent to which the emergence of the new punitiveness can be explained in terms of globalization, at a number of points it has been suggested that the link is not a necessary one, but that globalization may also be relevant in explaining why the new punitiveness has failed to emerge in some places and in identifying processes that might eventually check its spread. This section will expand briefly on these claims.

The opening section to this chapter tried to illustrate the reasons why globalization is capable of generating effects that, on the surface, are flatly contradictory. While at a macro-level globalization has coherence as a concept, both the processes that drive it at a micro-level and the reactions that these

Table 7.1 The new punitiveness: examples and characteristics of 'successful' penal policies

Examples: mandatory sentencing; sex offender registries; community notification; boot camps; penal austerity proposals; disenfranchisement of ex-prisoners; criminalization of 'nuisance' behaviours.

Characteristics
- Carry a clear symbolic aspect
- Consistent with a 'crime control' rather than 'due process' model of justice
- Emphasize image over substance
- Arise in response to exceptional, very serious cases
- Become highly mediatized as a result of these exceptional cases
- Are largely unsupported by empirical research, are simple to comprehend, can be understood by far more people than more complex responses to crime
- Assume a high public profile across different jurisdictions
- Lend themselves to quasi-political slogans ('three strikes and you're out')
- Are associated with advocates, moral entrepreneurs, individual victims, and politicians rather than experts or criminal justice practitioners
- Attract high levels of public support when placed on simplistic opinion polls
- Carry (or are perceived to carry) electoral benefits for politicians and political parties that support the policies
- Are rapidly adaptable from one country to another.

responses provoke are diverse. Therefore, while the aggregate effect may be to promote the construction and intensification of relationships across the planet, globalization does not otherwise behave as a unified force that pushes events in a single direction. Accordingly, it may be more useful to think in terms of a cluster of forces that emerge in different combinations in different settings and then interact to yield a variety of responses. Applied to the potential impact of globalization on the institution of punishment, it follows that there is no reason to expect that the emergence of a phenomenon such as the new punitiveness would be the exclusive outcome, nor to anticipate that it would spread universally; quite the opposite. It is far more likely that it would constitute one of a number of reactive strands in penal thinking and entirely feasible that, while global forces might be combining to produce fertile conditions for its appearance in some places, they might equally well be combining to neutralize its proliferation in others.

Proportionality and restraint

Turning to a specific example, it is important to note that there is more to penal policy development than merely a movement towards increased punitiveness; policies have not assumed a unidirectional movement towards a more punitive form of justice. Although a number of reforms such as mandatory sentencing have assumed a global scale, at least two counter-movements exist. One of these promotes proportional, retributive sentencing. A number of jurisdictions have moved to strengthen proportional sentencing in recent years by placing the principle of proportionality on a statutory footing. For example, the principle was codified in Canada in 1996, New Zealand in 2002 (Roberts, 2003), and in Finland (Lappi-Seppala, 2004). The Criminal Justice Act 2003 in England and Wales retains proportionality as a principle in sentencing, albeit one that is somewhat undermined by the consideration of offenders' criminal history (von Hirsch and Roberts, 2004). In addition to proportionality, several jurisdictions, including England and Wales, Canada, and New Zealand have also codified the principle of restraint with respect to the use of imprisonment. Both restraint and pro-portionality are highly inconsistent with the new punitiveness. However, that does not mean that the coincidental adoption of these principles across a number of jurisdictions is unconnected with globalization; just that their ascendancy is not the product of new punitiveness discourse. Rather, their prevalance is connected to the global spread of just deserts in sentencing and the infiltration of criminal justice settings by human rights ideology (see further van Zyl Smit, 2002a, b; van Zyl Smit and Ashworth, 2004). Although space limitations preclude a fuller discussion of the issue, it is worth pointing out that these reforms consti-tute evidence of the influence of elite rather than mass opinion.

Restorative justice

The more interesting and significant alternative to the new punitiveness concerns the global movement towards restorative justice. Restorative initiatives and reforms have proliferated in many countries, particularly at the level of juvenile justice (see Crawford and Newburn, 2003). In some respects, restorative justice has proliferated faster and wider than even the policies included under the 'new punitiveness' rubric. As Walgrave (2003) notes: 'Twenty years ago, "restorative justice" was a barely known notion, indicating some isolated experiments with anecdotal significance only and some sympathetic utopian ideas advanced by a few academics' (p. vii). In contrast to the high-profile punitive reforms (such as mandatory sentencing, sex offender registries, etc.), restorative justice has been more a product of local, grassroots developments. Canada offers a good example of this lag between local developments and the more visible statutory reforms. Developments at the statutory level pale in comparison with the amount of activity in restorative justice at the local level in Canada (see Roberts and Roach, 2003). Restorative justice programmes have long existed throughout the country, and include sentencing circles, circles of accountability and support, victim–offender reconciliation programmes, and the like.

Restorative programmes and policies have not attracted the kinds of media headlines associated with three-strikes sentencing laws, sex offender registries, and the like. Nor has restorative justice benefited from identification with a specific individual, although many punitive reforms emerged in response to an individual tragedy. Restorative justice has received almost no political 'lift' – no politician has included 'restoring offenders to the community and reconciling victims and offenders' as part of his or her electoral platform. In short, there has been simply no political advantage in promoting restorative rather than punitive criminal justice policies. Electoral advantage has been attributed to affirming the differences between, rather than reconciling, victims and offenders. We would argue that the drive behind restorative justice lies outside the ambit of formal criminal policy development, and is not the product of the same globalizing forces as punitive reforms, although it may result from others. The explanations for the proliferation of restorative initiatives over the past decade are beyond the scope of this chapter. For the present purposes we simply note that the globalization model that we have invoked to explain punitive criminal justice policies cannot account for all penal policy developments in the same manner.[12]

Summary and conclusion

To summarize, we see globalization forces as having affected the evolution of penal policies in Western jurisdictions in a number of ways. These forces create or facilitate creation of a policy environment in which punitive policies may thrive. This environment consists of a populace that is anxious about crime trends and lacks confidence in the criminal justice system. As well, through 'mediatization', public, professional, and political attention is focused on particular crimes such as sex offending, drug trafficking, and street robbery at the expense of other, equally serious problems. Public interest and attention then focus on attractive policies seen to respond to these offences. In the jurisdictions that have been under discussion here, globalization thus privileges certain penal policies – those characterized by punitiveness. These forces also accelerate the proliferation of specific policies and particular sanctions; they mediatize certain issues, and politicize the debate about how best to respond to crime. Globalization forces have clearly facilitated 'policy transfer', to use a phrase employed by Newburn and Sparks in a recent (2004) volume. This has resulted in the proliferation of a variety of punitive policies in a number of countries. We would summarize the consequences of globalization on penal policy-making in three principal ways: (i) homogenization or harmonization of problems and responses across a diversity of jurisdictions; (ii) acceleration of penal policy transfer across jurisdictions; (iii) promotion of short-term punitive policies at the expense of longer-term, evidence-based policies.

Notes

1   This chapter is a revised version of a paper presented at the *Global Governance and the Search for Justice International Conference* held at the University of Sheffield, UK, 29 April–1 May 2003.
2   Estella Baker would like to thank the Department of Law at the University of Leicester by whom she was then employed for financial support to attend the original conference.
3   There are also signs that they are surfacing elsewhere: see Krajewski (2004).
4   For example, the term itself did not come into currency until the 1980s (Twining, 2000: 3), two decades after it was originally coined (Waters, 2001: 2).
5   A fact that itself is, of course, not unconnected with the universalizing forces of global capitalism.
6   Similar conclusions emerge if Marshall's famous triad of state functions is used as the yardstick. He proposed that a successful state confers three benefits upon its citizens: economic stability, security, and protection of cultural identity (Marshall, 1950). But for the reasons that have just been given, the certainty with which the modern nation-state can promise to deliver any one of these things in the globalizing world is increasingly doubtful.
7   See, for example, Giddens' discussion of the democratization of the family (Giddens, 2002: 63).
8   Although the supposed comfort that can be drawn from their longevity may in fact be misplaced: see Giddens (2002).
9   For discussion see generally Asp (2002); Baker (1998); Harding (2000).
10 Polls reveal considerable support for crime prevention when prevention pro-grammes are made salient. However, the first reaction of the public, and the one that drives political initiatives, is rather punitive.
11 Perhaps the best example of this comes from New Zealand, where a referendum in 1999 asked the public whether 'there should be a reform of our justice system placing greater emphasis on the needs of victims, providing restitution and compensation for them and imposing minimum sentences and hard labour for all serious offenders' (see Roberts *et al.*, 2003).
12 Walgrave (2003) explains the breakthrough of restorative justice by reference to socio-cultural 'understreams' such as communitarianism, emancipation of indigenous people, and more academic movements such as feminism and critical criminology.

References

Ashworth, A. J. (2004) 'The Criminal Justice Act 2003: (2) Criminal Justice Reform: Principles, Human Rights and Public Protection', *Criminal Law Review*, 516–532.

Asp, P. (2002) 'Harmonisation and Co-operation within the Third Pillar – Built in Risks', in A. A. Dashwood, C. Hillion, J. R. Spencer and A. Ward (eds) *The Cambridge Yearbook of European Legal Studies 2001*, Volume 4, Oxford: Hart Publishing.

Baker, E. (1998) 'Taking European Criminal Law Seriously', *Criminal Law Review*, 361–380.

Beck, U. (1992) *Risk Society*, London: Sage.

Cole, G. (1991) 'Thinking about Crime: the Scope of the Problem, and Shifts in Public Policy', *The Public Perspective*, 2: 3–6.

Crawford, A. and Newburn, T. (2003) *Youth Offending and Restorative Justice. Implementing reform in youth justice*, Cullompton: Willan.

Edwards, A. and Gill, P. (2003) *Transnational Organised Crime: Perspectives on Global Security*, London: Routledge.

Findlay, M. (1999) *The Globalisation of Crime*, Cambridge: Cambridge University Press.

Garland, D. (1996) 'The Limits of the Sovereign State: Strategies of Crime Control in Contemporary Society', *British Journal of Criminology*, 36(4): 445–471.

Giddens, A. (1990) *The Consequences of Modernity*, Cambridge: Polity.

Giddens, A. (2002) *Runaway World: How Globalisation is Re-shaping our Lives* (2nd edn), London: Profile.

Giddens, A. (2004) '*Globalisation – The State of the Debate and the Challenge for Europe*', Lecture to launch ESCUS (the University of Sheffield European Social and Cultural Studies Centre), University of Sheffield, June 15.

Gros, J.-G. (2003) 'Trouble in Paradise: Crime and Collapsed States in the Age of Globalisation', *British Journal of Criminology*, 43(1): 63–80.

Harding, C. S. (2000) 'Exploring the Intersection of European and National Criminal Law', *European Law Review*, 25(4): 374–390.

Hough, M. and Roberts, J. V. (2004) *Confidence in Justice: An International Review*, ICPR Report Number 3, London: King's College.

Jones, T. and Newburn, T. (2004) 'The Convergence of US and UK Crime Control Policy: Exploring Substance and Process', in T. Newburn and R. Sparks (eds) *Criminal Justice and Political Cultures*, Cullompton: Willan.

Krajewski, K. (2004) 'Crime and Criminal Justice in Poland (Country Survey)', *European Journal of Criminology*, 1(3): 377–407.

Lappi-Seppala, T. (2004) *The Renewed Chapter 6 'On Sentencing' in the Finnish Penal Code*. Manuscript available from the author at: Tapio.lappi-seppala@om.fi.

Loader, I. and Sparks, R. (2002) 'Contemporary Landscapes of Crime, Order and Social Control: Governance, Risk and Globalisation', in M. Maguire, R. Morgan, and R. Reiner (eds) *The Oxford Handbook of Criminology* (3rd edn), Oxford: Oxford University Press.

Marshall, T. H. (1950) *Citizenship and Social Class*, Cambridge: Cambridge University Press.

MORI (2003) *Public Confidence in the Criminal Justice System*, London: MORI.

Nelken, D. (1997) 'The Globalisation of Crime and Criminal Justice: Prospects and Problems', *Current Legal Problems*, 50: 251–277.

Newburn, T. and Sparks, R. (2004) 'Criminal Justice and Political Cultures', in T. Newburn and R. Sparks (eds) *Criminal Justice and Political Cultures*, Cullompton: Willan.

Observer (2003) Crime Uncovered. A Nation under the Cosh? The truth about crime in Britain in 2003. *The Observer Magazine*, 27 April.

Pratt, J. (2003) 'The decline and renaissance of shame in modern penal systems', in B. Godfrey, C. Emsley and G. Dunstall (eds) *Comparative Histories of Crime*, Cullompton: Willan.

Renn, O. (1991) 'Risk Communication and the Social Amplification of Risk', in R. E. Kasperson and R. J. M. Stallen (eds) *Communicating Risks to the Public*, Deventer: Kluwer.

Renn, O. and Levine, D. (1991) 'Credibility and Trust in Risk Communication', in R. E. Kasperson and R. J. M. Stallen (eds) *Communicating Risks to the Public*, Deventer: Kluwer.

Roach, K. (1999) *Due Process and Victims' Rights*, Toronto: University of Toronto Press.

Roberts, J. V. (2003) 'An Analysis of the Statutory Statement of the Purposes and Principles of Sentencing in New Zealand', *Australia and New Zealand Journal of Criminology*, 36(3): 249–271.

Roberts, J. V. and Hough, M. (2005, in press) *Understanding Public Attitudes to Criminal Justice*, Maidenhead: Open University Press.

Roberts, J. V. and Roach, K. (2003) 'Restorative Justice in Canada: From Sentencing Circles to Sentencing Principles', in A. von Hirsch, J.V. Roberts, A.E. Bottoms, K. Roach and M. Schiff (eds) *Restorative and Criminal Justice. Competing or Reconcilable Paradigms?*, Oxford: Hart Publishing.

Roberts, J. V., Stalans, L. S., Indermaur, D. and Hough, M. (2003) *Penal Populism and Public Opinion: Lessons from Five Countries*, New York: Oxford University Press.

Robertson, R. (1992) *Globalisation*, London: Sage.

Rock, P. (2002) 'On Becoming a Crime Victim', in C. Hoyle and R. Young (eds) *New Visions of Crime Victims*, Oxford: Hart Publications.

Royal Society (1992) *Risk: Analysis, Perception and Management*, London: Royal Society.

Sherman, L. (2002) 'Trust and Confidence in Criminal Justice', *National Institute of Justice Journal*, 248: 22–31.

Tonry, M. (2004) *Punishment and Politics*, Cullompton: Willan.

Twining, W. (2000) *Globalisation and Legal Theory*, London: Butterworths.

van Zyl Smit, D. (2002a) 'Punishment and Human Rights in International Criminal Justice', *Human Rights Law Review*, 2(1): 1–17.

van Zyl Smit, D. (2002b) *Taking Life Imprisonment Seriously in National and International Law*, The Hague: Kluwer.

van Zyl Smit, D. and Ashworth, A. J. (2004) 'Disproportionate Sentences as Human Rights Violations', *Modern Law Review*, 67(4): 541–560.

von Hirsch, A. and Roberts, J.V. (2004) 'Legislating Sentencing Principles: The Provisions of the Criminal Justice Act 2003 relating to Sentencing Purposes and the Role of Previous Convictions', *Criminal Law Review*, in press.

von Hirsch, A., Bottoms, A.E., Burney, E. and Wikstrom, P.-O. (1999) *Criminal Deterrence: an Analysis of Recent Research*, Oxford: Hart Publishing.

Walgrave, L. (2003) 'Introduction', in L. Walgrave (ed.) *Repositioning Restorative Justice*, Cullompton: Willan.

Waters, M. (1995) *Globalisation*, London: Routledge.

Waters, M. (2001) *Globalisation* (2nd edn), London: Routledge.

8. Engaging with punitive attitudes towards crime and punishment. Some strategic lessons from England and Wales

Mick Ryan

Speaking to Conservative Party delegates, British Home Secretary Michael Howard declared:

> Prison works. It ensures that we are protected from murderers, muggers and rapists ... This may mean that more people will go to prison. I do not flinch from that. We shall no longer judge the success of our system of justice by a fall in our prison population. (Conservative Party Conference, 6 October 1993)

To emphasize the more punitive role intended for one of Britain's most celebrated penal exports, the probation service, whose traditional role had been to 'advise, assist and befriend' those offenders placed in its care, New Labour's Home Office Minister, Paul Boeteng, declared:

> We are moving away from a social work type of befriending model, no one should be under illusions about this ... we intend to form the national probation service on law enforcement. (*Hansard*, Standing Committee G. col 33, 4 April 2000)

At the beginning of this chapter we briefly focus on how penal policy was traditionally made in England and Wales in order to contrast it later with how penal policy is shaped in modern times. Clearly, each country has its own, wider political culture that helps to determine how the penal policy-making process works, so a degree of *specificity* is both evident and appropriate. However, as we move forward to consider modern times in England and Wales we make it clear there are also certain *commonalities*, that some of the factors now driving the penal policy-making process in England and Wales are also at work in other Western countries, factors that have ratcheted up the level of pain we now inflict on those who break the law. [↳ allows continuous linear motion in only one direction while preventing motion in the other direction.]

The bold outline of our position is that the policy-making process in England and Wales, and many other Western democracies, has changed; that in modern times the public voice is increasingly being heard, not least when policies on crime and punishment are on the agenda. The argument is that this development

139

should not be confused with populism *per se*; it represents something more enduring, and arguably more democratic, calling for a more considered, outward-looking political strategy from those groups campaigning for a progressive penal politics in punitive times.

Past times

The post-1945 political settlement in England and Wales was a hard-fought compromise between capital and labour that ushered in the social market economy and the modern welfare state directed at eradicating the five 'great evils' identified by Beveridge: want, squalor, idleness, disease, and ignorance.

This had some impact on liberalizing the overall direction of criminal justice policy. Ordinary Labour Party supporters recognized that those at the sharp end of the criminal justice system had been touched by one or more of these evils, and therefore deserved a measure of welfare and support rather than simple punishment. However, it is fair to say that the opportunity to secure a really progressive penal policy was lost, not least because while Labour's rank and file understood the impact of deprivation well enough, they were not entirely convinced that all offenders were simply the hapless victims of circumstance, and there was a widespread suspicion of the influence of 'do-gooders' in the Parliamentary Labour Party who had supported liberal policies such as the abolition of corporal punishment in 1948 (Ryan 1983).

The modest reforms Labour did succeed in pushing through after 1945, and those secured by subsequent Conservative governments between 1951 and 1964, including the partial abolition of capital punishment, are also partly to be explained by the *deferential* character of the policy-making process in England and Wales. What we wish to draw attention to here is Gabriel Almond and Sidney Verba's observation that well into the 1960s Britain's political culture was uncharacteristically deferential (Almond and Verba, 1963). This allowed politicians, civil servants, insider pressure groups and so-called 'experts' serving on government advisory bodies almost a free hand when it came to making major policies. There was a widespread feeling among the general public that the 'men from the Ministry' knew best.

This top-down policy-making process, buttressed by political deference and party loyalty, and reinforced by the threat of the Official Secrets Act (1911), was nowhere more obvious than in the Home Office, where ministers, advised by senior civil servants, academic experts like Sir Leon Radzinowicz of the Cambridge Institute of Criminology, and senior judges, made criminal justice policy as they thought appropriate. True, this elite *ensemble* could not entirely ignore the public voice(s) on penal matters, but this was attended to, not in order to accommodate it, but rather to circumvent it. As for those operatives who actually ran the criminal justice system, be they local magistrates, police officers, prison warders, or even prison governors, their wishes were also almost wholly ignored. Indeed, those who daily ran the criminal justice system, especially the prisons, were patronized in the extreme (Lewis, 1997). As for the victims of crime, they were mostly left out of the equation altogether (Rock, 1990).

Explaining this highly deferential political culture requires a wider canvas than we have available. Suffice it to say for our present purpose that this entrenched top-down way of doing business came under threat in the late 1960s and early 1970s from two directions. First, the impact of the counter-culture was significant. Alternative groups across a whole range of policy areas began to make themselves heard. The 'experts' were now said to be prisoners on the inside, mental patients themselves, claimants on welfare benefits, not political and administrative elites and their expert advisors in Whitehall. While the impact of this explosion was arguably greater in America and some other European countries than in England and Wales, the effect here was clearly discernible with the arrival of the militant prisoners' group, PROP, Radical Alternatives to Prison (RAP), and Up Against the Law, groups which all confronted the way that criminal justice policy had traditionally been made and, even more telling, the political assumptions on which it operated.

Modern times

Second, while the counter-culture did have some policy implications in England and Wales, the prison system was destabilized throughout the 1970s for a start, it was paralleled after 1975, and then finally subsumed, by the rise of a very British moment of populism, known colloquially as 'Thatcherism'. While not populism in its purest form – British political culture was still too deferential for that – Mrs Thatcher's politics (she was elected to lead the Conservative Party in 1975) did contain some of the essential ingredients of populism.

In the first place, and most crucially, like all populist movements, Thatcherism set itself against the prevailing political hegemony, against the system, not just against particular policies (Canovan, 1999; Taggart, 1996). In this case it was against the social market economy and the welfare state of the post-war years, arguing instead for the dynamic promise of unfettered markets and more self-help to replace the 'nanny' welfare state which had destroyed, or so it was argued by the New Right, ordinary people's self-respect and starved the economy of the necessary additional purchasing power to secure sustained economic growth. The political basis of the post-war settlement therefore had to be renegotiated, even if this meant emasculating the trade union movement through the courts and on the streets.

In the second place, Thatcher's message was addressed directly to the people, above the heads of those consensually minded political and administrative elites who were held responsible for the current mess; that shifting, largely unaccountable, elite *ensemble* of metropolitan opinion-formers who had so arrogantly ignored the people. It was 'the people of Britain', Mrs Thatcher once famously said, that she was listening to on crime and punishment, not to the academy, administrative elites running the Home Office Research Unit, or self-interested pressure groups, like the Howard League for Penal Reform (Ryan, 2003).

This had enormous popular appeal in the 1970s as Britain wrestled with rising unemployment, record and escalating inflation, crumbling inner cities, and rising crime rates, and Mrs Thatcher swept into power in 1979 with support from all classes. But in particular, her direct, albeit simple appeal, not just on the economy but also on law and order, had a strong resonance among the many working-class people who switched their party loyalties and voted Conservative on this issue perhaps more than any other (Taylor, 1981).

In the context of penal policy *per se*, Thatcher's electoral success led to a sustained attack on the established liberal agenda as the rhetoric of neoclassicism overtook that of welfare. Longer sentences were delivered for repeat offenders and drug traffickers, securing parole was made more difficult and the conditions of parole tighter, and there was a succession of free votes in Parliament on the re-introduction of capital punishment. Furthermore, while the demand that 'life sentences should mean life' was resisted, the Court of Appeal was given additional powers to increase sentences handed out by the lower courts if they were thought to have been too lenient. The search for alternatives to custody was sidelined in 1984 when the government announced a huge programme of prison building, the biggest since mid-Victorian times, and by the new Home Secretary's repeated assurances to the judiciary and the public that all those the courts chose to imprison would be accommodated. Into the 1990s, Home Secretary Michael Howard famously declared that prison regimes were to be 'austere' (Ryan and Sim, 1999). So the pain of imprisonment was also intentionally ratcheted up, while the government endorsed incapacitation theory, adopting, at a bellicose Conservative Party conference, the slogan 'Prison Works'.

For many commentators this phase in British penal history is regarded as the beginning of Modern Times, so to speak, the birth of a new 'punitive populism' (Bottoms, 1995). This view is partly supported by the official statistics. That is to say, when the Conservatives took office in 1978 the prison population stood at 49,000; when they left in 1997 the figure was 67,000 and rising. Furthermore, it is still rising in 2004 at around 74,000, reflecting, it is argued ironically, New Labour's success since 1997 at being 'tougher on criminals than on the causes of crime'. The days when a British Home Secretary – in the mid-1970s – viewed the prospect of a prison population of around 40,000 as something of a policy disaster have long gone (Ryan, 1983).

So the punitive drift in Britain since the late 1970s, under both the major political parties, is apparently easy to verify. However, so baldly stated this sug-gests far too simple a link between the Conservatives and New Labour. Furthermore, to imply that the congruence between the major political parties is underpinned by a shared commitment to populism is analytically crude and misleading: it ignores other important changes to our political culture. What we mean by this is that Thatcher's appeal to 'the people of Britain' can indeed be defined as a populist *moment*. It elided in a very instrumental way public anxieties about 'law and order' with a whole range of other social and economic tensions in Britain in the 1970s as the Tories deliberately sought to unpack (and reorder) the post-war settlement between capital and labour. The politics of New Labour, however, are far removed from this fundamental struggle. Indeed, under Blair, New Labour enthusiastically embraced the new order, the market economy, and voted to remove Clause 4 from its constitution, carefully distancing itself from the trade unions. Furthermore, employment levels during New Labour's term in office have been at an all-time high, there has been sustained economic growth, and inflation rates are at their lowest since the 1960s. New Labour's pitch is therefore a far cry from the disaffected *populist moments* that have traditionally been mobilized at times of political crisis in Britain, as in the 1970s, that reject the established order of things.

Setting the record straight

Part of the reason for mislabelling New Labour as *populist* stems from the fact that those of us working in the field of criminal justice take our political institutions and processes too much for granted; we ignore other more significant changes that are taking place in our political culture. We forget, for example, that the political parties we have become familiar with in western Europe (and elsewhere) were the creations of the mid-nineteenth century. They were formed in response to the enfranchizement of the masses and were designed to present the voting public with competing sets of public policy choices. In an age when grand narratives dominated political discourse, these public policy choices came to span the spectrum from the far left to the far right.

These new political parties were led by social and political elites that held considerable sway in determining policies and governed largely untroubled by the public at large, or indeed, even by the organized political parties that worked to sustain them in power. True, the parties on the left, the British Labour Party and the German Social Democratic Party, for example, had mechanisms in place to make their party leaders accountable to the rank and file, but these arrangements were more often honoured in their breach than in their observance.

However, two changes to this way of doing business – and we must remember that it continued for over a century – are evident. In the first place, grand narratives are becoming less relevant, so the choices offered to the public are less clear cut. This inevitably reduces party and voter loyalty – switching support from one party to another is not a big issue. In these circumstances the *pragmatic*, non-ideological preferences of the voter as consumer (rather than a mere follower) become paramount, and party leaders are required increasingly to pay attention to them if they are to secure re-election (Hogg and Brown, 1998). Also, the pull of political deference has diminished. As people no longer blindly follow 'their party' whatever it offers, so they are also less inclined to defer to social and political elites or experts who now have to justify their policies; more than ever before, they are being held to account.

What this means for students of crime and punishment is that policy-making in many Western democracies is far less of an exclusive, top-down business than it once was. Politicians are required to *engage* with the public in a manner that a generation ago would have been unheard of in most Western democracies. To put the same thing more directly, the wider public nowadays refuses to be air-brushed out of the policy-making equation; the idea that difficult questions – domestic or foreign – can be left to a handful of clever people – mostly clever 'chaps' – in the Home Office or the Foreign Office is no longer an option.

To denigrate New Labour politicians, or the current Conservative leadership for that matter, for responding to this long-term, arguably democratic shift in our political culture as 'populist' is not only seriously to misuse this term, it also blurs our strategic thinking. But perhaps this should not surprise us. As Michael Kazin has wisely reminded us in his widely read social history of America, 'The habit of branding as "populist" everything from Bruce Springstein to Rush Limbugh to loose fitting trousers … also has a history' (Kazin, 1995: 5).

The rise of the public voice(s)

The rise of the public voice(s) in Western democracies has been extensively researched across several continents by Robert Inglehart, and the changes in England and Wales have parallels elsewhere. Inglehart's compelling argument is that:

> Mass publics have played a role in national politics for a long time of course, through the ballot box and in other ways. Current changes enable them to play an increasingly active role in formulating policy, and to engage in what might be called 'elite challenging' as opposed to 'elite directed' activities. Elite directed participation is largely a matter of elites mobilizing mass support through established organisations such as political parties … The newer elite challenging style of politics gives the public an increasingly important role in making specific decisions, not just a [mere] choice between two or more sets of decision makers. (Inglehart, 1997: 3)

In the particular context of criminal justice, David Garland is therefore at least partly correct to have observed that the policy making process has become profoundly *populist*, or as an educated political scientist, I would have it, *democratized*; that public opinion now counts as much as 'the views of experts' who are now apparently 'increasingly disenfranchised' (Garland 2001).

However, what is driving this long-term change is not simply a climate of fear in late modernity among some sections of the middle classes (Garland, 2001; Young, 1999), but a mixture of better education and the reach of the new technologies. These give ordinary people, and not just the middle classes, better access to critical information which they are more prepared to use. This does not necessarily, even usually, take the form of mobilizing through formal political institutions, or even, through the traditional network of attendant advisory committees comprising the great and the good, but rather through ad hoc groups which, more often than not in modern times, cut right across party lines and operate on politicians directly through the media.

The most stunning – shocking, perhaps – example of this in Britain in recent years was the campaign against paedophiles on the Paulsgrove council housing estate in the city of Portsmouth in 2000. This followed the tragic abduction and murder of young Sarah Payne in the adjacent county of Sussex. Militant residents claimed that the local council was dumping paedophiles on their doorsteps with no warning or protection, so with the support of the sensationalist tabloid newspapers like the *News of the World* these 'misfits' were 'outed' and hunted down by vigilantes. Small children – some could barely walk – were encouraged to march under banners which proclaimed, 'Kill the paedophiles'.

This sort of direct political pressure on decision-makers is increasing at the same time as political participation in the formal political system is declining. For example, just a year or so after the Paulsgrove affair the British general election recorded its lowest turnout of registered voters since 1918.

Of course, the residents of Paulsgrove, wrongly perceiving every paedophile as a maniacal killer, sometimes identified quite the wrong people to attack and failed to understand the legal restraints – let alone the practical ones – on tracking such offenders in the context of the European Convention of Human Rights. However, the crucial point is that like many other public mobilizations, around environmental issues for example, these protests are a highly potent communication between people and governments in modern democracies. Politicians have to pay more attention to them. They can no longer count on people just deferring to their judgement, or that of 'experts', or rely on 'their' supporters to endorse them at the ballot box at the next general election, come what may.

This attention to the public voice has been reinforced by other changes in the governance of criminal justice. In most Western democracies the state no longer claims a monopoly on securing safer communities. Increasingly voluntary and for-profit agencies are at work, often in partnership with state and a myriad local agencies, delivering criminal justice services to the public from running prisons to organizing victim and witness support schemes (Garland, 1996). The state cannot invite in the active citizen and then continue to exclude the public voice from debating some of the sensitive issues. Ordinary people want more ownership of 'their' democracy than in the past.

Of course, and it is important that we stress this point, politicians should not simply 'give in' to popular demands on matters of crime and punishment. The truth of the matter is that representative democracy is simply a set of institutional arrangements and processes for reconciling often very different opinions and interests, including what we loosely call public opinion. So compromises with informed opinions – so loathed by populists proper who want simple, unambiguous solutions – have to be made. And to a degree this has always been the case. On the question of capital punishment in the 1950s, for example, the Commons was for getting rid of it, as was the National Council for the Abolition of the Death Penalty; the House of Lords on the other hand was in favour of keeping it, as was a clear majority of the public. The messy compromise, which really satisfied no one, was the distinction between capital and non-capital murders eventually enshrined in the Homicide Act (1957).

However, the long-term changes we have identified indicate that the manner in which modern democracies operate has significantly increased the pressure on today's politicians and their advisors to accommodate public opinion within existing institutional arrangements and processes more than was once required or expected. This, if I may borrow (and adapt) from Canovan (1999), is the sometimes 'illiberal shadow' that is now cast across modern democracies, even more strongly than in the nineteenth century when Alexis de Tocqueville warned against the 'tyranny of the majority' (Tocqueville, 1998). Of course public opinion is a social construct, but that is not the point. The issue is that public opinion, however it is put together, now carries more clout than in the past, and this has been one of the key factors – *though not the only one* – helping to undermine what elsewhere Pratt (2002) has characterized as the culture of liberal forbearance (if not tolerance) in modern Western societies, relentlessly cranking up the punitive agenda (see also the introduction to this volume). To denigrate politicians as being *populist* for having to accommodate this long-term change in our political culture, to accuse them of simply being opportunistic, though no doubt some of them occasionally are, is wilfully to overlook the very significant change that has taken place in the context in which policy debates are now conducted in most Western democracies.

The most recent and telling example of this pressure on politicians in England and Wales came early in 2004. This concerned the issue of migrant workers. Under the terms of the Treaty of Nice signed in 2000 a number of eastern European countries, most notably Poland, were due to join the European Union in the spring of 2004. This threatened, or that at least is what the tabloids claimed, the whole fabric of Britain's welfare state. Tens of thousands of Polish workers, and even more threateningly, deviant Roma people from other eastern European countries, were said to be poised to flood the country and live off our generous welfare benefits which they had not even begun to contribute towards. From a position of being very relaxed about this influx of workers – the government judged it to be broadly beneficial to the British economy – New Labour was forced to rush emergency measures through Parliament to restrict the welfare rights of those eastern Europe people who might come to secure work. Although it is to the government's credit that it did not totally 'give in' to public opinion, which had been whipped into a frenzy on this issue by tabloids like the *Daily Mail*, there is no doubt that the welfare rights of migrants from the accession countries are now far more restricted than the government had originally thought was either necessary or justified.

Some strategic consequences

The rise of the public voice(s) seems to us to be irreversible; it is deeply rooted across most Western democracies and is unlikely to be rolled back (Hallsworth, 2002). Just think back to the massive, world-wide demonstrations in 2002 against the war in Iraq. Modern technologies reinforce it. Live talk shows, interactive digital television, the internet, all encourage the public voice. Just about any old 'riff-raff' now can now get air time, and if this eludes you for some reason, then email the Prime Minister who in January 2004 began conducting his 'Big Conversation' with the British people.

While it may not be accurate, as we have sought to argue, to crudely dismiss this as *populism*, the consequence of having to engage with what appears to be an increasingly punitive public voice is hardly encouraging. However, there is more hope than progressive forces might imagine.

In the first place, Hough and Roberts (1998) remind us that, if properly informed, the British public is not as punitive as is generally thought, or as the popular press frequently represent it as being. Given the relevant information, public opinion on sentencing does not greatly differ from the opinions of the judiciary. Second, the same authors also point out that the public's knowledge of existing sentencing practices in Britain is very limited; the British judiciary is much more punitive than ordinary people perceive it to be, handing out very harsh sentences across the board. Governments, and the judiciary for that matter, need to be much more proactive in making sure that this is known to the public, as they should be more proactive in pointing out that in spite of what sensationalist tabloids would have us believe, the crime rate for many offences is on the decrease rather than the increase, a trend that is true of several other Western democracies (Roberts *et al.*, 2003).

Responsible politicians might also point out the cost of hardline law-and-order policies that play to the gallery. Attaching these costs to published legislative proposals is one practical suggestion (Roberts *et al.*, 2003). So governments and those running the criminal justice system need to find more imaginative ways of joining in the public debate, of presenting information about crime and punishment in ways that is about something more than simply trying to justify an increase in their own budgets.

As for pressure groups, and in England and Wales there is a plethora of such groups lobbying for a more progressive penal politics, they need to acknowledge more than anyone else that modern democracies are changing. They can no longer rely on the 'top-down' way of doing business which once so characterized the British style; of cosy Whitehall seminars and discreet departmental committees where socially well connected amateurs and professional experts together enjoyed the close attention of liberally minded civil servants and ministers in formulating penal policy. These groups must now engage with the wider public, lobbying *outwards* rather than *inwards*. Just talking to one another, celebrating their role as part of a progressive 'moral community', is no longer an option (Rutherford, 1995).

This will mean taking advantage of recent technologies to embrace new styles of lobbying. For example, if modestly resourced and highly diverse groups of young people can mobilize globally, across frontiers from Seattle to Genoa, and contest world trade negotiations then there is no real reason why the penal lobby in Britain cannot engage more widely, to contest the power of the sensationalist press to manufacture their very own construction of the 'public voice'. I do not take this to be an agreeable task, in Britain particularly, which has a vociferous right-wing populist press. Who would rather not tread the corridors of Whitehall than encounter vigilantes in Paulsgrove and engage the former editor of the *News of the World*, Rebekah Wade, or the proprietor of the *Sun*, Rupert Murdoch?

Nor is it any easy task. The internet, for example, has many inchoate, [beginning/immature/start] regressive sites, but engaging with these is necessary. It is no longer good enough for the penal lobby to make sure that the right people are in the right places. The right people are already in the right places in England and Wales. Pressure groups spokespersons have taken up government appointments helping to run our prisons and the Youth Justice Board and, conversely, senior civil servants and liberal ex-ministers turn up as office holders in pressure groups like the Howard League and the Prison Reform Trust with monotonous regularity (Ryan, 2003). And this can still count in policy terms, in some instances. But more generally the strategic need to is to engage with structuring the public voice(s), not in trying to deftly circumvent it (them), which is no longer an option.

Simply despairing about 'populism' in learned academic journals, and we have literally been swamped by such material across several continents, is not always a particularly perceptive or helpful response to the wider political forces that are now at work changing the way in which public policy is being made in modern democracies. It suggests, in the British case at least, an enduring social snobbery: a last-ditch defence mounted by an increasingly isolated academic and administrative elite against the idea that ordinary people are entitled to have their say. This is no basis on which to build a lasting, progressive criminal justice strategy in more punitive times.

What is required instead is that we engage in more political education outside of the academy and beyond the lobby; nothing more, nothing less. But crucially, this engagement has to be informed by a theory that pays more attention to the wider political processes that shape criminal justice policy; one that appreciates that nowadays it is negotiated across a complex series of penal networks (and actors) rather than being simply handed down and executed by the state from the centre. Our politicians seem to have woken up to this new reality more quickly than many academic criminologists. But to end on a more positive – even hopeful – note, our call for a theory with an eye to its strategic potential confirms our instinctive political belief that the punitive tide can be turned, the irresistible rise of the public voice(s) notwithstanding. Indeed, we would argue that the space opened up by the emergence of more fragmented and dispersed penal networks that others sketch in this collection is testimony to the potential space for resistance.

References

Almond, G. and Verba, S. (1963) *The Civic Culture*, New Jersey: Princeton Press.

Bottoms, A. (1995) 'The Politics and Philosophy of Sentencing', in C. Clarkson and R. Morgan (eds) *The Politics of Sentencing Reform*, Oxford: Clarendon.

Canovan, M. (1999) 'Trust the People! Populism and the Two faces of Democracy', *Political Studies*, 47: 2–16.

Garland, D. (1996) 'The Limits of the Sovereign State: Strategies of Crime Control in Contemporary Society', *British Journal of Criminology*, 30: 449–474.

Garland, D. (2001) *The Culture of Control: Crime and Social Order in Contemporary Society*, Oxford: Oxford University Press.

Hallsworth, S. (2002) 'The Case for a Postmodern Penality: Reconsidered and Reaffirmed', *Theoretical Criminology*, 6(2): 145–163.

Hogg, R. and Brown, D. (1998) *Rethinking Law and Order*, London: Pluto.

Hough, M. and Roberts, J. (1998) *Attitudes Towards Punishment: Findings from the British Crime Survey*. Home Office Research Study 197, London: Home Office.

Inglehart, R. (1977) *The Silent Revolution*, Princeton: Princeton University Press.

Kazin, M. (1995) *The Populist Persuasion*, Ithaca: Cornell University Press.

Lewis, D. (1997) *Hidden Agendas*, London: Hamish Hamilton.

Pratt, J. (2002) *Punishment and Civilisation*, London: Sage.

Roberts, J., Stalans, J., Indermaur, D. and Hough, M. (2003) *Penal Populism and Public Opinion. Lessons from Five Continents*, Oxford: Oxford University Press.

Rock, P. (1990) *Helping Victims of Crime*, Oxford: Clarendon.

Rutherford, A. (1995) *Transforming Criminal Justice Policy*, Winchester: Waterside Press.

Ryan, M. (1983) *The Politics of Penal Reform*, London: Longman.

Ryan, M. (2003) *Penal Policy and Political Culture in England and Wales*, Winchester: Waterside Press.

Ryan, M. and Sim, J. (1999) 'Power, Punishment and Prisons in England and Wales', in R. Weiss and N. South (eds) *Comparing Prisons*, Amsterdam: Gordon and Breach.

Taggart, P. (1996) *The New Populism and the New Politics: New Parties in Sweden in a Comparative Perspective*, London: Macmillan.

Taylor, I. (1981) *Law and Order Arguments for Socialism*, London: Macmillan.

Tocqueville, A. de (1998 edn) *Democracy in America*, Ware: Wordsworth.

Young, J. (1999) *The Exclusive Society*, London: Sage.

punitive: inflicting punishment

9. The ad and the form: punitiveness and technological culture

Katja Franko Aas[1]

On 12 October 2001, Senior US District Judge Bruce S. Jenkins delivered a speech entitled 'For thinking press 1, for compassion press 2, for judgment press 3'. In his speech, Jenkins compared judicial sentencing under the US Federal Sentencing Guidelines to talking to a pre-programmed computer chip, quite like computer chips that we encounter in other spheres of our lives.

> In the field of sentencing, it is almost like pressing one for thinking and finding that pre-thinking is all that is available, that compassion is not available at all, and that local hands-on judgement is not wanted ... It appears to me that in this computer age there is a subtle change in the manner in which we think and act. We forget that the computer is just a tool. It is supposed to help – not substitute for thought ... It can add up figures, but can't evaluate the assumptions for which the figures stand. Its judgement is no judgement at all. *There is no algorithm for human judgement.* Press one. Press two. Press three. (Jenkins, 2002; emphasis added)

→ a precise rule/set of rules specifying how to solve some problem

Jenkins' impassioned observations are echoed in remarks made by a number of decision-makers who have compared the work of penal professionals to machines and computers (Simon, 1995; Franko Aas, 2005). The diminishing space for hands-on judgment, expressed by Jenkins, has also been addressed in research findings about risk culture as well as being described as a general trait of modernity (Feeley and Simon, 1992; Christie, 1993; Ericson and Haggerty, 1997).

to consider/examine speech or writing

On the other hand, popular punitive discourse about crime often appears to be a direct opposite of the unemotional, computer-like nature of penal systems (Garland, 2001; Sparks, 2001; Pratt, 2002). While technological systems are 'cold', rational, and managed, populist speech is 'heated', unrestrained, and irrational. The popular thus represents what is excluded from technical jargon. While systems are technical, self-referential, and drained of events, popular sentiments about crime appear emotional and focused on dramas of loss and victimization produced on the television screen and evoked in inflammatory speech by politicians.[2]

opinions/tender feeling/ emotion

This chapter suggests that the above observations, while plausible, tend to overlook a vital aspect of these two seemingly contrasting discourses – namely, their *mediated* nature. Both discourses – populist speech and administrative

reasonable/ valuable

decision-making are transmitted through certain media and shaped by specific styles of communication. While the technical nature of the administrative discourse and the populist punitive discourse may appear opposed at the level of content, I will suggest that they are not exclusive when assessed in terms of their communicational style. This chapter attempts to bridge the dichotomy between the technical and the populist by studying the two by reference to their specific *styles or techniques* of communication (Sparks, 2001: 198). Understanding the communicational aspects of penal discourse allows us to see the populist and the technical not as diametrically opposed, but rather as two related fields with certain common traits and embedded in a shared cultural context, particularly the context of the information society and the 'information order' (Lash, 2002).

To examine these issues we need to consider the types of knowledge with which penal systems operate and establish what distinguishes such knowledge from populist discourse. Staheli (2003) describes the popular in terms of its *wide accessibility* and that it is *easily understandable*. It denotes a sphere that is different from that occupied by elites and experts and consequently has a certain resonance with popular culture, itself constructed as the opposite of high or elite culture. In academic circles, the notion of popular punitiveness almost exclusively tends to have negative connotations, while promoters of popular (or populist) views tend to see themselves as giving voice to the people.[3] Most observers of contemporary crime politics would probably agree that it has become unsympathetic to various forms of expert talk about crime, and has embraced 'the average citizen' and the victim as the privileged subject or 'expert' (Garland, 2001; Haggerty, 2004). Criminologists and other sociologically trained experts are thus positioned as promoters of 'high' knowledge, which is not easily understandable or 'easily quotable' (Staheli, 2003: 280).

The marginalization of traditional criminological expertise is not reserved to political discourse about crime only, but has been described as a trend within penal systems as well. Garland (2001: 150), for example, describes 'the declining influence of social expertise' as a defining trait of contemporary penality. Similarly, Haggerty (2004: 211) describes criminology as a 'displaced expertise' – displaced both by the 'highly symbolic public discourse about crime' as well as by the 'neo-liberal forms of governance which have made traditional forms of criminological knowledge and preferred sites of intervention increasingly superfluous to the practice of governance' (ibid.). The declining influence of traditional criminological expertise thus takes place on two levels. From the perspective of populist discourse, criminological discourse is discarded as elitist, as 'high' knowledge, distant from people's feelings. From the perspective of penal institutions, this same knowledge is in a number of settings replaced by forms of governance that promise to be more efficient and technically operational.

This chapter suggests that the two displacements, although different in their objectives, share a common disregard not only for the *content* of the old, welfarist penal policies, but first and foremost, a disregard for their *form of communication*. While traditional criminological expertise relies heavily on scientific discourses about crime and causes of crime, the communicational environment of contemporary information societies is badly suited for handling complex scientific discourses and narratives (Lash, 2002). In what follows, an argument will be made that the demands for accessibility and understandability of penal knowledge are not only demands of the populist press, but also demands directed to penal institutions which increasingly are required to open themselves to auditors, accountants, system managers, and others uninitiated in the traditional penal expertise. Consequently, complex explanatory narratives tend to be compressed into shorter, instantly understandable messages and pieces of information. Standardized, 'informational' knowledge (Lash, 2002) thus becomes a privileged form of communication, marginalizing alternative styles of expression and unregulated forms of narration. Furthermore, it will be suggested that the breaking down of the modernist penal discourse cannot be adequately explained simply as being postmodern (Hallsworth, 2002). Although fragmented and non-linear, the new modes of communication reveal traits of an emerging order – termed by Lash (2002) as 'informational order' – rather than postmodern disorder.

The purpose of this chapter is therefore to explore how an analysis of the information order could shed some light on the dynamics between the populist and the technical in contemporary penality. What follows is first an analysis of *forms* as a distinct communicational technique characteristic, but not exclusive, to risk communication, followed by an analysis of political *advertisement* as a typified communicational style of populist speech.

The form

In *The Great War and Modern Memory* (1975), historian Paul Fussel traces one of the first examples of the use of forms: the British Field Service Post Cards in World War I. To control public anxiety about war at home, these cards were given to soldiers wounded in battle. The soldiers were instructed to circle the appropriate phrase and send them back home without any additional writing on them.

I have been admitted into hospital	
Sick	and am doing well.
Wounded	and hope to be discharged soon.

According to Fussel (1975: 185):

> The Field Service Post Card has the honor of being the first wide-spread exemplar of that kind of document which uniquely characterizes the modern world: the 'Form'. It is the progenitor of all modern forms on which you fill in things or cross out things or check off things, from police traffic summonses to 'questionnaires' and income-tax blanks. When the Field Service Post Card was devised, the novelty of its brassy self-sufficiency, as well as its implications about the uniform identity of human creatures, amused the sophisticated and the gentle alike.

Needless to say, British soldiers soon developed techniques of underlining that ironicized and undermined the one-dimensionality of the cards.[4]

Formalization can be described as one of the main characteristics of contemporary risk thinking, marked by the proliferation of various risk assessment forms, prison classification forms, forms for assessment of suicide risk, etc. Formalization is also strongly present in some recent sentencing reforms, particularly in the spread of the sentencing guidelines model in the United States (Franko Aas, 2005). Just like risk assessment forms, sentencing guidelines structure professional knowledge in order to achieve greater order and predictability. It has been argued that one of the main characteristics of contemporary risk societies is that they are constantly refining the rules regarding how knowledge is communicated. Knowledge formats define how professionals within the system should think and act and there is a pervasive sense of distrust of alternative forms of knowledge (Giddens, 1990; Ericson and Haggerty, 1997). What facilitates the growth of forms is the technological framework at hand. Information technologies are vital in institutionalizing a more predictable mode of governance, thus establishing a new cultural style of communication about crime and punishment.

> Computers allow the development of new formats of risk communication, as well as instant dispersal of knowledge of risk to interested institutions … *The databases rather than individual bureaucrat become the basis for governance through knowledge.* Knowledgeability becomes systematic, operating at collective and institutional more than individual level. (Ericson and Haggerty, 1997: 13; emphasis added)

Here, we can see an important change from the past, where penal professionals and their knowledge were viewed as the main resource of the system. Now, however, this same knowledge is viewed with suspicion, as a possible source of disorder and unpredictability that needs constant monitoring (Ericson and Haggerty, 1997; Franko Aas, 2005).

The point here is that the nature of professional knowledge itself is being transformed. Knowledge itself (or rather, its content) becomes, in many ways, *secondary* to the format (Ericson and Haggerty, 1997). Forms simplify choices, they create transparency and predictability, they ease the classification and processing of data, and last but not least, they are the tools of control and surveillance. They are the tools that enable a shift of discretion and power from professionals to administrators. The force of managerialism is deeply dependent on a structured and formatted view of reality (Bottoms, 1995). Managerial control in contemporary penal systems is based on limiting the access of certain groups to introduce alternative types of knowledge and language that do not correspond with closed-ended formats and classifications. Therefore, the ideological struggles following the fall of rehabilitation and the rise of competing paradigms are not only struggles about the *content* of penal knowledge, they are, perhaps even more crucially, struggles about the *format* and nature of knowledge. In the end, these struggles have to a considerable extent legitimized and insti-tutionalized structured and formalized thinking as an ideal of penal professionalism.[5]

Forms promise predictability and transparency of penal decisions, according to clear and unequivocal standards. They facilitate accumulation of great amounts of information concerning criminal justice decisions; the information which, precisely because of its standardized form, is capable of being stored, analysed, and communicated in the penal system. Not only risk assessment forms but also sentencing guidelines can be better understood when viewed in this perspective. The guidelines are, albeit an extreme, part of a general trend towards regulating the minutiae of penal decision-making and exercise of discretion. In the extreme, the US Federal Sentencing Guidelines have more than 900 pages, and have on average 60 amendments per year.[6] Even though the original concern behind the guidelines was to address the problems of sentencing disparity, they later became used as a tool for facilitating managerial planning and the allocation of resources. In a number of states a major benefit from the guidelines has been the development of computer-based population simulation models that project the amount of money needed to support a state's sentencing policy (Lubitz and Ross, 2001). Guidelines make it easier to predict sentencing outcomes and, therefore, and correctional costs.[7]

Sentencing commissions are thus becoming vital centres of correctional resource management and sentencing data gathering. Judges are required to fill out forms or worksheets for each sentence they impose. In some states the manual forms are now replaced by electronic worksheet systems. The system helps judges and other users to determine the right guidelines application. The completed forms can then be submitted electronically to the commissions. Sentencing forms in many respects resemble Ericson and Haggerty's (1997: 364) description of 'forms about forms', the purpose of which is to regulate and supervise the uses of other forms. If the role of the guidelines is to standardize the sentencing process, the task of worksheets is to further ensure that the process and the reporting about it are uniform. Sentencing commissions are thus becoming important managers of sentencing information and furthermore, controllers of uni-form collection of this information, which is increasingly collected and transmitted through electronic systems.

An interesting aspect of sentencing guidelines is that their form has been able to adapt to a variety of goals and philosophies (Lubitz and Ross, 2001), while preserving the same structural framework. They are being used to implement both populistic policies, the goals of more efficient system management and, to some extent, attempts to limit prison growth. The Minnesota Sentencing Commission, for example, added public safety and more severe punishment of violent offenders as the number one priority of the guidelines system, even though the guidelines were originally designed as a 'just deserts' system. However, while the discourses and objectives behind the guidelines vary, the technique (or rather the format) largely remains the same. Perhaps guidelines can best be described as tools for administrative *communication* – for information gathering, auditing, and accountability – rather than instruments for *symbolic* exchange of discourses about punishment. Their role and the role of sentencing commissions is to gather information for the purposes of further analysis, to supervise compliance rates, to make budgetary calculations, prison population forecasts, etc., rather than address the issues of why and how one should punish. Stith and Cabranes put it this way:

[T]he sentencing hearing today can be nearly unintelligible to victims, defendants, and observers, and even to the very lawyers and judges involved in the proceeding. Too often, when it is all over, neither the judge nor the lawyers are able to explain coherently, much less justify or defend, the sentence imposed. (Stith and Cabranes, 1998: 5)

A report about a guideline hearing in *The Washington Post* (6 Oct. 1996)[8] further exemplifies the phenomenon:

'The court finds that the base offense level is 20,' the judge began. 'Pursuant to Guidelines 2K2.1(b)(4), the offense level is increased by two levels [to 22] ... The Court notes that the criminal convictions ... result in the total criminal history category score of 18. At the time of the instant offense ... the defendant was serving a parole sentence in two causes of action. And pursuant to Sentencing Guidelines 4A1.1 (D), 2 points are therefore added. The total criminal history points is 20. And according to the Sentencing Guidelines Chapter 5, Part A, 20 criminal history points establish a criminal history category of 6 ... [As a result] the guideline range for imprisonment is 84 to 105 months.

Guidelines clearly have problems justifying sentencing decisions and creating credible narratives about crime and punishment. Therefore, as much as guidelines and forms can be seen as a continuity of the Weberian theme of rationalization and rule-governed behaviour,[9] an essentially modern trend, I would like to suggest that they also have qualities that distinguish them markedly from previous decision-making tools. The Weberian world of modernity, although constantly striving for greater predictability, was still focused on discourses and symbolic exchange. On the other hand, the world of information societies, in which guidelines and risk instruments are embedded, is centred on communication of information, and marked by the absence of narratives (Lash, 2002). The technological and cultural contexts in which the guidelines and risk assessment forms emerge and are implemented, influence the nature of knowledge that these decision-making tools generate. Thus, while there are clear lines of continuity with modernity, there are also clear points of discontinuity.

The crisis of narration

Guidelines and risk assessment forms represent a certain break with traditional modes of decision-making, which are essentially connected to written texts and oral communication. With the formalization of crime control, penal power is losing its ability to *create a narrative*. The matrix grids and formulas reduce the penal vocabulary to a limited menu of terms and expressions. They produce a code of language which is unable to express complex thoughts and ideas to the public and actors in the penal process. As Simon (1995: 20) points out, the oral elements of previous epochs helped to 'provide an anchor for punishment in the world outside the penal system' that is now increasingly absent. Guidelines reduce the 'range and quantity of knowledge that can be produced about acts of political significance' (ibid.). Penal discourse thus increasingly becomes standardized, addressing 'standard offenders' through a standard menu of expressions (Franko Aas, 2005).

Barry (2001) points out that while standardization used to be considered a problem for engineers, it now plays a crucial role in political and economic life. Standardization, it could be argued, is not only a technical but also a political project.[10] In our contemporary, increasingly interconnected and reflexive world, objects and processes need to be standardized in order to be compared, communicated about, and traded with. Once externalized and standardized, knowledge and processes can be lifted out and dissociated from particular individuals. It is no longer necessary that a thinking process is something that, by its very nature, happens in a decision-maker's *interior*. As Lash (2002) argues, in a technological culture, reflexivity no longer takes place inside a subject.

> There is an outsourcing of the flux of inner experience onto the flows of images, media and information in the external world. The unconscious itself is outsourced into the world ... Even reflexivity is outsourced, is externalized. It is no longer a *reflection from the interior* in an effective conversation within the self, but an externalized gloss on activities and events to others. Reflexivity becomes *communicational*. (Lash, 2002: 208; emphasis added)

In the case of penal decision-making, this means that thoughts concerning penal decisions need to be communicated further in the system. The thoughts that resist formalization and are not, or cannot, be communicated are, in a way, rendered irrelevant or at least viewed with suspicion. They constitute an anomaly in a cultural landscape where communication of information is of primary importance. Penal knowledge, therefore, needs to be 'able to travel' (Franko Aas, 2004). Knowledge needs to be accessible to outsiders in order to accommodate the demands for information sharing, transparency, and accountability.

Some authors present the crisis of narration as a general trait of contemporary culture. Manovich (2001) suggests that today, narrative is increasingly being replaced by the database as the privileged form of cultural expression. A database organizes information through a markedly different ontology than narratives. A database is a medium for storing and organizing *information* rather than discursive knowledge (Franko Aas, 2004). Information should be distinguished from knowledge since it is objectivated, it is 'byte-like' and compressed (Lash, 2002). Information is different from the discourse or the narrative because it is produced in a much shorter time span and, therefore, leaves little time for reflection. While narratives are designed to be read from the beginning to the end, the database imposes no such limitations on its users. Every item of information is isolated in its self-sufficiency. Lash (2002: 3) argues that information is, in a sense, 'indexical' – 'it has effect on you without the sort of legitimating argument that you are presented with in discourse'.

Forms and guidelines are, as argued above, not primarily characterized by their theoretical consistency in the sense of conforming to a distinct and consistent scientific narrative. They are characterized precisely by their lack of narration. They are what Simon (1995) calls 'power without narrative'. They are organized in such a way that they have no distinct beginning, middle, or end. Thematically, they have no development that organizes them into a sequence. Forms are marked by what Manovich (2001) describes as the 'database logic'. They appear as collections of items upon which the user can perform various operations characterized by additivity rather than causality, which has been traditionally the privileged logic of social scientific discourse (Lash, 2002).

> Causal relations in social science and the causality in the classical narrative privilege the monologic and centralized power of the Gutenberg age. This is the power of the cause over the effect, the classifier over the classified. Linear relations thus speak in terms of B because of A, and A over B. Additive relations speak of A *and* B. Of A and B discontinuously: of A *connecting to* B discontinuously. (Lash, 2002: 180; emphasis in original)

The objective is, according to Lash (2002), not to answer the question why – not to explain, but rather to act. Forms and guidelines are therefore marked by their *operationality*. They are instruments for action rather than for understanding (Franko Aas, 2004).

In a way, creators of forms are beholden to the same philosophy as computer programmers: the creation of a predictable and self-contained world. They are trying to keep the 'rules of the game' as clear as possible. Surprises and ambiguities are not welcome. The 'success' of the form therefore lies in its timelessness and disembeddedness – its insistence that people and their circumstances can be turned into *objects of information,* independent of the subjects that give them meaning. They insist that there is no 'mystery' behind decision-making and that information contained in penal decisions could and should be prescribed in advance. Poster (1990) points out that the effectiveness of the database, and one could say the same for the form, reside in its non-ambiguous structure and the elimination of cultural context. A database relies upon the reduction of information and elimination of ambiguity in language. 'A database arranges information in rigidly defined categories – speed and efficiency of the database vary directly with the fixity of the form in which information appears in it' (ibid.: 96). Writing and speech, on the other hand, are highly *contextual* modes of communication which encode rich cultural materials. The difference has important implications for the types of knowledge and subjectivity that are promoted by information technology and, consequently, also by guidelines and forms.

Communication through forms is essentially carried out through the process of coding and objectification of language: information should have the same meaning independent of space and time. The individual relationship between the knower and the object of knowledge, therefore, needs to be broken. In the context of a penal system, that means that a decision-maker is no longer encouraged to produce data that only he or she, with personal knowledge of persons or events, can interpret. Rather, the system focuses on standardized items that can 'travel' without difficulty. Offenders, therefore, have to be made independent of their social context and dissociated from the decision-makers, in order to be handled by the computer (or indeed to be made legible to the emerging information order).

Castel (1991) argues that by making intervention policies impersonal, and by breaking the direct relationship between a practitioner and a subject of control, practitioners tend to be reduced to suppliers of information to management. With the help of computerized data processing, administrators can achieve autonomy from practitioners.[11] Castel observes that practitioners' roles become auxiliary to that of the manager to whom they simply provide information, which is then processed and distributed in the system. Thus, '[t]hey no longer control the usage of the data they produce' (ibid.: 293). 'The relation which directly connected the fact of possessing a knowledge of a subject and a possibility of intervening upon him or her (for better or for worse) is shattered' (ibid.: 293). Technological mediation of knowledge leads to a fundamental transformation of penal expertise, detaching it to some extent from penal experts (the sole possessors of 'high' knowledge with unique possibilities to solve certain problems), and bringing it closer to the demands for accessibility and understandability.

Haggerty (2004) argues that the changes in the knowledge structure of penal systems, and the consequent growth of 'technoscientific knowledge' (ibid.: 222), may be an important reason behind the diminishing power of criminological expertise to influence penal policy. Criminological expertise, traditionally focused on addressing individual and social problems, is now replaced by 'technical expertise applied on a routine basis by low-ranking professionals' (ibid.: 218). The focus is on information gathering, efficient system management, and resource allocation. Haggerty describes the case of the New York City Probation Department where low-level probationers now report to computerized information kiosks rather than to human beings.

> Such technologies assist in transforming what was originally envisioned as a 'helping' profession into an agency engaging in routine forms of technological surveillance, with individual officers taking it on trust that their monitoring tools accurately depict the physical location (and occasionally the sobriety) of their virtual charges. (Haggerty, 2004: 223)

Similarly, Judge Jenkins' speech, quoted at the opening of this chapter, highlights the dichotomy between two distinct approaches to sentencing and judicial thinking: one that focuses on concrete cases and relies on 'hands-on' experience, and, on the other hand, there is the type of thought, embodied in guidelines and forms, that sees procedures and categories as its primary point of reference and justification. In the latter case, the compatibility of this type of reasoning with computers is not simply a matter of literary comparisons, but also increasingly of practical necessity.

The ad

As we have seen, the world of mass media and crime politics often appears at odds with the unemotive, calculative rationality of forms and administrative decision-making. The emotive nature of political discourse about crime is often attributed to television as a medium. Criminological analysis has become over the past two decades thoroughly aware of the significance of the fact that political discourse is to a large extent taking place on television, and that the nature of TV as a medium shapes the content of its messages (Meyrowitz, 1986; Ericson *et al.*, 1991; Sparks, 2001). As Haggerty (2004: 221) suggests:

> Whereas print media allow for greater analysis and contextualization of issues, television relies on a symbolic logic more concerned with effect than evidence. This is fueled by television's need for dramatic visual images and sound-bite commentary that fit the template of the 60-second news story. As such, television encourages the development of a post-rational polity characterized by efforts to win people's hearts more than convince their minds …

Haggerty also identifies another vital aspect of televised crime discourse – namely the time aspect. Not only do televised messages attempt to 'win people's hearts more than convince their minds' (ibid.), they also have to fit into the mould of a '60-second news story'. A number of contemporary observers have noted that time has become one of the most precious commodities in the information age. Hence, the argument, most notably argued by Paul Virillo, about the ascendance of 'fast time' and correspondingly, the demise of 'slow time' that allows for distanced contemplation. As Hylland Eriksen (2001: 69) writes:

> The great scarce resource for all purveyors of information – from advertisers to authors – is *the attention of others*. When an ever increasing amount of information has to be squeezed into the relatively constant amount of time each of us has at our disposal, the span of attention necessarily decreases. Television has paved the way. As viewers get accustomed to taking in more and more compressed information, it can be compressed even further. (emphasis in original)

While extended narrative moments may be granted to victims of crime (provided, of course, that they can present their story in a media-friendly manner), the same attention span is seldom given to politicians. While they may well produce long speeches about crime, these narratives are seldom reported by the media, unless they contain a slogan. What is unique about political slogans is their self-sufficiency and de-contextualization. A good slogan presents a message or a theme that has instant meaning and appeals to the audience. The messages that slogans contain can 'travel' and are universal in their application regardless of the constraints of time and space. Politicians in Oslo, for example, talk of 'zero tolerance', sometimes without even feeling the need to translate the message. Slogans can stand isolated as a newspaper headline, a line on a campaign poster, or in a newspaper ad. The trend is exacerbated by politicians' preference for television over other media because of 'the assumed size and breadth of television's audience and the impact of its images' (Ericson *et al.*, 1991: 31).

The time aspect is crucial since it inevitably affects the nature of the messages that are allowed to appear on television. And while the emotional nature of television as a medium may account for much of the populist nature of political crime speech, the brevity of the messages is less often mentioned. However, I would like to suggest that the time aspect of communication is vital for understanding contemporary media. Contemporary discourse about crime is not only more emotional and symbolic, but also more *fragmented* and *compressed*. Our analysis of the form may therefore also carry some relevance for the understanding of political discourse. Communicating through short, self-contained, easily understandable communicational entities is not confined to administrative decision-making, but has rather become a general trait of contemporary culture. And just as the form is marked by its additive logic, the same has also been claimed about contemporary media field. According to Lash (2002: 180), we live in a society of the 'ad', where the media and cultural sphere can best be pictured as a 'mosaic' – a 'decorative assemblage' – where the focus is on the *visual*, rather than on linear causality characteristic of narrative cultural expression. Ericson *et al.* (1991: 29) make a similar observation while differentiating between various media:

> The newspaper page layout allows for a mosaic-like, creative juxtaposition on a given page, although the overall presentation in print is linear and sequential, especially within the story. In contrast, television and radio are much more mosaic-like in their presentation as well as between items. They make a collage of very brief (ten- to fifteen-second) clips from sources and journalists to capture a sense of what has gone on and who the key players seem to be.

The inclusion of marketing techniques and marketing style of communication (Butler and Collins, 1999), personified by 'a focus on slick presentation, the prominent role of campaign consultants, and an emphasis on marketing of image' (Farrell *et al.*, 2001: 12), also propels this process forward. Hence, the 'preference for "sound-bites", "spin" and slogans' (Sparks, 2001: 199) and a move from content to rhetoric (Sparks, 2001: 201). Politicians – and to a much lesser extent other penal actors such as the police – have become more professional communicators; professional in a sense that they are adopting techniques of media management and developing a media-friendly communicational style in order to convey their messages. What might be described as a 'media-friendly commentator' always needs to be willing to comment, providing 'information at all places at all times' (Poster, 1990: 70). However, the comments have to be short and concise: 'byte-like' to use Lash's (2002) term. As the media attention span becomes increasingly shorter, the political messages also correspondingly become shorter and easier to grasp, culminating in the political ad as the most obvious example of the trend.

Political advertising is only one, though increasingly prominent, part of political marketing strategies. Although originally a US phenomenon, political advertisements have certain qualities which exemplify the contemporary mediation of politics, namely, its communicational style. Political marketing techniques, used to produce political ads, constitute voters as consumers and politicians as 'products', sold with a specific image. Just as companies advertise their products and imbue them with a specific image, so too politicians have to sell themselves to the electorate (Newman, 1999).[12] Willie Horton ads, used by

George Bush in the 1988 US election, are probably one of the best known examples of ads about crime as a vehicle of political communication. Playing on racial fears, Bush used the ads to portray his opponent Michael Dukakis as 'soft on crime'. The ads asserted that when Dukakis was governor of Massachusetts, a black convicted criminal William Horton was paroled and went on to commit a number of serious offences.

As with the form, the ad too, offers 'information that travels' and can be easily understood by a variety of audiences. The expressive nature of its messages makes TV accessible to almost everyone, while print is better suited for conveying abstract concepts accessible only to the educated (Meyrowitz, 1986). Similarly Ericson *et al.* (1991: 220) argue that because 'television news items are brief and the audience is assumed to have "zero knowledge about a subject", journalists must engage in selecting news pictures which can be expected to have "instant meaning"'. With TV even children can participate in the adult cultural sphere (Meyrowitz, 1986). Since every second of TV time and every inch of newspaper space is very expensive, messages have to be kept short. Brevity is itself a key feature of the ad. TV ads are usually not more than 30 seconds long, which makes it difficult to develop nuanced arguments, and even more difficult to answer simplifications presented by others. As Diamond and Bates (1992) write in their analysis of the 1988 US elections, where Willie Horton so prominently featured:

> In the 1988 Bush furlough ad, the voice-over says that Dukakis 'gave weekend furloughs to first-degree murderers not eligible for parole' while the text on the screen tells viewers that '268 escaped' and 'many are still at large.' But as reporters discovered, only 4 of the 268 escapees were first-degree murderers, and only 3 escapees – none of them murderers – were still at large. This truth might have been difficult for the Dukakis campaign to explain in thirty seconds. (1992: 378)

As in risk communication, we can mark here a similar reliance on and awareness of the usefulness of numbers as a form of communication. Numbers carry an air of 'objectivity' and seem to need no interpretation (think of Tony Blair's now-infamous 45-minute claim about Iraq).

According to Lash (2002: 184), contemporary media no longer have a pedagogical function. The nature of communication is no longer a linear political discourse. The media, rather, encourage experiences of cultural belonging, recognition, and participation, thus fundamentally changing the nature of community and political participation. What Lash (2002: 184) terms 'deep participation', encouraged by contemporary media, is markedly different from citizenship and prior forms of political participation. While traditionally media were places for representation of political discourse and education of citizens, now, Lash argues, media become *participatory* devices, places of shared experience.

> In the press the first items we turn to are what we know in order to 're-cognize' our experience. Newspapers no longer *represent* human association: they become *an 'aspect' of human association'*. Newspapers are

no longer pedagogical devices to produce citizens. They lead to participation in a sense much more cultural than political. (Lash, 2002: 184;
emphasis in original)

Political messages thus increasingly resemble lifestyle commercials, presenting
candidates as people who make other people feel good about themselves, aided
by attractive images and seductive music.

A similar point about the changing nature of representation or a 'crisis of
representation' is made by Poster (1990). Following Baudrillard, he argues that to
understand a phenomenon such as a TV advertisement, one should not look at it
from the traditional view of representational logic and truthfulness. To suggest
that political commercials or Coca-Cola commercials are misleading would be
missing the point. Few consumers believe that their life will become sexier if they
drink Coke instead of water. According to Baudrillard, the commodity in the
consumer society represents a mode of communication which is a departure from
the traditional understanding of the sign. Advertisement represents, albeit in an
extreme form, the tendency of media to remake language and communication
patterns. Words no longer have a stable meaning. 'Floating signifiers, which have
no relation to the product, are set in play … in a manner that optimizes viewers'
attention without arousing critical awareness' (Poster, 1990: 63). Or as Lash (2002:
184) argues:

> The semiotics of the advert consist of neither discourse nor narrative, but a
> graphic, mosaic, 'condensed and displaced form', opening this 'deep
> participation'. The Gutenberg age gives us the book, consumed under
> conditions of contemplation. In the electronic age we read the newspaper,
> watch television, browse on the Internet, under conditions of distraction.
> Deep participation takes place, paradoxically, under conditions of
> distraction.

The tendency is certainly to a large extent reflected in the emotive nature of media
discourses about crime, where those who argue from the traditional standpoint of
representational logic often seem out of place. In the information order
'truthfulness' and logical discourse cease to be of primary importance, since what
is at stake is participation in a shared cultural experience. The images and
messages produced in the media landscape are always open to manipulation.
They are a 'play' of signs rather than a matter of 'truth', an experience rather than
a discourse, a matter of creating images rather than presenting arguments.

Therefore, contemporary populist discourse about crime seems to be more
about adopting a certain image of 'toughness', rather than being a matter of
presenting consistent and salient crime policies to the electorate. Newburn and
Jones (forthcoming) argue that the Willie Horton story had a profound impact on
Bill Clinton's, and consequently also New Labour's, penal policies. The tough-on-
crime stance became 'a *sine qua non* for campaign success' (ibid.: 25). However,
Newburn and Jones point out that the lessons the British left learned from
Clinton's successful presidential campaign are not primarily about the content of
penal policies, but rather about images, political language, and communicational
style.

Blair clearly also brought home with him important lessons about the language of politics. It is no coincidence that the soundbite that Blair is most lastingly remembered for – 'tough on crime and tough on the causes of crime' – was uttered just three days after his return from North America …

[A]t least in part the emergence of New Labour penal populism involved lesson-drawing from the American New Democrats. In this regard, the 'Willie Horton affair' has and continues to cast a long shadow over British penal politics. (ibid.: 26, 27)

Conclusion

To summarize the discussion, this chapter has developed an argument about the 'crisis of narration' in contemporary penal discourse, exemplified by forms and political ads. I have argued that the antinomy between the technical, unemotional nature of administrative penality and the emotional populist discourse can be partly bridged by situating these practices within the contemporary field of media culture and the information order. Both the ad and the form are techniques of communication that do not favour traditional social scientific modes of narration and linear logic. In the ad and in the form the focus is on brief, compressed, and instantly understandable items of communication which can easily 'travel' in time and space, rather than on creation of complex, uninterrupted narratives.

While this crisis of narration may have a distinct postmodern theme, I would like to suggest, following Lash (2002), that it could be more adequately described as *informational*. In the information order, information – with its distinct qualities – becomes the organizing principle of communication. In this type of order, the punitive and the instrumental are 'translatable' into each other through the common language made of compressed and self-referential messages, isolated slogans and numbers that need minimum interpretation and can be easily understood by experts and non-experts alike. Perhaps, most crucially, the language is marked by the short attention span it requires from the audience/recipients of information. In ads and in forms, information is presented in easily understandable packages, ready for 'consumption'.[13] The focus is on action rather than on reflection, on operationality rather than on understanding. The ad and the form thus seem to have an elective affinity to the immediacy of contemporary punitive culture, rather than to the more complex rationalities of penal welfarism.

The issue of the decline of criminological expertise (Haggerty, 2004; Garland, 2001) is therefore also an issue of changing parameters of communication. The rise of the informational order can be described as the crisis of Cartesian culture, where criminologists and social scientists were constituted as 'knowing subjects' (Poster, 1990: 12) with the privileged access to specific types of knowledge and, therefore, also power. The forms and the guidelines represent a break with the perception that a decision-maker is the main locus of power. Now, the authority lies in the system, while decision-makers are 'construed as inherently non-self-sufficient entities' (Bauman, 1992: 90) that require additional help in order to make decisions. The US Sentencing Commission, for example, operates a 'hotline' for judges, probation officers, and prosecutors in order to help them with correct guideline application (Stith and Cabranes, 1997: 1258).

While it is common to describe contemporary punitive discourse as being not only more emotional but also as having become more symbolic, in the long run we may need to address further the very nature of penal symbolism and emotivism. The symbolic and the emotive in penal discourse are crucially shaped by the nature of the channels through which the discourse is communicated. One can therefore wonder about the ability of contemporary media, which is essentially monologic and focused on representational form rather than on content, to convey symbolic messages. This certainly seems to be an argument made by Baudrillard and other observers (Merrin, 1999; Lash, 2002), who rather than seeing contemporary media as conveyors of the symbolic, describe them as its negation. In his usual provocative style, Baudrillard forces us to ask whether symbolic exchange can take place through 'speech without response' (1981: 170) – in a world where any response is 'fully anticipated and neutralized in advance', or is 'television killing the art of symbolic exchange' (Merrin, 1999: 130)?

Notes

1   The author would like to thank Nils Christie, Hedda Geirtsen, Helene Oppen Gundhus, Simon Hallsworth, Heidi Mork Lomell, John Pratt, and Lill Scherdin for their comments.
2   The term 'populist punitiveness' is, according to Bottoms (1995: 40), 'intended to convey the notion of politicians tapping into, and using for their own purposes, what they believe to be the public's generally punitive stance'.
3   The label of 'liberal elitism' in crime debates is perceived as negative for two reasons: the liberal denotes the lacking of a wish to punish, while the elitist denotes distance from 'the people'. The label of 'liberal elitism' was, for example, given to Michael Dukakis and to certain sections of the liberal press in the 1988 US presidential election where, as we shall see later, the Willie Horton case played a prominent role (Anderson, 1995).
4   The reference reported in Simon (1995).
5   Particularly in the US context, the growth of formalized decision-making has been part of a broader movement trying to create a less discretionary and also less discriminatory penal system. Paradoxically, however, the cost of increased formality and reflexivity may also be increased incarceration (Caplow and Simon, 1999). In a system focused on formal rules, police and other correctional agents more often choose to process cases forward, rather than exercise their discretion and drop the charges (ibid.).
6   The source is http://www.sentencing.org/facts.htm
7   Reitz (2001) reports that the above-mentioned prison projections of sentencing policies have sometimes had a sobering effect on legislators, who realized the costs of various sentencing policies. On the other hand, prison projections were used in the federal system simply to correctly predict the amount of resources needed to implement the draconian federal sentencing legislation.
8   Reported in Stith and Cabranes (1997: 1264).
9   One could in a way look at sentencing guidelines as a final realization of Weber's idea of 'law without gaps' and judge as automaton 'into which legal documents and fees are stuffed at the top and in order that it may spill forth the verdict at the bottom

along with the reasons, read mechanically from codified paragraphs' (Weber, 1968: 978).

10   Barry (2001) suggests that the reason for the extraordinary technicality of the issues that are usually addressed by EU institutions is that these institutions basically do not function as traditional state institutions. The primary job of EU institutions is to set forth the conditions within which a certain degree of standardization (or harmonization) can take place.

11   This is not say that the process has gone without resistance or that it has been by any means complete. American judges in particular have been fervent opponents of formalization (Franko Aas, 2005). Similarly, Kemshall and Maguire (2001) describe that while there clearly has been a move towards standardized risk evaluation, there is also a strong cultural resistance to these practices on the 'ground level', and a continuing belief in the salience of the modernist project.

12   There are important differences between various countries in the extent to which marketing techniques have been adopted by politicians. While the US clearly stands at the forefront of the development, other Western countries have not been immune either (for an overview of related literature, see Newman, 1999).

13   My intention here is not to claim that people are simply passive when consuming media. As Poster (1990: 46) writes, 'media promote forms of self-constitution by viewers that profoundly engage them'.

References

Anderson, D. C. (1995) *Crime and the Politics of Hysteria: How the William Horton Story Changed American Justice*, New York: Times Books, Random House.

Barry, A. (2001) *Political Machines: Governing a Technological Society*, London and New York: The Athlone Press.

Baudrillard, J. (1981) *For a Critique of the Political Economy of the Sign*, St Louis: Telos.

Bauman, Z. (1992) 'Life World and Expertise: Social Production of Dependency', in N. Stehr and R. Ericson (eds) *The Culture and Power of Knowledge: Inquiries into Contemporary Societies*, Berlin and New York: Walter de Gruyter, pp. 81–106.

Bottoms, A. (1995) 'The Philosophy and Politics of Punishment and Sentencing', in C. Clarkson and R. Morgan (eds) *The Politics of Sentencing Reform*, Oxford: Clarendon Press, pp. 17–50.

Butler, P. and N. Collins (1999) 'The Marketing Colonization of Political Campaigning', in B. I. Newman (ed.) *Handbook of Political Marketing*, London: Sage, pp. 41–54.

Caplow, T. and J. Simon (1999) *Understanding Prison Policy and Population Trends*, Chicago: University of Chicago Press.

Castel, R. (1991) 'From Dangerousness to Risk', in G. Burchell, C. Gordon and P. Miller (eds) *The Foucault Effect: Studies in Governmentality*, London: Harvester/Wheatsheaf.

Christie, N. (1993) *Crime Control as Industry: Towards GULAGS, Western Style*, London and New York: Routledge.

Diamond, E. and S. Bates (1992) *The Spot: The Rise of Political Advertising on Television*, Cambridge, MA and London: MIT Press.

Ericson, R. V. and K. D. Haggerty (1997) *Policing the Risk Society*, Oxford: Clarendon Press.

Ericson, R. V., P. M. Baranek and J. B. L. Chan (1991) *Representing Order: Crime, Law, and Justice in the News Media*, Milton Keynes: Open University Press.

Farrell, D. M., R. Kolodny and S. Medvic (2001) 'Parties and Campaign Professionals in a Digital Age', *Press/Politics*, 6(4): 11–30.

Feeley, M. M. and J. Simon (1992) 'The New Penology: Notes on the Emerging Strategy of Corrections and its Implications', *Criminology*, 30(4): 449–473.

Franko Aas, K. (2004) 'From Narrative to Database: Technological Change and Penal Culture', *Punishment & Society*, 6(4): 379–393.

Franko Aas, K. (2005) *Sentencing in the Age of Information: From Faust to Macintosh*, GlassHouse Press, Cavendish Publishing: forthcoming.

Fussel, P. (1975) *The Great War and Modern Memory*, New York: Oxford.

Garland, D. (2001) *The Culture of Control: Crime and Social Order in Contemporary Society*, Oxford: Oxford University Press.

Giddens, A. (1990) *The Consequences of Modernity*, Cambridge: Polity Press.

Haggerty, K. D. (2004) 'Displaced Expertise: Three Constraints on the Policy-relevance of Criminological Thought', *Theoretical Criminology*, 8(2): 211–231.

Hallsworth, S. (2002) 'The Case for a Postmodern Penality', *Theoretical Criminology*, 6(2): 145–163.

Hylland Eriksen, T. (2001) *Tyranny of the Moment: Fast and Slow Time in the Information Age*, London and Sterling, VA: Pluto Press.

Jenkins, B. S. (2002) 'For Thinking Press 1, for Compassion Press 2, for Judgment Press 3', in *Vital Speeches of the Day* (15 January 2002).

Kemshall, H. and M. Maguire (2001) 'Public Protection, Partnership and Risk Penality: The Multi-agency Risk Management of Sexual and Violent Offenders, *Punishment & Society*, 3(2): 237–264.

Lash, S. (2002) *Critique of Information*, London, Thousand Oaks, New Delhi: Sage Publications.

Lubitz, R. L. and T. W. Ross (2001) 'Sentencing Guidelines: Reflections on the Future', in *Sentencing & Corrections, Issues for the 21st Century*, National Institute of Justice.

Manovich, L. (2001) *The Language of New Media*, Cambridge, MA and London: The MIT Press.

Merrin, W. (1999) 'Television is Killing the Art of Symbolic Exchange: Baudrillard's Theory of Communication', *Theory, Culture & Society*, 16(3): 119–140.

Meyrowitz, J. (1986) *No Sense of Place: The Impact of Electronic Media on Social Behavior*. New York: Oxford University Press.

Newburn, T. and T. Jones (forthcoming) 'Lesson-drawing and Penal Populism: The Long Shadow of Willie Horton' (draft of a paper).

Newman, B. I. (ed.) (1999) *Handbook of Political Marketing*, London, Thousand Oaks, New Delhi: Sage Publications.

Poster, M. (1990) *The Mode of Information: Poststructuralism and Social Context*, Cambridge: Polity Press.

Pratt, J. (2002) *Punishment and Civilization*, London, Thousand Oaks, New Delhi: Sage Publications.

Reitz, K. R. (2001) 'The Disassembly and Reassembly of U.S. Sentencing Practices', in M. Tonry and R. S. Frase (eds) *Sentencing and Sanctions in Western Countries*, New York: Oxford University Press.

Simon, J. (1995) *Disciplining Punishment: The Re-Form of Sentencing*, unpublished manuscript.

Sparks, R. (2001) 'Bringin' it all Back Home: Populism, Media Coverage and the Dynamics of Locality and Globality in the Politics of Crime Control', in K. Stenson and R. R. Sullivan (eds) *Crime, Risk and Justice*, Cullompton: Willan Publishing.

Staheli, U. (2003) 'The Popular in the Political System', *Cultural Studies*, 17(2): 275–299.

Stith, K. and J. A. Cabranes (1997) 'Judging Under the Federal Sentencing Guidelines', *Northwestern University Law Review*, 91(4): 1247–1283.

Stith, K. and J. A. Cabranes (1998) *Fear of Judging*, Chicago: University of Chicago Press.

Weber, M. (1968) *Economy and Society: An Outline of Interpretative Sociology* (G. Roth and C. Wittich, eds), New York: Bedminster Press.

10. Electronic monitoring, satellite tracking, and the new punitiveness in England and Wales

Mike Nellis

The whole wide world is no longer big enough to hide in. Everywhere is connected to everywhere else. Everywhere – the air of the most desolate desert, the wind above the waves of the most remote part of the oceans: *everywhere* – is laced with electronic chatter. We once believed that the world was packed, wingtip to wingtip, with invisible and omnipresent angels whispering the word of God to His entire creation, leaning through our skulls to speak to our souls. Now our flesh is continually swept by an invisible and omnipresent rain of information, quantum packets, strings of zeros and ones, on its way from somewhere to somewhere else. How different are our dreams? (McAuley, 2002:328)

The aim of this chapter is to explore and explain the significance of the electronic monitoring of offenders (henceforth EM) as it has developed in England and Wales, in the context of the well documented shift towards increased punishment that has occurred there (Tonry, 2004). EM currently entails the use of radio-frequency/landline telephone technology to know remotely but in real time whether tagged offenders abide by the conditions of a court-imposed curfew (usually made to their own home, overnight). Schemes of this kind were piloted in England and Wales in the 1990s, and deemed useful by the Home Office. Variants of this technology can monitor and measure the alcohol and drug intake of curfewed offenders but these are not yet in regular use in England and Wales. Voice verification monitoring permits the checking of an offender's presence at multiple rather than single locations – this has been tried on a small scale, mostly with young offenders. Satellite tracking – using Global Positioning System (GPS) satellites and the mobile telephone system – monitors movement and facilitates the specification of exclusion zones rather than mere presence at a particular location. Pilots of this began in September 2004. The New Labour government called EM 'the future of community punishment' shortly after its election (Home Office, 1997), and, counting the satellite tracking pilots, now runs (or rather contracts out to three private companies) nine distinct EM programmes. England and Wales is the European leader in the use of EM. Since 1999 (up to September 2004), 170,883 offenders had been tagged, for an average of four months each; there were upwards of 10,400 of them in the community on any given day.

Pratt's (2002: 177) formulation of the new punitiveness allows not only for the growth of mass incarceration and the renaissance of older, atavistic penalties such as public humiliation but also for the emergence of 'new possibilities of punishing which previously seemed to have no place in the civilised world'. EM is certainly new, and firmly associated in England and Wales with attempts to intensify the controlling elements in community penalties and to increase their enforceability. But the position of EM within the new punitiveness is in fact ambiguous and equivocal: whether and in what form it might earn a place in 'the civilized world' remains to be seen. Not all the narratives surrounding it have accepted that it is properly or sufficiently punitive, and it has had both utopian and dystopian aspirations projected onto it, as many new technologies have had in the past (Sturken and Thomas, 2004). Its resemblance to the pernicious forms of state surveillance envisaged by George Orwell (and even more so by other science fiction writers) was undoubtedly the basis on which the English probation service initially rejected it as a punitive step too far in community supervision. On the other hand, Tom Stacey, the electronic tag's originator in England, saw EM as potentially rehabilitative – believing that the wearing of an ankle tag would encourage prudence and responsibility on the part of an offender – and more reassuring to the public than existing welfare-based community penalties (Nellis, 1991). Furthermore, both Stacey and the Home Office, which legislated for EM-curfew orders in the Criminal Justice Act 1991, believed that it would make a significant contribution to reducing the use of imprisonment: EM can thus be understood, in this narrative, as an attempt to reduce the intensity and scale of incarcerative punishment.

Even within the sociology of punishment, when it has been addressed at all, EM has usually been understood as part of an actuarial, risk-oriented, managerialist approach to crime control, whose ethos of cost-efficient micro-regulation of offenders is generally hostile to the more viscerally punitive sensibilities that have indeed resurfaced in late modernity. Except among those who are animated by Orwellian anxieties – a dwindling band in the British public – EM has indeed become a relatively unemotive issue in (English) media debate, devoid of either the awe or anxiety one might have expected of an innovation that 30 years ago would have seemed to many like science fiction. So low-key has reaction to it become that politicians struggle to construct narratives of credibility with which to recommend it to the public – its efficacy as punishment is simply not self-evident. And while EM must be understood as a kind of punishment – it facilitates restrictions of personal liberty that would not otherwise be possible – cogent claims have been made that the technology *could* serve humane and constructive ends in penal reform (Whitfield, 1997, 2001). From this liberal humanist perspective EM, far from being constitutive of a new punitiveness, *could* actually help to hold it at bay and constitute a civilized and progressive response to crime in the twenty-first century. Others have seen symbiosis rather than strain between managerialist and viscerally punitive approaches to crime or, indeed, have seen potential for new and sophisticated forms of repression in managerial approaches alone, and in the search for 'technocorrections' with which it is now firmly associated (Fionda, 2000; Coyle, 2001). Certainly the expansion of surveillance – something that theorists of the new punitiveness have tended to neglect – had become a major focus of intellectual enquiry and political concern, even before the events of September 11th 2001 boosted interest in identity cards, biometric border controls, and intensified intelligence-gathering (Norris and Armstrong, 1999; Lyon, 2003). As Haggerty and Ericson (2000: 612) have written, 'today, surveillance is ... in keeping with the technological future hinted at by Orwell, but augmented by technologies he could not even have had nightmares about'.

This is the terrain with which I will be concerned. The deeper sociological reasons for the emergence of EM remain surprisingly underexplored, even as government commitment to it deepens and new variants of it are brought into play. This chapter will suggest that the advent of satellite tracking helps to shed light on the growth of EM more generally, which in turn enables tentative judgements to be made about EM's relationship to the new punitiveness and its place in our penal future.

Correctional reform and the emergence of electronic tracking

After several decades of *relative* stability, the scale and pace of change in the sentencing framework and organizational structures pertaining to the community supervision of offenders began to accelerate in the 1990s. This began under a Conservative government and continued apace under a New Labour government which took office in 1997 – a neoliberal ethos being common to both. The Criminal Justice Act 1991, although explicitly predicated on a commitment to reducing the size of the prison population, sought to shift the probation service away from its traditional social-work ethos to an ethos of 'punishment in the community' and to develop tougher community penalties that would have greater credibility with sentencers and public. The commitment to penal reductionism was short-lived: by 1993 it had been replaced by Home Secretary Michael Howard's 'prison works' doctrine (which encouraged prisoner numbers to rise) and a near-absolute belief that the probation service had nothing useful to offer. New Labour inherited a prison population of 62,000 and while not talking up the use of prison in quite the way Howard had done, showed no initial public commitment to slowing or reducing the numbers. Using a rhetoric of 'modernization', the new government initiated a welter of legislative and administrative reforms intended to bring criminal justice into line with neoliberal precepts. Modernization has in effect meant increasing central control over the implementation of criminal justice policy and an intensification of managerialism (Mclaughlin *et al.*, 2001; Nash and Ryan, 2003). In addition, there has been a heightened emphasis on the use of new technology, whose significance to the entire penal enterprise is perhaps only now becoming apparent.[1]

New Labour prioritized the reform of youth justice. The Crime and Disorder Act 1998 created a central body, the Youth Justice Board, to administer (via local youth offending teams) an array of custodial and (mostly new) community penalties. These included elements of restorative justice, coercive rehabilitation ('accept help and support now or be punished instead'), spatial exclusion (most notably in the form of anti-social behaviour orders which ban youngsters from areas where they have been causing trouble), as well as EM. The Criminal Justice and Court Services Act 2000 then centralized control of the probation service, promoted a narrowly conceived ideal of 'effective practice' (based on cognitive behavioural psychology), and while maintaining a wide range of distinct community penalties dropped the term 'probation order' to signify the government's growing commitment to detraditionalization. Major reviews of sentencing policy and court structure and resettlement practice (critically reviewed in Rex and Tonry, 2002; Tonry, 2003) led eventually to the Criminal Justice Act 2003, which introduced, for the first time, several 'seamless sentences' (mixes of custodial and community elements) and (for adults but not juveniles) blended all existing community penalties into a single generic community order which sentencers could tailor to individual cases on a mix-and-match basis, drawing from a menu of 12 requirements. The *Correctional Services Review* (Carter, 2003) developed these trends further, proposing the merger of the existing prison and probation services into a single National Offender Management Service (NOMS), and the creation of a purchaser–provider split in community supervision, to facilitate increased private and voluntary-sector competition for custodial and supervisory work. The *Review* accomplished a longstanding, but hitherto much resisted New Labour goal, namely the *de facto* abolition of the Probation Service, an organization whose enduring humanistic traditions looked increasingly anachronistic under New Labour's modernizing gaze. Little of the *Review* was liberal in the traditional penal sense, but its overriding aim was, for cost-effectiveness reasons, to place a ceiling on prison numbers of 80,000, rather than allowing them to drift inexorably upwards to 93,000 by 2008, as some Home Office projections had anticipated.

EM curfews have been increasingly significant in each of these phases in correctional reform. They were first piloted, on adults, in the context of the 'punishment in the community' strategy, and were portrayed then as a palpably tough community penalty, whether used alone or in conjunction with other rehabilitative measures (Home Office, 1988, 2000; Nellis, 1991; Fay, 1993). Further pilots followed in the mid-1990s, administered by private-sector organizations because of marked Probation Service hostility to the measure. These were translated into a national scheme by New Labour in 1999 and extended into an early release from prison scheme to help manage the rapidly rising numbers of short-sentence prisoners. Although initially used cautiously by prison governors, this rapidly became the bigger of the two schemes. The Criminal Justice and Court Services Act 2000 introduced EM for young offenders (as an element in bail, community sentences, and post-custody supervision) and sought to infuse EM into a wider range of adult community measures in order to make them more readily enforceable. These latter experiments were not a success – take-up was low – reflecting a dissonance between the government's strong ideological commitment to EM and its actual capacity to direct and engineer rapid changes of practice among sentencers and professionals at ground level (Bottomley *et al.*, 2004). Nonetheless, sentencers' confidence in the original EM curfew grew, and opposition to it declined within the Probation Service.

The significance of that decline, for the service itself, was slight – too little, too late (Nellis, 2003a, 2004a). England and Wales is the only European country to use the private sector to deliver EM,[2] and to maintain a degree of separation between it and 'social work' interventions with offenders (less so for juveniles than for adults). EM and the 'effective practice' initiative have never been integrated, for example, and have developed on parallel tracks within the Home Office. EM has tended to receive both stronger, and more regular, endorsements than probation in ministerial pronouncements on the future of community supervision; symbolically, as EM's star rose, probation's waned. References to 'a twenty-first-century electronic monitoring service for a twenty-first-century criminal justice system', and to England aspiring to being 'a world class lead[er] in EM' by Home Office officials (Toon, 2003; Snelgrove, 2003) indicate how emblematic of modernization EM has become.

The advent of satellite tracking

It was the *Correctional Services Review* (Carter, 2003), at whose core was the belief that a separate probation service could and should be dispensed with, which first outlined the rudiments of a strategy for existing forms of EM – and also announced the advent of a new form of it, satellite tracking, which had been used patchily in the USA since 1996.[3] In England and Wales it was to entail a combination of GPS satellites (for outdoor locations) and mobile telephony (for indoor locations) which between them could track and trace the movements of offenders on a 24/7 basis, either in real time or retrospectively. Over and above its intention to 'control the movement of offenders' (including monitoring the perimeter of specified exclusion zones), satellite tracking was intended 'to ensure offenders attend work or rehabilitation programmes [and to] provide the police with information on the behaviour of persistent offenders' (Carter, 2003: 28). Both it and exclusion zones had already been legislated for in the Criminal Justice and Court Services Act 2000, and had been loosely associated with the idea that if the whereabouts of dangerous paedophiles were always known to the penal authorities (including the police), murders like that of eight-year-old Sarah Payne would not occur. Suitably reliable and accurate technology – better than that originally used in the US – took a while to develop, but once it was available the Home Office (2004a: 13) confirmed that satellite tracking would indeed 'be an increasing feature of correctional services in the future'.

Further indications of this future's shape appeared in the Home Office Strategic Plan 2004–08, in July 2004. Written to win public support in the next general election, it explicitly played on post-September 11th insecurities, synthesizing a wide range of previously announced criminal justice (and immigration management) initiatives. The Prime Minister's foreword claimed that 'modernization' now required moving 'further and faster – from incremental to transformational change' (Blair, 2004: 5). At the Plan's heart was a strategic multi-agency focus on the alleged 5,000 prolific (formally called 'persistent') offenders who apparently commit 10 per cent of all crime. Under the new regime, these offenders would, at different points in their criminal careers, be subject to an array of interventions, including prison, drug treatment, and EM, and by so doing a 15 per cent reduction in crime was deemed feasible in four years. While partly rhetorical, this ambition did reflect genuine increases in police and local government powers to address crime and anti-social behaviour, a range of more punitive sentences and the availability of funds to create 3,000 new prison places (notionally to enable the 80,000 ceiling).

'To support all of the above and stay ahead of the criminal', the Home Secretary wrote (Blunkett, 2004: 10), 'we will harness new technology.' Instantiating this, Blair gave his imprimatur 'to a doubling of the [daily] capacity to use electronic tagging' (to 18,000), and to the introduction of 'satellite tracking for high risk offenders' (*idem*). The Strategic Plan called EM *'central* to the way we deal with offenders in the community' in a way that it had never been before, and clear pride was taken in being 'the largest user of tagging outside the USA' (Home Office, 2004b: 78; emphasis added). And although satellite tracking was to be piloted in select areas rather than launched immediately as a national scheme, a long-term commitment to its introduction *had already been made*:

> *Once the technology has been tested we will make tracking much more widely available.* This will radically intensify the supervision of offenders to help monitor compliance with exclusion orders, which we will activate as a newly-available community penalty, and will result in an increase in public protection. (*idem*; emphasis added)

The satellite tracking pilots were established in September 2004 in Greater Manchester, the West Midlands, and Hampshire areas. They were targeted on sex offenders released from prison, domestic violence offenders, and persistent offenders (both young adults and juveniles) and emphasized the usefulness of tracking not just for monitoring movement, but also in enforcing specified exclusion zones (around schools, playgrounds, and victims' homes, for example). It is recommended that exclusion and curfews are sometimes combined to give expression to what the Home Office calls its 'prison without walls' strategy (Home Office, 2004c: 6, 14). In October 2004, a related pilot was initiated for 'failed' asylum seekers (those awaiting deportation), the first use of EM in England outside a criminal justice setting.[5]

Understanding the emergence of EM

It still remains the case that 'EM is ... being implemented in a way that has outpaced current capacity to understand its implications and consequences' (Bottoms *et al.*, 2000: 247). Arguably, however, the emergence of tracking – monitoring *movement* rather than just *location* – will facilitate understanding of where the general impetus for this change is coming from, and what the contours of a new, twenty-first-century regime in community supervision may look like. Haggerty and Ericson's (2000) concept of 'the surveillant assemblage' – the increasingly, but imperfectly, integrated network of computerized data streams that electronically monitor the movements, trails, and traces of employees, consumers, and citizens (suspect or otherwise) in the contemporary world – is a useful resource for starting such an analysis. The first point to grasp is that while the electronic monitoring of offenders may seem (to penologists) to be a discrete, distinctive, and new development in criminal justice, the tagging and tracking of people, objects, and sometimes animals in order to check, regulate, or control their functioning and/or their movements, locations, and schedules (in single buildings or cities, whole countries – or the entire planet) is already widespread in many spheres. Fitting a person, object, or creature with a machine-readable identifier – a PIN, a tag, or a biometric, for example – and connecting them in some way to a computerized telecommunications network (local, national, or global) enables their whereabouts to be known remotely with extraordinary speed and accuracy. Instances include the increasingly ubiquitous tagging of goods for stock control purposes, plant equipment in the construction industry, cash-in-transit vehicles, vehicle security systems, farm animals (to prevent rustling), wild animals and birds (to do research), pets (using subcutaneous identity chips), containerized cargo, airport baggage, some parcels, employees in 'smart' workplaces, patients with Alzheimer's, new-born babies in hospitals (to prevent mix-ups and kidnapping), crime suspects, undercover police officers – as well as curfewed and satellite-tracked offenders. The movement of any or all of these entities can either be monitored in real time or retrospectively, and/or scanned and checked at the entry and exit points of designated zones or places (Jones, 2000). Management theorist Brian Bloomfield considers that

> we are witnessing a wholesale movement towards the institution of a world where every object whose movement is potentially problematic (as regards, for example, ownership, identity or organisation) may become subject to electronic surveillance, a world where all such objects will have a form of electronic or virtual identity. We will have the object – whether a human or a non-human – and its electronic tag – with the ordering of these objects in space and time mediated by electronic surveillance. (Bloomfield, 2001: 183)

The technical equipment used to monitor offenders is not developed for 'surveillance' as such; it is customized from components invented and developed for the systems that make information transfer and real-time global communication possible, and benefits from constant technological innovation in that larger system. The developmental needs of corporate capitalism and nation-states (or sub-divisions thereof) for enhanced performance in the creation of profit and security drive techno-scientific innovation. Within this, the military, and specifically the American military, have often played a catalytic role (Reynolds, 2000; Chinn, 2001). The market for EM (in the broadest sense) has now become sufficiently large to sustain a number of specialist companies who, along with the international private prison and private security providers, are integral elements of 'the global commercial-corrections complex' (Lilly, 1992; Lilly and Knepper, 1993). One of them, the Israel-based Dmatek (whose subsidiary, Elmo-Tech, supplies EM equipment to law-enforcement agencies around the world, including Britain) recently envisioned its market to its shareholders in the following way:

> We believe that people-related electronic monitoring will gradually spread into more and more areas of modern society. Electronic monitoring based applications will provide better, faster and more cost-effective solutions to everyday tasks and enable services which are not available today for lack of technological means.

> We expect the use of electronic monitoring in the corrections market to grow faster in the coming years – as the need is evident, as the system is proven to be cost-effective and the solution is becoming accepted in more countries around the world. We anticipate the medical field to be the next emergent adopter of the technology, on an even bigger scale. (Dmatek, 2002: no page number)

Even companies like Dmatek are dependent on larger developments in telecommunications systems for new business opportunities. Significantly, it has been upgrades to the 26-year old NAVSTAR GPS[6] and the technical ability to mesh it with the mobile phone system (undertaken to facilitate a range of navigational improvements) that have made the tracking of individual offenders possible (Enge, 2004). The tagging and tracking of offenders has become a possibility simply because of 'the converging technologies of computerisation and telecommunications … tagging is not in any way different to these developments; *indeed, in many cases it is realized through them'* (Bloomfield, 2001: 195; emphasis added).

EM can thus be understood, in part, as the exploitation of the new global electronic environment – the milieu described by Paul McCauley in the quote that heads this chapter – for law enforcement purposes. It makes possible the penal regulation of mobile and dispersed individuals in a way not *humanly* possible before. Zygmunt Bauman is thus slightly offbeam when he says that *immobilization* (typifed by imprisonment) is the logically perfect punishment to inflict in contemporary society, where an individual's sense of being free is inextricably entwined with the 'right' to personal mobility. 'Being prohibited from moving is [certainly] a potent symbol of impotence' (Bauman, 1998: 122); but to lose one's anonymity whether in crowded or empty, public or private spaces – to be regulated by unseen agents *even while one is moving, no matter where one is* (as can happen with satellite tracking) – is surely spectacularly punitive as well, and perhaps all the more unnerving because no previous generation of offenders has experienced it.

Two further points of relevance to EM can be derived from the surveillant potential of telecommunications: one to do with simulation, the other to do with time. Contemporary forms of surveillance increasingly involve simulation (rather than a direct gaze) in that the locations and movements being monitored can be digitally represented on computer screens in a variety of graphic forms. Remotely sensed – and automatically captured – data can, for example, be blended with digital mapping techniques (such as Geographical Information Systems) to create two- or even three-dimensional representations of the zones being monitored. There are vast commercial, civil, and military uses for such technology – missile guidance systems are one of the latter – and it might be argued that law enforcement has come relatively late to it. There is no doubt that it 'allows locations and patterns of flows to be precisely defined, surveilled and virtually simulated against a global geometry of precise, digital, time-space coordinates' (Graham, 1999: 133). This in turn affords 'radically new possibilities for tracking and social control' (*idem*: 135).

Regarding time, telecommunication technologies aim to 'overcome [the limitations of] space and distance by minimising time constraints' (Bloomfield, 2001: 32). They enable awareness, and sometimes action in real time, or a close approximation of it. This process is largely commercially driven. Late modern notions of efficiency require, metaphorically speaking, 'business at the speed of thought' (Gates, 2000). New temporal standards emerge, then diffuse outward from commerce to governance and culture more generally, heightening expectations about the pace at which 'social problems' can be addressed and legislation enacted, and upturning hitherto stable assumptions about what might be rendered do-able, or knowable, in real time. Within crime control agencies, there are now constant pressures to 'speed up' basic administrative processes – to increase rapid access to information (on databases), to accelerate decision-making, and to reduce delay – and to monitor the locations and schedules of offenders subject to community penalties (Nellis, 2003b). Compared with prison, the traditional spatial and temporal restrictions placed on an offender in the community have of necessity been somewhat limited (Nellis, 2004b). Immersion in the telecommunications environment changes that, by making possible personalized surveillance packages around particular individuals. Whether used to curfew or track, EM renders an offender's whereabouts, in whole or in part, knowable in real time. Non-compliance (absence from a specified location, presence in a specified exclusion zone) is knowable instantly, and even if it cannot be acted upon instantly, there is an electronic record of the moment(s) at which infractions occurred, available for later use in warnings or prosecution (Albrecht, 2003).

Most commentators on telecommunications accept that the technology does indeed have the potential to create dystopian, hyperregulated social environments, while acknowledging that it is not technology alone that might bring this about. Technology only creates *possibility*, including, in this instance, the possibility of supplanting older ways of dealing with lawbreakers, and the organizational forms in which they are embedded. It is politics – and the knowledge, sensibilities, hopes, fears, and ambitions that fuel politics – which creates *actuality*. The relationship between technology and politics is, however, complicated by the fact that, as David Nye (2004: 170) puts it, 'a technology's symbolic meanings may determine its uses'. Technologies (and EM is emphatically not an exception) are invariably embedded in narratives that already pre-package their supposed social utility and moral meaning. These are not immutable – far from it – but in the first instance, politicians have to work with and/or against a range of these pre-given meanings in order to fabricate a compelling narrative of their own. In England, the New Labour government has grasped that the surveillant potential of computerized telecommunications systems gives them new choices in the crime control field – choices to regulate offender behaviour in wholly new ways, to dispense with some of the old ways, or to combine the two in creative or destructive ways. While their determination to make EM central to their conception of community supervision is absolute, they have not in fact found it easy, in the face of what Bottoms (1995) calls 'populist punitiveness', to build a narrative in which EM penalties are accepted as a credible means of crime control.

'Populist punitiveness' and EM

The extent to which vindictiveness towards offenders is widespread in the general public is debatable, but it is patently articulated in influential – or at least vociferous – sections of the media (Hancock, 2004; Tonry, 2004). The introduction of EM for juveniles in February 2002 was greeted with derision in many conservative newspapers. The alleged failures of the Home Detention Curfew (HDC) scheme were seized upon by both the Conservative opposition and conservative newspapers to castigate the government, and while it was the early-release aspect of HDC, rather than EM itself, that was being criticized, the technology was tainted by association.[7] More recently, the Conservative Party (led by Michael Howard, the former Home Secretary who promoted 'prison works') took to portraying EM as a gimmicky intervention to which the government subscribes only because it is is too pusillanimous to build sufficient numbers of prisons. Some of this is mere political point-scoring, but the tenor of anticipated Conservative criticism has nonetheless set limits on the ways in which government can present EM to the public, and does serve to weaken its credibility. This has been particularly evident in respect of satellite tracking.

Media coverage of satellite tracking has thus far been entirely reactive to official initiatives – around the Carter Report, the local elections in May 2004, the Strategic Plan and, most recently, the launch of the pilot schemes – and in that sense the government might well be said to be setting, even controlling, the agenda. Each time, however, the image of satellite tracking has been slanted to offset the risk of being portrayed as 'soft on crime', and that has entailed making concessions, at least to the language of populist punitiveness. The Home Office has, by turns, underplayed the novelty of satellite tracking, linked it to already familiar penal concepts, split attention between it and something equally interesting (lie detectors for sex offenders), and blended it into a broad 'high-tech' strategy for dealing with crime. The Home Secretary's core description of satellite tracking as 'a way of keeping tabs on people' and a 'prison without bars' bears out Sturken and Thomas's (2004: 7) point that 'we talk about and represent contemporary technologies ... through metaphors and representations that defined technologies of the past'. More futuristic narratives were logically available – promoting the minister's new-found capacity to commandeer hardware in orbit above the Earth as evidence of rather exceptional potency and determination in the fight against crime, for example – but these were eschewed. Mundaneness prevailed, with Home Secretary Blunkett carefully emphasizing that tracking would even be used on 'very minor offences (sic) where we are worried about people being on community sentences but where our jails would simply be filled up in an unnecessary fashion'.

Radio, TV, and press coverage was widespread at the time of each event, but invariably gave as much prominence to derisive comments from a Conservative Opposition spokesman – who implied that the government's plans put the public at risk – as to the Home Secretary's views:

There may be sensible reasons for tagging certain prisoners. But we should not tag prisoners and let them out of jail early simply to free up space in our overcrowded prisons. *He* [Blunkett] *should build more.* This decision by the

Home Secretary is a last-minute response from a man who has run out of ideas and whose prisons are at crisis point. What kind of message does this send out to criminals, as well as the victims of crime? (David Davies, quoted in the *Daily Telegraph*, 29 May 2004: 12; emphasis added)

Subsequently, the government neutralized the threat of populist punitiveness by co-opting it, packaging the Strategic Plan as an assault on the lingering liberal sentiments that were impeding the creation of safe and secure societies in a post-September 11th world. This effectively robbed Conservative politicians of *their* platform. Nonetheless, conservative newspapers remained ambivalent about satellite tracking, with *The Times*, for example, welcoming tracking as 'the cutting edge of developments in law and order' in its main news report, but registering scepticism in its editorial:

The plan to monitor all 5000 [prolific] offenders with the tags and satellite tracking already posed for sex offenders ... deserves the benefit of the doubt. In principle it would create a 'prison without bars' in which offenders could take part in rehabilitation programmes designed to reduce recidivism. In practice, however, the technology remains unproven as a crime preventer and *could simply create an alternative to prison so unthreatening as to encourage rather than deter crime* ... If more prisons are needed, untested technology is not the answer. (*The Times*, 20 July 2004; emphasis added)

By the time of the launch itself, the press had in some respects become more sympathetic to the idea of satellite tracking, but none of the conservative papers were reconciled to the principle of artificially stabilizing the prison population. The *Sun* (3 September 2004) ran a headline, '24-hour Satellite Patrol on Beasts: sky spy stops pervs and crooks striking again', likening the technology to 'Tom Cruise's movie "Minority Report" in which cops arrest criminals before they reoffend' and claiming that 'it harnesses techniques used by the RAF to direct laser guided missiles in Iraq'. In *Sun* terms, these are definite boosts to tracking's credibility – yet its editorial expressed 'Nagging Doubts' about releasing paedophiles at all. The *Daily Star* (3 September 2004) editorial, headed 'Keep Jails AND Tags', welcomed the use of 'cutting-edge technology to fight against crime', compared it with earlier 'breakthroughs' like CCTV and DNA profiling, but claimed that although 'this project will deter [offenders] from committing further offences ... Mr Blunkett mustn't dispense with tried and trusted measures – like prison.' The *Daily Mail* (3 September 2004) was arguably the most hostile, portraying the initiative as 'another bit of high-tech headline grabbing gadgetry', mocking GPS's limitations 'around tall buildings and tunnels', and reminding readers that 'thousands of crimes have already been committed by offenders released early from jail wearing existing tags'. Among the broadsheets, the *Daily Telegraph* was similarly scathing:

Mr Blunkett said the technology 'will allow us to develop and promote the tough community sentences which are vital if we are to prevent re-offending'. In other words, we have yet to see the alternatives to custody that will command the confidence of the public. We have been promised these for years, but they, too, are expensive to develop, and there is the suspicion that the money is not available for them either. He should rely less on technology that purports to offer virtual incarceration and opt instead for the real thing by building a few more prisons – with bars. (*Daily Telegraph*, 3 September 2004)

The Strategic Plan may never be implemented as written. Already the plan to introduce NOMS – the centrepiece of the Carter report – has been postponed (but not abandoned) after massive criticism of the scale and pace of the proposed reforms. Even with a rich array of tough community penalties and greater control over sentencer discretion, the prison population may not 'stabilize' at 80,000, in which case EM, including satellite tracking, could still develop in tandem with it, lower down the tariff, as a normal and commonplace characteristic – perhaps *the* defining attribute – of community supervision, to which, just occasionally, rehabilitative or educational measures might be tacked on.

Conclusion

EM is undeniably new but in its present forms it does not entirely embody all the characteristics of the new punitiveness – and, significantly, it has been dismissed in some quarters as not punitive enough. Thus far, however, this has done no more than limit the scale of its development – it has not discredited it. To fully understand why EM is becoming so prominent in penal debate in England and Wales and how it fits with the undeniably harsh trends in British penal policy, it helps to acknowledge that there are still three distinct and competing discourses in play within 'western European' penality (Peters, 1988; Rutherford, 1993; Feeley and Simon, 1994; Cavadino *et al.*, 2000; Scheerer, 2001). These writers do not wholly concur on the characteristics of the three discourses, but there is sufficient affinity between them to believe that they are making robust and realistic distinctions. The terms 'punitive-repressive', 'managerial-surveillant', and 'humanistic-rehabilitative' readily signify the ethos of each discourse. There are national variations among them, points of overlap between them, and tensions, inconsistences, and gradations of opinion within them. All these factors make a difference to the precise way in which penal politics play out, but I am concerned here with the bigger picture, with the probable and possible trajectories of each discourse, and the more general impact that each has on the others.

Punitive-repressive discourse aims to maximize the delivery of pain to offenders. It tends to privilege the use of imprisonment, either for short periods to teach errant young people a lesson, or for natural life in the case of some murderers. Some within this discourse subscribe to capital punishment, and sometimes corporal punishment. It can be both elitist or populist, although punitive elites in democracies often justify their sentiments by appealing to the allegedly visceral instincts of ordinary, decent citizens. The suffering of crime victims is invariably cited as a moral basis for inflicting equivalent or greater suffering on the offender. There tends to be no belief that offenders are reformable or redeemable, merely that they can be frightened (deterred) into law-abidingness or have their spirits broken, in or out of prison. The fiscal costs of punishment are largely dismissed as irrelevant, although it is imagined that costs would be reduced if prisons were made more austere. In the past, community penalties have mostly figured in the punitive-repressive discourse as objects of derision – they have not been regarded as meaningful punishments, and if they were to be used they should be visibly humiliating, enforced on a zero-tolerance basis and always backed by imprisonment. EM, to the chagrin and surprise of some of its supporters, has not been seen as significantly different from other community penalties; at best, even with satellite tracking, scepticism prevails.

Managerial-surveillant discourse elaborates on the technocratic rationality – the logical and unemotional configuration of means and ends – which Max Weber identified as the defining characteristic of modernity. Since the late twentieth century the body of knowledge called 'new public management' – glossed simply as 'managerialism' by a number of commentators – has given refined and sophisticated expression to it. It imports concepts, practices, and standards from the commercial world as part of a strategy for improving the efficiency and effectiveness of putatively ailing public services. It embodies neoliberal values, favouring command and control structures, competition, commodification, and marketization. By setting tight targets and deadlines, specifying outcomes, constantly monitoring their attainment, perhaps penalizing their non-attainment, traditional organizational cultures can be 're-engineered'. Moral judgement never matters: the human objects of managerialist attention are neither bad nor good – they are merely manipulable. Cost-efficiency becomes an end in itself, superseding values that have hitherto given purpose to an organization and motivated its professional staff. Surveillance (in the broad sense of information gathering) is integral to the operation of managerialism (Dandeker, 1990; Jones, 2000). Scheerer (2001: 251) further observes that it 'gives a boon to technical controls that display some kind of elective affinity to it' and sees just 'such an elective affinity between managerialism and electronic monitoring'.

Humanistic-rehabilitative discourse articulates a belief that criminality can be educated or counselled out of individual offenders, especially if certain kinds of practical help with employment, accommodation, addiction, and family relationships are also offered, and if equality of opportunity prevails. It concedes that offenders may have to be coerced, even imprisoned, but such constraints are only defensible in the service of higher moral ends, and their worst 'side-effects' are deliberately ameliorated to ensure attainment of those ends. The Probation Service built its mid-to-late twentieth-century identity around these beliefs, its interventions ranging from 'tough love' to psychologically based behavioural interventions. Latterly, restorative justice and a commitment to human rights have been encompassed by this discourse, partly in response to allegations of Eurocentric bias in the traditional construction of humanistic values (Lyotard, 1991; Margalit, 1996). Such values can be expressed in secular language, but defences of their relevance to criminal justice – in terms of the redeemability of even the worst of offenders – are increasingly underpinned by theological insights (Gorringe, 2004). While generally anxious about the intrusiveness of surveillance, the more confident versions of humanistic-rehabilitative discourse claim that techno-scientific developments can and indeed must be used for civilized ends – medicine most obviously, but EM too, within limits.

With these discourses in mind, it can be said that EM (in the broadest sense) is primarily grounded in, and expressive of, the managerial-surveillant enterprise – it facilitates the efficient, fine-grained regulation of human action in time and space. As a cutting-edge technology, it appeals to politicians who are self-conscious modernizers, affording both new possibilities and a chance to repudiate the encumbrances of tradition. This is the basis of EM's growing prominence in New Labour's penal strategy. It has been used, discursively, to erode confidence in merely humanistic interventions (such as those run by the Probation Service) and in that sense alone it has arguably contributed to the birth of the new punitiveness, because the incremental removal of the ethical constraints traditionally supplied by humanism does tend to unleash the atavistic. But the vision of social order implicit in techno-scientific managerialism (of which EM is an aspect) is not itself atavistic – as Pratt (2002: 187) rightly observes, managerialist precepts tend 'to provide a buffer against the outright domination of popular sentiment on penal development'. That does not mean, however, that the managerialist vision is not alarming in its own right. It points towards a future dominated by what Lyotard (1991) calls 'the inhuman' – the relentless reduction of human beings to mere units of productivity or consumption, in particular the eradication of empathy, reflection, and discretion in public (administrative and legal) life and its replacement by purely rule-based operations. Highly managerialized organizations (such as contemporary criminal justice agencies) tend inexorably towards rule-based governance – demanding simple obedience and discouraging independent thought and action – but computerized monitoring technology greatly amplifies the capacity for it (Jones, 2000). What Lianos and Douglas (2000) call 'automated socio-technical environments' already exist; EM systems are prototypical examples.

Nonetheless, while it is possible to envisage a totalitarian trajectory for managerialism, independent of, and perhaps at odds with, the momentum of the new punitiveness (see Los, 2003), perceived weaknesses in the current forms of EM will continue to invite criticism. Two aspects of contemporary EM mean that it does fall short of what, from a punitive-repressive perspective, a serious punishment should be. Firstly, despite past references to it as 'electronic incarceration', 'electronic ball and chain', 'virtual prison', 'home detention', and most recently 'prison without bars'– it is not a properly incapacitative penalty. As with traditional community penalties, the offender's consent and cooperation (however coerced or reluctant) are necessary to make it workable. Tags can be removed, and locational regulations ignored – or crimes can be committed while the tag is being worn. Surveillance-based compliance with a community penalty may well be more onerous than incentive-based, trust-based, and threat-based compliance (the traditional means of securing compliance with community penalties), but it does not dispense with an offender's willingness to act prudently and responsibly (Nellis, 2004c). There is thus a sense in which, compared with the locks, bolts and bars of prison, EM leaves an offender 'free'.

Secondly, and paradoxically in the light of the first, EM may also seem 'unpunitive' because only a difference of degree is perceived between the kind of surveillant regulation which it entails and the routine and commonplace regulation which ordinary citizens themselves nowadays experience. To a greater or lesser degree, surveillance makes us all 'unfree'. The capacity to pinpoint and locate offenders is not a particularly distinctive phenomenon in late modernity. Our willingness to be watched by ubiquitous CCTV systems, our collective immersion in telecommunication and financial networks, our participation in managerialized workplaces mean that we are all somewhat locatable and traceable, and by and large we are seduced by the narratives that present this as convenience, reassurance, and pleasure. While there is still a subjectively distinctive difference between court-ordered locatability and the self-imposed locatability and traceability entailed by cellphones, credit cards, car-locator devices, and child-safety tracking systems, EM in its present law-enforcement forms can seem to lack the necessary degree of 'less eligibility' that makes punishment publicly plausible (Sparks, 1996).

In the light of this, even while the managerial-surveillant discourse remains ascendant, it is likely that the 'punitive weight' of EM will eventually be increased. Shorn of humanizing civilities, coarsened by media-hyped anxieties about crime, a combination of political demand and new thinking from research and development sites within the 'commercial-corrections complex' may well stimulate the development of more onerous and meticulous forms of EM, or generate still more innovative technologies of behavioural regulation (derived, say, from gene therapy, neurology, or psychopharmacology). At its most mundane, the 'toughening' of EM – akin to the processes that 'toughened' probation and community service in the late twentieth century – may entail a lengthening of curfew hours, a lengthening of the period subject to EM, or, perhaps, visibly humiliating tags. Beyond that, far more speculatively, lies the possibility of unremovable (implanted?) tags which give electric shocks if the perimeters of exclusion zones are breached, or which inject slow-acting thought- or mood-altering drugs. Given the contribution allegedly made by a 'Spiderman' comic to EM's American origins (Fox, 1987), we should not disparage the role of science fiction in stimulating the techno-correctional imagination in the longer term (Sobchack, 2004) – or of warning us of what is to come. 'As Bill Gates of Microsoft has said, people tend to overestimate the changes that will take place in the next two years, but they also tend to underestimate the changes that will take place within the next ten years' (Scheerer, 2001: 248). In its original manifestation in England, EM took criminology by surprise – and we are still catching up. That should not happen again.

Notes

1 Publications such as the *Police Science and Technology Strategy* (Home Office, 2003), as well as the Home Office's own website, testify to the burgeoning importance of new technology. So too does the emergence of *Criminal Justice Management*, an independent bi-monthly magazine from the GovNet Communications group. It circulates widely among criminal justice personnel, and its annual London-based conference is becoming a key fixture for policy-makers and commercial and technical interests in criminal justice.

2 In 1999 the Home Office divided England and Wales into four regions and after a process of competitive tendering awarded three companies contracts to deliver EM: Securicor in the north, Premier in the Midlands and London, and Reliance in the

south. After 2005, there will be five regions. New providers may or may not emerge, possibly from the USA, which Martin Narey, the Commissioner for Correctional Services, has visited to encourage private contractors to show an interest in the commercial opportunities created by the emergence of NOMS.

3   The satellite tracking of offenders began in the USA, experimentally, in 1996. Numbers increased from 40 to 1200 by 2002 (700 of them in Florida) (Renzema, 1999; 2000; personal communication 11 March 2002). See Nellis and Lilly (2004) for an update on GPS tracking in the USA.

4   Sarah's murder prompted major public debate on whether to release sex offenders from prison and how to manage them in the community. 'Populist punitive' demands for an equivalent of America's 'Megan's Law' (full public/local knowledge of offenders' whereabouts) were deflected by the creation of new joint police/probation collaborative arrangements to intensively supervise such offenders, the Multi-Agency Public Protection Panels. These agencies may play a part in decisions on whom to use GPS tracking.

5   The Asylum and Immigration (Treatment of Claimants etc.) Act 2004 indicates that EM will be linked to bail, and could be used to enforce a 'residence restriction' (akin to a curfew), a 'reporting restriction' (presence at a location to which they have been directed to go), and/or an 'employment restriction' (presence at a place of work, or the prevention of employment). Asylum-seeker support groups are hostile to the use of EM, which they see as the wholly unethical application of a criminal justice measure to a non-criminal group of people (Beynon, 2004).

6   The GPS system was created by the US Department of Defense in 1978, to serve the navigational needs of 40,000 military (army, navy, airforce) users (Enge, 2004). Civil and commercial uses were always anticipated, although the whole system is still run from the Schriever Airforce base in Colorado. Civil use began in the 1980s, and increased rapidly as the full network of 24 satellites and associated ground stations necessary for continuous service came into being. Only 8 per cent of the network's users are now military. Western Europe is developing its own system of geolocation satellites, called Galileo, to be operational by 2010.

7   Some conservative newspapers persistently disparage EM by associating it with particularly 'undeserving' offenders (Nellis, 2003c). The decision to release two known racist offenders on Home Detention Curfew (the early release scheme), even though it was within the rules, was condemned in the *Daily Mail* (25 January 2003). The more routine cases receiving HDC , and the high rates of compliance, are rarely reported. The extension of the HDC early release period to 135 days in April 2003, for example, was dismissed as 'crackpot' by the *Daily Express* (11 April 2004), under a headline which announced 'Villains to Leave Prison Even Earlier'.

References

Albrecht, H-J (2003) 'The Place of Electronic Monitoring in The Development of Criminal Punishment and Systems of Sanctions', in M. Mayer, R. Haverkamp and R. Levy (eds) *Will Electronic Monitoring Have a Future in Europe?*, Freiburg: Max Planck Institute: 249–264.

Bauman, Z. (1998) *Globalisation: The Human Consequences*, Cambridge: Polity Press.

Beynon, R. (2004) 'Big Brother's Heavy Hand', *Bulletin of the Joint Council for the Welfare of Immigrants*, Autumn 2004: 6–7.

Blair, T. (2004) 'Foreword', in *Confident Communities in a Secure Society: The Home Office Strategic Plan 2004–08*, London: The Stationery Office, Cm 6287.

Bloomfield, B. (2001) 'In the Right Place at the Right Time: Electronic Tagging and Problems of Social Order/disorder', *The Sociological Review*, 49(2): 174–201.

Blunkett, D. (2004) 'Foreword', in *Confident Communities in a Secure Society: The Home Office Strategic Plan 2004–08*, London: The Stationery Office, Cm 6287.

Bottomley, K., Hucklesby, A. and Mair, G. (2004) *The New Uses of Electronic Monitoring: Findings from the Implementation Phase*, London: National Association of Probation Officers.

Bottoms, A. E. (1995b) 'The Philosophy and Politics of Punishment and Sentencing', in C. Clarkson and R. Morgan (eds) *The Politics of Sentencing Reform*, Oxford: Clarendon Press.

Bottoms, A. E., Rex, S. and Gelsthorpe, L. (2000) 'Concluding Reflections', in A. E. Bottoms, S. Rex and L. Gelsthorpe (2000) (eds) *Community Penalties: Change and Challenges*, Cullompton: Willan: 226–240.

Carter, P. (2003) *Managing Offenders, Reducing Crime: A New Approach*, London: Cabinet Office (*The Correctional Services Review*).

Cavadino, M., Crow, I. and Dignan, J. (2000) *Criminal Justice 2000: Strategies for a New Century*, Winchester: Waterside.

Chinn, W. (2001) 'Technology, Industry and War 1945–1991', in G. Jensen and A. Wiest (eds) *War in the Age of Technology*, London: New York University Press: 42–65.

Coyle, A. (2001) 'Technocorrections – A Vision of the Post Modern Prison', *Prison Service Journal*, 134: 2–4.

Dandeker, C. (1990) *Surveillance, Power and Modernity*, Cambridge: Polity Press.

Davies, S. (1996) *Big Brother: Britain's Web of Surveillance and the New Technological Order*. London: Pan.

Dmatek (2002) *Annual Report 2002*, Tel Aviv: Dmatek.

Enge, P. (2004) 'Retooling the Global Positioning System', *Scientific American*, May 2004: 64–71.

Fay, S. J. (1993) 'The Rise and Fall of Tagging as a Criminal Justice Measure in Britain', *International Journal of the Sociology of Law*, 21: 301–317.

Feeley, M. and Simon, J. (1994) 'Actuarial Justice: The Emerging New Criminal Law', in D. Nelken (ed.) *The Future(s) of Criminology*, London: Sage, 173–201.

Fionda, J. (2000) 'New Managerialism, Credibility and the Sanitisation of Criminal Justice', in P. Green and P. Rutherford (eds) *Criminal Policy in Transition*, Oxford: Hart Publishing, 109–130.

Fox, R. G. (1987) 'Dr Schwitzgebel's Machine Revisited: Electronic Monitoring of Offenders', *Australian and New Zealand Journal of Criminology*, 20: 131–147.

Gates, B. (2000) *Business at the Speed of Thought*, Harmondsworth: Penguin.

Gorringe, T. (2004) *Crime*, London: SPCK.

Graham, S. (1999) 'Geographies of Surveillant Stimulation', in M. Crang, P. Crang and J. May (eds) *Virtual Geographies: Bodies, Space and Relations*, London: Routledge, 131–148.

Haggerty, K. and Ericson, R. (2000) 'The Surveillant Assemblage', *British Journal of Sociology*, 51(4): 605–622.

Hancock, L. (2004) 'Criminal Justice, Public Opinion, Fear and Popular Politics', in J. Muncie and D. Wilson (eds) *Student Handbook of Criminal Justice and Criminology*, London: Cavendish, 51–66.

Home Office (1988) *Punishment, Custody and the Community*, London: Home Office, Cm. 424.

Home Office (1990) *Crime, Justice and Protecting the Public*, London: Home Office, Cm. 965.

Home Office (1997) *Electronic Monitoring: The Future of Community Punishment*, Home Office Press Release, 12 September.

Home Office (2003) *Police Science and Technology Strategy 2003–2008*, London: Home Office.

Home Office (2004a) *Reducing Crime, Changing Lives: The Government's Plans for Transforming the Management of Offenders*, London: Home Office.

Home Office (2004b) *Confident Communities in a Secure Society: The Home Office Strategic Plan 2004–08*, London: The Stationery Office, Cm 6287.

Home Office (2004c) *Guidance on the Piloting of Satellite Tracking Technology to Monitor Exclusion Orders and Prisoners on Licence*, London: Home Office.

Jones, R. (2000) 'Digital Rule: Punishment, Control and Technology', *Punishment and Society*, 2(1): 5–22.

Lianos, M. and Douglas, M. (2000) 'Dangerisation and the End of Deviance: The Institutional Environment', in D. Garland and R. Sparks (eds) *Criminology and Social Theory*, Oxford: Oxford University Press, 103–126.

Lilly, J. R. (1992) 'Selling Justice: Electronic Monitoring and the Security Industry', *Justice Quarterly*, 9(3): 493–503.

Lilly, J. R. and Knepper, P. (1993) 'The Corrections-Commercial Complex', *Crime and Delinquency*, 39(2): 150–166.

Los, M. (2003) 'The Technologies of Total Domination', *Surveillance and Society*, 2(1): 15–38. http://www.surveillance-and-society.org.

Lyon, D. (2003) *Surveillance After September 11*, Cambridge: Polity Press.

Lyotard, J-F (1991) *The Inhuman: Reflections on Time*, Oxford: Blackwell.

Margalit, A. (1996) *The Decent Society*, Harvard: Harvard University Press.

McAuley, P. (2002) *Whole Wide World*, London: Harper Collins.

Mclaughlin, E., Muncie, J. and Hughes, G. (2001) 'The Permanent Revolution; New Labour, New Public Management and the Modernisation of Criminal Justice', *Criminal Justice*, 1(3): 301–318.

Nash, M. and Ryan, M. (2003) 'Modernising and Joining-Up Government: The Case of the Prison and Probation Services', *Contemporary Politics*, 9(2): 157–169.

Nellis, M. (1991) 'The Electronic Monitoring of Offenders in England and Wales: Recent Developments and Future Prospects', *British Journal of Criminology*, 31(2): 165–185.

Nellis, M. (2003a) 'Electronic Monitoring and the Future of the Probation Service', in W. H. Chui and M. Nellis (eds) *Moving Probation Forward: Evidence Arguments and Practice*, Harlow: Longmans, 245–257.

Nellis, M. (2003b) 'Community Justice, Time and the New National Probation Service', *Howard Journal*, 41(4): 59–86.

Nellis, M. (2003c) 'News Media and Popular Cultural Representations of Electronic Monitoring in England and Wales', in *Howard Journal*, 42(1): 1–31.

Nellis, M. (2004a) '"I Know Where You Live": Electronic Monitoring and Penal Policy in England and Wales 1999–2004', *British Journal of Community Justice*, 2(3): 33–59.

Nellis, M. (2004b) 'The "Tracking" Controversy: The Roots of Mentoring and Electronic Monitoring', *Youth Justice*, 4(2): 77–99.

Nellis, M. (2004c) 'Electronic Monitoring and the Community Supervision of Offenders', in A. E. Bottoms, S. Rex and G. Robinson (eds) *Alternatives to Prison*, Cullompton: Willan, 224–247.

Nellis, M. and Lilly, B. (2004) 'GPS Tracking: What America and England Might Learn from Each Other', *Journal of Offender Monitoring*, 17(2): 5–26.

Norris, C. and Armstrong, G. (1999) 'The Maximum Surveillance Society: *The Rise of CCTV*', Oxford: Berg.

Nye, D. (2004) 'Technological Prediction: a Promethean Problem', in M. Sturken, D. Thomas and S. J. Ball-Rokeach (eds) *Technological Visions: The Hopes and Fears that Shape New Technology*, Philadelphia: Temple University Press, 159–176.

Peters, A. G. (1988) 'Main Currents in Criminal Law Theory', in Jan van Dyjk *et al.* (eds) *Criminal Law in Action*, Deventer: Kluwer, 19–36.

Pratt, J. (2002) *Punishment and Civilisation*, London: Sage.

Rex, S. and Tonry, M. (eds) (2002) *Reform and Punishment: The Future of Sentencing*, Cullompton: Willan.

Reynolds, D. (2000) *One World Divisible: A Global History Since 1945*, Harmondsworth: Penguin.

Rutherford, A. (1993) *Criminal Justice and the Pursuit of Decency*, Oxford: Oxford University Press.

Scheerer, S. (2000) 'Three Trends into the New Millennium: The Managerial, the Populist and the Road Towards Global Justice', in P. Green and A. Rutherford (eds) *Criminal Justice in Transition*, Oxford: Hart Publishing, 243–260.

Snelgrove, B. (2003) 'Electronic Monitoring: Meeting the Needs of our Stakeholders', paper presented at Bidder's Conference for Contracts and Tenders, London, 21 July.

Sobchack, V. (2004) 'Science Fiction Film and the Technological Imagination', in M. Sturken, D. Thomas and S. J. Ball-Rokeach (eds) *Technological Visions: The Hopes and Fears that Shape New Technology*, Philadelphia: Temple University Press, 145–158.

Sparks, R. (1996) 'Penal Austerity: The Doctrine of Less Eligibility Reborn?', in R. Matthews and P. Francis (eds) *Prisons 2000: An International Perspective on the Current State and Future of Imprisonment*, Basingstoke: Macmillan, 74–93.

Stacey, T. (1989) 'Why Tagging Should be Used to Reduce Incarceration', *Social Work Today*, 20 April: 18–19.

Sturken, M. and Thomas, D. (2004) 'Technological Visions and the Rhetoric of the New', in M. Sturken, D. Thomas and S. J. Ball-Rokeach (eds) *Technological Visions: The Hopes and Fears that Shape New Technology*, Philadelphia: Temple University Press, 1–18.

Tonry, M. (2003) (ed) *Confronting Crime: Crime Control under New Labour*, Cullompton: Willan.

Tonry, M. (2004) *Punishment and Politics: Evidence and Emulation in the Making of English Crime Control Policy*, Cullompton: Willan.

Toon, J. (2003) 'Electronic Monitoring: The Now and the Not Yet', paper presented at Bidder's Conference for Contracts and Tenders, London, 21 July.

Whitfield, D. (1997) *Tackling the Tag: The Electronic Monitoring of Offenders*, Winchester: Waterside Press.

Whitfield, D. (2001) *The Magic Bracelet: Offender Supervision and Technology*, Winchester: Waterside Press.

Part 3

Non-punitive Societies

11. Levels of punitiveness in Scandinavia: description and explanations

Ulla V. Bondeson

In this chapter I will examine the thesis of Pratt in *Punishment and Civilization* (2002: 146) that penal policy in modern society departed from the civilizing process at the beginning of the 1980s, but with Scandinavia as an exception. His arguments, to support the contention that the Scandinavian countries had some built-in defences against this, were that (i) the welfare structure of these countries was open and consultative, and (ii) the Scandinavian countries enjoyed high levels of functional democratization.

I will begin by presenting crime rates as set out in official statistics and victimization studies to see whether criminality is different in Scandinavia compared with other European countries (Scandinavia is here defined as including Denmark, Finland, Norway, and Sweden). Criminal justice policy will be studied mainly by reference to imprisonment rates to investigate whether they are different and whether there has been a change in the last few decades. Fear of crime and punitive attitudes will then be examined in order to study how they are related to criminality and criminal justice policy, and the media will be introduced as an intervening variable. The welfare model will be analysed for any influence it may have on crime rates and/or criminal justice policy; community involvement will be examined and, finally, other interpretations of changes in criminal policy will be presented.

Crime rates

An updated overview of 'Crime and the Reaction to Crime in Scandinavia' has been written by von Hofer (2004) and serves as a useful introduction. According to official statistics, crime rates have been increasing in all the Scandinavian countries at least since the beginning of the 1960s. Westfelt (2001) compared crime trends in Scandinavia with those in Austria, England and Wales, France, Germany, and the Netherlands. The Scandinavian countries all exhibit much the same increasing trends for the crimes of theft and assault as the other nations of Europe. Several authors have also noted a striking similarity between the trends over the past 50 years, despite different criminal justice systems (see also Bondeson, 1998a).

Clearance rates have fallen in the Scandinavian as well as in other European countries, approximately halving over the past 50 years. While the above five Western European countries started off at a somewhat higher level than the Scandinavian countries, they all end up in year 2000 at about the same level; hence the drop has been more accentuated for the other European countries (von Hofer, 2004). The curves for Norway, Denmark, and Sweden have fairly parallel courses, with a decrease from around 40 to 20 per cent, while Finland has had a clearance rate almost double that of the other Nordic countries. These falling curves may be interpreted as a drop in police efficiency but other factors may also be contributing.

When making cross-national comparisons of levels of crime, victimization studies are usually considered to be a better instrument than official statistics, due to variations in the collection and production of statistics in different countries. Those studies, carried out at different intervals in the individual Scandinavian countries, seem to be in accordance with the official statistics inasmuch as Sweden ranks highest, closely followed by Denmark, with Finland and Norway on a lower level (Bondeson, 2003: 22–23). Comparing all eleven offence types, the Danish and Swedish level come very close to the average for Europe (van Kesteren *et al.*, 2000). Thus, both the rank order and the level of criminality seem to be corroborated by victimization studies compared with official statistics.

Criminal justice policy

The punitiveness of the criminal justice systems will be mainly illustrated here by imprisonment rates. Prison populations have been fairly stable in Denmark, Norway, and Sweden over the past 50 years. Finland has been a remarkable exception, with extremely high levels of incarceration of about 200 per 100,000 of population around 40 years ago, which have since reduced to about the same level as the other Nordic countries. The dramatic reduction in the use of imprisonment has been explained by concerted actions by the correctional and political elites (Lappi-Seppälä, 2000), influenced in part by criminological research showing the exceptional nature of high Finnish imprisonment rates, partly due to very long sentences. The decisive factor was the attitudinal readiness of the civil service, judiciary, and the prison authorities from that time to use all available means in order to bring down the number of prisoners (see also Christie, 2000: 48–52).

However, over a period the number of prison sentences has increased in Scandinavia, most in Denmark and least in Sweden. The difference in correctional statistics can be accounted for by the shortening of the sentences. Prison sentences imposed are longer in Sweden and Finland than in Denmark and Norway. There has been an increase in the number of prisoners over the five-year period 1997–2001 of about 10 per cent, with the exception of Denmark (Nordisk Statistik, 2003).

The detention rates per 100,000 inhabitants have been around 60 in Scandinavia, almost 50 per cent less than the average of other European countries. In 2000 the incarceration rates were 64 in Denmark, 63 in Sweden, 57 in Norway, and 52 in Finland (European Sourcebook, 2003: 196). More detailed comparison between the Scandinavian countries is difficult due to yearly fluctuations: in 2001 the same figures were 58 in Denmark, 69 in Sweden, 58 in Norway, and 60 in Finland (Barclay and Tavares, 2003:7). Comparing the prison populations per 100,000 population from 2000 to 2003, there are increases in all the Scandinavian countries, with Sweden and Denmark ending up at the highest level of 72 (von Hofer, 2004).

No clear change in penal trends can be discerned, though, from the beginning of the 1980s. Sentences, however, have become more extended, particularly those related to drug crimes. This has also lately led to partial overcrowding where prisoners have had to share cells, a new phenomenon in most Scandinavian countries, at least in the post-war period. Another indicator of a more repressive criminal policy over recent years can be seen in the increasing number of sentences to life imprisonment, particularly in Sweden and Finland. The number of 'lifers' at the end of 2003 was 17 in Denmark, 100 in Finland, and 123 in Sweden, but none in Norway, which abolished this sanction in 1981 (it should be observed that a life sentence in Scandinavia traditionally does not mean a lifetime). In Sweden the pronounced treatment ideology has been partially abandoned by a philosophy called the 'penal value of crime'. This underlines the traditional proportionality principle but adds that treatment is an important element in corrections but not as a justification of punishment.

Generally, prisons in Scandinavia remain small and to a certain extent open. They usually have a capacity of under 50 places and not more than 500. Staffing levels are generally high. Perhaps this is one of the reasons why interaction between staff and inmates is less antagonistic in Scandinavian prisons than has been demonstrated in American prisons. However, clear signs of criminal subcultures and a prisonization process have been confirmed in all types of correctional institutions in Sweden (Bondeson, 1989). Recidivism rates are also very high: more than four in five reoffend by way of serious crimes within a ten-year period. In a survival analysis, prisonization is also causally related to recidivism (ibid.: 277–293).

Despite several correctional reforms, much constancy in the patterns of the criminal subcultures in the Scandinavian countries can be observed. The number of foreign prisoners has been greater in Sweden than in the other Nordic countries. The increasing proportion of foreigners in the prison population in that country seems to be making for a tougher climate in prisons at the moment, and has become a highly charged issue due to some dramatic escapes from closed prisons.

Explanations of crime rates and criminal policy

A first conclusion seems to be that crime rates are not related to criminal justice policy. For more than half a century registered criminality has been increasing drastically although the criminal justice systems have remained very much the same. Also, while crime rates in Scandinavia seem to be around the European average, the imprisonment rates are much lower. This general independence of crime and criminal justice policy has previously been noted by several authors (Blumstein, 1997; Shinkai and Zvekic, 1999).

Fear of crime and punitive attitudes

Pratt (2002: 182) states that there seems little doubt that the public mood became more sharply punitive from around 1980 onwards than had been the case in the previous 20 years, and refers to Walker and Hough (1988). Roberts *et al.* (2003) similarly point to a penal populism from the mid-1980s. They declare that public opinion has played a pivotal role in the sentencing reforms designed to increase prison numbers that have been proposed or enacted in the five countries included in their study: the United States, the United Kingdom, Canada, Australia, and New Zealand.

An interesting question is whether fear of crime and punitive attitudes are less pronounced in the Scandinavian countries despite similar crime levels to other European countries. Feelings of security measured by the question, 'How safe do you feel walking alone after dark in the area where you live?' (Eurobarometer 58.0; see European Commission, 2003), show that Denmark, Finland, and Sweden have much higher levels of security than the average of other European countries. Danish respondents particularly have an exceptionally large percentage answering that they feel very safe (60 per cent). My earlier comparative study of the Nordic countries also demonstrates that Danes express the highest levels of security, with Norway on an average level (Bondeson, 2003: 77–78). Although there has been an increase in the feelings of insecurity in Denmark, Sweden and Finland from 1996 to 2002, they still remain on a much lower level than the average European level (Denmark 15 per cent, Finland 19 per cent, and Sweden 21 per cent while EU 15 has 35 per cent).

However, when the question is formulated as to whether respondents fear being victims of specific crimes, the picture changes dramatically. Here Sweden and Finland in particular but also Denmark show much higher perceived levels of risk of theft but also of burglary, and for the two first countries also, for risk of assault as well as risk of robbery. Hence, there is little covariation between the different questions of security. People can evidently see the risk of being victimized without feeling afraid of, for example, going out alone at night. Could the Scandinavian attitude be seen as a more enlightened and rational approach? The answer to this question is complicated when it is taken into account that police numbers are much lower in the Scandinavian countries than in most other European countries, amounting to about half the size per capita (see European Sourcebook, 2003: 30, where the four Scandinavian countries form a cluster lower than all the other European countries).

As to punitive attitudes, Pratt points out that these have become harsher in many countries since the 1980s (2002: 163). Again, different kinds of questions evidently give divergent results. The general question whether sentencing is too harsh or too mild always seems to produce the result that the public thinks sentencing is too mild. But when more specific questions are asked, respondents give much more moderate answers. This is evident from my Scandinavian survey, which asked 'What is your general opinion about the severity of punishment in this country?'. More than two-thirds of those questioned answered that it was too mild and only 2 per cent that is was too severe (Bondeson, 2003: 96 ff.). The highest figures for criticizing leniency can be observed in Sweden, where a toughening of punitive attitudes could be seen over time. Milder attitudes in Finland should probably be seen against a stricter penal policy that prevailed there at the time.

However, a very different picture emerges from another question concerning the criminal status and perceived seriousness of 15 crimes or deviant acts. The respondents were asked to state whether each was an offence, and if so what type of punishment it should receive. The wide distribution of answers on a scale of eight different types of punishment indicates that there is little correspondence between public opinion and criminal justice policy. Here people rated more acts less severely rather than more severely compared with judicial opinion (ibid.: 68 ff). In other words, the general public in the Scandinavian countries seem more tolerant and less punitive than their judges.

In an earlier study it was also found that public opinion was less repressive than judicial opinion. However, judges perceived ordinary people to be more severe than they really were (Bondeson, 1980), and were therefore giving unnecessarily punitive sentences because they thought that this was what the public wanted. For a summary of studies showing that the public is not harsher than the courts and that criminal justice professionals and politicians have an exaggerated view of the punitiveness of the public, see Roberts and Stalans (2000: 210–213).

In my own Scandinavian studies, people have always demonstrated a great willingness to accept alternative sanctions to imprisonment, even being prepared to consider sanctions not yet on the statute books. Compensatory damages as an alternative to imprisonment is, for example, accepted as a possible alternative by as much as 60 per cent in Norway and Sweden although such a sanction does not exist (Bondeson, 2003: 100–102). This is not unique to Scandinavia: for example, several reports from the Home Office show similar results, which again seems to indicate that the British general public are not necessarily very punitive (Kershaw *et al.*, 2001).

Focusing upon the treatment of youth criminality, some divergent results emerge. The International Crime Victimization Study asked respondents to choose which of a variety of sanctions they felt to be most suitable for a 20-year-old male found guilty of his *second* burglary, this time stealing a colour television set in the process. Given the choice between fine, prison sentence, community service, suspended sentence, or any other sentence, 16 per cent of the Finnish respondents chose a prison sentence, 18 per cent of the Norwegians, 20 per cent of the Danish, and 26 per cent of the Swedish. Here the Scandinavian countries do not deviate much from the European average, contrasting with England and Wales and the USA, where prison sentences are advocated to a much greater extent, in fact by more than half (van Kesteren *et al.*, 2000: 219). The Eurobarometer (European Commission, 2003), however, gives the Scandinavian countries a different profile on the question 'Do you agree that the following are effective ways of reducing the amount of crime committed by young people?'. The proportion of respondents choosing the alternative 'tougher jail sentences' shows Sweden on the lowest level, followed by Denmark and then Finland, all below the average of the European countries. There does not seem to be any evident interpretation of the different results.

It thus seems possible that a milder criminal policy could partly be explained by less fear of crime and less punitive attitudes in the Scandinavian public. The media act as an important intervening variable (cf. Garland, 2000; Cavender, 2004). Again it is possible that the media in Nordic countries exercise a more restraining role, relatively speaking. Ethical rules for journalists are probably stricter than in many other countries. In Sweden, for example, crime journalists are not supposed to give the names or photographs of suspected criminals, and journalists have been invited by the Swedish Crime Preventive Council to participate in classes in criminology. There also seems to be a significant absence of the tabloid press in Scandinavia, a factor noted by Lappi-Seppälä (2000) in his analysis of what allowed the Finnish prison population to decline so much. In other words, whether it is because of language differences or other reasons, media moguls have kept away from Scandinavia. As a result, the mass media anti-crime and more punishment campaigns, so prevalent in Britain and Australia especially, have had less presence or impact in these North European countries.

Welfare model and functional democracy

The provocative question now is whether the Scandinavian welfare model could be a factor in creating the milder criminal policy. It can first be stated that the welfare level does not seem to have had any impact on the crime level. It seems quite realistic, though, to assume that welfare has had an impact on the criminal justice system.

It might be worthwhile to investigate whether the total expenditures on crime prevention measures and on the correctional system have been different in the Scandinavian countries as compared with other European countries. However, such statistics do not seem to be available. It appears reasonable to conclude that the ideology of the welfare model with its emphasis on rational and humanitarian belief systems would also impact on the criminal justice system. A welfare model implies that every citizen should have a decent standard of living and that there should be no great inequality between different social groups, and also that there should be solidarity among people. The solidarity principle should also include the less privileged, i.e. the socially and economically poorest groups, which generally are considerably over-represented in our prisons (Friestad and Skog Hansen, 2004).

Whether the criminal justice policy is also a rational decision-making process could be discussed (see Bondeson, 1998b). As an example of this, and also of the way in which intellectuals and academics may have a more direct influence on policy in Scandinavia than elsewhere, I refer to my investigation of correctional institutions in Sweden (Bondeson, 1974, the Swedish version; and 1989, the revised English version with a follow-up study). The then Minister of Justice declared that the research had demonstrated the detrimental effects of imprisonment and hence, that the number of prisoners should be reduced over a period of years from about 5,000 to 1,000. The following year there were also 1,000 fewer sentences of imprisonment although this decreasing trend was stopped with a new minister of justice.

As another example of how criminological research has influenced criminal policy, my Swedish version of the book *Alternatives to Imprisonment* (Bondeson,

1977; English editions 1994 and 2002) indicated that probation with institutionalization had a much higher recidivism rate than ordinary probation: 61 per cent as against 30 per cent, a difference that remained significant when using a quasi-experimental design. It was then decided to abolish this particular form of probation. However, these two examples of rational criminal justice policy in Sweden should probably be regarded as exceptions.

Another possible interpretation of the greater tolerance in the Nordic public might be what Pratt (2002: 146) has called high levels of functional democratization in the Scandinavian societies: 'everyone was made to feel that they had a role to play and were involved in the country's social and economic development'. One relevant example of this is that the prisoner movement groups (KRUM, etc.) in the Nordic countries were open to the general public and many intellectuals were active in them. This led, at least in the 1970s to much debate about prison conditions. This was particularly the case in Sweden in 1970 when about 2,000 prisoners participated in hunger strikes in 35 prisons. Central negotiations took place between prisoners and the Department of Correction (Mathiesen, 1972; see also Bondeson, 1974: 454–469). The Swedish Information Service circulated worldwide a leaflet entitled 'Prison Democracy in Sweden'. However, the negotiations broke down, with new hunger strikes as a result and with the authorities trying to stop the discussions going on in the media. Greater success was achieved with the creation of community links to the prison, and official reports pointed out that it promoted a better understanding outside the prison of the problems and aims of the establishment.

Another illustration of functional democratization can be seen in the Eurobarometer (European Commission, 2003), demonstrating how participation in a neighbourhood watch scheme has exceptionally high support in Sweden, Denmark, and Finland, while at the same time in these countries there is little support for the idea that private individuals and organizations should share responsibility for crime prevention with the police. It is a pity that Norway is not included in the Eurobarometer since this country has a reputation for an unusually strong emphasis upon locally based democracy ('near democracy'). One would thus expect an even greater level of participation in the neighbourhood watch scheme in this country.

The Nordic countries are all characterized by having fairly homogenous populations, well educated and with a high standard of living. The macro-values are dominated by leftism and egalitarianism. People are secularized to a high degree but still influenced by Protestant values, being often strict and moralistic. *The Law of Jante*, written by the Norwegian novelist Sandemose based on his Danish home town, expresses such a Nordic ethos of fundamental equality, conformity, and oppression. The first of the 'Ten Commandments' is as follows: 'Thou shalt not think you are a somebody' (see further Bondeson, 2003: 261–262).

When we compare the Nordic countries, Denmark shows on many questions a lower degree of Puritanism than the other Nordic countries. The Danes are more liberal on issues related to the criminalization of different types of drugs and different sexual activities. At the same time they show an exceptionally low acceptance of illegal behaviour. On several questions concerning community sentiment towards punishment, they also show a higher degree of punitiveness (ibid.: 59–78 and 96–106). It is as if they draw a more narrow space of what is not permitted but within this limited area they are stricter.

Comparing Denmark and Sweden, it seems as if their different history could give some explanation of the different moral climates. A range of moral and social movements appear over time to have been more influential in Sweden than in Denmark. Many so-called reform movements, all more or less influenced by Lutheran values, but still in opposition to the dominant society, were very important in the nineteenth century. These social movements had a determining effect through puritanical ideas and organizational culture on the growing labour movement, principally reformatory in character, leading to the first Social Democratic parties in the 1870s to 1880s. One of these movements, teetotalism, was particularly strong in Sweden as well as in Norway at that time.

Other interpretations of changes in criminal justice policy

Two articles will now be reviewed that try to describe the development of criminal policy in the last century. In a historical article, 'Towards a Rational and Humane Criminal Policy', Lahti (2000) argues for the existence of a Scandinavian criminal justice policy. He is aware of the fact that there has not been any uniform criminal justice policy common to the various Nordic countries but nevertheless he believes it is possible to discern certain essential similarities among them. He also points to Nordic cooperation and refers to Article 5 of the Nordic Cooperation Agreement (1962), which states that the contracting parties should aim for mutually consistent provisions on criminal offences and their sanctions. He starts by pointing out the sociological school in penal law inspired by von Liszt that impacted upon many European countries, particularly Scandinavia. The individual preventive ideas were dominant in Scandinavia for most of the first half of the twentieth century. They led to individualized sanctions taking into consideration the needs of the offender. Lahti points out that criminological research showed that the treatment was not effective, by showing that certain treatments were better than others in decreasing recidivism, but he fails to mention that the research also showed the detrimental effects of many of the treatments. The negative effects shown in this research led to the abolition of many of the indefinite sanctions which also seemed to be contrary to important legal principles such as proportionality and equality. As a result, we saw first in Finland (1976) and then in Sweden (1985) neoclassical proposals where emphasis was laid on justice, legal security, and humaneness as legal principles in the criminal justice system, while at the same time putting value on the general preventive effects of the penal law. Lahti further discusses the internationalization and Europeanization of criminal policy to judge whether this development is a threat or an opportunity. He refers to Delmas-Marty (1995), stating that the European criminal justice policy is on the way towards both harmonization and unification. Again, if we are trying to guard against the inroads of populism in particular jurisdictions, then it may be added that one way to achieve this might be through unification of criminal penal policies between groups of states: creating a corporate barrier against populism and punitiveness.

A political analysis of 'Law and Order as a Leftist Project' with particular emphasis on the case of Sweden has been presented by Tham (2001). He takes Sweden as the welfare state *par excellence*, remarking that Swedish crime policy was internationally renowned in the 1960s and 1970s, especially in the field of corrections. 'At that time, crime policy was characterized by social engineering, by belief in rehabilitation and by humanitarian values.' He speaks about a 'tendency towards abolitionism', characteristic of the 1970s, which disappeared when the Social Democrats returned to power in 1982. He claims that the 1980s were marked by an expansion of penal law and that 'just deserts were introduced as a guiding principle for sanctioning' (p. 411). An even tougher crime policy under the Social Democratic governments returning to power in 1994 is illustrated by several changes in legislation and practice. Since then, for example, prison inmates sentenced to more than two years become eligible for parole only after two-thirds of the sentence has been served, instead of half, as before; and pardons for those with life sentences are much more restricted.

What explanations could be given for the Social Democratic regimes' changing policy? Rising crime rates and also fear of crime are dismissed. The author seems to believe that the economic crisis witnessed in Sweden in the early 1990s offers one explanation. While the Swedish model was traditionally built on a full employment policy, this became weakened and the welfare state was reduced. The Social Democratic Party tried to redefine Sweden as a drug-free society: 'the strict drug policy has become a means for reinforcing a threatened national identity' (p. 415). Other examples of 'symbolic politics' that are mentioned include the treatment of youth, violence, child pornography, and sexual services. 'As models, zero tolerance, new moralism and the morality of the market seem to reinforce one another' (p. 418). Tham also illustrates how decreasing levels of inequality shifted into an increasing inequality at the beginning of the 1980s. This can provide an explanation of the increasing status anxiety and general insecurity in the lower social classes, resulting in a call for law and order. With an electorate losing faith and with the nation-state and its culture reducing in importance, the Social Democratic Party has broken with Scandinavian traditions and has made the issue of crime control a political one, more concerned with the government of the moral order.

Conclusions

Pratt (2002) seems correct when he states that a sharpening of criminal justice policy takes place in many countries in the early 1980s but that Scandinavia appears more or less to be an exception. Crime rates have been on the increase in the Nordic countries as well as in other European countries, to about the same level. Fear of crime, though, remains on a lower level in Scandinavia. Also punitive attitudes seem to be less repressive in the Nordic countries. In addition, the media play a somewhat more responsible role in our countries than in many Anglo-Saxon countries where they tend to encourage more fear and suspicion.

Imprisonment rates have stayed very much on a lower, similar Scandinavian level. The general welfare model has not reduced crime levels but seems to have had somewhat of a softening effect on criminal justice policy.

A certain rational component can be seen in the criminal justice policy process in so far as during last century several Nordic commissions, commenting upon high recidivism rates for released prisoners, have advocated that as few persons as possible should be sentenced to imprisonment and that the sentences should be as short as possible. There are also some examples of criminological research affecting criminal justice policy, at least in the short run.

Historically, long-standing Social Democratic regimes with an ideology of full employment and solidarity have had an effect in the way of taking care of the weakest citizens in society. Those persons ending up in our prisons usually belong to the least privileged groups and should thus be embraced by the solidarity principle.

Historical explanations may be of interest since social values seem to change very slowly. Trend analyses of a great number of questions show surprising constancy over at least two decades in my studies (Bondeson, 2003: 239–260). Similarly, Togeby (2002), analysing data from the European Value Studies from 1990 to 1999, finds both gross and net changes small for such a relatively long period. Also Hellevik (1996: 17), analysing similar Norwegian data from 1985 to 1993, concludes that 'you are struck by the almost unbelievable stability in many of the time series'. However, such a 'relative constancy' of similar opinions in the United States has also been observed by American scholars (see Warr, 1995). Likewise, Flanagan and Longmire (1996: 10) have characterized major aspects of public opinion concerning crime and justice issues over time as primarily having a 'remarkable temporal stability in many aspects of public attitudes, including perceptions of crime, fear of crime, evaluations of the police, the role of the government spending in fighting crime, gun control and drug control policy'. In other words, relative constancy in public opinion is not unique to Scandinavia. But constancy in public opinion in say, the United States, which reveals much greater fears and anxieties, may only increase social divisions, intolerance, mistrust, and demands for tougher punishment. The constancy of public opinion in Scandinavia may have ultimately had a different impact: stronger interdependencies and levels of trust – and thereby greater tolerance of others and possibly an in-built cultural resistance to the new punitiveness.

In more recent years, however, we have heard more moralistic tones from our governments. A tendency to a sharpened criminal justice policy can also be observed simultaneously with a questioning of the welfare state as economies have weakened. However, a comparative study by Juul (2002) shows continued strong support for the welfare state in the Scandinavian countries, but somewhat weaker in the young generation. If the younger generations are less committed to the welfare state, there is also evidence that they are less committed to the tolerance characteristic of these Scandinavian countries (see Bondeson, 2003: 96–102 and 109–121). Very high levels of absence from work in the Nordic countries have lately been criticized and looked upon as a way of profiting from too generous sick-leave provisions. This might possibly be interpreted as support for Habermas' (1981) theory of the bureaucracy's colonization of our life values, in the sense that the system's technocratic administration takes over the participatory democracy's resources of meaning, solidarity and identity (see further Bondeson, 2003: 269). At the same time, given the centrality of the particular nature of the Scandinavian welfare state to its culture of tolerance, and the sense of unity and trust brought about by functional democratization, these differing values of young people may possibly be early indicators that the low levels of punitiveness and of imprisonment rates characteristic of this region will ultimately be in jeopardy.

References

Barclay, G. and Tavares, C. (2003) *International comparisons of criminal justice statistics 2001*. Home Office Statistical Bulletin, Issue 12/03. 24 October, London: Home Office.

Blumstein, A. (1997) 'The US Criminal Justice Conundrum: Rising Prison Populations and Stable Crime Rates', in *Prison Population in Europe and in North America*, Helsinki: Department of Prison Administration of the Ministry of Justice of Finland.

Bondeson, U. V. (1974) *Fången in fångsamhället*, Malmö: P.A. Nordstedt and Söners förlag.

Bondeson, U. V. (1977) *Kriminalvård i frihet – Intention och verklighet*, Stockholm: LiberFörlag.

Bondeson, U. V. (1980) 'Rättsmedvetandet rörande brottens straffvärde och domarens straffmätning' ('Public Consciousness of the Penal Value of Crime and the Meting out of Punishment by the Judges'), in E. Kühlhorn (ed.) *Påföljdsval, straffmätning och straffvärde*, Stockholm: Brottsförebyggande rådet, 2, pp. 54–71.

Bondeson, U. V. (1989) *Prisoners in Prison Societies*, New Brunswick and Oxford: Transactions Publishers.

Bondeson, U. V. (1994) *Alternatives to Imprisonment: Intentions and Reality*, Boulder: Westview Press.

Bondeson, U. V. (1998a) 'Global Trends in Corrections', *Annales Internationales de Criminologie*, 36: 91–116.

Bondeson, U. V. (1998b) 'Interplay between Criminological Research and Criminal Policy', in *Festschrift für Kaiser*, Berlin: Duncker and Humblot, pp. 57–69.

Bondeson, U. (2002) *Alternatives to Imprisonment: Intentions and Reality*, New Brunswick, NJ, and London: Transaction Publishers.

Bondeson, U. V. (2003) *Nordic Moral Climates. Value Continuities and Discontinuities in Denmark, Finland, Norway, and Sweden*, New Brunswick and London: Transaction Publishers.

Cavender, G. (2004) 'Media and Crime Policy', *Punishment and Society*, 6(3): 335–348.

Christie, N. (2000) *Crime Control as Industry*, London and New York: Routledge.

Crime Prevention in the Nordic Context – The Nordic Model (2001) Stockholm: Brottsförebyggande rådet.

Delmas-Marty, M. (1995) *The Criminal Process and Human Rights. Towards a European Consciousness*, The Hague: Kluwer Law International.

European Commission (2002) *Public Opinion Regarding Security and Victimisation in the EU*. Contact with drugs related problems. Eurobarometer surveys no. 44.3 (1996) and 54:1 (2000) (Drugs Co-ordination Unit. Directorate General for Justice and Home Affairs). http://europa.eu.int/comm/public_opinion/archives/eb/ebs_145_100.pdf

European Commission (2003) *Analysis of Public Attitudes to Insecurity, Fear of Crime and Crime Prevention*. Results of Eurobarometer 58.0 (Autumn 2002). Brussels, 25 April 2003. DG PRESS B/1/UTM D(2003). http://europa.eu.int/comm/public_opinion/archives/ebs/ebs_181_sum_en.pdf

European Sourcebook of Crime and Criminal Justice Statistics – 2003 (2003) (2nd edn) Onderzoek en beleid 212, The Hague: Boom Juridische uitgevers.

Flanagan, T. J. and D. R. Longmire (eds) (1996) *Americans View Crime and Justice*, Thousand Oaks: Sage Publications.

Friestad, C. and Skog Hansen, I.L. (2004) *Levekår blant innsatte ('Living conditions among inmates')*, Fafo-rapport 429, Oslo: Fafo. http://www.fafo.no/pub/rapp/429/429.pdf

Garland, D. (2000) 'The Culture of High Crime Societies. Some Preconditions of Recent 'Law and Order' Policies', *British Journal of Criminology*, 40: 347–375.

Habermas, J. (1981) *Theorie des Kommunikativen Handelns*, Frankfurt am Main: Suhrkamp.

Hellevik, O. (1996) *Nordmenn og det gode liv* ('Norwegians and the Good Life'), Oslo: Universitetsforlaget.

Hofer, H. von (2003) 'Crime and Punishment in Sweden: Historical Criminal Justice Statititcs 1750–2000', *Journal of Scandinavian Studies in Criminology and Crime Prevention*, 4: 162–179.

Hofer, H. von (2004) 'Crime and the Reaction to Crime in Scandinavia', *Journal of Scandinavian Studies in Criminology and Crime Prevention* (forthcoming, vol. 5:2).

Juul, S. (2002) *Modernitet, Velfærd og Solidaritet ('Modernity, Welfare and Solidarity')*, Copenhagen: Hans Reitzels Forlag.

Kershaw, C. *et al.* (2001) *The 2001 British Crime Survey: First Results, England and Wales*. London: Home Office.

Kesteren, J. van, Mayhew, P. and Nieuwbeerta, P. (2000) *Criminal Victimisation in Seventeen Industrialised Countries. Key findings from the 2000 International Crime Victims Survey*. Onderzoek en beleid 187, The Hague: NSCR/WODC.

Lahti, R. (2000) 'Towards a Rational and Humane Criminal Policy – Trends in Scandinavian Penal Thinking', *Journal of Scandinavian Criminology and Crime Prevention*, 1: 141–155.

Lappi-Seppälä, T. (2000) 'The Fall of the Finnish Prison Population', *Journal of Scandinavian Studies in Criminology and Crime Prevention*, 1: 27–40.

Mathiesen, T. (1972) *Det ofullgångna ('The Unfinished')*, Stockholm: Wahlström and Widstrand.

Nordic Criminal Statistics 1950–2000 (2003) S. Falck, H. von Hofer and A. Storgaard (eds) Report 2003:3, Department of Criminology, Stockholm: Stockholm University.

Nordisk statistik för kriminalvården i Danmark, Finland, Norge och Sverige 1997–2001 ('Nordic Prison and Probation Statistics 1997–2001'), Norrköping: Kriminalvårdsstyrelsen.

Pratt, J. (2002) *Punishment and Civilization*, London: Sage.

Roberts, J. V. and Stalans, L. J. (2000) *Public Opinion, Crime and Criminal Justice*, Boulder, CO: Westview Press.

Roberts, J. V., Stalans, L. J., Indermaur. D. and Hough, M. (2003) *Penal Populism and Public Opinion. Lessons from Five Countries*, Oxford: Oxford University Press.

Shinkai, H. and Zvekic, U. (1999) 'Punishment', in G. Newman (ed.) *Global Report on Crime and Justice* published for the UN Office for Drug Control and Crime Prevention, Center for International Crime Prevention, New York/Oxford: Oxford University Press, pp. 89–120.

Tham, H. (2001) 'Law and order as a leftist project. The case of Sweden', *Punishment and Society*, 3: 409–426.

Togeby, L. (2002) 'Hvilke værdier ændrer sig, hvornår og hos hvem?' in P. Gundelach (ed.) *Danskernes værdier1981–1999* ('Danish values 1981–1999'), Copenhagen: Hans Reitzels Forlag.

Walker, N. and Hough, M. (eds) (1988) *Public Attitudes to Sentencing*, Aldershot: Gower.

Warr, M. (1995) 'The Polls – Poll Trends', *Public Opinion Quarterly*, 59: 296–310.

Westfelt, L. (2001) 'The Netherlands in an International Perspective', in F. W. M. Huls, M. M. Schreuders, Ter Horst-van Breukelen and F. P. van Tulder (eds) *Crime and Law Enforcement, Developments and interrelations*, Part I, The Hague: WODC, pp. 199–214.

12. Missing the punitive turn? Canadian criminal justice, 'balance', and penal modernism

Jeffrey Meyer and Pat O'Malley

Criminology, particularly of the critical sort, is a discipline besotted with catastrophic change (O'Malley, 2000). But a change has come over the way in which catastrophes are characterized. In an earlier generation of criminology, most of the imagined catastrophes were progressively revolutionary in nature and implication. In the 1960s and 1970s, crises of one sort or another were about to precipitate major changes in modern capitalism and its criminal justice apparatuses. Staggering under fiscal and legitimation crises, the capitalist state was dramatically restructuring. Decarceration was one of these changes, informal justice another. Both were predicted to empty the prisons, lighten the hand of criminal justice, and reduce or externalize the criminal justice expenditures. Thirty or forty years later, another – but radically different – crisis has been detected by critical criminologists. The 1960s now have been made to appear as a 'golden age' of penal modernism in which a therapeutic correctionalism was 'hegemonic'. The new catastrophe is a Dark Age of criminal justice characterised by 'economies of excess', 'decivilizing processes', 'populist vengeance', and so on – in short, the 'death of penal modernism'. It is seen to be replaced by exclusionary regimes characterized by savage punishments, mass imprisonment, and incapacitation. It is said to be driven by a punitive state that in turn is responding to the failure of penal modernism to reduce crime, and by the demands of a disillusioned and angry populace.

In large measure, we would argue, this account of our criminological present suffers from the same exaggerating tendencies that afflicted radical criminology 40 years ago. As then, such characterizations are drawn overwhelmingly in relation to evidence from the United States and Britain, as David Garland (2001: 212) has candidly admitted. But even with respect to these countries, the account conveniently ignores many developments of a distinctly different type. These would seem hard to square with the 'decivilizing process' identified by John Pratt (2002) and Barry Vaughan (2000), the collapse of penal modernism diagnosed by David Garland (2001) or the emergence of an 'economy of excess' located by Simon Hallsworth (2000). A polar opposite 'positive' and 'integrative' account, scarcely less plausible, could be constructed around the high-profile influence of restorative justice and its re-integrative ethic of justice (Braithwaite, 2003: 12–15); the emergence of a new era of 'therapeutic jurisprudence' developed in (of all places) the United States drug courts (Nolan, 1998); and the creation of enterprising prisoner schemes in which offenders participate in the drawing up of their own road map to a decent future (O'Malley, 1999). One response to such contrary observations has been to suggest that we are in an era of 'volatile and contradictory punishment' (O'Malley, 1999; Garland, 1996). Both punitive and ameliorative penal responses are said to be present, but their dominance alternates according to short-term political exigencies. Yet this account too may be a characterization that draws a stronger contrast with preceding eras of criminal justice than can fully be justified. After all, there were many criminologists of the 1960s who lamented the resilience and strength of the punitive and repressive urge even as others pointed to the triumph of scientific corrections (e.g. Cressey, 1961; Galtung, 1961; Morris and Hawkins, 1969).

As noted earlier, the accuracy of accounts of a new punitive age may be geographically bounded. In turn, we could speculate that much of the punitive change in the United States is an effect not of major structural reconfigurations of the sort mapped out by Garland, Pratt, and others, but of the specific phenomenon of a highly racialized and enduring drug problem, quite possibly sustained and exacerbated by that other peculiarly American institution, the 'War on Drugs'. It is not our intention to explore such specific possibilities here. We raise them, rather, to suggest that a more modest criminology than one identifying a global punitive turn might take Garland's cue and consider the characteristics and contexts of specific criminal justice regimes. There are indications that the stark contrast between a 'golden age' of the 1960s and a contemporary abandonment of penal modernism is simply inapplicable to countries such as Canada and Australia. In both countries, for example, the recent development of risk-based interventions in criminal justice bears witness to the resilience and resistance of the welfare professions and their knowledges (O'Malley, 2001). Many of the 'risk factors' that are part and parcel of the emergent era of crime control turn out to be little more than the 'causes of crime' central to the sociologies and psychologies of the 1960s. As Gervais (2002: 191–6) has argued, there is a strong 'neo-social' presence in Canadian crime prevention strategies, in which the (traditional sociological) causes of crime and welfare-style interventions have become increasingly prominent issues since the early 1990s. Even more recently, the government of Canada has stressed that a 'social development approach continues to be the driving force in Canada's criminal justice system'. In this approach, crime prevention through social development 'is an approach to crime reduction that deals with underlying causes of crime and recognizes the complex social, economic, and cultural factors that contribute to crime and victimization' (Correctional Services of Canada, 2003a: 12). As we will elaborate shortly, closely linked to this is an undertow of criticism of United States' policies and practices, precisely those identified with the 'death of the social', that is indicative of considerable resistance in Canadian government to the type of punitive turn said to be occurring in the US.

In this light, we turn to an analysis of whether there has been a punitive turn in Canadian criminal justice. In the following section we briefly review the period prior to the early 1970s, taking this as the baseline from which any punitive turn can be assessed. This review suggests that, far from a golden age of penal modernism, Canadian criminal justice in the period leading up to 1970 was marked *both* by discourses of penal modernism *and* by punitive discourses and high rates of imprisonment. Much the same has been true for the period after the 1970s, which – if anything – has been characterized by an increased faith in penal reformism, although punitive discourses have also remained active. In the past 20 years, the example set by the 'failure' of increasingly punitive practices in the United States acts has been mobilized in favour of sustaining and promoting a 'balanced' strategy that regards both punishment and correction as central aims of criminal justice.

Was there a golden age in Canada?

The period prior to the mid-1970s has been made to appear as one in which scientific correctionalism was 'hegemonic', in which punishment was seen as a regrettable hangover from former days, and in which 'protecting the public was rarely the motivating theme of policy making' (Garland, 2001: 12). In practice, official discourse and statistics make it clear that no such hegemonic state of affairs existed in Canada. Looking back on this 'era', Canada's first government document on sentencing notes that:

> A striking omission from the Criminal Code, one which dates from its inception in 1892, is the lack of any statement of the purposes and principles which underlie the criminal law in general, and sentencing in particular. This lack of formal Parliamentary guidance has resulted in a situation whereby it cannot be said that there is a clear, nationally-applicable set of standards or principles ... (Canada, 1984: 33)

This reflected an assumption that 'no social institution as important or complex as the criminal law can afford the luxury of picking just one purpose – intellectually simple and satisfying though that selection might be' (Canada, 1982: 40). Not surprisingly, evidence exists to demonstrate the place of at least three or four different official policy directions: rehabilitation, protection, retribution, and deterrence were all officially part of the scene (Cousineau and Veevers, 1972: 10–31). Certainly by the late 1950s, it was clear that rehabilitation had become a major policy aim, and that, in the words of Canada's Attorney General and Justice Minister, 'it seems to be clear that the entire period of deprivation of liberty should be directed toward preparation of the offender to assume again a normal life in the community as a law abiding citizen' (Fulton, 1958: 265).[1] However, he was equally clear that 'this does not mean that our prisons would cease to be places of punishment for the offender. There is, and there must remain, in the prison sentence an aspect of punishment which requires a certain amount of discipline and a certain lack of comfort' (Fulton, 1958: 270). The point was reiterated a decade later in the report of the Canadian Committee on Corrections (Canada, 1969: 18), which stressed that 'the Committee believes that traditionally punishment has been over-stressed as a means of crime prevention, yet it does not deny the necessity for punishment as a sanction'. The Committee also accepted that 'in some cases the person may be so dangerous as to justify his segregation from the community for periods up to the whole of his life' (Canada, 1969: 18). As this also indicates, contrary to current depictions, punishment and correction were not only regarded as complementary, but as joined by an emphasis on the protection of society. Thus in words prefiguring those of the 'risk-focused' 1990s, the Solicitor General of Canada (Goyer, 1972: 7) proposed establishing 'criteria to assure ourselves that inmates which are a serious threat to society are not liberated'.

Accordingly, Canadian corrections were characterized by a considerable emphasis on imprisonment. As Cousineau and Veevers (1972: 10) show, in Canada throughout the 1950s and 1960s the rate of incarceration of adults was one of the highest in the world, and – at 240 per 100,000 – exceeded that of the United States by 20 per cent. Moreover, while it was officially recognized that rehabilitation was most effective where penal conditions matched those of the outside world, a large proportion of those prisoners (in 1959, 54 per cent) were held in maximum-security conditions. In keeping with the increasing emphasis on rehabilitation, by the end of the 1960s, this figure had declined substantially (to 35 per cent), although rates of imprisonment still exceeded those of the United States.

It is against this rather heterogeneous or eclectic backdrop that any current trends towards increased punitiveness must be compared. But Canada was not about to perform a major volte-face in the direction of punishment after the early 1970s. Rather, both the rates of imprisonment and the proportion of offenders in maximum security were to continue declining through the 1980s and 1990s. By 1995, only 20 per cent of prisoners were held in maximum-security institutions, and the rates of imprisonment had fallen well beneath those of the United States.

Was there a Canadian 'punitive turn'?

In a close analysis of changing patterns of criminal between 1984 and 1990, Hatt and his colleagues concluded that with respect to legislation, at least, Canada did not exemplify the neoconservative, law-and-order mentality expressed in the United States and Great Britain (Hatt et al., 1992: 245–60). A clause-by-clause review of all criminal legislation enacted by Brian Mulroney's Progressive Conservative government revealed that most criminal legislation introduced in Canada during this time was replicated from prior Liberal government initiatives, and there was little evidence of changes of course during these critical six years. Even with a more conservative regime in power, any differences between the 1970s and the 1990s were subtle, and evidence of drastic change towards a law-and-order approach is lacking – despite the occasional outburst of rhetoric about being tough on crime and being concerned with social and economic efficiency (Hatt et al., 1992: 257). From an official standpoint, therefore, it is broadly accurate to say that Canada's criminal justice system continued a policy based on punishment and correction. A self-styled 'balanced' philosophy was strengthened during these years that is still prominent in early twenty-first-century correctional policy (Canada, 2002: 3–5). Even if some criminal sanctions were justified by retributive aims, the government of Canada into the 1980s and beyond asserted that the 'acceptance of retributive justifications for punishment implies neither rejection of utilitarian justifications for such punishment, nor the acceptance of harsh, cruel or vindictive forms or levels of punishment' (Canada, 1982: 41). In the final analysis there is an official understanding that 'pursuing two sometimes conflicting purposes for criminal law, directs attention to the need to devise an approach for defining the proper point of balance between these two purposes' (Canada, 1982: 41). This 'balanced' approach has proven quite resilient, and indeed has come to be regarded as distinctly Canadian – in contradistinction, that is, to the policies and practices across the border.

'The Canadian way' and a 'balanced approach'. Governance in the 1990s

During the 1990s, Canada's federal government, under the leadership of Liberal Prime Minister Jean Chrétien, began the task of establishing a distinctive 'Canadian way' for dealing with social problems into the twenty-first-century. The Canadian way is said to be a distinctive orientation that embodies and promotes policies that are comprehensive and committed to the liberal values of opportunity, diversity, and inclusion (Chrétien, 2000). In the realm of criminal justice, it is argued that there is a need to see policies balance the rights and freedoms of society, victims, and offenders in as representative a manner as possible. Within this nationalist framework, 'balance' has become an important category in contemporary Canadian policies, albeit that its precise meaning was quite variable. Thus while balance was to exist between punishment and correction, and between offenders and victims, it was also averred that:

> While prison may be the right place – the only place – for some criminals, it is also the wrong place for others. There is no hard evidence to show that locking people up has a deterrent effect, or reduces crime, or even the rate of re-offending. A balanced system is needed to keep our communities safe and secure – one that gets tough with violent, high-risk offenders but also finds alternatives to incarceration for non-violent, low-risk offenders. (Canada, 2001a)

In pushing this line, it was urged that 'we have two choices – go the way of the US and build more prisons, or develop meaningful, lasting alternatives to incarceration for low-risk offenders who can be better managed in the community' (Canada, 2001a). This echoed remarks made earlier by Patrick Gagnon, Parliamentary Secretary to the Solicitor General of Canada in 1995:

> We will continue to follow a balanced, comprehensive plan of action, a plan that gets tough with violent crime but that also emphasizes dealing with the factors that cause crime. The Government's efforts to fight and prevent crime are comprehensive and far-reaching. While dealing with violent crime will continue as a priority, we realize that we must also address the causes of crime if we are to really build safer communities. We know that harsher penalties alone do not solve crime. If this was true, the United States would be one of the safest countries in the world. We know this is simply not the case. (Gagnon, 1995: 30)

This ongoing critique of United States developments has been repeated endlessly, almost invariably with a stress on the contrast with Canada, and almost invariably explicitly rejecting a punitive turn. Thus in pointing to the 'currently unacceptable' rate of imprisonment in Canada, the Canadian correctional service stressed that the:

> United States is a good example of what happens when governments rely too heavily on incarceration. It has one of the highest incarceration rates in the world and it is still not a safer place to live ... Canada is not the United States. We need a made-in-Canada solution, consistent with Canadian values and beliefs. (Correctional Service of Canada, 2001a: 3)[2]

A 'balanced approach' thus takes its place specifically as part of the contrast between the (implicitly) unbalanced or lopsided emphasis on punitiveness that is held to characterize the US, and the circumspection and moderation that is distinctively Canadian. Such balance is also held to apply to the need to retain a focus on dealing with the social determinants of crime. Accordingly, welfare discourses that aim to address 'root causes' of crime still maintain a central place in Canadian justice (Correctional Service of Canada, 2003a: 12). There is a continuing faith and investment in therapeutic intervention. Thus programming for even the most serious offenders is said to be readily available. For example, there are currently 196 social programmes to address the 'needs' of child sexual abuse offenders in Canada, available in both community settings and correctional environments (Health Canada, 2002). Treatment of violent offenders in Canada has also received increasing amounts of attention over the last few years, with the development of increasing numbers and varieties of specialized treatment programmes (Correctional Service of Canada, 1999a: iii).

More broadly, in Canada's federal penitentiaries there exists a whole battery of social programmes designed to attend to the welfare of prisoners in general (Correctional Service of Canada, 1993). According to the Correctional Service, in 2000–2001 it spent Can $85.7 million on providing correctional programmes to federal offenders. 'These ranged from substance abuse treatment, living skills and family violence programs to education and employment programs' (Correctional Service of Canada, 2002b: 1). Legislation requires that the Correctional Service of Canada 'provide every inmate with essential health care, and reasonable access to non-essential mental health care that will contribute to the inmate's rehabilitation and successful reintegration into the community' and to 'deliver essential health services comparable to provincial and community standards, notwithstanding the constraints inherent in the correctional environment' (Correctional Service of Canada, 2002a: 2–4). Secondary and post-secondary education is available in all federal institutions 'to provide offenders with provincially accredited or certified programs which meet their identified education needs to assist them to reintegrate into the community as law-abiding citizens' (Correctional Service of Canada, 1999b: 1). There are occupational development programmes premised on promoting time-management skills, 'pro-social' behaviours, and marketable skills for reintegration (Correctional Service of Canada, 2004). There are ethno-cultural and spiritual support pro-grammes and a wide variety of dietary accommodations that allow offenders the freedom to practise a special diet if they so choose (Correctional Service of Canada, 2001c). Visitor programmes 'encourage [offenders] to develop and maintain positive community and family relationships that will assist them to prepare for reintegration as law-abiding citizens' (Correctional Service of Canada, 2001d: 1). One such programme, in place since the 1980s, enables offenders to spend periods of up to three days with their family in private, home-like settings located on institutional grounds

Apart from these general programmes and entitlements, there are many programmes to meet the 'special needs' of aboriginals, women, and offenders serving long sentences. Aboriginal offenders, who are over-represented in Canada's federal penitentiary system, have officially received extensive attention over the years to the point that there is now an Aboriginal Initiatives Branch in the Correctional Service of Canada (Correctional Service of Canada, 2003b). The Branch is 'mandated to create partnerships and strategies that enhance the safe and timely reintegration of Aboriginal offenders into the community' (Correctional Service of Canada, 2003b). The Department of the Solicitor General, in collaborative partnership with Aboriginal communities, aims to 'develop and support innovative projects to examine offender treatment and services within the context of restorative justice and healing. Examples include the Hollow Water Community Holistic Healing Circle in Manitoba and the Maison Waskeskun House in Montreal.' The Correctional Service has also 'developed culturally appropriate substance abuse programs; Native liaison services; traditional cultural and spiritual programs within prisons; Elders' services; mandatory cross-cultural training for corrections staff; and post-release programs and services' to accommodate the welfare of Aboriginal offenders (Correctional Service of Canada, 2002c: 1–2).

Long-term prisoners, those serving sentences of ten years or longer, have become the focus of increasing attention, being regarded as 'a unique group requiring special approaches to the provision of programs and services' (Correctional Service of Canada, 1998: 10). In 1991, Corrections Canada implemented recommendations made by the Task Force on Long Term Sentences to manage and facilitate long-term offenders in four stages: adaptation (coming to grips with the reality of confinement), integration (to the prison environment), preparation (for release in a progressive manner), and reintegration (back into the community) to accommodate particular needs (Correctional Service of Canada, 1998). Through the Life-Line Concept, long-term offenders are given assistance to 'make more productive use of [their] time while in custody with a view to increasing the likelihood of timely release and safe reintegration to the community' (Correctional Service of Canada, 1998: 1). In some cases, 'lifers' are encouraged to become 'career role models', and to maximize their time and privileges by helping new inmates adapt, integrate, and prepare for eventual release (Correctional Service of Canada, 1998). In sum, there is a great deal of social programming and individual accommodation found in Canada's federal penitentiary system.

This is, of course, not to be starry-eyed in any way. Official discourse is the site of much distortion. As the chapter by Dawn Moore and Kelly Hannah-Moffat in this volume shows, for example, these technocratic and therapeutic interventions are often punitive in operation. Even where the policy is genuinely meant to be effected, the translation into practice is always prone to intended and unintended transformations, many of them focused on increasing security at the expense of programmes 'on paper'. But, as countless critical criminologists documented, the same was true for the welfare sanctions of the 1960s and 1970s. Our point is to engage at the level of the concerns of the 'punitive turn' theorists, that is, with official policy and discourse. However we regard this relationship between discourse and practice, it is difficult to conclude other than that, far from disappearing or even having become marginalized, 'penal modernism' appears as strong or stronger than ever as a central ethos of official discourse on Canadian criminal justice.

Canadian incarceration: a 40-year comparative analysis

One of the fundamental claims made in the punitive turn thesis is that the use of incarceration has dramatically increased since the 'golden era', and especially during the last decade we have entered an era of 'mass imprisonment'. However, if we take a 40-year comparative snapshot using official statistics for adult offenders over two five-year periods (Table 12.1), we can see that the ratio of federal offenders to total adult population in Canada has remained relatively stable.

Table 12.1 Federal incarceration rates (five year periods compared, 1957–61, 1997–2001)

	1997	1998	1999	2000	2001
Total number of federal offenders	13,759	13,170	12,974	12,732	12,811
Rate per 100,000 population	60	57	56	54	53
	1957	1958	1959	1960	1961
Total number of federal offenders	5,432	5,770	6,295	6,344	6,738
Rate per 100,000 population	50	52	55	55	57

Table 12.2 Provincial incarceration rates (five year periods compared, 1957–61, 1997–2001)

	1997	1998	1999	2000	2001
Total number of provincial offenders	18,955	19,220	18,634	18,815	19,262
Rate per 100,000 population	83	83	80	80	80
	1957	1958	1959	1960	1961
Total number of provincial offenders	9,739	11,192	11,166	10,896	11,821
Rate per 100,000 population	89	101	98	94	101

In the provincial context, and contrary to the punitive turn thesis, there is a lower proportion of adults incarcerated today than there was during the 'golden era' (see Table 12.2).

Thus one of the most significant claims – that there has been a drastic increase in the use of imprisonment – is simply not the case in Canada. With respect to federal institutions – in which the more serious offenders serve their time – a downward trend is visible, in keeping with official commentaries that regard current rates of incarceration as 'unacceptably high' (Doob and Marinos, 1995). As Roberts and his colleagues also report (2003: 17), in the decade ending in 1995, incarceration rates and average sentences remained 'remarkably stable'.

The abolition of capital punishment

The return of the death penalty in the United States has figured large in many of the accounts of current penality. The proximity of Canada to the US – and the saturation of Canadian media and politics with the politics of American criminal justice – could therefore be seen as creating pressures for the return of capital punishment. However, it would again appear that the American example is regarded as deeply problematic across the border. With the exception of certain classes of treason, the death penalty was abolished in Canada in 1976, with Bill C-84 on a free vote. In 1987, a free vote regarding the reinstatement of the death penalty resulted in parliamentarians voting by an increased margin to maintain the abolition of the death penalty. In 1998, Canada's Parliament removed the last remaining death penalty provisions with the passing of the National Defence (Amendment) Act. As noted by the Department of Justice, the abolition of the death penalty is considered to be a principle of 'fundamental justice', and Canada has played a key role in denouncing the use of capital punishment at the international level (Canada 2003a). In *United States* v. *Burns* [2001] 1 S.C.R. 283 the Supreme Court of Canada unanimously decided that before extraditing a fugitive, the Charter of Rights and Freedoms requires that there be assurances the death penalty will not be imposed. The Supreme Court has said that this ruling is a constitutional requirement under the Charter of Rights and Freedoms that must be followed in all but exceptional cases. Under the Charter, it was ruled, the death penalty is considered to be cruel and unusual punishment.

Mandatory minimum sentences

According to Gabor and Crutcher, as of 1999 the Canadian Criminal Code contained 29 offences with mandatory minimum sentences, of which 19 were created in 1995 alone under Bill C-68, a package of firearms legislation (Gabor and Crutcher, 2002: 1). In Canada, mandatory minimum sentences apply to first- and second-degree murder, high treason, impaired driving and related offences, various firearms offences, betting and bookmaking, and living off the avails of child prostitution. In 1999, there were nine private members' bills proposing mandatory minimum sentences, in 2000 there were five, and for part of 2001 there were six (Gabor and Crutcher, 2002: 43). Pressure thus still exists for a more punitive stance. Yet a private member's bill, after all, requires just one member to move it, and its very existence indicates that the government did not support it. In all cases the motions failed. While Canada's Criminal Code may contain a few mandatory minimum sentences for highly moralized, but statistically marginal, offences, the advocacy for mandatory minimum sentences comes from only a small number of parliamentarians.[3] Moreover, mandatory minimum laws in Canada do not appear to endorse the same level of severity expressed by their parallels in the United States. In contrast to the United States, for example, Canada does not have any mandatory sentences for any drug offence. In the United States Anti-Drug Abuse Acts of 1986 and 1988:

> a 5 to 40-year sentence, without probation or parole, was mandated for first offenders convicted of possession with intent to distribute small quantities of designated substances. The sentence was 10 years to life for larger quantities. The 1988 Amendments increased mandatory minimum sentences, imposed these sentences for even smaller quantities, and prescribed especially tough sentences for first-time offenders possessing crack and other cocaine-based substances. (Gabor and Crutcher, 2002: 17)

Canada does not have any mandatory minimum sentences for drug trafficking. Despite the threat of possible life imprisonment in Canada, the median length of a drug trafficking sentence in 1996–97 was four months (Canada, 1999).

The Correctional Service of Canada mandate, mission, and core values

In general, the body in charge of implementing the final stages of Canada's criminal justice system does not indicate a punitive sentiment in its legislative responsibilities. The two official mandates for the Canadian Correctional Service (2003a: 9) are: to 'carry out sentences imposed by the courts through the safe and humane custody and supervision of offenders'; and 'assisting the rehabilitation of offenders and their reintegration into the community as law-abiding citizens through the provision of programs in penitentiaries and in the community'. The political desire to deliver rehabilitation to offenders while they are incarcerated still has considerable salience in Canada, and there is a clear acceptance of the workability of reformist efforts.[4] On the topic of incapacitation and rehabilitation, a recent publication from the Solicitor General of Canada regarding the 'Influences on Canadian Correctional Reform' notes that, 'although rehabilitation has generally been discredited as a legitimate justification for *sentencing* an offender to imprisonment, no major report has ever recommended an end to rehabilitation as a goal of *corrections*' (Canada, 2002: 18–19).

The report goes on to say that 'even in an era of financial restraint, most corrections professionals, academics, and even members of the public still support the principle of rehabilitation, perhaps simply on the grounds that it would be irresponsible and cynical to give up so soon' (Canada, 2002: 18). On the topic of incapacitation and deterrence, the report suggests that 'corrections should not try to increase the deterrent effect by making the conditions of confinement more unpleasant and austere than necessary' (Canada, 2002: 19). It is recommended that when deterrence is used as a rationale to guide judgment, it 'seems more appropriate to do so by making the sentence longer, within the appropriate limits' rather than making conditions in prison more austere (Canada, 2002: 19). In sum, the report declares the 'deterrent function of corrections arises from the fact of incarceration, and not the conditions of confinement' in Canada (Canada, 2002: 19).

Penal populism and Canadian public opinion

Populist governments routinely deploy public opinion in the attempt to legitimate 'crackdowns' on crime and draconian sentencing. As a rule this is a robust finding, and it has been relied upon in the new criminological literature as the official justification for the punitive turn. Some sociologists, such as David Garland (2001: 145–46), have moved even further to argue that such popular support is not an artefact, but is evidence of a changing experience and consciousness of crime. Especially among the middle-class professionals, he argues that this emergent awareness of crime has played a key role in driving justice away from penal modernism. Neither the evidence of Canadian public opinion, nor of politicians' attempts to mobilize this, suggests a similar pattern in this country. The evidence produced by the government suggests that the general public in Canada does not support the abandonment of rehabilitation, or for that matter a more punitive orientation as a replacement. According to research sponsored by the Department of the Solicitor General, 'over the past 25 years, fear of criminal victimization has remained relatively steady with a small decline in recent years. On average, 31% of adult Canadians reported being afraid.' (Canada, 2001b: 1) While the study notes that women are more afraid than men, and acknowledges the limitations in accurately researching perceptions, this study tentatively demonstrates that crime is not considered a very significant issue for Canadians. Certainly this is how government bureaucracies have represented matters: 'although almost one of three Canadians expresses fear of crime, dealing with crime is not seen as a high government priority. In a recent survey, only two percent of respondents saw crime as an area that the government should focus on, far behind issues of health care, education and the economy.' (Canada, 2001b: 1) It is found, and advertised, that studies:

> examining the attitudes of the public to the criminal justice system have shown that Canadians are not very supportive of 'get tough' policies. Public support for capital punishment has fallen to a historic low and the majority of survey respondents prefer parole to incarcerating offenders until the end of their sentences. Support for punitive interventions and negative attitudes toward the criminal justice system however, are associated with fear of crime. People who report the highest fear levels showed the most support for incarceration and the greatest opposition to rehabilitation. (Canada, 2001b: 1–2)

These research findings have provided three policy implications, which the department officially acknowledges and is currently addressing. The first is that 'most Canadians feel safe in their communities. Conveying these findings to the public is important to counter-balance media portrayals of crime as a pervasive problem.' The second is that 'compared to other issues, the majority of Canadians do not view crime as a priority issue for the government. This information is helpful in ensuring that the government's response to the crime problem is kept in perspective.' And third, support for 'get tough' remedies for dealing with crime is not very strong. 'Most Canadians agree with the view that rehabilitation and parole are important methods for reducing reoffending. Continued development of supervised release and rehabilitation programs is encouraged' (Canada, 2001b: 2).

This finding tallies with the evidence of other studies, notably those reported by Roberts and his colleagues, which have found that in Canada penal populism has 'limited influence', and indeed that public opinion on sentencing, while always in favour of more severe sentences, had changed little since the early 1970s (Roberts *et al.*, 2003: 28, 39). Whatever the 'true' picture of Canadian public opinion, what matters here is that the key government departments are representing this in ways that minimize any tendency toward a populist vendetta or support for increased punishment.

Canadian drug policy: a balanced approach case study

As in most countries, the regulation of drugs has become increasingly contentious in recent years, and is a topic of debate currently being addressed in Canada's legislature. Both the House of Commons and the Senate have commissioned special committees[5] with Orders of Reference to consolidate the state of knowledge on drugs, and to provide recommendations with respect to how the Government of Canada can better approach the regulation of drugs – whether drugs are defined as illicit or otherwise. Although official concern for illicit drugs dramatically increased after the United States declared war on drugs, the Canadian approach for addressing and controlling drugs is culturally different than that south of the border.

The introduction of Canada's first National Drug Strategy in 1987 and its following amendments have been premised explicitly on a 'balanced approach' mentality so as to articulate the idea that drug use and abuse are not just a judicial issue but also, and more primarily, a health and social issue. Thus, in a specific context, while prison officially might be regarded as a good place for drug traffickers, it is seen as the wrong place for petty drug users, and especially drug users arrested for seeking to buy drugs (House of Commons Special Committee on Non-Medical Use of Drugs, 2002; Senate Special Committee on Illegal Drugs, 2002). According to Herb Gray, Solicitor General of Canada in 1993:

> The drug trade is dependent on demand and only by developing preventative strategies that strike at the underlying factors that lead people to use drugs in the first place can we curb drug abuse and trafficking. These factors, or root causes, such as sexual abuse, broken homes, illiteracy,

physical abuse, and lack of parental guidance are more social problems than they are problems of crime. (Library of Parliament, 1993: 10)

As reaffirmed by the House of Commons Special Committee on Non-Medical Use of Drugs (2002: 5), 'overall, the Committee believes that the harmful use of substances, and dependence, are primarily public health issues that must be addressed within a public health framework'. In its final analysis the Committee proposes that cannabis in particular be decriminalized in Canada. Supporting this view, yet pushing more strongly for the legalization of cannabis, the Senate Special Committee on Illegal Drugs declared that 'only offences involving significant direct danger to others should be matters of criminal law' (2002: 29), and that 'the main social costs of cannabis [and other drugs in Canada] are a result of public policy choices, and primarily its continued criminalization' (2002: 33–34). In short, punishment in such instances is regarded as part of the problem rather than part of the solution, in strong contrast to the American 'War on Drugs' mentality. Indeed, once again there is an explicit rejection of the US approach:

In our view, it is clear that if the aim of public policy is to diminish con-sumption and supply of drugs, specifically cannabis, all signs indicate complete failure ... One of the reasons for this failure is the excessive emphasis placed on criminal law in a context where prohibition of use and a drug-free society appear to remain the omnipresent and determining direction of current public policies. (Senate Special Committee On Illegal Drugs, 2002: 33–34)

This statement advances more than a mere critique of the shortcomings of current prohibitionist policies, and the limits of the criminal justice system. This state-ment encourages Canadian leadership to recognize that control does not necessarily result from the imposition of some 'excessive', all-encompassing approach – such as law enforcement. The net result is that existing Canadian policies regarding cannabis are seen by the Senate Committee as too restrictive and as such require a more holistic and balanced approach. According to the Senate Special Committee:

We think that a public policy on psychoactive substances must be both integrated and adaptable, target at-risk uses and behaviours and abuses based on a public health approach that neither trivializes nor marginalizes users. Implementation of such a policy must be multifaceted. (2002: 34)

This position has been sustained despite considerable United States' media and official opposition.

Conclusions: cultural lag or glocalisation?

Canadian criminal justice cannot be subsumed under a general model of a global punitive turn. As has become clear in this analysis, policies and official discourses are turning as much and perhaps more to the forms of intervention characteristic of penal modernism. While attention has been paid to official discourse, as seen, a wide array of indicators continue to show declining severity in punishment and a downward trend in incarceration. These continue into the present day. As of 2001, the incarceration rate had slipped to 116 per 100,000, which takes it down to about one-sixth of that in the United States, and has now declined below the rate in the United Kingdom (125 per 100,000) for the first time in decades. Prison populations have declined about 10 per cent since the mid-1990s, new admissions to federal institutions have declined by 16.5 per cent in the same period, and the average time spent in custody has tracked a similar course. Does this reflect a society averse to punishment? Doubtfully, for it has been seen already that Canada has exhibited very high rates of incarceration by international standards, and only comparatively recently have these declined below the rising rates in the UK and US. In sum, it could be said that Canada has followed a fairly steady course over the past half-century, with some increasing emphasis on decarceration and improving the availability of 'welfare sanctions' since the early 1990s.

It may, of course, be argued that we are witnessing some variant of the 'cultural lag' thesis, and that Canada – late on the scene with respect to de-emphasizing punishment, will be late on the scene taking the punitive turn. The possibility has to be recognized, and a new conservative government could change matters – although this did not occur in the 1990s. But elsewhere the punitive turn supposedly dates from the 1970s. Thirty years and counting seems a rather lengthy cultural lag, especially when the exemplar of punitive justice is just across a very long and still quite permeable border, when the mass media have long been saturated with criminal justice news and dramatizations from the US, and when the tide seems still to be running fairly strongly against harsher and less reformist sanctions. Even more important, the US response to crime is officially regarded as having failed. In particular, the move toward punitive rationalities and mass incarceration have been represented as counterproductive. Evidence of this failure, in turn, is linked with a nationalist discourse on the 'Canadian way'. This taps into strongly valorized cultural images of Canada as a civilized and 'peaceable kingdom', often specifically contrasted with the United States. To the extent that the punitive turn is associated with globalizing processes, then we have to entertain the possibility that Canadian criminal justice has been insulated from this by a 'glocalizing' reaction: the assertion of regional or national autonomy in the face of global pressures. However, we are not arguing that this kind of response has created, or even shaped in any active fashion, the nature of the local penal agenda. Rather, it is more that it has been mobilized in such a way that a long-term pattern, itself characterized by a modest tendency towards increased penal modernism but equally by internationally high rates of imprisonment, has been preserved. It is a pattern in which punishment and penal modernism are articulated together in a relatively robust configuration that has resisted hegemonizing either the modernism imagined to be characteristic of the 'golden era', or the punitive programming imagined to be characteristic of the present. 'Balance' has been the sign under which successive Canadian governments have sustained this assemblage.

Notes

1 Of course, the reality was somewhat different. Commenting on this scenario more than a decade later, one member of the National Parole Board notes that 'most offenders still pass through the correctional system relatively untouched by programs of rehabilitation' (Outerbridge 1970: 280).

2 Many similar comments abound, often repeating this identical theme almost verbatim: 'The USA has one of the highest incarceration rates in the world (682 per 100,000), yet it is not a safer place to live' (Canada, 2001a: 14).

3 As an index of the marginality of such sentences, as of June 2002, there was a total of 313 designated 'dangerous offenders' in Canada, but of these only 13 were serving mandatory sentences. In the period from 1990 through 1999, an average of only 22 dangerous offenders were designated each year out of an average of about 4,000 offenders sentenced to terms of imprisonment in federal institutions.

4 According to the Department of the Solicitor General (Canada, 2002: 19), the disfavour of rehabilitation was premised 'on two fronts: first, that rehabilitation had been costly and ineffective, and, second, that it had caused more cruelty and longer punishment than the intentionally "punitive" model which had preceded it'. After reviewing research evidence on this matter, the authors conclude that 'we are of the view then, that it cannot be concluded that rehabilitation is ineffective. The evidence is too sparse, and the actual attempts to design, fund, and carry out a rehabilitative model for corrections have, to date, been inconsistent and incomplete' (2002: 20).

5 A special committee, unlike a standing committee, has a set lifespan and is only designed to take a snapshot review on the current social context. In Canada, parliamentary work is primarily conducted through committees rather than sessions of Parliament.

References

Braithwaite, J. (2003) 'What's wrong with the sociology of punishment?', *Theoretical Criminology*, 7: 5–28.

Canada (Government of) (1969) *Report of the Canadian Committee on Corrections, toward Unity: Criminal Justice and Corrections*, Ottawa: Information Canada.

Canada (Government of) (1982) *The Criminal Law in Canadian Society*, Ottawa: Solicitor General.

Canada (Government of) (1984) *Sentencing*, Ottawa: Solicitor General.

Canada, (Government of) (1999) *Illicit Drugs and Crime in Canada* (85-002-XIE Vol. 19 no. 1), Ottawa: Statistics Canada.

Canada (Government of) (2001a) *The Government's Balanced Approach 2001*, Ottawa: Correctional Service of Canada. http://www.csc-scc.gc.ca/text/pubed/feuilles/govbal_e.shtml

Canada (Government of) (2001b) *Public Fear of Crime and Perceptions of the Criminal Justice System*, Ottawa: Solicitor General.

Canada (Government of) (2002) *Influences on Canadian Correctional Reform: Working Paper of the Correctional Law Review 1986–1998*, Ottawa: Solicitor General.

Canada (Government of) (2003a) Newsroom Fact Sheet: Capital Punishment in Canada. http://canada.justice.gc.ca/en/news/fs/2003/doc_30896.html

Canada (Government of) (2003b) Talk About Justice: Human Rights in Canada and Abroad – Case Summaries http://www.justice.gc.ca/en/ps/sg/p1/ti/cssm.html

Chrétien, J. (2000) *The Canadian Way in the 21st Century*, Ottawa: Prime Minister's Office.

Correctional Service of Canada (1993) *Contributing to the Protection of Society through Assistance and Control: An Overview of Canada's Correctional Service*, Ottawa: Correctional Service of Canada.

Correctional Service of Canada (1998) *Implementing the Life Line Concept: Report of the Task Force on Long Term Offenders*, Ottawa: Correctional Service of Canada.

Correctional Service of Canada (1999a) *Anger Management Programming for Federal Male Inmates: An Effective Intervention*, Ottawa: Correctional Service of Canada.

Correctional Service of Canada (1999b) *Commissioner's Directive: Education of Offenders*, Ottawa: Correctional Service of Canada.

Correctional Service of Canada (2001a) *Speakers' Kit: The Government's Balanced Approach, Key Messages*, Ottawa: Correctional Service of Canada.

Correctional Service of Canada (2001b) *Commissioner's Directive: Use of Force*, Ottawa: Correctional Service of Canada.

Correctional Service of Canada (2001c) *Commissioner's Directive: Ethnocultural Offender Programs*, Ottawa: Correctional Service of Canada.

Correctional Service of Canada (2001d) *Commissioner's Directive: Visiting*, Ottawa: Correctional Service of Canada.

Correctional Service of Canada (2002a) *Standards for Health Services*, Ottawa: Correctional Service of Canada.

Correctional Service of Canada (2002b) *Backgrounders: Offender Rehabilitation*, Ottawa: Correctional Service of Canada.

Correctional Service of Canada (2002c) *Backgrounders: Aboriginal Offenders*, Ottawa: Correctional Service of Canada.

Correctional Service of Canada (2003a) *Estimates Part 3 – Report on Plans and Priorities*, Ottawa: Correctional Service of Canada.

Correctional Service of Canada (2003b) *Aboriginal Initiatives Branch*, Ottawa: Correctional Service of Canada.

Correctional Service of Canada (2004) *Corcan: The Commitment Behind Our Products*, Ottawa: Correctional Service of Canada.

Cousineau, D. and J. Veevers (1972) 'Incarceration as a Response to Crime: The Utilization of Canadian Prisons', *Canadian Journal of Criminology and Corrections*, 14: 10–31.

Cressey, D. (1961) 'Introduction', in D. Cressey (ed.) *The Prison. Studies in Institutional Organization and Change*, New York: Holt, Rinehart and Winston.

Doob, A. and Marinos, V. (1995) 'Reconceptualizing Punishment. Understanding the Limitations of the Use of Intermediate Punishments', *Roundtable*, 2: 413–33.

Fulton, D. (1958) 'The Limits of our Imagination Alone Restrict the Effective Contribution that the Private Citizen Can Make', *Canadian Journal of Corrections*, 1–2: 264–272.

Gabor, T. and Crutcher, N. (2002) *Mandatory Minimum Penalties: Their Effects on Crime, Sentencing Disparities, and Justice System Expenditures*, Ottawa: Justice Canada.

Gagnon, P. (1995) 'Speaking Notes for Patrick Gagnon, M.P, Parliamentary Secretary to the Solicitor General of Canada, Public Discussion on the Federal Justice System Closing Remarks'. www.sgc.gc.ca

Galtung, J. (1960) 'Prison: The Organization of a Dilemma', in D. Cressey (ed.) *The Prison. Studies in Institutional Organization and Change*, New York: Holt, Rinehart and Winston.

Garland, D. (1996) 'The Limits of the Sovereign State: Strategies of Crime Control in Contemporary Society', *British Journal of Criminology*, 36: 445–471.

Garland, D. (2001) *The Culture of Control*, Oxford: Oxford University Press.

Gervais, C. (2002) 'Governing Crime Through Prevention in Late Twentieth Century Canada', unpublished Doctoral Thesis, Department of Sociology and Anthropology, Carleton University, Canada.

Goyer, J-P (1972) 'Address by the Honourable Jean-Pierre Goyer Solicitor General of Canada: Address at the Club Richelieu d'Ottawa', Ottawa: Solicitor General.

Hallsworth, S. (2000) 'Rethinking the Punitive Turn. Economies of Excess and the Criminology of the Other', *Punishment and Society*, 2: 145–60.

Hatt, K., Caputo, T. and Perry, B. (1992) 'Criminal Justice Policy under Mulroney, 1984–90: Neo-conservatism, eh?', *Canadian Public Policy*, 18: 245–260.

Health Canada (2002) *National Inventory of Treatment Programs for Child Sexual Abuse Offenders*, Ottawa: National Clearinghouse on Family Violence, Family Violence Prevention Unit, Population and Public Health Branch.

Hogarth, J. (1967) 'Towards the Improvement of Sentencing in Canada', *Canadian Journal of Corrections*, 9: 122–136.

House of Commons Special Committee on Non-Medical Use of Drugs (2002) *Policy for the New Millennium: Working Together to Redefine Canada's Drug Strategy, Report of the Special Committee on Non-Medical Use of Drugs*, Ottawa: House of Commons.

Library of Parliament (1993) *Illegal Drugs and Drug Trafficking*. Ottawa: Library of Parliament.

Linden, R. (1996) *Criminology: A Canadian Perspective* (3rd edn), Toronto: Harcourt Brace Canada.

Morris, N. and Hawkins, G. (1969*) The Honest Politician's Guide to Crime Control*, Chicago: University of Chicago Press.

Nolan, J (1998) *The Therapeutic State: Justifying Government at Century's End*, New York: York University Press.

O'Malley, P. (1999) 'Volatile and Contradictory Punishment', *Theoretical Criminology*, 3: 175–196.

O'Malley, P. (2000) 'Criminologies of Catastrophe? Understanding Criminal Justice on the Edge of the New Millennium', *The Australian and New Zealand Journal of Criminology*, 33: 153–167.

O'Malley, P. (2001) 'Risk, Crime and Prudentialism Revisited', in K. Stenson and R. Sullivan (eds) *Crime, Risk and Justice*, Cullompton: Willan.

Outerbridge, W. (1970) 'Unity and Credibility in Corrections', *Canadian Journal of Corrections*, 12: 274–284.

Pratt, J. (2002) 'Emotive and Ostentatious Punishment. Its Decline and Resurgence in Modern Society', *Punishment and Society*, 2: 417–441.

Roberts, J., Stalans, L., Indermauer, D. and Hough, M. (2003) *Penal Populism and Public Opinion. Lessons from Five Countries*, Oxford: Oxford University Press.

Senate Special Committee on Illegal Drugs (2002) *Cannabis: Our Position for a Canadian Public Policy*, Ottawa: Senate of Canada.

Vaughan B. (2000) 'The Civilizing Process and the Janus-face of Modern Punishment', *Theoretical Criminology*, 4: 71–91.

13. When is a society non-punitive? The Italian case

David Nelken

This collective volume takes its starting point from the editors' concern about recent developments in criminal justice systems in which the growth of imprisonment has been accompanied not simply by longer prison sentences but by penal laws which seem to abandon long-standing limits to punishment in modern societies. For many scholars this change is seen as a concomitant of the globally influenced move to neoliberalism[1] in the workings of economics and politics. But, for others, the fact that punishment is going up worldwide in places with different types of economic and political systems, including those which are far from 'modern', suggests that imitation is more important than underlying conditions (Pavarini, 2004). The mechanisms that link variations in economics, politics, and culture are also somewhat opaque. The main way this works in Anglo-American type societies seems to be that when the state is challenged by the pressures of globalization, politicians choose to adopt penological approaches that downgrade the status of criminal justice professionals in favour of ill-informed and intolerant public opinion. The editors of this collection, however, rightly note that such mechanisms may not be universal and that the developments that worry them are in any case differently advanced in different parts of the world. They were therefore especially interested in contributions that aimed to explain punishment trends in what they describe as 'non-punitive societies'.

The reason why this chapter about Italy is located with other case studies of so-called non-punitive societies (Scandinavia and Canada) is that it was commissioned as a result of talks I gave at Sydney and Melbourne Universities in July 2003 entitled 'Getting it Right or Getting Away with Murder? The Response to Juvenile Delinquency in Italy'. I argued then that the Italian approach to juvenile justice was much more lenient than that represented by Anglo-American juvenile justice systems. This will also be the central claim of the present chapter. But, in keeping with the overall plan of the volume, I shall try to relate this issue to larger questions about the Italian criminal justice system and the study of punitiveness and leniency more generally. Although I shall make selective reference to various aspects of Italian criminal justice, there will not be space here for any attempt to provide detailed descriptions of the law and practice of either the adult or the juvenile justice systems.[2] On the other hand, however, although knowledge of the specific laws and procedures of other jurisdictions is certainly a prerequisite for describing their functioning, it is unlikely by itself to provide the answer to the questions posed by this volume. What is needed is insight into how practices of punitiveness or leniency in the Italian (or any other) criminal justice system may be fairly compared with those with which the reader may be more familiar (Nelken, 2000a, 2002). The challenge, as always in comparative research, is to be sure we are comparing like with like. This sort of analysis is more difficult to find.

In my attempt to meet this challenge I shall first ask what is involved in calling a society punitive or non-punitive and indicate some of the problems of measuring punitiveness cross-nationally and cross-culturally. I go on to suggest that the level of imprisonment and general level of harshness of the Italian system is within the norm for Continental Europe, but that its approach to juvenile delinquency does stand out as relatively lenient. In the remainder of the chapter I discuss whether alleged wider trends towards neoliberalism have affected the juvenile justice system and conclude that, at least as far as the reaction to Italian youngsters is concerned, they have not yet done so. I shall only try to deal with a few of the issues raised by comparative research into punitiveness. In particular I do not have the space to examine the assumption, which underlies much of the academic response to growing punitiveness, that more lenient practices are necessarily and always a 'good thing'. But this chapter does imply that, as much as in any analysis of punitiveness, any evaluation of non-punitiveness also needs to take carefully into account its causes, conditions, and consequences.[3]

Comparing levels of punitiveness: some preliminary considerations

What data should we use to decide whether Italy (or anywhere else) is a non-punitive society, or whether it too has been affected by the new punitiveness? There are many aspects to the alleged rise of punitiveness.[4] Within the criminal justice system these range from the lack of proportionality in sentencing, to the use of humiliating and psychologically destructive sanctions. In general society there is the rise of vigilantism, the endorsement of populist calls for revenge, the social and economic exclusion of offenders, accompanied by the malign neglect of the poor. While, as we shall see, no comparison of punishment can limit itself to the criminal justice system as such, embracing a wider perspective does make it more difficult to measure differences. There are big differences in the way in which in some societies the state retreats from responsibility on some fronts yet hardens its response to crime on others. Is the reduced role of the state part of what is to be explained or part of the explanation? With respect to the 'parcelling out' of the risks of modern life, in Italy it is only recently that 'the state' has come to be seen as responsible for reducing the level of street crime (Nelken, 2000b). But it is now the central or local state itself, especially in dealing with illegal immigration, which is adopting something of the new punitiveness style in ideas and practices.

The editors invited contributors to present information about changes in levels of imprisonment, together with whatever other relevant evidence is available concerning recent legislation and current administrative practices. They also suggested the particular importance of policy-making. Indeed they define 'non-punitive societies' as those societies that 'remain exceptions to these trends, still have low rates of imprisonment, and seem to place a value on professional expertise in planning penal policy'. It could be helpful, however, to think a little more about what we mean both by punitiveness and non-punitiveness. Are they two points on the same continuum? In other words, does the explanation of non-punitiveness involve considering the same variables as those assumed to be responsible for punitiveness? The editors appear to be conceptualizing non-punitiveness as an 'absence'; more specifically as the absence of what they see as the neoliberal-inspired drive to punitiveness.[5] More than this, non-punitiveness is taken to be the 'normal' or default case in which sufficient heed is given to policy-makers and experts. But for a more complete analysis we also need to look for 'presence', for the special factors that explain high levels of punitivenesss, especially in the US, and, on the other hand, the many and varied specific factors that explain which societies have particularly low levels of punishment.

Following the broad definitions of punitiveness set out by the editors, we shall need to examine both quantitative and qualitative indicators. We have to consider levels of 'punitiveness' not only as shown by rates of imprisonment but also in relation to the many other ways in which 'harshness' can characterize the treatment of offenders (Whitman, 2003). While it has become conventional to rely mainly on rates of imprisonment as the measure of relative levels of punitiveness in different societies, those who have made their careers studying comparative prison statistics tell us that 'the imprisonment rate is only a very weak indicator of punitiveness' (Kommer, 2004: 9). At the least we need to it break this up into a series of more specific measures of the use of prison at different stages for different purposes (ibid.). Other problems of comparability range from the way crimes are defined to the types of sentences available. From an interpretative point of view it is risky to use rates of imprisonment (or rates of other legal processes) to prove the existence of postulated processes of punishment or leniency (or anything else) because the significance we read into these rates depends on our first understanding the processes which produce them (Nelken, 1994, 1997a).[6]

As so often, problems of measurement also point to larger theoretical issues. If we are really interested in gauging societal levels of punitiveness, how are we to measure other types of punishment and practices of official social control not involving prison? Going beyond this, what significance should we attach to changes in patterns of so called 'informal' social control? It is curious that the cutbacks on 'disciplinary' forms of social control by 'psy' experts, social workers, and others, which are a defining feature of all definitions of neoliberalism, are rarely counted as part of a reduction in the overall punishment equation. But it is not easy, or even useful, to draw a line between state and non-state sanctioning systems, or the formal and the informal. Some factors which shape the mix of punitiveness and leniency may play a role in all of these – as in the role of Catholic instruction and values in Italy. Should we not also consider differences in the growth of surveillance and situational prevention as an aspect of the development of greater punitiveness? These measures cannot be classified as 'stigmatizing punishments'. But there would be a strong argument for taking them into account in terms of the way they tend to replace expenditure on more 'social' forms of prevention, and the types of exclusionary messages they send to the collectivity. Much of the reliance placed on imprisonment rates, despite their ambiguities, should be attributed only to the ready availability of such cross-national sets of data as compared with the more 'soft' evidence available concerning other features of punitiveness.

Trying to relate what happens within and without the formal system raises yet more questions. Does harsh treatment in the penal system necessarily reflect harsh application of social sanctions in social life? It could be the case that a relatively open and mobile society would be more likely to operate harsh official penalties precisely because of the lack of bite of secondary group norms. Conversely, a society with a low level of official punishment may be one characterized by a high use of vendetta. Where 'exit' from group requirements is difficult it may be common to find tolerance of (certain) forms of breaches of state rules. But, if harshness in official sanctions may or may not correspond to harshness elsewhere, what happens to our comparisons of punitiveness?

As this suggests, it is far from obvious that punitiveness means the same thing when treated as an objective or else as a subjective phenomenon. It is one thing to focus on allegedly objective differences in penal outcomes; quite another to characterize given penal or governmental projects. Are we mainly interested in the causes and conditions of variations in levels of punishment, irrespective of the intentions of those involved? Or are we trying to explain why members of a given society think they are being punitive or non-punitive? Leniency could be an unintended side-effect of dealing with prohibited conduct outside the criminal law, through using regulatory regimes, welfare interventions, or restitution programmes (Italy is a country which, relatively speaking, makes little use of these alternatives).[7] Or else, apparently lenient outcomes could be a consequence, desired or otherwise, of inefficiency, delay and the limited resources devoted to criminal justice (this seems important in the Italian case). If leniency is to be studied as a deliberate choice to reduce punitiveness, we shall need to investigate the exercise of 'mildness', 'tolerance', or 'forgiveness', and decisions not to intervene penally in relation to certain offenders or offences. It will also be important to try to grasp internal debates about leniency and the use of words and phrases that indicate when certain practices of leniency are considered to have gone too far. It is significant that in Italy there are many expressions, including *perdonismo* and *buonismo*, which indicate over-forgiveness, as well as the strange term *garanzie pelosi* ('hairy procedural rights'), which refers to attempts to pay lip service to due process which really aim to block trial processes.

If we do not keep the objective and subjective aspects of punishment regimes distinct, our search for 'non-punitive societies' risks succumbing to the so-called 'orientalist' temptation to describe 'other' societies in terms of their relevance to ourselves. The analytic categories we use may not be salient (or the only ones salient) for the society we are purporting to represent (Cain, 2000). Take for instance the underlying idea of this collection that there exist 'non-punitive societies' from which we can and need to learn from in order to become less punitive. Are we sure we are comparing like with like? We need to attend to crucial differences between the ideal and actual forms taken by social control in so-called 'state societies' and those where 'civil society' is and is supposed to be its locus (Melossi, 1990).

When we speak of non-punitive societies, for example, the term 'society' could be meant to describe the country as a whole, or intended rather to be taken in the restricted sense of 'public opinion' , as opposed to state officialdom. The editors suggest that the current drive to punitiveness is the result of giving less weight to the experts. But the alternatives of 'professional expertise' versus 'populist politics' may tell us more about the 'starting point' of Anglo-American societies and their cycles of punitiveness and leniency than about the societies we want to use as a foil or counterpoint. As should later become clear, the key to lenient practices in Italy does not lie necessarily in the 'value placed on professional expertise in planning penal policy', but more on a variety of historical factors that shape the functioning of adult and juvenile systems of criminal justice in relation to wider aspects of political and social life.

However convenient it may be for collaborative comparative exercises or comparative criminal justice textbooks, we must even be cautious about talking about 'Italy' as a place distinct from the rest of the world, characterized by its own unique approach to punishment (Nelken, 2005). Not all that goes on in Italy is specifically Italian, but rather reflects or relates to larger identities such as that of the civil law, Catholicism, southern Europe, modern capitalism, etc. Italy has undergone and is undergoing change (after all, the invention of Fascism can hardly be taken as a sign of essential non-punitiveness). And, ever more, as this volume rightly presupposes, Italy is affected by worldwide changes (Nelken, 1997b, 2003a, 2004). On the other hand, national governments and legal jurisdictions do try to mark their boundaries in relation to elsewhere. For present purposes one of the most interesting examples of this is the way, once comparative incarceration rates began to be published, countries such as Finland, Holland (and even to some extent Italy) have tried to adjust the numbers of those sent to prison so as to remain within the European average. For Finland the goal was to reduce numbers; the Dutch minister of justice, on the other hand, justified his prison-building programme of the 1980s on the basis that his country was too far beneath the average. Hence it must be a mistake to assume that levels of punishment are necessarily culturally 'embedded' in the country in which they are found (Nelken, 2005).

Even within a society we should also not assume that punitiveness and non-punitiveness necessarily come as complete packages (in this chapter I shall be drawing a distinction between adult and juvenile justice in Italy). Seen comparatively, a country that is relatively harsh in dealing with a given type of offence may not be so in responding to another. In Italy, for example, some types of financial crime are pursued with more rigour than in the UK, but the reverse is true for juvenile delinquency. Southern European countries are considered relatively lax in their approach to law enforcement, but these are the countries in which recent immigrants, convicted of relatively minor crimes, currently make up the highest proportion of modern prison populations. Historical changes also affect the boundaries of punitiveness. Since the last world war, modern industrial societies have become more tolerant and inclusive of some sorts of deviance, e.g. sexual deviance, while less willing to respond with assistance to those accused of conventional crime (Young, 1999).

The best antidote to 'orientalism' is to try to learn about the society in question in its own terms. This undoubtedly requires examining what local practitioners say they are trying to do, and taking on board what local experts say is happening. In this chapter I shall make reference to some of the best theoretical criminologists, such as Dario Melossi and Massimo Pavarini, as well as leading experts on the juvenile justice system, such as Uberto Gatti, Gaetano de Leo, and Duccio Scatolera. But at the same time, we should not expect local experts to speak with one voice, nor to possess the whole picture. They are unlikely to have the answers to questions coming from our 'starting point' (Nelken, 2000b). On the contrary, as far as the theme of the present collection is concerned, far from seeing it as an exception to present trends, many Italian commentators see Italy as very much affected by the spread of neoliberal American ideas about punishment. In a recent broad-ranging discussion, Massimo Pavarini describes the recent rise in punitiveness as a worldwide trend from which not even the Third World (let alone Italy) is exempt (Pavarini, 2004). He argues that it is impossible to find an explanatory common denominator for this rise. Even if the growth of crime were taken to be the cause (and not the consequence), the rise of crime is not well correlated with increases in imprisonment worldwide. The only explanation he can offer is that of emulation of neoliberal ideas even when these are not necessarily conditioned by local developments.

But if emulation helps explain the rise of punitiveness, it can also provoke calls for resistance. Take, for example, the following description of what is happening in Italy, which forms part of the presentation of a recent conference on prisons in 2004 organized by the pressure group Antigone (an activist organization of lawyers, academics, and others concerned with prison reform, comparable with the Howard League in the UK):[8]

> Set against a background characterized by neo-liberal deregulation of the economy and systematic attack on the welfare system and principles of social solidarity, we are witnessing on the one hand a reduction in the penal control of criminal activities linked to businesses' behaviour and the exercise of power by dominant social groups. This is put into action under cover of misuse of the principle of 'due process' bent to the logic of protecting the most powerful that brings about reduction in punitiveness not so as to create a penal system that is more tolerant and democratic but towards reinforcing privileges. This produces the result that, on the other hand, there is increased repression of so-called street crimes by means of making sanctions more rigorous and a wider resort to prison. This process, which is accompanied by an increase in the resources destined to repressive apparatuses and social control in the face of reductions in expenditure on social welfare expertise, moves us in an authoritarian direction and shows the tendency characteristic of non-egalitarian societies to reduce social questions and underlying criminal phenomena to simple questions of public order to be regulated exclusively through the use of the criminal law. Immigrants are among the social groups most marginalized and hit by this trend ... as well as drug addicts and those committing 'micro-crimes' in urban centres ... With the intention to create a facile political consensus this repressive tendency is beginning to extend itself also to other categories of offenders such as simple users of drugs as well as juveniles for whom laws have been put forward that make the relevant punishments much harsher.

Most (though, interestingly, not all) of this account would be familiar to observers of Anglo-American criminal justice systems and would seem to echo the editors' fears about growing punitiveness. This summary of developments even includes juvenile justice among the areas being subject to increased punitiveness. Does this mean that neoliberalism is sweeping all before it? If so, what is this chapter doing here? In my view this description, while accurately describing a series of developments that go in the direction of increasing (some) types of punishment, tells us less about how far this tendency has yet been realized in practice. For these engaged commentators want to stress the dangers of following certain trends, which they describe as if they were universal, transferable, and already in the processes of being transferred (see also Di Georgi, 2002, 2004). But we should not confuse the question whether Italy is also being influenced by neoliberal developments or models with the issue of whether Italian practices of punishment are currently less punitive than those adopted for example in the US or other Anglo-American societies. I would argue that they are, and especially so in the case of juvenile justice.

The Italian criminal justice system in comparative perspective

Even though the number of people in prison in Italy is slowly rising, in part because of an increase in conviction rates often involving foreign-born offenders (Sollivetti, 2004: 21), the level of imprisonment remains much less than that of the US, and near the European average of around 100 prisoners per 100,000 of the population. Ways of treating prisoners, though far from ideal, are also less harsh than in the US. This suggests that rather than explaining what is different about Italy we should be concentrating on America as the exception (at least since its prison rates soared at the end of the 1970s). On the other hand, Italy does arrive at its average position in its own way. It has one of the lowest rates of convicted prisoners in Europe. But it comes out high in terms of gross sentences of imprisonment and has one of the highest average detention periods (Kommer, 2004). Many of those in prison are waiting final sentence in the three-stage trial system. The Italian situation cannot be understood without taking into account the many complex procedures and delays that characterize all these stages, which mean that trials often fail to be completed because they overrun set time limits – so-called prescription periods. The large variety of measures of mercy or conditional forgiveness which undo the effects of a sentence or punishment are also important and in some ways unique.

We could of course choose to treat such features of penal procedure and organizational practice as themselves aspects of Italy's low level of punitiveness. And, following the shock of the anti-corruption investigations of the early 1990s, there has been a cut-back in the open use of governmental amnesties and indulgences. But to say that delay always represents a deliberate choice to be non-punitive would be stretching things. And there is another side to this reduction of imprisonment numbers through attrition. Compared with common-law countries, in Italy there is a relatively high risk of being exposed to the criminal process even for relatively powerful groups such as politicians, administrators, and businessmen (as well of course for the poor and marginal groups who are the normal fodder of the criminal courts). It is the irregular immigrants and drug dealers who fill the prisons. But the powerful quite often get a taste of pre-trial stigmatization (and suicide is not uncommon) even if they usually get off in the end. Malcolm Feeley, a leading scholar of the American criminal process, famously argued that 'the process is the punishment' (Feeley, 1979). If we were to compare Italy with the US in these terms, the pains of the process would certainly loom larger in Italy. For a leading Italian criminologist, Dario Melossi, the elites in Italy 'rule by leniency' (Melossi, 1994) rather than ' governing through crime' as is allegedly done in the US. Certainly this is true in comparison with the US. In relation to other European countries, however, deciding whether or not Italy is a more or less punitive society depends on how much we focus on the process or the outcome of sentencing.

Italian leniency, insofar as it exists, is not a result of economy in the use of the criminal law. Commentators agree that its legal system tries to deal with too many matters through the criminal law, whilst efforts at depenalization have made little headway as yet. In common-law countries many forms of conduct that, in Italy are at least theoretically regulated by criminal law, would be the subject of administrative or civil law. In addition, penal law plays a crucial role in political life that would not find an easy parallel in common-law countries. For almost 15 years a central political issue has been the battle between some of the judges trying to deal with political corruption and financial crime and the later counter-attack by some politicians. In the Tangentopoli investigations of the early 1990s, prosecuting judges destroyed all the governing political parties simply by successfully applying the criminal law. Beyond politics, in much of economic and social life, compliance with the rules of the group often takes precedence over obedience to what are seen as rigid and inflexible state rules. Rather than changing the rules, they are collusively evaded. So the potential risk of criminal prosecution is ever present. Yet, despite this, the current premier and longest-lasting post-war Italian prime minister is Silvio Berlusconi, who is himself a former major beneficiary of largesse from the disgraced Socialist Party. Although he has been investigated and tried for a range of crimes, he has succeeded in avoiding final conviction, often by exploiting the possibilities of delaying trial procedures, and is currently locked into a battle for legitimacy with the penal judges (Nelken, 2003b).

Whatever the extent of actual or menaced punishment of the 'upperworld', by contrast there is very much less politically exploited public fear of conventional crime as compared to that which characterizes many common-law countries (and a noticeable lack of tabloid-driven media crime panics). Part of the explanation here is that, compared with common-law countries, judges and judicial prosecutors have a larger role in defining the crime problem, whereas the police are given little chance to act as spokespeople. Victims are much more rarely the focus of concern than in common-law countries (in this Catholic culture their role is to show forgiveness). And it is still the 'state', and the collective values it protects, rather than the 'community' as a set of locally based individuals, which vindicates itself through criminal law. Until the 1990s, crimes as serious as robbery, burglary, and even rape were actually called 'micro-crimes', so as to contrast them with the forms of crime that threatened the state itself, such as corruption, political terrorism, or organized crime (Nelken, 2000b).

But, as the Antigone presentation points out, things have been changing since the 1990s, and the new term is 'street' crime or 'diffuse' crime. Parties forming part of Berlusconi's ruling coalition, such as the Northern Leagues or the National Alliance former Fascist party, are now revealing some authoritarian leanings. They tend to minimize police brutality, have recently relaxed the law restricting torture, and are planning to re-criminalize soft drugs. Politicians are also well aware that it is politically popular to pass measures that tighten up the control of irregular immigrants even if the effects of these measures is frequently only to make them more vulnerable to economic exploitation. Now that local mayors are elected by direct vote they also have reason to play on the 'fear of crime'. Yet we are still far from 'law and order' politics. The current prime minister has made it his priority to make it more difficult to obtain convictions for white-collar crime. But some of the procedural reforms he has sponsored can also make it more awkward to impose convictions in more conventional crime cases. And there is remarkable cross-party support for what Anglo-American legal culture would describe as 'due process' legal procedures (the so-called *garanzie*) in the penal process, even when these inevitably exact a price in terms of 'reducing crime control' to all but the most flagrant cases.

The juvenile justice system: getting away with murder?

Whatever conclusions we draw about the degree of punitiveness of the adult system, both insiders and outsiders agree that the Italian system of juvenile justice is one of the most lenient in the world.[9] Consistent with the role of this chapter, some experienced Italian commentators even attribute this to the benevolence of the general public. Thus Duccio Scatolera speaks of what he calls the 'benevolent tolerance' that often accompanies the view taken of small-scale criminality by young Italians (Scatolera, 2004: 400). He argues that the propensity to tolerate such criminal behaviour increased in recent times once the authors of such behaviour no longer belonged exclusively to the marginalized classes at risk (ibid.). In the UK, leading critical criminologists and specialists in youth justice (including its comparative aspects) such as John Pitts and John Muncie have also held up the Italian case as a model of non-punitiveness from which England and Wales could learn.

In a country with a population the size of Britain there are many fewer prosecutions and many fewer convictions of young people. At any given time there are no more than around 500 young people in prison. Only around 3,000 young people (aged 14–18) are sentenced to prison each year, compared with the 10,000 or more people in the same age group sentenced to prison in Britain yearly (and the proportion in the United States is of course many times higher). What is as remarkable is that the number of young people sent to prison in Italy has been going down steadily from the around 7,000 sent to prison annually in the 1960s. Despite the demographic decline in the relevant age group there has been an increase in the number of reported crimes by young people, as well as a particular increase in the proportion of violent offences being reported. But the number of Italian-born youngsters sentenced to prison has declined so as to become almost negligible; though prison is still used by some southern Italian courts for young men convicted of violent crimes such as armed robbery. On the other hand, it has increasingly been used in the 1990s in dealing with young unaccompanied immigrants accused of drug dealing or property offences, or gypsy girls accused of recent pick-pocketing, these are held in custody both before and after the final sentence is passed. Scatolera concludes, 'but for immigrants and drug addicts, penal correctional ideology for young people would be exhausted for lack of human material on which to exercise itself' (Scatolera, 2004: 401).

The first explanation for this leniency lies in the law itself. The work of the juvenile court is largely shaped by a Juvenile Justice Reform Act passed in 1989. This requires that prison use be avoided to the utmost and, more in general, that care be taken in legal proceedings not to interrupt the normal process of growing up. Once a criminal case is put forward by the prosecutor there are a series of trial stages in which it is possible to make decisions before arriving at a full public trial. The judges can use a variety of ordinances to oblige the youth to remain at home at certain times or not to frequent certain places. Otherwise the main measures possible (at various of the trial stages) are: declaring the offence 'irrelevant' (as being trivial and occasional); conferring a 'judicial pardon' (a long established possibility for adults and youths alike); and imposing a new form of pre-trial probation called *messa alla prova*, or 'putting you to the test'. With this disposal, final trial is delayed to see if the youth complies with a court-approved programme focused on schooling, work, voluntary work (often organized by the local Church), and, if necessary, psychological counselling.

Compared with Anglo-American jurisdictions there is relatively little going on in terms of positive interventions in children's lives. Fines or other punishments are also rarely used. Arrangements for restitution and compensation to the victim, though theoretically possible, are rare; mediation schemes have recently been introduced in some court districts on an experimental and voluntary basis but their authorization under the 1989 reform is somewhat controversial. It should be noted that the 1989 Act was a procedural reform (made necessary by a larger procedural reform for adults introduced in the same year), so no new substantive penalties could be introduced. The new measures it introduced are all, formally speaking, ways of postponing or avoiding the need for trial. Thus prison remains – in theory at least – the standard post-trial sentence, even if it is rarely imposed and most prison sentences handed down are suspended. Paradoxically, one reason the system sends few children to prison could be that children do not have the opportunity to fail social interventions and thus move up the ladder of penal severity. Delay in dealing with cases, sometimes deliberate but often not, also helps.

The 'putting you to the test' form of pre-trial probation is the most innovative element in the 1989 reform, and, despite being procedural, does involve social intervention as an alternative to prison. 'Putting to the test' schemes are administered by social workers employed by the Justice Ministry, often with the help of local government social workers. These programmes can run for up to three years, for crimes carrying a potential prison sentence of twelve years or more (the average imposed is around one year), and up to one year for lesser crimes (here the average is eight months). They can and often do involve some use of (non-secure) community homes, which are also used outside such schemes. However, resource considerations limit the use of social interventions especially in the poorer parts of the country. Currently there are no more than about 2,000 cases a year of pre-trial probation. The Ministry of Justice is encouraging larger use of such interventions. It deems well over 70 per cent of them to be successful. But the criterion it uses is that the judge has decided at the end of the programme that there is no need to hold 'the trial': there is no official follow-up of later recidivism. The limited research evidence available suggests an almost 40 per cent recidivism rate within the conventional two-year follow up (Scivoletto, 1999).

One of the most striking features of this form of pre-trial probation is the fact that no type of crime is excluded. Cases of murder by young people are therefore also eligible for the scheme and most cases (especially in the north and centre of Italy) are dealt with in this way. Thus, not only are young people in Italy not sent to prison for cases of murder, but, because this is a pre-trial measure, if they successfully pass the test they do not even get a criminal conviction. Certainly they are not 'getting away' with murder in the sense that nothing is done in such cases. But, in the context of thinking about punitiveness, there can be little doubt that the measures taken for dealing with such young people give little importance to the need for denunciation, retribution, deterrence, or any aim other than putting the child first.

Even in Italy, however, the response to juvenile crime is not always lenient, and the exceptions are instructive in showing the limits and hence conditions of non-punitiveness. We have already seen that certain categories of youngsters, such as immigrants and gypsies, do not get to benefit from much of the leniency, ending up relatively more often in prison and benefiting less often from pre-trial probation. This is explained by the authorities as having to do with the difficulty of organizing programmes without the background of a (law-abiding) home base. Individual cases may also test the limits. Since 2000 there have been a series of well-publicized scandals in which teenagers or young adults have murdered their fathers or mothers. The case that attracted most media attention was that of Erica and Omar, who together killed Erica's mother and younger brother for apparently the most futile of motives. Both young lovers were from good families in the north of Italy. Erica in particular came from a well-off, professional, and apparently model religious family background (and attended a religious school). Erica's mother had recently left work to be more available for her children, and her younger brother's last school essay had been full of love for his sister. The sentences they received at first instance were 16 years and 14 years respectively. Public opinion was struck by the way these youngsters originally tried to blame the crime on foreigners, by the lack of excusing circumstances, and the fact that Erica in particular failed to make the public admission of contrition expected in such cases. It was shocking to think that this crime might have happened to any of them.

The fact that such lengthy sentences were imposed without public protest helps explain why, as the Antigone presentation indicated, Justice Minister Roberto Castelli (a member of the populist Northern Leagues party in Berlusconi's coalition government) thought he could make himself spokesman for public alarm over such serious cases of youth crime. His draft law introduced in 2003 proposed (along with other changes to the system) to exclude serious crimes such as murder or sexual offences from the ambit of pre-trial probation.

But it is just as significant that (as Antigone neglected to mention) Castelli's bill failed at the first parliamentary hurdle, with even his colleagues in his own parliamentary majority refusing to follow him. Most cases of murder by young people still do not even end up with a conviction, let alone prison.

Leniency and neoliberalism in Italy

We have seen so far that the adult criminal justice system generates a prison rate in line with the rest of Europe. Its non-punitiveness consists in the way it manages to remain within the norm despite an inflated statute book and attempts to criminalize the powerful as well as the powerless. Juvenile justice is a more clear case of leniency. Should we say that juvenile justice is an area of punishment that is in general an exception to such trends? Not according to Francis Bailleau and Yves Cartuyvels (2003), two criminologists from Continental Europe who have for some years been running a comparative juvenile justice project for the Council of Europe. For them, 'the paradigm of control and risk management and reduction that is associated with neo-liberal reasoning is on a roll in Europe', although they do admit that 'cultural mediations give it a different complexion according to the country concerned'. Their aim is therefore to engage other European criminologists in the common task of examining how far juvenile justice systems have been driven in the direction of greater punitiveness by neo-liberal trends.[10]

'The hypothesis' which Francis Bailleau and Yves Cartuyvels say they want to 'substantiate and validate' is 'the dominance of a managerial and risk-reducing rationale associated with a neo-liberal plan'. As they see it, the 1980s were a time:

> when growing feelings of fear of crime, the subjective expression of social insecurity and surges of 'victim-mindedness', etc., combined with a number of other factors: deteriorating conditions of access to employment for less educated young people, a crisis in or transformation of ties with the social sphere, a change in our relations with norms as a reflection of the rise of individualism, and the questioning of the Social State's collective solidarity-oriented plan … Today a majority of governments feel that each individual is responsible for her/his own trajectory or fate, it is counterproductive to want to reduce social inequality, and in the field of public law and order a society must legitimately content itself with managing the harmful effects of deviance at the lowest possible cost. It must strive to reduce the social risks and troubles that are connected to deviance without considering and even less so taking charge of the collective causes of such individual deviations.

According to Bailleau and Cartuyvels (2003), the 'neo-liberal plan' has at least the following elements:

1. An inversion of the dialectic of responsibility. The youthful offender or child in jeopardy, a victim of social injustices to be emancipated or resocialized, has been forgotten. In her/his stead the child who is

    responsible for her/his movements and summoned to bear responsibility for and repair the social and economic consequences of her/his actions has taken centre stage in the theatre of the media and politics.

2. Youth deviancy ties in with the problems of other figures of insecurity or risk groups, such as foreigners, drug addicts, sexual delinquents, etc. As a means to the 'transfer of anxiety' its function is to create a diversion with regard to other mechanisms of social insecurity that the State chooses not to, or is no longer able to, treat. Law and order discourse is hence targeted at 'special groups', 'urban gangs' or other 'hard cores' of deviancy whose numerical importance is inversely proportionate to the media coverage that they receive.

3. Criminal justice responses increasingly involve a 'punitive' practice that relies on the principle of 'zero tolerance' and condones the isolation or detention of these marginalized minorities, which are doubtless deviant with regard to the dominant values of the middle classes, but are above all poor. But, although there are tougher criminal sanctions for high-risk cases/figures, a non-stigmatizing ('soft') penal approach is used for lower-risk cases/figures, and diversion for unlawful acts committed by the privileged classes.

4. There is a move to proactive, early control, a rise in the adoption of managerial language and emphasis given to the importance of speed. 'Real time control' represents a move from 'protection time' to 'prevention time'.

5. There is a return to communities and localities and a growing tendency to look to private players, via public–private cooperation agreements. The emphasis in the legal system is on productivity, where proper working of the system (by means of various procedures of decongestion, diversion or acceleration) takes precedence over the 'due process of law', and where the job insecurity of staff working on a contract basis prevails over the stability of a long-term status that would allow extended intervention backed up by good knowledge of the local environment…

I have quoted at length from this very valuable working hypothesis because it serves as such a good summary of relevant trends, as well as providing a yardstick against which to measure the alleged effects of neoliberalism on juvenile justice in Italy. But, as we have seen, there is not much in it that fits the current system. It is true that Gaetano di Leo, its academic architect, promoted the 1989 reform using the language of 'responsibilization' rather than welfare. But there is little real interest in making children responsible to the 'community'. The system remains firmly in the hands of professional judges, assisted by honorary judges with relevant expertise, and relies on social workers for its interventions. Those who run the system operate with an ostensibly welfare ethos within a generally legalistic framework,[11] as is illustrated by the following, not untypical, comment by an Italian juvenile court judge in the north:[12]

We are dealing with a youth who is growing up who has committed a crime. What is in the interest of society ... even if it doesn't care about the child himself? That the child doesn't become a determined delinquent! Because otherwise it's a cost for society in all senses, hence we must invest the maximum potential to make sure he doesn't commit more crimes ... Whether this ends up as indulgence or over-forgiveness remains to be seen. Some juvenile court judges may tend to say the youth is always right. But I don't agree with that. I don't think the average judge thinks like that. Certainly they don't think it's always the youth's fault. In general every time you see a youth who has committed a crime you'll find in his biography a reason for that crime. Always. I have never seen one who is a child of a '*good family*'. Maybe he comes from a good family in the sense that they have lots of money but that's not what I mean. Hence these are all youths with big problems and dealing with these must be the best way of solving the problems youths represent for the legal system. Youth crime is in any case not an urgent problem because they are not so many such crimes. Crimes are not going up; at least to me it doesn't seem that they are. Then there are of course those isolated cases where young people kill their fathers or mothers. But, come to that, there are also cases where parents kill their children! (emphasis in original)

As far as the other elements of the neoliberal hypothesis are concerned, rather than going for 'early intervention', in the Italian system delay continues to be an essential element. In part this is an undesired result of complex procedures and under-staffing. But time is also explicitly used as a resource to see whether the child will 'grow out' of the behaviour before serious official intervention is necessary (the guiding assumption being that intervention is itself risky). Because of the independence of the judiciary there is not much talk of meeting organizationally defined targets. Respect is shown to legal processing for its own sake and little attention is given to the reduction of crime and recidivism. 'Scientific' evaluation of 'what works' is in any case not an important part of most social policy initiatives in Italy (as compared with political and party political point-scoring). Even the most praised aspect of the new juvenile procedure has not been given a rigorous assessment. Procedures 'work' in Italy because they are considered to be 'right', rather than, as in more pragmatic cultures, needing to be demonstrated to be right because they 'work'. As regards the move back to communities and localities, this was tried and abandoned in the 1980s, the independence of the judiciary undermining the idea of meeting organizationally defined targets.

Outside of the justice system properly speaking, and for much the same reasons which apply to the adult system, there is still little sign of a 'law and order discourse' focusing on problem groups of youth which are so central to Anglo-American cultures and now spreading elsewhere. Young people would be the least likely groups in Italy to be used for the 'transfer of anxiety'. The term 'juvenile delinquent' is not common currency and until only a few years ago it was hard to find discussions of youth crime in the mass media. Newspapers do now report some cases of murder as well as the not infrequent cases of serious assaults linked to perceived injuries to honour. They speak quite regularly about bullying at school (often attributed to power-hungry children from well-off families), and lament the extent of youthful drug dealing and consumption. But youth crime comes very low in the order of national worries.

The main aspect of the system which does appear to fit Bailleau and Cartuyvels' 'neoliberal plan' is the 'bifurcation' of response between Italian youngsters on the one hand, and young unaccompanied illegal immigrants and gypsy children, on the other. It is certainly of central importance that marginal immigrants are increasingly the target of both the adult and youth systems. Globalization and neoliberalism have certainly played a part in producing this problem. But, as far as prosecutors and judges are concerned, we seem to be facing less a strong choice in favour of criminalizing marginal immigrant youths[13] and more a result of a lack of political will and the organizational resources for finding interventions which fit their needs. The 1989 law was tailored to the typical situation of Italian youngsters. But young immigrants break the law because they need money for themselves and their relatives back home; even if the majority would be happy to work, by law they are not allowed to do so. Even so, there are some judges, prosecutors, and those in other roles, who are trying to find ways to produce a more constructive responses even for such difficult cases by making unaccompanied youngsters wards of court.

What conclusions may we draw about the relationship between neoliberalism and leniency in Italian juvenile justice? Certainly there is none of the 'continuing moral panic' that has been said to characterize the response to youth crime in England and Wales. But the current situation could change; the situation in France shows how immigrant youth can so easily come be constructed as a threat. I would not claim that thinking about neoliberalism is irrelevant to what is happening or to what might happen in the future. A focus on the effects of neoliberal trends does help us appreciate, for example, why cut-backs in welfare provision would be less likely to have the same effects in a system which does not invest heavily in social welfare interventions for young people but relies instead on family and extended family structures. Corporatist and group-based loyalties and values in Italy may also be helping to slow down the spread of consumerist individualistic values, even if they offer no resistance to the growth of consumption itself.

What I have mainly been trying to show, however, is the need not to let discussion of obstacles to the spread of neoliberalism in Italy distract us from many of the other important conditions that explain and sustain the relatively lenient response to youth crime. These factors range from the nature of youth crime to the role of youth in Italian society. There seems to be much less burglary in Italy than in the UK. Italian cities have few ghetto housing estates except in the south; crime rates are highest in the city centre, and the poor steal from the rich, not other poor people. The age structure is crucial. Youth crime ends at 18 but Italians live at home till well into their 30s, and even when economically independent many prefer to live with their parents until they marry. Against the background of the cultural emphasis on putting children first, the family and extended family can and do offer powerful incentives to children to conform as well as exercising a variety of soft sanctions. One Italian writer on the family has described this as 'a gilded prison'. Families are also crucial to finding employ-ment, especially in the small businesses that are the backbone of the Italian economy. Compared with many other industrial societies, the level of surveillance of the young is relatively high, and there is still little sign of the drinking culture that plays such a role in youth crime and disorder in Northern Europe. At the same time, there are lower expectations on the young to demonstrate their independence. Schools place less emphasis than in the UK or the US on competitiveness and are highly reluctant to exclude pupils. Italian children are trained to collaborate with the groups in which they find themselves. There are many other potentially significant social, religious, economic, political, legal, and cultural differences.[14] But those mentioned should be enough to show why we should seek to find out more about such historical and local specificities which condition any relative lack of punitiveness. Only in this way can our explanations take note both of what is 'present' in the society concerned and what is 'absent'.

Notes

1 What is meant by neoliberalism is itself contested. Some authors concentrate on the general socioeconomic impact of this phenomenon while others describe the specific mechanisms by which it supposedly affects particular aspects of criminal justice (where there can even be opposite effects with respect to different types of criminal behaviour). I shall simply assume the general definition used by the editors except when dealing with the details of how it is supposed to be transforming practices in juvenile justice.

2 Gatti and Verde (2002) may be consulted for an authoritative presentation of the Italian juvenile justice system which also relates it to a general typology of different ways of responding to crimes by juveniles.

3 As far as adult criminal justice in Italy is concerned, it should be borne in mind that at least three regions of the country are said to be largely under the control of organized crime groups. With respect to juvenile justice, leniency in handling juveniles must be related to their (over) dependence on the family, which it helps to reproduce.

4 See the editors' introduction.

5 See also Lacey and Zedner (1998).

6 The 'meaning' of institutions and practices can also vary enormously from one context to another. While the editors see the growing militarization of police forces as one indicator of the new punitiveness, in Italy the militarized police forces, especially the Carabinieri, continue to be voted as the institutions which citizens trust most, because they are thought to be most loyal to the state (Nelken, 1994).

7 It is not possible to say enough here to explain why this should be so. The approach to law in most Continental European countries, compared with to Anglo-American legal culture, is much more state-centred and more formally legal, and distinguishes more sharply between what is involved in criminal and civil type disposals. Crawford (2000) offers important insights into these differences. In Italy the state is still more formalistic than in France and less geared up to provide 'social policy' type interventions.

8 I am responsible for this and all the other translations from the Italian in this chapter.

9 But statistics of youth imprisonment show a large variation in levels of severity in which the Italian case is by no means the most lenient (Muncie, 2005).

10 Their previous effort to identify common moves towards greater repression in juvenile justice met with very mixed results. Few of the countries sampled in fact showed univocal trends in that direction (Bailleau and Cartuyvels, 2002).

11 This combination is certainly unusual. But the great criminologist Lemert (1986) was, I think, surprisingly ethnocentric in describing Italy's juvenile justice system (even that before the 1989 reform) as 'spurious' only because it did not resemble that which he knew in the US.

12 These observations were made in the course of discussing a 'vignette' describing an offence of medium seriousness, one of a set of hypothetical crime situations used as part of an ESRC-financed research in progress comparing juvenile justice in Italy and England and Wales. A few judges in the south were harsher in their evaluations of the current system, complaining about the drastic lack of resources. And the annual reports of many chief judges in the south regularly speak of an alarming rise of serious youth crimes related to local organized crime groups.

13 My research in various Italian juvenile courts suggests that though immigrants and gypsies are objectively discriminated against in the offer of pre-trial probation, they do benefit from the 'benevolent' deflationary measures in the 1989 law at least as often as Italian youngsters (sometimes even when the legal requirements may not be met). But this could be read less as benevolence than as an unwillingness to invest resources in trying to deal with their behaviour.

14 The role of the Catholic Church as an institution and of Catholic ideas of forgiveness is one of the most obvious issues which would need much more extensive analysis. The Church is not by any means identical with the role or ideology of most juvenile court judges; and in some respects, though less than in the past, it continues to sap legitimacy from the state in a way that contrasts importantly with the role of Protestant national churches. On the other hand, the juvenile courts rely heavily on local priests for organizing welfare interventions. And Catholic culture helps shape a large part of Italian thinking and behaviour even among those who see themselves as anti-clerical.

References

Bailleau, F. and Cartuyvels, Y. (2002) Special issue of *Deviance e Societé*.

Bailleau, F. and Cartuyvels, Y. (2003) 'Juvenile Penal Justice in Europe: Issues at Stake and Outlook', unpublished paper circulated to the members of the Council of Europe research group on juvenile justice.

Cain, M. (2000) 'Orientalism, Occidentalism and the Sociology of Crime', *British Journal of Criminology*, 40: 239–60.

Crawford, A. (2000) 'Justice de Proximitè: The Growth of 'Houses of Justice' and Victim/Offender Mediation in France: A Very UnFrench Legal Response?', *Social and Legal Studies*, 29.

Di Georgi, A. (2000) *Zero Tolleranza Strategie e pratiche della società di controllo*, Roma: Derive Approdi.

Di Georgi, A. (2002) *Il governo dell'eccedenza. Postfordismo e controllo della moltitudine*, Verona: Ombre Corte.

Feely, M. (1979) *The Process is the Punishment*, New York: Russell Sage Foundation.

Gatti, U. and Verde, A. (2002) 'Comparative Juvenile Justice: an Overview on Italy,' in J. Winterdik (ed.) *Juvenile Justice Systems: International Perspectives* (2nd edn), Toronto: Canadian Scholars Press, 297–320.

Kommer, M. (2004) 'Punitiveness in Europe Revisited', *European Society of Criminology Newsletter*, February 2004.

Lacey, N. and Zedner, L. (1998) 'Community in German Criminal Justice: A Significant Absence?', *Social and Legal Studies*, 7: 7–25.

Lemert, E. (1986) 'Juvenile Justice; Italian Style', *Law and Society Review*, 20: 509–544.

Melossi, D. (1990) *The State of Social Control*, Cambridge: Polity Press.

Melossi, D. (1994) 'The Economy of Illegalities: Normal Crimes, Elites and Social Control in Comparative Analysis', in D. Nelken (ed.) *The Futures of Criminology*, London: Sage, 202–219.

Muncie, J. (2005) 'The Globalisation of Juvenile Justice', *Theoretical Criminology* (forthcoming).

Nelken, D. (1994) 'Whom Can you Trust?', in D. Nelken (ed.) *The Futures of Criminology*, London: Sage, 220–244.

Nelken, D. (1997a) 'Puzzling out Legal Culture: A Comment on Blankenburg', in D. Nelken (ed.) *Comparing Legal Cultures*, Aldershot: Dartmouth, 58–88.

Nelken, D. (1997b) 'The Globalization of Crime and Criminal Justice: Prospects and Problems', in M. Freeman (ed.) *Law and Opinion at the end of the 20th Century*, Oxford: Oxford University Press, 251–279.

Nelken, D. (ed.) (2000a) *Contrasting Criminal Justice*, Aldershot: Dartmouth.

Nelken, D. (2000b) 'Telling Difference: Of Crime and Criminal Justice in Italy', in D. Nelken (ed.) *Contrasting Criminal Justice*, Aldershot: Dartmouth, 233–264.

Nelken, D. (2002) 'Comparing Criminal Justice', in M. Maguire *et al.* (eds) *The Oxford Handbook of Criminology* (3rd edn), Oxford: Oxford University Press, 175–202.

Nelken, D. (2003a) 'Crime's Changing Boundaries', in P. Cane and M. Tushent (eds) *Oxford Handbook of Legal Studies*, Oxford: Oxford University Press.

Nelken, D. (2003b) 'Legitimate Suspicion? Berlusconi and the Judges', in P. Segatti and J. Blondel (eds) *Politics in Italy 2003: The Second Berlusconi Government*, Oxford: Berghahn Books, 112–128.

Nelken, D. (2004) 'Globalisation and Crime', in P. Kennett (ed.) *Handbook of Comparative Social Policy*, London: Edward Elgar.

Nelken, D. (2005) 'Theorising the Embeddedness of Punishment', in D. Melossi, M. Sozzo and R. Sparks (eds) *Travels of the Criminal Question: Cultural Embeddedness and Diffusion*, Oxford: Hart Press.

Pavarini, M. (2004) 'Processi di Ricarcerizzazione nel Mondo (Ovvero del Dominio di un Certo "Punto di Vista")' *Questione Giustizia*, 2–3: 415–435.

Scatolera, D. (2004) 'Devianza Minorile e Coercizione Personale', in *Questione Giustizia*, 2–3: 397–411.

Scivoletto, C. (1999) *C'è Tempo per Punire. Percorsi di Probation*, Milano: Franco Angeli.

Sollivetti, L. (2004) *Italian Prison Statistics*, Department of Statistics, La Sapienza, Rome, 21.

Whitman, J. Q. (2003) *Harsh Justice: Criminal Punishment and the Widening Divide between America and Europe*, Oxford, Oxford University Press.

Young, J. (1999) *The Exclusive Society*, London: Sage.

Part 4

Explanations

14. Modernity and the punitive

Simon Hallsworth

In the last two decades the tariff of acceptable pain that could be legitimately directed towards deviant populations appears to have increased. This is evident particularly in the United States but its imprint can also be seen in other English-speaking jurisdictions such as the UK, Australia, and New Zealand, and, in a less pronounced form, in other European societies. This punitive turn has moved hand in hand with a significant shift in the way in which penal values have been conceived. From a modern penal economy where justice was imagined in terms that sought limits to pain, equivalence in sentencing, and which sought to invest productively in offenders, in the new punitiveness we witness the resurrection of an alternative economy premised upon values that emphasize the legitimacy of pain, visceral sentencing, and destructive punishment (Hallsworth, 2002).

In this chapter my aim will be directed at establishing the extent to which the constitutive forces out of which punitive expressions in general and the new punitiveness in particular can be traced back to the projects associated with modernity. Examining this relationship is by no means an issue without precedent.[1] Indeed, it is one that has preoccupied social theorists for some time. It would also appear to be a question to which an answer has been provided and around which a consensus now appears to crystallize. This holds that the seeds of penal excess are already present within modernity and under the right conditions will bloom and grow. This is the position that appears in its most developed form in Bauman's *Modernity and the Holocaust* (Bauman, 1989), a text that centres on demonstrating – to use Bauman's terms – that violence is not a stranger to modernity. On the contrary, it is, he argues, a 'legitimate resident in its house'. The question I want to pose here is whether penal excess is indeed an outgrowth of modernity, as Bauman's argument appears to suggest.

To explore this issue I will begin by critically considering the evidence used to substantiate the relation Bauman adduces to prove it. I will then reconsider modernity by rethinking its nature in terms of general economics, considering as I do the relationship of modernity to notions of expenditure in general and deficit expenditures in particular. While I will accept that modernity and violence partake of an intimate relationship, I will argue that punitive tendencies cannot be unproblematically identified with modernity as Bauman asserts. As I will show, when modern states transgress into punitive excess they are not evoking forces normally at play within the homogeneous pattern of development I will equate with modernity. Far from being beholden to distinctly 'modern' values, punitive excess derives its authority from transgressive heterogenaic forces normally suppressed in modernity – including state practice. To ground my argument I briefly reread fascist action as a heterogenaic movement that emerged outside of the homogeneous projects I equate with modernity, before attending to the socio-genesis of the new punitiveness in the contemporary United States.

Violence and modernity

Using Bauman's work on the holocaust as a case study, let us now consider how he interprets the relationship between violence and modernity, examining as we do what it is that separates violence modern-style from its 'less successful' premodern predecessors. Taken collectively, the violence-producing attributes of modernity, as defined by Bauman, can be summarized in the following way.

1. Modernity concentrates the means of violence in ways that make modern societies far more lethal than premodern social formations.

2. Modernity gives birth to a technology of violence that would surpass anything known to premodern regimes.

3. Modernity encourages forms of rational, coordinated, and dispassionate violence that makes modern states able to deliver its violence more capably.

4. Far from diminishing the possibility of violence through its civilizing processes, modernity makes its extreme exercise thinkable.

The concentration of violence within modernity

While Bauman does not dispute Elias's thesis of social pacification (Elias, 1978), the civilizing process, he argues, never eliminated violence from modern society. What the civilizing process heralded instead was a redeployment of violence and a 'redistribution of access' to it.

> … violence has been taken out of sight, rather than forced out of existence. It has become invisible, that is from the vantage point of the narrowly circumscribed and privatised personal experience. It has been enclosed instead in segregated and isolated territories, on the whole inaccessible to ordinary members of society; or evicted into the 'twilight areas', off-limits for a large majority (and the majority that counts) of society's members; or exported to distant places which are on the whole irrelevant for the life-business of civilised human beings (one can always cancel holiday bookings). (Bauman, 1989: 97)

It is precisely as a consequence of the civilizing process, specifically the monopoly of violence claimed by the sovereign territorial state, that would provide it with its terrifying and lethal capability. By removing violence from society, so were created the preconditions necessary for concentrating it in ways that would permit a level of domination no premodern society or absolutist ruler could ever imagine possessing.

The technological development of violence within modernity

The development of productive forces not only enhanced already existing methods of killing by perfecting their integral logic (modern artillery after all simply does what the cannon did but more effectively), it would also make possible more effective ways of killing. The use of the aeroplane to carry bombs that could be transported to annihilate populations located in entirely different countries exemplifies one aspect of the lethal potentiality latent within modernity; the development of the death camp system reveals another. While the civilizing process made possible the removal of violence from daily life on one hand, this removal was also:

> … intimately associated with a thorough-going militarization of inter-societal exchange and inner-societal production of order; standing armies and police forces brought together technically superior weapons and superior technology of bureaucratic management. For the last two centuries the number of people who have suffered violent death as a result of such militarization has been steadily growing to reach a volume unheard of before. (Bauman 1989: 99)

As Bauman observes, 'the holocaust absorbed an enormous volume of the means of coercion'. It would harness these means in ways that brought together both the coercive potential of the modern sovereign state with the technological means that modernization had also made possible. While the terrifying effectiveness of the death camp system remains a testimony to what this combination could accomplish, what makes the holocaust for Bauman a uniquely modern enterprise was the rational bureaucratic mode of operation that underpinned its organi-zation. This feature, however, is also a unique property of modernity.

The organization of violence within modernity

What made modern bureaucracies effective was that they reflected both in their organizational form and in their characteristic behaviour a fundamentally instrumental rational orientation to the world. Modern bureaucracies operate around conceptions of merit rather than status. This means that the problems they confront as organizations are resolved by those best suited to the task in hand. The impersonality and rational orientation of bureaucracies together with the hierarchical and functional division of labour that characterizes them, also provides them with a capacity to resolve designated tasks in ways that no other organizational form could ever aspire to achieve.

And if modern bureaucratic organizations encounter problems in the delivery of specific tasks, what distinguishes those of the present from those of the past is that the former are uniquely equipped by virtue of their rational orientation to resolve the problems they confront. Indeed, given their rational orientation they have an inherent capacity for reflexivity and self-learning that ensures that they not only solve problems, they continually improve on the solutions they adopt.

Placed at the disposal of violent states, this innate problem-solving orientation could be put to terrifying use. The holocaust for Bauman is a testimony to what this momentous power can be translated into. What distinguished it from other chronicles of 'emotions running amok, of lynching mobs, of soldiers looting and raping their way through the conquered towns' was that it was from the beginning an altogether rational and planned exercise. It was, moreover, one from which the irrational was systematically purged in its realization.

What the holocaust represented then was a distinctly modern way of murdering people *en masse*. What made it uniquely modern was that the techniques and practices used to perpetrate it were those made possible by distinctly modern bureaucratic methods. In effect the business of mass killing did not differ markedly from the techniques and practices that inform the conduct of any typically modern organization. This would tellingly include those established in the heart of government and not least capitalist business. In fact what the holocaust demonstrated was just how efficiently and effectively these already existing organizations could, with seemingly so little effort, and indeed with such chilling ease, find themselves actively complicit in the business of mass murder.

The mobilization of violence within modernity

What the factors we have considered so far attest to is that in modernity the state has a greater destructive capacity than it possessed in its premodern form. Its violence is more concentrated and more lethal when unleashed. But the means of violence are not the same as a propensity to exercise it. This point is important: just because states concentrate their violence more profoundly in modern times, this does not prove of itself that violence is more likely to be deployed within it (a point I will return to consider below). Aviation technology, by way of an example, developed rapidly after the Wright Brothers' pioneering flights, but this does not entail that planes would be delegated the task of carrying the explosives that would subsequently destroy cities such as Hamburg and Dresden. Indeed, if we follow the arguments of Elias and his followers, then it could be argued that modern states develop via the civilizing process an array of sensibilities that preclude violence from social life far more readily than could be observed in their premodern predecessors.

For Bauman, however, this argument counts for little. What allows him to position penal excess as a 'legitimate resident in the house of modernity' is not just that the means of violence are more developed but that modernity itself brings into being a way of gazing upon the world in ways that will ultimately license unspeakable horror. This he associates with what he considers to be the 'gardening gaze' modernity ushers in to being along with an associated tendency to self-perfection. This gaze is one directed at conceiving societies as gardens that require both tending and routine acts of weed clearance in order to stay healthy. Such a vision, however, also came hand in hand with another that conceived the social garden as a landscape that could be improved in line with utopian dreams. The engineering work unleashed in the name of building the utopian society, however, would require the elimination of that which was alien to the health and well-being of the garden itself and the design that underpins it – unhealthy species, society's weeds. What constitute weed formation in the social sense are heterogenaic populations. When state gardeners encounter these, then, in the name of creating a good society, they can find themselves subject to the violence the state warehouses. For Bauman therefore it was not simply the way the Nazis appropriated the fruits of scientific reason and problem-solving that made the holocaust possible. It was also the gardening logic that would render genocide *thinkable* as a social project.

Rethinking modernity

From these arguments it would appear rational to conclude that when we investigate the socio-genesis of the new punitiveness, it too can be explained as an invariable by-product of modernity. Indeed I would suggest (and have argued elsewhere) this is precisely how Christie (1988) (in part at least), not to say Feeley and Simon (1992), have sought in their own ways to account for 'gulags Western style'. These, they intimate, emerge as a consequence of what Christie terms 'the final subordination of law and order to regimes to the instrumental rational logic of the modern state'.

In what follows I want to contest this line of reasoning by arguing that penal excess does not emanate from modernity as Bauman suggests. It is not, in other words, a legitimate resident in its house. To develop this argument requires as a prerequisite that we distinguish our terms more clearly. As I will now show, much of what Bauman has to say about the violence-producing attributes of modernity relates less to modernity *per se* but to processes of modernization, which, I would argue, is a different thing.

Modernization is about the development of the productive forces within a given social formation. The state of development of these provides social formations with the institutional means they can then deploy to realize certain ends. What distinguishes industrial society from its predecessors was precisely the revolution it would witness in its productive forces. This would make possible technological breakthroughs that gave rise to the most prodigious and productive economic order humanity has ever known. It would also facilitate the development of complex solutions to many of the problems that had hitherto plagued it.

Placed at the service of social health, the instrumental rational problem-solving orientation of modern science and technology heralded huge break-throughs in the control of disease. Likewise, when placed at the service of the repressive apparatus, the self-same expertise would also license – as Bauman convincingly shows – an exponential development in the means of violence. Though these developments parallel the rise of the modern state, I would suggest that what we are talking about here are processes of *modernization*. Now this is not to dispute the argument that modern states are more dangerous because of what modernization makes possible; only to suggest that the argument here is about the development of repressive means – not about the capacity to use them.

Where I depart from Bauman is in his characterization of modernity: in particular, his equation of modernity with the 'gardening mentality' he identifies as key to the modern state's self-image and identity. By drawing this equation, Bauman is able to argue that Hitler's ambitions were not as aberrant to the kind of mentalities that modernity forged but entirely consistent with them. Like other dominant political elites, Hitler also wanted to engage in the business of grand design. The awesome power of the modern state became the tools he deployed to remake the social garden and by so doing bring it into line with his pre-established vision. The Jews in this were nothing other than a social species that had no place in the envisaged scheme, and so had to be removed. Science, technology, and bureaucracy did the rest.

Though this looks like a persuasive argument, it is one that is blind to a number of attributes inherent in modern state development that I would identify with modernity, but which do not figure in Bauman's approach. Rather than evoke Elias, however (as Pratt does in this volume), my aim will be to engage with the work of George Bataille. By looking at how he characterizes the modern industrial order it is possible to reread modernity in ways that depart significantly from those offered by Bauman. To get to this, however, requires a slight digression. More specifically we need to look again at society and its constitution.

The constitution of society

The social infrastructure of any social formation may be considered a product of two elements. First, the *homogeneous* part of society and, second, that which it excludes: its *heterogenaic* elements. The first of these spheres is most easily grasped in thought as it defines the everyday world in which we moderns tend to live. It comprises for Bataille the *homogenous* sphere of existence: a world given over to labour expended in the production of wealth accumulated for useful things. Homogeneity for Bataille (1988: 122) signifies:

> The commensurability of elements and an awareness of this commensurability: human relations are sustained by reduction to fixed rules based on the consciousness of the possible identity of delineable persons and situations; in principle all violence is excluded from this course of existence.

For Bataille production is the basis of homogeneous existence and within the world production makes as its own 'every useless element is excluded'. In homogeneous life, objects obtain the status of things whose value is only ascribed by virtue of their utility as elements within the productive process. Money, he argues, is the currency by which value is ascribed within the homogeneous order of things. It serves to 'make measure all work and make man a function of measurable products' (Bataille, 1988: 122–123).

This, the homogeneous sphere, is at once opposed to the order of the heterogenaic which defines the space of being beyond it. This, for Bataille is also the space of pure sovereignty, the full and intimate experience of which can only be obtained through deficit, unproductive expenditures. This plane of being includes the *sacred*, which also constitutes the realm of religion and magic things; all that society expels as waste and dejecta and which it constitutes as the *abject*; and forms of behaviour and affective states that transgress the normal rules of homogeneous existence. What all heterogenaic life has in common is that it is composed of unproductive expenditures, all of which provoke sharp, explosive, and intense responses. The elements of which it is composed are by nature disorderly and unruly. They neither add to nor maximize system utility in any tangible way. They represent in their totality a plenitude of energy which, far from being productively valorized into system growth, is instead luxuriously or catastrophically wasted.[2] The heterogenaic can include forms of life that provoke intense attraction as well as repulsion, horror or laughter, elation and dread. Potlatch, sacrifice, eroticism, riots, executions, and carnival, each, in their own way, provides an opening and thus a doorway into this realm. It is not only acts and behaviours, however, which constitute that which is heterogenaic. Some populations and social groups can also stand by virtue of various diacritical markers such as religion, culture, or colour, heterogenaic to the wider society in which they dwell. They can also provoke by their otherness sharp and explosive responses.

Redefining modernity

Societies can be differentiated from one another in terms of the relationship they establish between their homogeneous and heterogenaic parts. This relationship is fundamentally about the way societies expend and use their surpluses. Societies that are principally homogeneous are those that do not willingly squander what they produce, and which view excessive and destructive forms of deficit expenditure as alien to their nature. Societies that are principally heterogenaic are those that conversely concede and expend a considerable volume of their surpluses in the manner of deficit expenditure. Premodern social formations are principally heterogenaic, and by virtue of this fact are attached to economies characterized by excess.

To take the case of medieval societies, they were by nature orientated to squander considerable amounts of the surplus their economy produced on the development of sumptuous courts, and luxurious amenities such as palaces and cathedrals (Bataille 1998a). Religious life in particular consumed prodigious quantities of social wealth, as did the medieval court society. Within such a society excess was also finally woven into the fabric of society. Its mark can be seen in the procession of carnivals and festivals, in the cult of sumptuous luxury, and not least in the penal excess that defined medieval punishment.

Over time and in Western societies, the relationship between the homogeneous sphere and the orders of unproductive expenditure constitutive of heterogenaic existence undergoes a process of profound reconfiguration. The coming of the distinctly modern industrial order heralds the advent of a world which becomes *homogenous* and progressively *homogenizing*, the more so as it develops. This is capitalism, the enterprise society, a social type premised by nature on absorbing all excess forces in the direction of the unlimited development of its material wealth. This is a society that gives 'precedence to the use of its available resources to the expansion of enterprises and the increase in capital equipment' and which 'prefers an increase in wealth to its immediate use' (Bataille, 1989: 119). This is a society that 'does not look for anything illusory' and which turns its face away from that 'which causes one to tremble with fear or delight' (Bataille, 1989: 129). In such a society value is no longer associated or sought in forms of luxurious squandering. In this, the order of the positively productive, life is rather given over to 'an essential conquest' of a world which aspires to solve 'the problems that are posed by things' (Bataille, 1989: 130).

In such a society unproductive expenditure comes to appear progressively alien, primitive, dangerous, and taboo. As society homogenizes further, a dense web of prohibitions arises to delimit access to a heterogenaic order now confined like the contents of the unconscious to the margins of conscious and lived existence. 'Prohibitions', Bataille argues, 'preserve intact – if and when possible, in so far and for so long as possible – the world work organises and shelter it from the disturbances repeatedly provoked by death and sexuality' (Bataille, 1983). If capitalism makes possible a dynamic order of production, it is also a productive order which, by reducing the problem of life to the function of reducing life's material difficulties, can no longer touch the immediacy of existence that unproductive expenditure proffered as its gift. Where the premodern order offered the promise of restoring to the sacred world that which had been rendered profane by servile existence, in modernity such a relation of 'intimate participation' is lost. The shift from what Bataille terms an 'economy steeped in excess' towards the homogeneous and homogenizing 'restricted economy' is thus a movement also characterized by loss and profound alienation. Moreover, it is registered as such by those who have to confront its loss and who are destined to permanently desire access to a sovereignty that homogeneous life by its own nature can never bestow.

If we conceive the movement towards modernity as one from economies in which excess and unproductive expenditures prevail towards an enterprise society characterized by the dominance of a restricted economy, then clearly we must recognize that this journey is one with tremendous implications for the organization of social life. This also embraces penal structures and processes and the normative foundations around which they are organized.

Where once spectacular punishment could be visited upon the body of the condemned by the transgressive force of a sovereign whose authority was confirmed through its unbounded capacity to destroy, we move in modernity towards societies that both oppose and define themselves in opposition to such unproductive expenditure. In the homogeneous order of modernity, punishment is consequently no longer perpetrated though grandiose spectacles of violence, but in the form of a calculated performance premised upon conservation and utility. From a premodern order where punishment was itself located in the order of the heterogenaic, we see the business of punishment gradually relocated to a homogenous part of society, the nature of which also determines the method of its practice. In this movement, punishment ultimately becomes reconstructed into questions of reclamation achievable through the construction and unfolding of a legion of plans and programmes, interventions, and therapies. Discipline would provide the institutional means for reclaiming the fallen; while the panoptic order would become, as Foucault has shown, the chosen vehicle of its delivery.

The ontological engines that would provide the blueprints for such engineering were themselves derived from the epistemic space made possible by a homogeneous society committed only to the pursuit of the useful. These grand meta-narratives were themselves embedded in and products of the great secular escatologies that emerged from the Enlightenment, and from them would be derived the frameworks of intervention that a growing army of technicians would implement. In a world given over to the positively productive, it is by no means surprising that dreams of these secular engineers were also attached to utopian reveries. In these social imaginaries, social problems would come to be represented in terms that would associate well-being with the productive and the pathological with the order of unproductive heterogenaic life. The movement towards a restricted economy therefore was also a movement in the direction of a society whose engineers were destined from the beginning to imagine progress in homogeneous terms. The developing history of criminology as a discipline that aspired to rid the world of crime by reclaiming deviants for useful purposes was inevitable given the conditions of its birth.

At this point let me reconnect my analysis with the theme of this chapter – violence and its relationship to modernity. As we have seen from this exercise in general economics, it is entirely feasible to reread this relationship in ways that do not presuppose that violent penal excess follows unproblematically from within modernity if – as I am suggesting – we read modernity through Bataille's eyes. The modern project as I will now define it is about the arrival and development of a societal form that is by nature homogeneous and homogenizing, from which violence is normally precluded. This is consequently what I take modernity to be and how I propose to define it: *A social formation predicated on the development, extension and protection of its homogeneous part.*

Through the development of capitalist markets – externally and internally– and through the commodification of the social world more generally, capitalist societies impose tendential homogenization. Workers in this process become repositioned over time as consumers of the products they produce, while their representatives become absorbed into hegemonic blocs themselves complicit in further programmes of social homogenization (Jessop, 1990).

For those elements that resist homogenization or whose heterogeneity is such that they are not extended the right to homogenization, a proportion of the surplus is redirected into imperative forms charged with the function of removing them. Behaviour that appears heterogenaic and thus transgressive to the normal rules of homogeneous existence is in this process suppressed. This trend would lead to the emergence of laws designed to prohibit illegal drug use, working-class street life and various popular festivities and pastimes (on this see Cohen, 1979; Storch, 1976). Crime in this becomes a process associated with what the bourgeoisie would associate with unproductive expenditure. For those who continue to transgress and by so doing remain heterogenaic, further surplus is directed into the development of total institutions charged with the function of controlling and regulating them. This would lead, as Cohen's and Foucault's work indicates, to the development of the asylum, the workhouse, and the penitentiary: total institutions given over to the task of forcible homogenization through disciplinary means (Cohen, 1984; Foucault, 1977).

At this point an interesting contradiction within modernity becomes visible. On one hand, we observe in the behaviour of the homogeneous and homogenizing state projects designed explicitly with the function of removing heterogenaic forms. To realize their suppression, however, also requires that the dominant homogenizing force, the state, at times invokes the very violence it otherwise aspires to suppress. This I would suggest poses a real problem for the modern state and modern societies more generally. Moreover, it is a problem posed at an acute psychological as well as material level.

The general solution that modern states have tended to adopt has been to develop methods of imposing forms of homogenization that preclude violence while also aspiring to regulate the necessary violence that forcible homogenization might make necessary. Gramsci's work on the formation of hegemony, it could be observed, is directed specifically at identifying how this process occurs via the formation of historic blocs that aspire to stabilize capitalist accumulation through effectively drawing diverse class elements into a homogenizing centre (Gramsci, 1973). As for the violence that the state will sanction in the name of forcible homogeneous reduction, great care has traditionally been taken to ensure that when it is expressed it does not become a monstrous double to the 'bad' violence it confronts. Violence in the modern state *as a homogenising state* has to be hygienized, and by so doing, cleansed of its heterogenaic associations. A squaring of circles, in other words *has to occur* for the state to proceed in its homogeneous form. How, though, is this accomplished?

If, as Girard argues, violence is a force that permanently threatened to overreach itself and by so doing engulf a society that is then re-established in its fell image, steps must be initiated to prevent its lethal contagion. Premodern societies relied upon the cleansing rituals associated with sacrifice to ensure this (Girard, 1979). In the modern society of positive production the typical solution has been to shift away from overt violence or to obscure in various ways the violence the modern state will tolerate. Thus in modernity we witness the progressive abandonment of punishments that rely on direct physical force. At the same time, the violence that is tolerated becomes subject to a pervasive array of regulations designed to ensure that, when used, its exercise is never disproportionate. This is why issues of proportionality become steadily more important in the bourgeois state, as do conventions delimiting the use of what will be considered excessive force. Nor is it only overt displays of violence that are stilled. The homogeneous society also delimits the formation of punitive dispositions. It does not by nature routinely seek to elicit pleasures of a sadistic kind. The entire edifice of coercion is organized in ways that attempt to obscure the very violence that is otherwise being evoked.

Now this does not entail that repressive forces delegated with the task of homogeneous reduction do not exercise serious levels of violence, nor is this argument premised upon suggesting that what else might be done in the name of homogeneous reduction might not be itself oppressive. One can cite, for example, the compulsory sterilization for working-class women, or the subjugation of prisoners to various therapeutic interventions conducted in the name of forcible homogenization. My argument is not to defend the authoritarian inhumanities of the modern state but to draw out a key defining feature of it: *It is fearful of violence, the affective states with which it is associated, and typically places the strictest of controls upon its exercise.*

If this is the case and if this is the *typical* trajectory of modern state development, then violence *is not* a normal resident in modernity's house as Bauman argues. The homogeneous state can indeed be a violent state but its homogeneous existence must by nature leave it to regulate the very violence it sanctions while also experiencing the violence it sanctions as a transgressive act – in other words, as an act that violates an agreed limit. But if this is the case, what then explains the periodic outbreaks of penal excess in which modern states become involved? This of course also includes the new punitive tendencies that are the subject of this text.

One response might be to say that the state as a sovereign force always maintains for itself the right to retaliate against those that challenge its sovereignty. This is an argument made by Brown (2002) in his investigation into the dynamics of British colonial rule. This of course is why standing armies are maintained and why the repressive apparatus continues to develop even in peacetime. Such examples, however, do not deal with the issue at stake here, which is about the manifestations of punitive excess that occur in the context of societies otherwise committed to tendential homogenization.

My answer to this question would be to suggest that when we see states engaged in forms of punitive excess, we must see in such exercises a revocation of transgressive heterogenaic sovereign forces that modernity normally aspires to still. This is not to suggest that the forces that are licensed during such moments do not avail themselves of the repressive means made available by the modernization of the means of violence – or to suggest that such outbreaks are devoid of rationality. My point is that the wellsprings from which such violence arises do not originate within modernity. Let us consider at this point as a case study the rise of fascism. I will then consider the issue of the new punitiveness.

Fascism as a counter-modern movement

Despite the fact that the Nazis were always and from the beginning committed to a cult of violence illegible to the homogeneous life-world of the bourgeois state, Bauman overlooks this issue by drawing attention instead to the similarities that he believes bind them to modernity. Hitler is, as we have seen, in Bauman's terms, no more than a 'modern gardener', albeit one whose grand design betrays megalomaniac tendencies. He did not, Bauman is keen to stress, invent the deadly gaze that would permit societies to be seen as gardens that could be radically reshaped; it is one that modernity brought in to being.

Where I would suggest Bauman errs is in overlooking the violence that was itself intrinsic to the Nazi design, and indeed the radical heterogeneity of the Nazis as a party. This, however, is precisely what Bataille (1998b) concentrates upon and by so doing provides, I would suggest, a more accurate character-ization of the socio-genesis of penal excess in modern state than that provided by Bauman. Hitler and the Nazi Party were never, Bataille argues, part of the homogeneous order licensed by capitalist development. The Nazis rather emerged from and mobilized forces of transgressive violence typically precluded within modernity; and which were, from the beginning, radically heterogenaic even though, as we shall see, they were articulated to a project of extreme homogenization.

What fascism resolved were the contradictions inherent in German society in the period following World War I: a society torn asunder by civil war and class conflict, and whose political structures were unable by their own power to animate or condense the divergent social elements into a unitary homogeneous totality. What fascism offered was a way of re-establishing a fractured totality not by reassembling the social order around utilitarian principles intrinsic to normal bourgeois rule, but by evoking sacred forces normally precluded from capitalist states in their homogeneous form. The basis of fascist action resided in its successful capacity to harness heterogenaic powers that were traditionally associated with and mobilized by monarchical regimes (unquestioned and absolute allegiance to authority, the association between divinity and leadership). These were activated in the formation of parties dominated by leaders beholden to no principle of authority independent of the sovereignty they and they alone possessed. As Bataille (1998b: 130) notes:

> Heterogeneous fascist action belongs to the entire set of higher forms. It makes an appeal to sentiments traditionally defined as exulted and noble and tends to constitute authority as an unconditional principle, situated above any utilitarian judgement.

This animating force was then translated into a homogenizing project predicated upon an idealization of the nation as a sacred inclusive whole, but which also relied on a vicious negation of all forces that were not included within it. Fascism can therefore be considered a movement dedicated to the unification of a nation elevated to sacred status, but via imperative means premised upon a vicious exclusion of its heterogenaic elements in a movement that itself relied upon evoking violent heterogenaic forces. A negating rage condensed in the figure of the fascist leader animates the whole, which is then turned upon an outside ready-made for the scapegoating role it has been elected to perform by virtue of its own heterogeneity. By the animation of pollution fears and by the negation of its 'filth', so the purity of the whole is revealed and its absolute domination as a superior entity confirmed.

Now this perspective on fascism does not belie the calculating mentalities by which the Nazis perfected the tactics by which the negation of its outside would commence. These occurred – as Bauman and others have shown – via the mobilization of ordinary men operating in effectively neutral ways, in rational bureaucratic organizations. What this perspective offers – that Bauman does not – is an account of the innate heterogeneity inherent in Nazi practice from its beginning. This is an issue that Bauman ignores. However, and this where we disagree, the animating force is everything, as is an identification of that part of the social world from which it emanates. As I have sought to argue, this is from heterogenaic tendencies normally precluded within modernity – they do not spontaneously emanate from modernity itself. The Nazis were from the beginning committed to heterogenaic action and themselves emerged from within the heterogeneity of which they were a part.

After this extended but necessary digression into state heterology, let us now consider the object of analysis in this book – the new punitiveness. As I will now show, the violence that characterizes this, like fascism, does not emanate from within modernity in its homogeneous form but rather from the resurrection of violent heterogenaic forces normally precluded in modernity by the homogenizing projects to which it is normally attached.

The new punitiveness in lockdown America

Under the aegis of the welfare state mode of social regulation (Amin, 1994), heterogenaic elements were largely subsumed, as we have seen, by inclusive measures designed to incorporate workers by repositioning them as consumers within Fordist accumulation regimes. This included corporatist modes of governance and the extension of an extended system of benefits directed at supporting the inevitable losers. Under conditions of neoliberal accumulation, however, the tendency towards the incorporation of its outside by homogeneous reduction has been supplemented by an emergent logic predicated upon exclusion (Young, 1999). These exclusionary forces are themselves intrinsically bound up with a production of an outside which, through both material and symbolic processes, has become constructed as the raw material for punitive dispensation.

The notion of material production pertains to the processes at play within free market economics that naturally and systematically produce a population external to production (just as much as it would produce a population of winners in a winner-take-all economy). The concatenation of forces active within this economic and political process works to produce and systematically reproduce surplus and redundant populations who have been schooled to consume relentlessly but can no longer consume legitimately in the free market society.

The idea of symbolic production pertains to the successful programme of persecution by which these excluded populations are reconstructed as Other. Through the mediation of persecution texts promoted through recurrent moral panics, the excluded are accorded a monstrous status in the context of a society itself constructed first as society of victims (Simon, 2004), and then, seamlessly, as a community of avengers. The social consequences of sustained criminalization have been to produce and identify heterogenaic elements positioned as impure, permissive, and dangerous to what is represented as the pure homogeneity of the white nation of free consumers. At the symbolic level the threat adopts the form of a sacrificial crisis (Girard, 1979). This is embodied in the spectre of a contaminating violence associated with an urban underclass of predatory males which, unchecked, threaten to overreach their point of origin in the ghetto and by so doing invade the threatened community of victims. To use Lynch's terminology (this volume), what is constructed is a vision of an outside imagined in terms that literally equate it with dejecta and foul matter. This is human 'toxic waste' – heterogenaic matter that threatens to pollute that which is healthy and which can only be contained through the most extreme methods.

What is integral to underclass thinking – and I would suggest a key to punitive development – is that it sanctions a vision of order premised upon the utter opacity and incommensurability of worlds. It evokes a language of essentialized difference predicated upon a vision of the Other as that which cannot be reasoned with but which in its radical heterogenaic promiscuity poses a permanent threat to a public interpolated as insecure and security conscious. Integral to such persecution texts, we find a mobilization of what Douglas (1966: 13) terms 'pollution fears' about heterogenaic life and heterogenaic populations. In the case of the US this finds expression in the pathological fear and hatred expressed towards illegal drug use, the promiscuity of single-parent families headed by mothers (families in other words devoid of the governing authority of males (i.e the phallus), and the existing heterogeneity of the black population that would find itself uniquely constructed for what Wacquant describes as 'punitive tutelage' (Wacquant this volume).

The implicit theme of state emasculation at play in this imagery is further reinforced by the perceived failure of the inclusive programme homogenizing projects associated with welfare state capitalism. Again, it is not only the material failure of welfarism to curtail rising crime that is an issue. Homogenous projects in visions of neoconservative thinking belong to the category of soft and effeminizing trends that induce emasculation by leaving the good society vulnerable by undermining state sovereignty (and thus the rule of men).

These processes cumulatively provide the ground out of which authoritarian elements would surface keen to exploit the endemic insecurity licensed by the threat posed by an outside that appeared impervious to the 'soft' inclusive control mechanisms of homogeneous capitalist development. What the turn towards punitive measures offered was a way of resolving the sacrificial crisis by recourse to a purifying and purified display of violence. As with fascism (with which neoliberal governance shares some common features), the resolution sought was predicated on a radical and vicious expulsion of heterogenaic elements again justified by the state's invocation of violent impulses normally precluded from the homogenous part of life.

In this turn the nominally invisible machinery of the criminal justice system in its modern guise has become manifestly visible to the public. From a system whose 'curative' and reclamatory elements are normally embedded in a mysterious edifice of control premised upon plans and programmes that unfold in homogeneous time, the space of punishment has become gradually and incrementally relocated to the immanence of a transgressive heterogeneity. In this process punishment has become retranslated from a technical language monopolized by experts into the compressed and far more immediate populist discourse of judicial retribution (see Aas, this volume). In so doing, the business of punishment becomes relocated from the homogeneous to the heterogenaic part of society.

The resurrection of these deeply transgressive forces can be seen both in the semantics at play within the new punitiveness (zero tolerance, tough love, boot camp, indefinite detention, three strikes), but also in the practices that are intrinsically associated with them: disproportionate and visceral sentencing, the renaissance of the death penalty, and not least the resurrection of punishments predicated on degradation (Pratt, 2000).

Integral to all these practices I would suggest is the inherent transgressive forces that animate them; in particular, the mobilization of transgressive practices normally stilled in distinctly modern and homogeneous forms of social development. Now something is transgressive only if there is a pre-established rule to be transgressed in the first place (Jenks, 2003). This is the point of its pleasure. What animates the mobilization of the violent heterogenaic forces attached to the new punitiveness is not least an open invitation to the pleasure of a permitted transgression. Sadistic impulses, as we have seen, are normally precluded within homogeneous life in the homogenizing society. By suggesting through punitive appeals that pain delivery is acceptable, these normal rules are suspended and violated. This, in part, is what makes the reintroduction of the death penalty in the US such a powerful motif in its punitive turn. It revokes the very principle of the restricted economy which is not to expend unproductively. It partakes directly in what Bataille would term the 'violence of an unconditional consumption' (Bataille, 1993: 213). In its transgression the state invokes its own edgework, just as its functionaries and its audience are positioned as edgeworkers.

As with fascism, the spectre of the Other is recurrently deployed to mobilize latent insecurity and to channel the affective forces it unleashes in the direction of the negation of an outside from which the right to homogenization has been withdrawn. In opposition to the homogenizing categories at play in penal modernity that construct outsiders as raw material fit for homogeneous reduction (plans, therapies, discipline, etc.), we witness instead the (re)arrival of forms of penality characterized by deficit expenditure legitimated by a revanchist state in an economy of excess.

Far from being a singular response to a crisis – the failure of the homogenizing projects intrinsic to welfare state capitalism – it is difficult to escape the conclusion that the collective effervescence provoked by the continual mobilization of insecurity has now become intrinsic to late capitalist American society in its contemporary form. Indeed, as Simon (1997) has argued, crime control has indeed been stabilized as a mode of governance in and of itself. Integral to such rule is the continued attempt to elicit and mobilize violent heterogenaic forces by exploiting wider insecurity in a 'free world' represented as perennially insecure because it is presented as perennially threatened by a 'toxic' outside. Such forces are mobilized both in the name of defending the inside of society from the outside that its political and economic structures produce, and in the name of constituting through its violence the homogeneity (and domination) of the imagined American nation – or indeed empire (Hart and Negri, 2000). If this is indeed the case, then in late modern US we are also looking at the extraordinary production of a social formation *that cannot live without its enemies*. Having obliterated in state socialism the only real alternative to itself, free-market America in the age of its empire has had to identify other appropriate scapegoats as a reason for being. The process has certainly taken root and flourished in the construction of its mode of internal repression. It is by no means impossible, however, that in the identification of a new 'axis of evil' external to its borders such transgressive excess is also becoming intrinsic to the operation of its external repressive apparatus as the catastrophic war on terror indicates.

Conclusion

Before we consign modernity to the mountain of wreckage that Walter Benjamin's 'Angel of History' is forced to survey as she is propelled backwards into the future on the cold wind of progress, we need to be more aware of the limits and limitations of the criticisms that have been directed against it. We also need to be more aware of the dangers that might well accrue to a (post)modern world being erected around us. As this chapter has sought to argue, modernity may not in all respects be as guilty as charged. It its homogeneous form it was certainly repressive but has, built within it, an important array of pain- and violence-delimiting attributes. It is what happens when these are dispensed with that we must fear. For when these are invoked what we find is a resurrection of catastrophic, not to say transgressive, life forms we must rightly fear. This certainly makes me a proponent of catastrophe theory, to deploy O'Malley's terminology. But then catastrophes are unfolding as we speak and surely we need to know why.

Notes

1 I first approached this subject in a paper written for *Punishment and Society* in 2000. Then my aim was to challenge visions of penal excess as a product of the modernization of penal regimes as proposed by Christie (1988). This chapter (re)examines this issue and this relationship.
2 For this reason Bataille would term such excess 'the accursed share'. It is that surplus that all societies must find ways of losing and which they have to lose.

References

Amin, A. (1994) *Post-Fordism: A Reader*, Oxford: Blackwell.

Bataille, G. (1983) *Prehistoric Painting: Lascaux or the Birth of Art* (trans. A. Wainhouse), London: Macmillan.

Bataille, G. (1988) *The Accursed Share* Vol. 1 (trans. R. Hurley), New York: Zone Books.

Bataille, G. (1993) *The Accursed Share Vols II and III* (trans. R. Hurley), New York: Zone Books.

Bataille, G. (1998a) 'Sacrifice, the Festival and the Principles of the Sacred World', in F. Botting and A. Wilson (eds) *The Bataille Reader*, Oxford: Blackwell.

Bataille, G. (1998b) 'The Psychological Structure of Fascism', in F. Botting and A. Wilson (eds) *The Bataille Reader*, Oxford: Blackwell.

Bauman, Z. (1989) *Modernity and the Holocaust*, Cambridge: Polity Press.

Brown, M. (2002) 'The Politics of Penal Excess and the Echo of Colonial Penality', *Theoretical Criminology*, 4(4): 403–423.

Christie, N. (1988) *Crime as Industry: Towards Gulags Western Style*, London: Routledge.

Cohen, P. (1979) 'Policing the Working Class City', in B. Fine *et al.* (eds) *Capitalism and the Rule of Law*, London: Hutchinson.

Cohen, S. (1984) *Visions of Social Control, Crime, Punishment and Classification*, Cambridge: Polity Press.

Douglas, M. (1966) *Purity and Danger*, London: Routledge.

Elias, N. (1978) *The Civilizing Process*, Vol 1: *the History of Manners*. Oxford: Blackwell.

Feeley, M. and Simon, J. (1992) 'The New Penology, Notes on the Emerging Strategy of Corrections and its Implications', *Criminology*, 30(4): 452–74.

Feeley, M. and Simon, J. (1994) 'Actuarial Justice: the Emerging New Criminal Law', in D. Nelkin (ed.) *The Futures of Criminology*, London: Sage.

Foucault, M. (1977) *Discipline and Punish* (trans. A. Sheridan), London: Peregrine Books.

Girard, R. (1979) *Violence and the Sacred*, Baltimore: Johns Hopkins University Press.

Gramsci, A. (1973) *Selections from the Prison Notebooks*, London: Lawrence and Wishart.

Hallsworth, S. (2000) 'Rethinking the Punitive Turn: Economies of Excess and the Criminology of the Other', *Punishment and Society*, 2(2): 145–160.

Hallsworth, S. (2002) 'The Case for a Postmodern Penality', *Theoretical Criminology*, 6(2): 145–163.

Hardt, M. and Negri, A. (2000) *Empire*, Cambridge, MA: Harvard University Press.

Jenks, C. (2003) *Transgression*, London: Routledge.

Jessop, B. (1990) 'Regulation theories in retrospect and prospect', *Economy and Society*, 19(2), May.

Parenti, Christian (1998) *Lockdown America: Police and Prisons in the Age of Crisis*, New York: Verso.

Pratt, J. (2000) 'The Return of the Wheel Barrow Men; Or, the Arrival of Postmodern Penality', *British Journal of Criminology*, 40: 127–145.

Ryan, M. (1998) 'Penal Policy Making Towards the Millennium: Elites and Populists', *International Journal for the Sociology of Law*, 27: 1–22.

Simon, J. (1995) 'They Died with their Boots on: The Boot Camp and the Limits of Modern Penality', *Social Justice*, 22(1): 25–49.

Simon, J. (1997) 'Governing through Crime', in L. M. Friedman and G. Fisher (eds) *The Crime Conundrum: Essays on Criminal Justice*, pp. 171–189.

Storch, R. (1976) 'The Policeman as Domestic Missionary; Urban Discipline and Popular Culture in Northern England 1850–1880', *Journal of Social History*, 9: 4.

Wilson, J. Q. and Herrnstein, R. J. (1985) *Crime and Human Nature*, New York: Simon & Schuster.

Young, J. (1999) *The Exclusive Society: Social Exclusion, Crime and Difference in Late Modernity*, London: Sage.

15. Elias, punishment, and decivilization

John Pratt

In *The Culture of Control*, David Garland (2001: 3) writes that:

> recent developments in crime control and criminal justice are so puzzling
> because they appear to involve a sudden and startling reversal of the settled
> historical pattern ... The modernizing processes that, until recently, seemed
> so well established in this realm – above all the long-term tendencies
> towards 'rationalization' and 'civilization' – now look as if they have been
> thrown into reverse. Not even the most inventive reading of Foucault, Marx,
> Durkheim and Elias on punishment could have predicted these
> possibilities.

Garland is referring here to the dramatic impact the new punitiveness has made:
in the United Kingdom and the United States in particular, but by extension as
well, and in varying degrees, in the other main English-speaking societies. I am
certain he is correct in his reference to the way in which these changes do not seem
to fit the theoretical precepts of the first three members of this famous quartet.
Thus, as regards Foucault (1978), instead of the discreet normalization through
discipline and surveillance that for him were the hallmarks of punishment in
modern societies, some of these new trends seem to be based more around the
characteristics of premodern societies (Pratt, 2000). Furthermore, these emotive
and expressive sanctions which deliberately provoke human sensibilities rather
than suppress them, seem to run counter to the kernel of 'rationality' that is
epistemologically embedded in Foucault's later work on governmentality (see
Foucault, 1991). It is also clear that the dramatic acceleration of prison populations across these societies seems to defy any of the operational logics that had
until recently been developed around the prison as a way of restricting its intake
– that they were too expensive and did not 'work' in the sense of retraining and
reforming prisoners. Now, it may be that they do indeed 'work', but on very
different precepts: they work in the sense that they simply incapacitate. In other
words, such developments point to a different set of rationalities operating
around the prison, based on ambivalence towards the wastage of human life in
this way, which again does not seem to fit within Foucault's *oeuvre*.

Equally, the way in which these developments are being driven by a new
culture of punishment, a new tolerance of high imprisonment rates irrespective of

their cost, seems to undermine the economistic explanations so central to Marx and neo-Marxists. And Durkheim, so confident of the prowess of the modernizing forces of the late nineteenth century which would have the effect of keeping emotive sentiment firmly in check as respected civil servants charted the course of penal affairs, would indeed be puzzled by these trends which can now prioritize expressions of public opinion to the complete exclusion in some cases of any input from scientific expertise (see Zimring (1996) on the passage of the Californian 'three-strikes' law). However, and with respect to Garland, I think it is not the case that these punitive reversals cannot be explained or predicted by Elias: indeed, the purpose of this chapter is to situate the new punitiveness within an Eliasian theoretical framework. In these respects, there would seem to be rather more to recent penal development than 'reversals' (cf. O'Malley, 1999): although, as will be argued in this chapter, both reversals and continuities do indeed seem to fit within Elias' precepts – in particular the concept of 'decivilization' (see Elias, 1984, 1996). However, before elaborating on this, it is necessary to give consideration to its counterpart of 'civilization', 'since the notion of reversal only make sense if one can be confident that the processs was previously moving in a structured way in a recognizable direction' (Mennell, 1990: 210).

Elias and the the civilizing process

In Elias (1984), the term 'civilized' differs from its normative, common-sensical associations regarding notions of human and social betterment and advancement and the attainment of ever higher standards of tolerance and sensibility. In contrast, for him, what was understood as 'civilized' represented only the current and contingent configuration of three characteristics, operating on different levels but associated with the long-term historical development of Western societies from the thirteenth century onwards. First, in relation to *state process*, there is the growth of the central state's monopolistic control of the use of legitimate violence and the raising of taxes. In these respects, the state's exclusive ability to act in these ways meant that it came to have sole responsibility for defence and the protection of national boundaries from external threat as well as responsibility for the settlement of internal conflict. As a result, the increasing authority of the state meant that when disputes arose, citizens would ultimately assume that the state would act on their behalf rather than attempt to redress such matters themselves. Second, in relation to *socio-genesis*, we find an increase in the scale and scope of what Elias refers to as 'interdependencies' between citizens as a result of the heterogeneous division of labour now characteristic of Western social arrangements. These were then accelerated in the shift from rural to urban life from the late eighteenth century. In these respects, the more differentiated the social functions of modernity became, the larger the number of people 'on whom the individual constantly depends in all actions, from the simplest and most commonplace to the more complex and uncommon' (Elias, 1984: 445). These interdependencies then necessitated restrictions on impulsive behaviour and aggression. Third, in relation to *psychogenesis*, we find, among individual citizens, the internalization of restraint. This relates to keeping displays of emotion in check and suppressed to the point where such behaviour becomes part of an individual's *habitus*, or becomes second nature to them. Such displays would increasingly be seen as shocking, distasteful, or inappropriate. This would then lead to a raising of the thresholds of shame and embarrassment, with the result that citizens developed a growing sensibility towards 'disturbing events'. In probably the most well known sections of *The Civilizing Process*, Elias (1984: 48–178) draws on the changing historical detail of manners books to demonstrate the way in which this led to distaste and repulsion for a growing range of behaviours, from the public performance of bodily functions to the slaughter of animals for food. Such activities came to be suppressed altogether or otherwise hidden from public view in the 'civilized' world.

Here then are some of the channels through which the idea of 'civilization', in Elias' use of this term, came to be developed. However, it is important to avoid the impression that there is some simplistic reiterative fit between the historical development of these societies (and penal trends within them) and the civilizing process. First, while characteristics of the civilizing process can be sketched in at a very general level, their particular details will vary from society to society, depending on what Elias referred to as 'the local centrifugal forces' appertaining to each one. Second, it is evident that the growing 'sensitivities' to disturbing events (and a concomitant growth in sympathy for the sufferings of others) are not distributed evenly among all classes and in relation to all such events. Middle-class elites, significant figures in reform groups of the nineteenth and twentieth centuries, displayed such sensitivities far in advance of other sectors (e.g. in relation to the abolition of slavery and child welfare). On the other hand, hostility towards and lack of empathy for some groups may have encouraged their isolation and removal (e.g. the mentally ill); in contrast (certainly in Britain), sensitivity to the suffering of animals seems to have run well in advance of that for most humans (Cunningham, 1980). Third, *The Civilizing Process* ends around the mid-nineteenth century and is unable to address the significance of features quite specific to social development in the civilized world thereafter. As will be seen later, of particular importance for our purposes is the way in which the monopolistic powers of the central state ultimately came to be exercised through modern bureaucracies – and were steadily extended from the raising of taxes and the use of legal force across broad areas of public policy. Such investment in specialist expertise, characteristic of the division of labour in 'the civilized world', particularly during the nineteenth and much of the twentieth centuries, thus led to ordinary people being largely shut out of any involvement in these areas of governance.

This then leads to a fourth qualification. Ordinary people became detached from governance in these areas not simply as a result of bureaucratization but because, in addition, the distaste for some of the more disturbing areas of public life that were being administered in this way (e.g. hospitals, mental institutions, prisons) made them anyway more reluctant to become involved. Indeed, the habitus of self-restraint that prompted these sensibilities (characteristic of the civilizing process) and the sense of detachment and non-involvement that this generates can turn into moral indifference. For Bauman (1989) this is seen as one of the causes of the holocaust. In what had become the accepted habitus of the civilized world, most German people did what they had been trained to do. They looked the other way and 'saw nothing' of the horrific events taking place around them. In these respects, and notwithstanding important differences in how 'civilized' is understood by Bauman and Elias,[1] it is evident that the qualities of the civilizing process itself are no guarantee of a civilized end product (and that Elias' work is not based on some teleological notion of human and societal betterment, as has been a regular line of criticism).

Decivilizing

These are qualifications that relate to the civilizing process itself and the impact its characteristics are likely to have. For Elias, however, this process could be reversed at any time by war, social catastrophe, and so on. Under these circumstances, 'decivilizing' then begins to take place. For Fletcher (1997: 82–7), there are three main characteristics to this: a shift away from self-restraint towards restraint imposed by external authorities; the development of behaviour and sensibilities that generate the emergence of less even, stable, and differentiated patterns of restraint; and a contraction in the scope of mutual identification between constituent groups and individuals. When these occur they are likely to be accompanied by a decrease in the state monopoly of violence, a shortening of interdependencies, and a concomitant rise of fear, danger, and incalculability. Elias himself recognized that the ominous portents surrounding him as he completed his work in Nazi Germany were indeed an indicator that the civilizing process contained no guarantee of its own continuity. At that time, though, he only made some oblique references to this.[2] It is only in his later work, notably *The Germans* (Elias, 1996), and the work of leading Elias commentators such as Mennell (1990) and Fletcher (1997) that these possibilities of reversal receive more detailed consideration, although, again, not without some ambiguity. In Elias (1996), the Nazi period is referred to as 'the breakdown of civilization' with frequent references to 'barbarization', 'barbarism' etc. While normatively this is an entirely accurate depiction of this period (and also seems to imply, despite disavowals to the contrary,[3] that normative values do find their way into his work) within Elias' theoretical precepts he thus seems to be implying that this was conduct characteristic of decivilizing rather than civilizing processes.

Nonetheless, while under sufficient conditions of catastrophe or social collapse, 'decivilizing' tendencies may completely eclipse civilizing counterparts and lead to a total and exclusive reversal of this process, more generally, at least in contemporary Western societies, it would seem that one of the consequences of the civilizing process itself – bureaucratization – provides for some residual embedding of governmental authority and certainty. This is likely to be a bulwark against any wholesale disintegration of the social order brought about by these tendencies. Equally, human capacities for learning are also likely to present such a barrier. As Fletcher (1997: 83) puts the matter, social processes under decivilizing conditions:

> do not simply reverse and go backwards, as it were, down the path along which they have already travelled. It is extremely unlikely that the

composite relations of the networks of interdependencies go into 'reverse' to the same degree, resulting in a different composition of the new configuration.

There are significant implications to these qualifiers. Barring some sort of extraordinary collapse, such as the aftermath of nuclear war, the civilizing process becomes less contingent and more of an ongoing process of development. In which case, the effects that decivilizing trends may have are likely to be partial, and may occur within particular configurations[4] of the more general parameters of the civilizing process. On this basis, what is likely to happen is that 'civilizing and decivilizing processes [will] occur *simultaneously* in particular societies, and not simply in the same or different societies at different points in time' (Dunning and Mennell, 1996: xv; emphasis added). And, if we extend this argument, the implications are that we are likely to see the emergence of new practices, behaviours, and cultural values that represent *a fusion* of these influences rather than the exclusive ascendancy of one or the other.

The nazification of Germany would seem to be a particularly good illustration of this point (rather than the Bauman argument that the civilizing process in itself can lead to this scale of catastrophe; and rather than explaining this era as the product of a decivilizing reversal of the civilizing process). It thus represents the specific outcome of these two processes running in tandem at that critical period in German history. It was the combination of the technological prowess and bureaucratic efficiency of the civilizing process as it had developed in Germany, and the hatred of Jews and other outsider groups brought by on by decivilizing influences, that culminated in the holocaust (Elias, 1996; Fletcher, 1997). Military defeat in 1918 followed by social and economic collapse in the 1920s broke down tolerance and self-restraint, and allowed myth and fantasy to take a hold on popular consciousness. Hitler thus appeared as a kind of 'magic man' who claimed that he could restore that country to greatness after its humiliating defeat in war: the way to do this was by protecting the purity of German national identity through channelling anxieties and insecurities into the seductive pull of a rigid and secure social order. As a result, we then find a deepening of the interdependencies between those judged to be 'racially pure', but at the same time a contraction of interdependencies as the increasing numbers who fell outside of this standard were denied sympathy or sensitivity. The need to defend this purity at all costs against external and internal threats then allowed a tolerance of barbarities, brutalities, and the withdrawal of the rule of law, resulting in genocide. Importantly, though, the hatred, intolerance, and blind obedience that had developed out of these decivilizing trends was then put into practical effect through a 'consolidated state monopoly of violence and an economy which was not in decline, but part of a highly specialized division of social functions and long chains of interdependency utilizing rationally planned and organized bureaucracies' (Fletcher, 1997: 172): characteristics of the civilizing process itself. As Mennell (1992: 249) chillingly puts the matter:

> that the camps were able to slaughter on such a huge scale depended on a vast social organization, most people involved in which squeezed no triggers, turned no taps, perhaps saw no camps and set eyes upon few

victims. They sat, like Adolf Eichmann, in a highly controlled manner at desks, working out railway timetables.

Punishment in the civilized world

Penal trends over much of the nineteenth and twentieth centuries can be interpreted as bearing close correspondence to the characteristics of the civilizing process. Thus, in relation to state process, what we see is the gradual assumption of the monopolistic control of the power to punish by central state authorities, which had been completed by the late nineteenth century in most of these societies. The consequences of this were that, first, all the remnants of the pre-modern carnival of punishment – all the local, informal sanctioning of miscreants – fell into disuse as this power was strengthened and consolidated in the bureaucratic organizations of the state. Second, monopolistic state control meant that the form that punishment took was increasingly standardized within jurisdictions instead of being fragmented and differentiated as before. Third, the general public became increasingly excluded from any formal involvement or influence on penal affairs. For example, previously free to wander around prisons and gaols (sometimes paying for the privilege to do so), by the late nineteenth century they had been almost totally shut out of them. It was now thought that the latter should not be allowed to interfere with prison administration – it was being turned into a professional activity to be undertaken by those trained for it. Punishment and penal affairs thereby became matters that were beyond the experience and capability of the general public to comprehend. In such ways, a firm dividing line was placed between the bureaucratic administration of penal affairs and the general public. By the same token, this consolidation of the power to punish in state organizations also meant that public knowledge of prisons would be controlled and channelled through them. Thus, in Britain, by the end of the nineteenth century the free-ranging and well published debates among prison governors, chaplains, social commentators, penal reformers, and so on about prison policy that had been characteristic of the mid-nineteenth century (Pratt, 2003) had evaporated. The overarching powers of the central prison bureaucracy were consolidated and extended under the provisions of the Prisons Act 1865. Thereafter, the prison establishment largely spoke with one voice, instead of the assemblage of claims and counter-claims that it had consisted of up to then.

In relation to socio-genesis, the concentration of penal power in state organizations saw the growth of interdependencies between penal officials and criminals, within the configuration both now inhabited, with the general public left largely outside of this. By the same token, the administration of punishment became an increasingly specialized activity, drawing on scientific knowledge and expertise to understand and act on criminality, rather than the emotive, expressive sentiments of the general public. In this way, the purposes of punishment changed from denunciation and deterrence characteristic of the mid-nineteenth century to those based around more objective, detached, scientific rationalities. On this basis, the reform and reintegration of criminals, rather than their permanent banishment or exclusion, became the main focus of punishment, particularly in the post-1945 period. The social distance between penal officials and criminals thus began to narrow (even if the distance between criminals and the general public remained much wider). As a result, the pejorative language of denunciation of the nineteenth century (criminals should be 'hated', according to Stephen, 1883) gave way to more sympathetic expressions of understanding for them by the mid-twentieth ('criminals have certainly injured their fellows, but perhaps society has unwittingly injured them'; Glover, 1956: 267). Equally we see advances in the levels of shame and embarrassment amongst penal officials. Hence the discomfort of Prison Commissioner Alexander Paterson on seeing Dartmoor prisoners in 1909: '[their] drab uniforms were plastered with broad arrows, their heads were closely shaven … not even a safety razor was allowed, so that in addition to the stubble on their heads, their faces were covered with a dirty moss, representing the growth of hair that a pair of clippers would not remove' (Ruck, 1951: 11). Indeed, as the ethos of reform became more embedded in penal development and the essentials of prison life (clothing, hygiene, diet) were steadily ameliorated (Pratt, 2002), those societies which seemed not to be following this course began to be seen as shameful and uncivilized. Attitudes to the 'uncivilized' Southern United States are an example of this, with its history of vigilantism, lynchings, and brutal prison conditions (the headline in *Time Magazine* 13 September 1943 was 'Georgia's Middle Ages', referring to a feature on that state's prisons).

In relation to psychogenesis, to what extent were 'ordinary people' prepared to accept the rational, scientific administration of punishment by government bureaucracies, with their own more emotive sentiments largely shut out of the formal penal framework that had been established? Certainly, by mid-twentieth century, the formal language of the penal professionals had come to be very different from that of their own, which on occasion threw off self restraint in angry outbursts of rage and hatred (outside courtrooms, for example) against particularly notorious criminals. Having said this, it should be noted that public opposition to the death penalty (at least in opinion polls) reached its highest levels in Britain and the United States in the 1930s (see Pratt, 2002). In addition, outrage at brutalities in the Southern United States was not just confined to elite groups – the 1934 movie *I am a Fugitive from a Chain Gang* attracted large crowds and galvinized a broad band of opinion against the injustices it portrayed. Furthermore, in Britain, until the 1930s, governments had been reluctant to widen the eligibility for indefinite prison terms to include sex offenders against children *because of public opposition to this particularly severe sentence* (Pratt, 1997). Even prison escapers, at least up to the 1950s, might be celebrated as heroes – little men, prepared to take on the overbearing state authorities – rather than reviled as the dangerous monsters they are considered today (Emmett, 2004). In this period, then, it is possible to discern distinct traces of sympathy and sensitivity to criminals and prisoners as well as the anger and resentment in the public mood that we have become familiar with today.

Nonetheless, the more general feeling seems to have been one of indifference rather than involvement – so long as the distasteful events of crime and punishment did not intrude on the lives of 'ordinary people'. Indeed, there was pressure to have the presence of punishment removed from everyday life, as the Report of the English Prison Commissioners (1947: 11) notes: 'the difficulty is that while it may be generally agreed that the Commissioners ought to acquire adequate accomodation for prisoners, any specific attempt to do so almost invariably meets with a firm local conviction that they should do it somewhere else'. In effect, it was as if the general public had come to expect and accept that punishing criminals was an area of political governance that was fenced off from them. Again, we might expect this to be the case, since for a good part of the twentieth century crime risks seemed manageable and largely under control within the existing framework of administration that had been extended for this (in so far as it is possible to ascertain in the absence of an omnipresent mass media and a much more cautious tabloid press[5]). This meant that under these circumstances, knowledge of crime problems was likely to be based on individual experience or from other local community sources, thereby making these risks more calculable and knowable (Giddens, 1990). In this way, the conditions necessary for a culture of forbearance, if not tolerance, were in place.

Overall, then, around 1970, a set of penal arrangements had been established, at least in the main English-speaking countries, whereby the power to punish was vested almost exclusively in the state and exercised through its bureaucratic and administrative organs of government. Punishment had become largely remote and anonymous, and for the most part made understandable to the general public (in so far as their indifference prompted any interest in such affairs) by the bureaucratic forces in control of it. This certainly did not mean that it was 'civilized' in the common-sense usage of this term, since privations and brutalities within the prisons could simply be hidden from view (Pratt, 2002). What it did mean, though, was that punishment of this kind had become one of the hallmarks of a society that liked to think it was civilized.

Post-1970: civilizing and decivilizing trends

Nonetheless, this framework of punishment was dependent for its existence on the particular configuration of the civilizing process across these societies around 1970. Any changes to this would bring about changes in the assembly of penal arrangements that it had previously made possible. What we have since seen, to a greater or lesser extent in these Anglo-American countries (but in few other European ones to the same degree) is the emergence of two competing sets of developments, consistent with the supposition that civilizing and decivilizing trends can run together rather than be mutually exclusive. On the one hand, we see an accentuation of the characteristics of the civilizing process: notably, trends towards globalization, technological development and mass communication are likely to strengthen interdependencies (through transnational trade, new international alliances, and so on) and increase identification with and tolerance of citizens from other countries as these societies become more heterogeneous. Similarly, the increasingly cosmopolitan and pluralistic nature of societies in the post-1970s period is likely to lead to an increase in tolerance of minority groups and differing personal arrangements regarding marriage, sexual preferences, and so on. As well, though, some aspects of the civilizing process can be seen as double-edged and as having the potential to bring about non-civilized consequences. Globalization, for example, not only fosters international alliances and leads to interdependencies between states, but it also leads to a weakening of the sovereignty of nation-states. Furthermore, the transcending of national boundaries as a result of trade agreements, etc., has led to massive population movements (particularly from the Eastern bloc and Third World countries) taking place, with the potential to further undermine the social stability of all these societies. Heterogeneity may be welcomed in some circles, but for many it seems threatening and unfamiliar, leading to contracting and more shallow inter-dependencies with these 'strangers'. Similarly, the technological prowess associated with the civilizing process enables mass communication industries to become our main source of knowledge of risks, making them thereby seem broader and more incalculable.

In addition, these developments coincide with decivilizing trends (fitting Fletcher's criteria) which have been brought about by the political, economic, and social changes of this period. Thus, with the ascendancy of neoliberal polities across all these societies, the authority of the central state is reconfigured and begins to be fragmented. It has come to assume a more residual role in governance than was previously the case. Providing protection from risks and dangers of various kinds may now be undertaken by the private or voluntary sectors, as citizens increasingly have to accept responsibility for such matters themselves (Garland, 1996). At the same time, government bureaucracies have regularly been criticized for their remoteness, expense, inefficiency and, in particular, their inability to solve the social problems and issues for which they had assumed responsibility in the post-war period. Again, though, one of the features of neoliberal politics, which has also been instrumental in its political success, is the way in which governments have acknowledged this and have been prepared to develop alternative modes of governance, that are now no longer privileged around the idea of a strong central state working at one with its own bureaucratic organizations, with ordinary people excluded from this framework. Instead, the emphasis has been on their empowerment, while simultaneously attempting to make government bureaucracies more transparent and accountable.

As this has occurred, interdependencies have been dramatically restructured. As Bauman (2001), Beck (1992), and Fukuyama (1995) have all noted, these wide-ranging changes have led to the erosion of many of the long-standing institutions and cultural expectations that had become deeply embedded in these societies: for example, the movement away from identities that were constructed around the rituals of durable and certain class cultures towards a world where one's identity is more contingent and is forged through consumption rituals. Equally, in relation to family life, not only has average family size declined dramatically, but in addition, what has now assumed the almost 'normal' status of family break-up makes for impermanent, transient sets of relationships. On this, Beck has posed the following questions:

> Ask yourself what actually is a family nowadays? What does it mean? Of course, there are children, my children, our children. But even parenthood, the core of family life, is beginning to disintegrate under conditions of divorce ... [G]randmothers and grandfathers get included and excluded without any means of participating in the decisions of their sons and daughters. (quoted by Bauman, 2001: 6)

The effects of this reversal of the trend towards a centralized state authority which had assumed overall management for the risks threatening its population, and the breaking up of previously secure and wide-ranging interdependencies, lead to a preoccupation with new areas of danger, vulnerability, and uncertainty. Risks increasingly seem incalculable and unpredictable. For example, the growing visibility of women in public space makes them more vulnerable to attack from 'strangers', to which the existing authorities seem to have no answer or solution. In other words, these new areas of experience require constant negotiation and awareness of the perils they might contain. It is as if all the road maps of everyday life which the state had previously drawn up on our behalf have been removed; in the new ones that replace them, the state only sketches in vague landmarks around which we must then undertake our own cartography. Yet the same process which makes interdependencies more diffuse and insubstantial is also likely to unify them against common, easily identifiable enemies who seem to put us further at risk, whether these be particular types of criminal or new categories of unwanted citizens, such as refugees, apparently making unwarranted claims on restricted state resources. Under these circumstances, the habitus of self-restraint begins to give way to more unrestrained outlets of emotion, as all the old assurances which had allowed us to take uncertainties or vicissitudes in our stride, or to tolerate those whose conduct or character seemed undesirable, begin to unravel. Indeed, we now live in an era of road rage, air rage, hospital rage, and so on – as if, without the social solidity of the pre-1970 period, *ad hoc* outbursts of anger can now become our response to delays, frustrations, and inconveniences; and a new intolerance – zero tolerance – of those not making a contribution to social well-being.

Against this backcloth, it becomes possible to see how the new punitiveness emerged. We have a loss of state authority, the breakdown of previously existing interdependencies, and the dangers individual citizens face seem to grow and become more incalculable. There is less self-restraint on the part of individuals but a simultaneous yearning for stronger and clearer responses from the state. Thus, in relation to crime, as its reporting in the official statistics escalated during the expansion of the mass media in the 1970s and 1980s, so it came to be represented as a problem out of control, beyond the existing modalities of governance and of increasing alarm to the general public (hence the way in which law and order has become such an important political issue in this period – and only in this period it would seem[6] – across these societies). Again, as such matters were opened up to political debate and scrutiny rather than left to be quietly administered by the penal bureaucracies, so sentencing and parole practices and the efficiency of the judicial authorities began to be regularly challenged, revealing the gulf that existed between court-imposed sentences and the reality of prison terms after parole, remission, etc., had been taken into account. This only gave further grounds for public suspicion and distrust of the bureaucratic organ–izations which were meant to be managing these distasteful features on their behalf. It was around these suspicions that popular movements such as 'Truth in Sentencing' began to emerge, rather slowly at first in the late 1970s, but later with gathering speed and momentum, until this slogan, with others, was turned into a populist rallying call against a supposedly out-of-touch liberal bureaucracy and judiciary.

In such ways, a large-scale insatiable sense of fear and anxiety has been created over this period, with a yearning for security and certainty, which has always proved to be elusive as new risks and dangers reveal themselves. Thus, paradoxically, at a time when governmental authority has been contracting and it no longer claims to have the solution to all the difficulties we are likely to face, it generates popular demands for a strong, central government that can provide remedies to what seem to be our biggest dangers, and which also seem to be the most easily solvable: crime and punishment problems. They at least seem the most easily solvable when common-sense knowledge, based on anecdotes, memories, and folklore begins to displace scientific rationalities and expertise as the mode of knowledge through which such matters are formally addressed.

The new punitiveness and its effects

What, though, are the particular effects of these changes within the penal configuration? In relation to the central state, while the authority of its own bureaucratic organizations has indeed become fragmented and discredited, this has hardly resulted in its complete collapse. What we see instead is a recon-figuration of the channels through which it governs. Thus, in the post-1970s period, at least in relation to the ownership of penal power, a new kind of state authority emerges: one now framed more around the relationship between government and the general public, with a reduced role for the penal bureau-cracies in the leadership of developments here. Previous public indifference has given way to demands for involvement and consultation at various levels of penal affairs. It is as if the initial political successes of neoliberalism over the last quarter of a century as a result of the ability of politicians such as Margaret Thatcher to speak to the anxieties and aspirations of 'ordinary people', simul-taneously bypassing government departments – about law and order matters and a whole range of others as well – come to be solidified in the form of an accepted acknowledgement of public anxieties and expectations that these will now be addressed by politicians (rather than deflected by bureaucrats). Even so, it would seem that the balance of forces within this new axis of power has begun to change: as governments become more populist (recognizing that this is the route to electoral success), and as the concerns and anxieties of the general public are not only unabated but seem to gather momentum, politicians no longer simply acknowledge the public mood or representations of this (Bottoms, 1995) but instead allow themselves to be led by it (Pratt, 2002; Freiberg, 2003).

In this way, we find the use of political mechanisms such as plebiscites and referenda which provide for more direct injections of public sentiment on policy development, sometimes to the exclusion of bureaucratic and expert opinion altogether, with the effect of creating a new axis of penal power (Zimring, 1996; Pratt and Clark, 2005). Thus in the New Zealand general election of 1999, there was a 91.75 per cent vote in favour of the following Citizens Initiated Referendum: 'should there be a reform of our justice system placing greater emphasis on the needs of victims, providing restitution and compensation for them and imposing minimum sentences and hard labour for all serious violent offences?' Notwithstanding its inherent contradictions, breaches of human rights and inconsistencies, the referendum was then heavily influential in the development of subsequent penal legislation which, in particular, proscribed and encouraged the use of much longer prison terms for some groups of offenders. Indeed, immediately on the passing of this legislation, the Justice Minister telephoned the organizer of the referendum to congratulate him (Pratt and Clark, 2005).

Furthermore, within this new axis of power, the formal language of punishment reflects new cultural values. Instead of a predominance of talk of reform and rehabilitation (which bore the stamp of the influence of liberal elites within the bureaucratic establishment), we become much more familiar with the emotive, unrestrained language of 'three strikes', 'zero tolerance', 'life means life', and so on, language deliberately designed to incorporate public anger and resentment – and particularly aimed at those criminals whose risks seem incalculable and who constitute the greatest dangers to us (for example, the new laws in the United States relating to sexual predators). Groups such as these are no longer thought to be in need of scientific scrutiny and examination. Instead, they become fantastic, irredeemable devils who have to be degraded and then excluded from the rest of us for as long as possible. Hence, as well, the adjustments that have been made to penal policies in the last 15 to 20 years as citizens demand that they have involvement in their sentencing and parole hearings and receive notification of the release of particular groups of ex-prisoners.

However, and in contrast to the emotive emblems of the new punitiveness, there are also important counter-trends which channel these sentiments into strategic effect and which, overall, provide a very uneven picture. As the partiality and particularity of these trends indicate, the current interconnection between civilizing and decivilizing influences is going to be experienced differentially across these societies, depending on (a) how advanced the former had previously been and (b) the degree to which the latter now erodes it. At a general level, the enhanced bureaucratic rationalism and scientific expertise indicative of the civilizing process become increasingly necessary to manage the growth in the prison population generated by decivilizing influences and the new punitiveness it produces. Equally, the use of actuarial techniques in parole adjudications is designed to minimize the risks of early release. In the aftermath of the new penal laws in New Zealand, the parole applications of those serving prison terms of seven years or more are assessed actuarially (although those serving two years or less are given automatic release on completing half their sentence).

Nonetheless, in other sectors of the penal configuration, there still seems to be something of an immunity to these new sentiments. Within the prison establishment itself, where there is much less scope for public penetration and scrutiny, notwithstanding what at times seem to be rather tokenistic attempts to prize open previously closed-off penal arrangements by making various segments of them more publicly accountable through inspection and so on, sanitized language and the ameliorative trends continue to a large extent. The emphasis on prison programmes and case and unit management are the latest attempts to rationalize prison work and reform prisoners. Similarly, prison authorities have been prepared to recognize the vulnerability of particular groups of prisoners and have continued to improve dietary, hygiene, and clothing arrangements (in recent years, 'slopping out' has come to an end in England and nearly so in New Zealand, for example). All this has happened despite periodic references to the need for more 'spartan'or austere prison regimes; or others based on some notion of turning the penal clock back and reintroducing penal strategies from the past.[7]

On the other hand, in parts of the United States, these continuing trends of amelioration and sanitization have been reversed. In Georgia, for example, prisoners' heads are now shaved on arrival, they must wear pressed uniforms labelled 'state prisoner', prison rations have been reduced, and there are to be no hot meals, amid a range of other trends detailed in the introduction to this book designed to increase the social distance between the prisoner and the prison authorities (see Pratt, 2002: 178–9). In this region, we might surmise that where the attributes of the civilizing process had only had a short and precarious history, it is not sufficiently embedded to resist decivilizing influences and moves more quickly and more extensively into reverse than elsewhere. Then more generally, across the USA, we see the development of 'Supermax' prison conditions (housing nearly two per cent of its prison population; King, 1999) where human contact and sensory stimuli are reduced to an absolute minimum: indicative of a reassertion, to an extreme degree, of the previous established/outsider relationship between the prison authorities and prisoners. Perhaps, though, we should expect these kinds of developments in a society where risk, danger, and insecurity seem more pronounced than in these other societies: penal intolerance escalates the prison population of that country to hitherto unparalleled heights in the civilized world; this then leads to attendant adjustments to prison regimes, particularly when their stark realities of deprivation can be glossed over with the language of expertise associated with the civilizing process (see Lynch, this volume, in relation to both Supermax prisons and the death penalty in the US). Indeed, placement in a Supermax may be referred to in relatively benign terms as 'administrative segregation'; the prisoners are referred to here as 'inmates'; their cases are reviewed once a week by 'treatment program supervisors'; misbehaviour in the cell leads to the inmate being 'extracted' from it (presumably to some other even more remote enclave).[8] In Georgia and some of the other Southern states, the localized effects of the civilizing process have been more easily reversed and old-style ideas and practices are relegitimated. Here, though, the effects of decivilizing impulses are significantly camouflaged by the language of the civilizing process. It is as if the prison bureaucracies adjust themselves and are prepared to move towards new horizons of emotional pain and deprivation in accordance with the new penal culture, but then formally address this in such a way that public sensitivities will not be shocked or disturbed. The invocation of known practices from the past, within their customary localities, seems to be acceptable. On the other hand, the more futuristic possibilities of punishing taking place across the USA in Supermax are spoken of more delicately. The South had always had an uneasy association with the civilizing process; but the USA as a whole would still seem to need the cloak of civilized standards to legitimate what it does.

Overall, though, the dramatic emphasis and attention on the prison which sees it move from the place of last resort that it had occupied around 1970 to one that creeps progressively back towards the centre of the penal systems of these countries represents the main consequence of the combined effects of civilizing and decivilizing processes at the present time, bearing in mind that the pace of this is highly localized. Nonetheless, the security offered by prison may not in itself be sufficient to contain and soak up the new punitiveness. These sentiments can run through other penal outlets. Over the same period, we have seen the return of punishments that involve public shaming and humiliation in parts of the United States and Australia; or again, the reappearance of chain gangs in the United States, previously thought to have been consigned to history after many decades of struggle to achieve this (Sellin, 1976). As a weak and fragmented state loses its monopolistic hold on the power to punish, or where the state's authority was particularly underdeveloped; and when this takes place in conjunction with increased sense of risk and insecurity alongside a lowering of the threshold of shame and embarrassment (so that such sights become tolerable once again to an onlooking public), then, as with the prisons regimes in Georgia, this can lead to the reactivation of readily available local cultural heritages: a clear reversal, then, of penal development, as opposed to modifications reflecting the competing influences of both civilizing and decivilizing processes. Again, where there are not such formal penal outlets available in the community to soak up and assuage no public sentiments, then extra-legal penal activity may be the product. Hence the emergence of activities such as the distribution of naming-and-shaming posters distributed around neighbourhoods, which alert the community to troublemakers, ex-prisoners, and so on, and, at the same time, vigilante activities. These came to a crescendo in Britain in anti-paedophile activities in the summer of 2000. It is surely significant that they took place there much more extensively than in any similar country because of the presence of a stronger, unified central penal bureaucracy than elsewhere; and because, as well, the British government had refused to extend provision for community notification registers to the general public. With no legitimate outlet for their punitive sentiments, they found expression in vigilantism.

There are other possibilities, though, as a result of the decline in the authority and ambit of the state. In jurisdictions with recent colonial histories such as New Zealand, Australia, and Canada, this decivilizing trend is fused with an extension of interdependencies to include ethnic minorities, thus continuing the civilizing process. This then allows for the reintroduction of varieties of indigenous justice practices, which attract the support of sections of the liberal bureaucracies and are then represented as restorative justice. In this way, it is not simply authoritarian forces moving into this void – the whole space is open for contestation at present: although, again, the growing power of this culture of intolerance would seem to suggest that the impact of the new punitiveness is likely to outweigh other more liberal sensitivities.

Finally, to return to the starting point of this chapter, I have tried to demonstrate that the penal reversals of recent years in the main English-speaking world – and the continuities as well – do indeed fit within the main tenets of Elias' work. More specifically, what we see emerging in this area across these societies are the contingent effects of long-term civilizing trends now running in conjunction with more recent decivilizing tendencies. The overall result has been the dramatic realignment over the last 20 years of the assumptions, the values, and understandings of the forms punishment should take in societies that like to think of themselves as civilized.

Notes

1 See Fletcher (1997: 166–71) for an extended commentary on this point; essentially, Bauman too seems to make the assumption that 'civilization' in Elias' work is some kind of normative construct, and it is on this basis that he develops his critique of both Elias and our faith in the ability of civilization to guarantee civilized end products.

2 In particular, 'the issues raised by the book have their origins less in scholarly tradition, in the narrow sense of the word, than in the experiences in whose shadow we all live, experiences of the crisis and transformation of Western civilization as it has existed hitherto' (Elias, 1984: xvii); and 'the armour of civilized conduct would crumble very rapidly if, through a change in society, the degree of insecurity that existed earlier were to break in upon us again, and if danger became as incalculable as once it was. Corresponding fears would burst the limits set to them today' (Elias, 1984: 307).

3 As Fletcher (1997: 45) puts the matter, 'there is some residual ambiguity surrounding the concept of civilization used by Elias. It is not completely clear whether the normative aspect of the term features in his work – he does not place "civilization" in inverted commas to indicate a normative valuation.'

4 Elias (1984: 214) uses the analogy of the dance to explain this concept: 'the image of the mobile configurations of interdependent people on a dance floor perhaps makes it easier to imagine states, cities, families and also capitalist, communist and feudal systems as figurations. Like every other social figuration, a dance figuration is relatively independent of the specific individuals forming it here and now, but not of individuals as such ... Just as the small dance figurations change – becoming now slower, now quicker – so too, gradually or more suddenly, do the large figurations which we call societies.'

5 On the differential nature of risk assessment and the role of the mass media in this in the pre-war and post-war periods, see Pratt (1997: 56).

6 One speaker in the Canadian federal parliament in the debate on the abolition of the death penalty in 1975 proclaimed that 'the cry for law and order has been the cry of nearly every tyrant in history' (Pratt, 2002: 32). The significance of the comment lies in the way in which it represented an era (coming to an end) where matters of law and order had little place on party political agendas, and were addressed by penal and justice officials 'behind the scenes'. Only tyrants such as Hitler had broken this code of political conduct up to that point.

7 For example, the shaming punishments in Australia are confined to remote frontier regions; see Pratt (2000).

8 Kurki and Morris (2001: 399) write as follows of extractions: 'five men dressed, armed and protected rather like Darth Vader enter your cell and with a large plastic shield pin you to the wall. This facilitates two of them safely chaining your feet together and your arms together at the wrist behind your back. You are then removed from your cell. The extraction is complete.'

References

Bauman, Z. (1989) *Modernity and the Holocaust*, Cambridge: Polity Press.

Bauman, Z. (2001) *Liquid Modernity*, Cambridge: Polity Press.

Beck, U. (1992) *Risk Society*, Oxford: Basil Blackwell.

Bottoms, A. E. (1995) 'The Politics and Philosophy of Sentencing', in C. Clarkson and R. Morgan (eds) *The Politics of Sentencing*, Oxford: Clarendon Press, 170–90.

Cunningham, H. (1980) *Leisure in the Industrial Revolution*, London: Routledge.

Dunning, E. and Mennell, S. (1996) 'Introduction', in N. Elias, *The Germans*, Cambridge: Polity Press, 1–20.

Elias, N. (1984) *The Civilizing Process*, Oxford: Blackwell (original edition 1939).

Elias, N. (1996) *The Germans*, Cambridge: Polity Press.

Emmett, A. (2004) *From Romantic Outlaw to Dangerous Monster: A Sociological History of Prison Escapers*, Wellington: Victoria University MA thesis.

Fletcher, J. (1997) *Violence and Civilization*, Cambridge: Polity Press.

Foucault, M. (1978) *Discipline and Punish*, London: Allen Lane.

Foucault, M. (1991) 'Governmentality', in C. Burchell *et al.* (eds) *The Foucault Effect*, Hemel Hempstead: Harvester Wheatsheaf.

Freiberg, A. (2003) 'The Four Pillars of Justice', *Australian and New Zealand Journal of Criminology*, 36: 223–230.

Fukuyama, F. (1995) *Trust: The Social Virtues and the Creation of Prosperity*, New York: Free Press.

Garland, D. (1996) 'The Limits of the Sovereign State', *British Journal of Criminology*, 36(4): 445–71.

Garland, D. (2001) *The Culture of Control*, Oxford: Oxford University Press.

Giddens, A. (1990) *The Consequences of Modernity*, Cambridge: Polity Press.

Glover, E. (1956) *Probation and Reeducation*, London: RKP.

King, R. (1999) 'The Rise and Rise of Supermax', *Punishment and Society* 1: 163–86.

Kurki, L. and Morris, N. (2001) 'The Purposes, Practices and Problems of Supermax Prisons', *Crime and Justice*, 21: 385–424.

Mennell, S. (1990) 'Decivilizing Processes: Theoretical Significance and Some Lines of Research', *International Sociology*, 5: 205–233.

Mennell, S. (1992) *Norbert Elias: An Introduction*, Oxford: Blackwell.

O'Malley, P. (1999) 'Volatile and Contradictory Punishments', *Theoretical Criminology*, 3: 175–96.

Report of the Prison Commissioners (1947) London: PP (1947–8), Cmd. 7475.

Pratt, J. (1997) *Governing the Dangerous*, Sydney: Federation Press.

Pratt, J. (2000) 'The Return of the Wheelbarrow Men', *British Journal of Criminology*, 40: 127–45.

Pratt, J. (2002) *Punishment and Civilization*, London: Sage.

Pratt, J. (2003) 'The Decline and Renaissance of Shaming in Modern Penal Systems', in B. Godfrey, C. Elmsley and G. Dunstall (eds) *Comparative Histories of Crime*, Cullompton: Willan, 178–94.

Pratt, J. and Clark, M. (2005) 'Penal Populism in New Zealand', *Punishment and Society* (in press).

Ruch, S. K. (1951) *Paterson on Prisons. The Collected Papers of Sir Alexander Paterson*, London: Frederick Muller.

Sellin, T. (1976) *Slavery and the Penal System*, New York: Elsevier.

Stephen, J. (1883) *History of the English Criminal Law*, London: Butterworths.

Zimring, F. (1996) 'Populism, Democratic Government and the Decline of Expert Authority', *Pacific Law Journal*, 28: 243–56.

16. Liberal exclusions and the new punitiveness

Mark Brown

This chapter engages with the theme of the new punitiveness at the level of the political. Much writing on past and recent penal trends has tended to pitch its analysis in such a way that large areas of political thought and action disappear from view. Consider for a moment the ubiquity of the following terms in recent writing on penal matters: 'modernity', 'late-modernity', 'late-capitalism', 'neoliberalism', 'governmentality'. We can apprehend distinct political meanings or associations in each. Yet in a curious sleight of hand these conceptual-analytical structures draw attention down onto the penal subject while simultaneously achieving a radical decentring of the political agent. Modernity, late-modernity, or neoliberalism thus become essentialized concepts, hollowed out of the very detail, character, dispute, idiosyncrasy, assumption, and referents that make (or made) them features of lived experience. Instead, we are liable to speak of penal modernism's key tenets – rationality, scientism, and restraint – or of neoliberalism's tropes of rationality and choice. Of course, this is not to say that political voices are not heard at all, for much if not the majority of contemporary penal theorizing is developed out of an analysis of discourse and texts. But this textual analysis has its own important silences that I will mention again in a moment. My aim in writing this chapter has therefore been to find a way to re-insert the political agent and some idea of a non-essentialized political analytic into contemporary debates about penal trends – in this case, the possible rise of a new punitiveness. In so doing I hope I may begin to clear up some important omissions of attention in contemporary penal theory.

Before embarking on this course, two prefatory remarks are in order. The first concerns the object of my interest in this chapter, liberalism. The question might reasonably be posed, why liberalism? And why should we be interested in the sort of extended discussion of it that will follow here? To begin with, I would say because liberalism and neoliberalism have emerged as key theoretical constructs in the explanation of recent trends and disruptions in the punitive field (see e.g., O'Malley, 1992, 2004; Rose, 1996, 2000). But perhaps more importantly, I believe that a close look at liberalism is important because the terms 'liberalism' and 'neoliberalism' have been bandied around with a remarkable lack of attention to the content of their structures. The term neoliberalism, particularly, has become ubiquitous in theoretical discourse on punishment, yet few writers pay the scantest regard to the political philosophy it references. This has produced at least three sorts of problems, and possibly more. Firstly, the student of punishment has been left to impute some content into the categories 'liberalism' and 'neoliberalism' based upon only the vaguest guidance: these political terms must, it seems, be in some way connected with ideas about personal responsibility, autonomy, the virtues of the market, and so on. But *precisely* how and why is often left unclear. Moreover, where liberalism has in fact received more detailed treatment, such as in the work of Mariana Valverde (1996) or Mitchell Dean (1999, 2002), it has occurred outside the mainstream of criminological discussion, in the study of government more generally. Secondly, and partly due to the lack of any real debate over the contours of liberal theory within the punishment literature, there seems to have been ample scope for writers to conflate and confuse the terms liberalism and neoliberalism. Pat O'Malley argues in respect of neo-liberalism that '[w]e need to understand this theoretically in order to develop a normative political response' (2004: 187). I agree fully, and this chapter aims to develop just such a theoretical understanding. But I cannot completely agree with his characterization of what neoliberalism is. To my eye, what he briefly describes as free market and social authoritarian principles, combining with a faith in individualism and constraints on central government, looks like little more than a definition of mid-nineteenth-century authoritarian liberalism, such as that elaborated by James Fitzjames Stephen (1873). Could it be that the *neo*liberalism O'Malley (2004) describes is less 'neo' than simply a *variety* of nineteenth-century liberalism, albeit one derived from Hobbes rather than Locke? Finally, while liberalism has received sustained attention in the work of Mitchell Dean (1999, 2002), his approach has been so strongly framed within a Foucauldian analytic of governmentality that liberalism's political content, its foundational character as a system of politics and government, has been emasculated. What this governmentality analysis leaves behind is an image of liberalism as little more than a kind of heuristic, problem-solving model of governance, perhaps at best a form of rationality. This chapter aims to address each of these three problems in an extended explanation and discussion of liberal thought that will, I hope, provide the necessary backdrop to an informed analysis of recent penal trends.

The second prefatory point I need to make concerns method. I remarked above that contemporary methods of textual analysis carry within them important silences. I do not claim any special expertise to decipher the epistemological bases of these methods, but I am able to observe the manifest paradox that methods resting upon analyses of texts clearly eschew certain types of text. Take the example of liberalism (or neoliberalism for that matter). The texts used to represent liberal thought tend to be the reports of prison inspectorates, the dossiers of prison administrators, the schedules and manuals of therapists, the occasional parliamentary speech, government white papers, and so on. What is missing here is attention to the thoughts, writings, and political doctrines established by liberalism's architects. For all of liberalism's analytic centrality, and so familiarity to readers and thinkers on punishment and social control, who among us can name five or six prominent nineteenth-century liberal theorists? Who can point to the main points of contention between John Stuart Mill and his furious opponent James Fitzjames Stephen? The fact that we can't, I believe, says something. Perhaps our ignorance and the silence it produces are due to the influence of French historical and philosophical methods – principally through Michel Foucault – where, since the Annales school, political history has been disdained. Perhaps it was Foucault's disconnection of meaning from discourse, his interest in discourses as elements in a system to be mapped, and his sense that forms rather than rationalizations would account for change, that has led to the decline in interest in how liberalism has been explained and justified. Whatever the reason, it is a part of my argument here that we cannot begin to understand what makes a new punitiveness possible unless we understand the spaces that might be provided for it within the principal philosophy underpinning contemporary Western statecraft.

The remainder of this chapter will develop this broad argument in detail and breaks fairly neatly into two parts. The first examines liberalism from three important angles: as a movement in popular ideas and politics; as a political philosophy demanding coherent description and defence; and, finally, as a philosophy that guided colonial government as well as government at its point of origin, which is commonly referred to as the 'metropolitan centre'. This part of the chapter will show how liberalism developed not simply as a doctrine of political organization but so too as an account of the necessary virtues of political subjects. Where a culture seemed bereft of such virtues, as in so many colonial locations, liberal thinkers such as John Stuart Mill recommended despotic government as a means of quickly transforming a society and its colonial subjects. It is the model of colonial exclusion developed within liberal thought of this time that provides the space, I believe, into which radical forms of punishment and exclusion in contemporary Western societies have been able to move. The second part of the chapter will show how this has been effected, beginning with an account of the relationship between what I will define as the 'new punitiveness' and colonial strategies of exclusion, and then moving to examine in more detail how specific punishments do, or don't, fit this analysis.

Liberalism and the colonial legacy

The past 150 years have seen liberal thought shift from the periphery to the very centre of modern Western political culture. Party political distinctions between Labour and Conservative, or Republican and Democrat, represent little more than scuffles over the detail of how an agreed liberal project should best be implemented. Across the board in Western societies there is a wide-ranging commitment to the liberal principles of democracy, rights, the rule of law and the market (Bellamy, 1992; King, 1999). Stephen Holmes (1993: 4) provides the following useful definition of liberalism:

> liberalism's four core norms or values are *personal security* (the monopolization of legitimate violence by agents of the state who are themselves monitored and regulated by law), *impartiality* (a single system of law applied equally to all), *individual liberty* (a broad sphere of freedom from collective or governmental supervision, including freedom of conscience, the right to be different, the right to pursue ideals one's neighbour thinks wrong, the freedom to travel and emigrate, and so forth), and *democracy* or

the right to participate in law making by means of elections and public discussions through a free press.

However, if we are to understand why such a structure of politico-ethical principles has risen to the very centre of Western statecraft, it is necessary to look to its nineteenth-century origins. In doing so it will become apparent that liberalism, or perhaps more accurately, British liberalism, emerged as a project of social transformation and nation-building. Its key aims and principles are thus closely tied to nineteenth-century ideas about nationalism and the qualifications for political and economic participation. British liberalism of this era also built upon a bedrock of principles laid down over more than 200 years, most notably by John Locke. The remainder of this section is thus broken into three parts. The first will trace the emergence in Britain of liberalism as a politico-ethical philosophy.[1] This will be followed by a closer look at the sustained attempt by John Stuart Mill to establish a liberal political doctrine, providing a bedrock of principle to new ideas about government and statecraft. The final part of this section will consider the case of British colonialism and its central and crucial role as a counterpoint to the ideal societies imagined in the doctrine of Mill.

Liberalism and social transformation

Britain entered the nineteenth century poised on the cusp of change. The Industrial Revolution, embodying the shift from an agrarian to industrial economy and the massive shifts in population and social structure it induced, was shortly to usher in a set of political changes that would establish a framework for modern Western states that has survived up to the present day. A series of changes initiated in the first part of the century began to shake the traditional social order, reflected most notably in the 1832 Reform Act, an initiative that extended for the first time a limited political franchise to the middle classes. An emerging liberal theory played a key role in this process of social transformation and would eventually provide the principled doctrinal basis, as well as an institutional political structure (in the form of the Liberal Party established progressively through the mid-nineteenth century) for its elaboration. At the heart of early British liberalism was a belief in the primacy of liberty, notwithstanding the fact that there remained considerable dispute as to what constituted liberty and whether it should more properly be defined in positive or negative terms. At a practical level, however, liberal thought of this period was worked out and developed through its connection with important political struggles. It was tied, for instance, to a reformist mission to reshape the structure of British society, to topple the edifice of traditional aristocratic power, and to extend political rights to the British demos. Yet such projects themselves created new sorts of social problems and so liberal thinkers were forced to combine with their analysis of social structures an account of the agency of political subjects. Importantly in this respect, it was widely believed that as desirable as structural changes were, they carried within them the seeds of social disorder, anarchy, and unreasoned government. Thus, liberalism began as much a theory of personal ethics as a theory of politics. Under this, the extension of political citizenship was to be balanced by a carefully worked-out programme of social and individual discipline that would enmesh and bind the new political classes to the new social order. Clearly, then, liberalism was from its inception an inclusionary political project: one in which political rights would be progressively granted to various social classes (the middle classes, then lower classes) and status groups (men first, then women) as each group was drawn into a modernizing civil society and nation-state.

The principles that would bind this new polity together were worked out and elaborated through the ideas of *virtue* and *character*. They were instilled in young Britons through the institutions of education and religious instruction, and through a wide variety of morality plays and tales. For the newly enfranchised worker they were acquired and reinforced through a series of institutions, such as mechanics institutes, workers associations, cooperative societies and the like, as well as, of course, through the dominance of an increasingly evangelical Christianity. Each sought to shape and mould the individual subjectivity of new, modern Britons around notions of progress, industry, civilization, and proper values. The Victorian 'character' received a special status and priority in this process and its development was guided through precise and intricate techniques of character development. Richard Bellamy (1992: 10) has succinctly described some of the important elements of Victorian character and one of its expert tutors, Samuel Smiles:

> Far from being a licence for the unrestricted satisfaction of one's wants and desires, 'character' consisted in the ability to rise above sensual, animal instincts and passions through the force of will. A variety of conventional Victorian middle-class virtues clustered around this key concept. These included, to cite some of those gathered together by the high priest of Victorian 'character' building – Samuel Smiles (1812–1905) – self-culture, self-control, energy, industry, frugality, thrift, prudence, patience, perseverance, honesty, integrity, temperance, sobriety, independence, manliness and duty.

Thus, as liberalism developed it meshed ideas about political structure with a set of assumptions about the necessary virtues of political subjects. It worked back and forward between the practical demands of parliamentary politics and the principled need for a coherent doctrine upon which political practices might be grounded. British liberalism thus first emerged as a project dedicated to redrawing the boundaries of British politics, boundaries that defined lines of political inclusion and exclusion. But while liberalism sought to redraw these lines, its leading thinkers remained committed to the idea that some degree of political exclusion was both necessary and desirable. But how was such a ploy to be achieved?

The structure of liberal doctrine

The chief architect of this new structure, this redrawing of the grounds upon which political inclusion and exclusion could be justified, was John Stuart Mill. Widely regarded as the 'father of modern liberalism' (Eisenach, 1998), Mill drew together these ideals of political reform and their important connection with the changing roles of both government and political subjects.[2] In three short works, *Utilitarianism* (1861–3), *On Liberty* (1859), and *Representative Government* (1861) (collected in Mill, 1972), Mill set out the moral, political and pragmatic ground upon which a structure of liberal doctrine could be erected. Following his father, James Mill, he argued in *Utilitarianism* that any theory of human action must have at its base the idea of utility. By this he meant:

> that pleasure, and freedom from pain, are the only things desirable as ends; and that all desirable things (which are as numerous in the utilitarian as in any other scheme) are desirable either from the pleasure inherent in themselves, or as means to the promotion of pleasure and prevention of pain. (Mill, 1972: 6)

These presumptions were reflected in ideas like the Greatest Happiness Principle, wherein Mill argued that all humans should strive for 'an existence exempt as far as possible from pain, and as rich as possible in enjoyments, both in the point of quantity and quality' (p. 11). At a societal level, the proper course of action, he believed, should be that which promotes the greater good while at the same time minimizing, to the greatest extent possible, any collateral pain. Utilitarianism, therefore, provided an abstract theory of action upon which liberalism could be grounded. In *On Liberty* he dealt with the question of how these ideas might operate in practice and, particularly, with the question of 'the nature and limits of the power which can be legitimately exercised by society over the individual' (p. 65). Prefacing a theme to which he would return often, Mill counterpointed the idea of individual liberty with that of authority, or the power of the state, arguing that '[t]he struggle between Liberty and Authority is the most conspicuous feature of the portions of history with which we are earliest familiar' (p. 65). His aim in *On Liberty* was to work out a system of government and social organization in which individual liberty would be protected from what he saw as the twin vices of despotism and paternalism.

He did so, in a quite unique fashion, by distinguishing the spheres of internal and external action (Capaldi, 1998). The inner sphere or domain of life was the personal, a sphere activated by free will and leading to individuals' shaping their own lives, their personal character, and their virtues. It was a sphere, as Capaldi has observed, characterized by freedom, but it was a very special kind of freedom that Mill had in mind. To be free was to exercise autonomy and while this autonomy could not be directly seen or measured, it could be evinced by the important behavioural characteristics of self-discipline, choice, and responsibility. Freedom, on this view, would operate at both individual and social levels. In modern parlance we might refer to it as something akin to self-actualization. At the individual level it was instantiated by choice itself: the person who did not choose their own course but allowed circumstances or others to guide them had, in Mill's view, 'no need of any other faculty than the ape-like one of imitation' (Mills, 1972: 117). In the social sphere, society, such freedom was necessary and desirable because the fully developed individual became more valuable not just to him or herself but to others also. The role of government was to protect this inner sphere, but equally the political subject bore a *responsibility* to develop their character in ways that promoted self-discipline. Personal freedom and autonomy were in some sense then both the product of government – it could encourage the development of self-disciplined subjects through the extension of special protections and the tutelary institutions of education and the like – and the product of a personal obligation held by all political subjects towards self-improvement.

Mill contrasted this idea of freedom, which operated within the inner sphere, with liberty in the outer or external sphere. Liberty thus represented release from the overbearing control and interference of government over action. Consistent with his utilitarian assumptions, Mill then argued that 'The only purpose for which power can be rightfully exercised over any member of a civilised community, against his will, is to prevent harm to others' (p. 73). Two important points are raised here. The first concerns the sphere in which harm may take place. This is limited to the external sphere, meaning that an individual's thoughts, preferences, beliefs, and the like were sacrosanct. So too would be individual actions that harmed only the individual him or herself: simply having disagreeable thoughts or taking personally harmful actions would be no justification for government interference. Secondly, and importantly for this discussion, there should be noted in Mill's description above the important qualification, 'civilised community'. This notion should be understood as operating upon two levels, both of which pertain to the capacity of individuals to develop autonomy in the internal sphere. Children, clearly, could not be expected to exercise proper choices and to take responsibility seriously, and so the limits of government action upon their liberty should be less stringent. At the same time, however, paternalistic government intervention in the lives of children could be justified only to the extent that it assisted them to develop those virtuous forms of action that characterized the autonomous individual. The same applied to what Mill termed 'barbarians':

> For the same reason [as applied to children] we may leave out of consideration those backward states of society in which the race itself may be considered as if in its nonage. The early difficulties in the way of spontaneous progress are so great, that there is seldom any choice of means of overcoming them; and a ruler full of the spirit of improvement is warranted in the use of any expedients that will attain an end, perhaps otherwise unattainable. Despotism is a legitimate mode of government in dealing with Barbarians, provided the end be their improvement, and the means justified by actually effecting that end. Liberty, as a principle, has no application to any state of things anterior to the time when mankind have become capable of being improved by free and equal discussion. (Mill, 1972: 73)

Here, then, emerge the first exclusions in an otherwise highly modern and progressive conception of individual lives and personal and cultural difference. In contrast to the exclusions of mid-nineteenth-century Britain's emerging parliamentary democracy, Mill's liberal formulation was grounded in clear philosophical reasoning and argument. The Victorian notion of character, so well articulated by the populist Samuel Smiles, is in Mill transformed into a doctrine of individuality, shorn of its repressive overtones and presented as a form of moral and ethical elevation. Yet despite these affirmations of the virtues of personal freedom and liberty, Mill is working not to rub out the line of political inclusion and exclusion but simply to shift it. In *Representative Government* he clarifies further the important relationship between inner freedom and political liberty: liberty should not be thought of as a form of natural right, for it is entirely conditional upon the capacity of an individual – or indeed a society – to demonstrate the inner freedom (autonomy) necessary to sustain political participation. It is worth quoting him again here, for the individual and social conditions that for him justify political exclusion are crucial to understanding contemporary liberalism's inheritance:

> a people may be unwilling or unable to fulfil the duties which a particular form of government requires of them. A rude people, though in some degree alive to the benefits of civilised society, may be unable to practice the forbearance which it demands: their passions may be too violent, or their personal pride too exacting, to forgo private conflict, and leave to the laws the avenging of their real or supposed wrongs. In such a case, a civilised government, to be really advantageous to them, will require to be in a considerable degree despotic: to be one over which they do not themselves exercise control, and one which imposes a great amount of forcible restraint upon their actions … But however little blame may be due to those in whom these mental habits have grown up, and however the habits may be ultimately conquerable by better government, yet while they exist a people so disposed cannot be governed with as little power exercised over them as a people whose sympathies are on the side of the law. (Mill, 1972: 178–9)

Implicit in this catalogue of personal and social conditions is the idea that freedom and liberty denote but two forms of government: freedom, the self-government of the senses and faculties; and liberty, the self-government of a people through representative institutions. Clearly illustrated in the passage above is Mill's view that people must be self-governing in the inner sphere before they may be capable of doing what is required to maintain a system of representative government and to comply with its demands. Thus, he argues, an individual or a people may wish for representative institutions, but unless they are prepared to exercise a requisite self-discipline and personal autonomy they will be incapable of keeping it for long. Mill sees virtue and character as implicit requirements for political participation. They serve as barriers to entry and their measure establishes the line of political inclusion and exclusion. Political citizenship thus cannot be thought of as an abstract right, but only in its connection with the personal capacities and qualifications that make participation rational and meaningful.

Liberalism, political exclusion, and the colonial subject

It is all but impossible to understand the structure of liberal thought being described here without an appreciation of the crucial role played in it by empire. When John Stuart Mill speaks of 'barbarous' or 'rude' peoples, he is not referring to Britain's working classes. He is, rather, referring to the populations of what he regarded as uncivilized tracts, many of whom were governed by Britain in its colonial dependencies. As an examiner in the East India Company for more than 20 years, Mill had an intimate knowledge of colonial governance and the impact of early liberal endeavours – such as Macaulay's model penal code and minute on education – on colonial rule. It is arguable that his structuring of liberal principles into those governing internal and external spheres of life draws heavily upon his knowledge of the difficulties of British rule in India. Post-colonial scholars have given attention to the way liberalism worked in colonial contexts and it is my contention here that the peculiar forms of exclusion they identify assist us in understanding the new turn to punitiveness in contemporary Western society.

There are two aspects to the analysis I wish to develop here. The first concerns liberal doctrine itself, and I have dwelt so long on the social conditions of early British liberalism and Mill's formulation of a liberal theory of self and government so that the point here may be made quickly. The second aspect is concerned less with liberal doctrine itself than with the way it was drawn upon in the process of colonial governance and used, much more purposively than in Mill, to constitute a distinct colonial subject of exclusion. Uday Mehta (1999) traces back to John Locke the liberal tactic through which exclusionary practices of colonialism emerge and find their justification. At the heart of liberalism lies what may be described as an ontological universalism, an assumption that all humans are born equal and thus are equally capable of and eligible for freedom, political participation, and the like. In this, liberalism makes no distinction among individuals on the grounds of race, gender, or religion. Yet Mehta also notes that as soon as this universal guarantee is given it is as swiftly rescinded, for Locke quickly argues that for political institutions to function properly individuals must be able to give *reasoned consent*. Here, then, the universal assumption of rationality is qualified by a socio-behavioural criterion that shifts us from potential (born rational) to capacity (able to give consent). For both Locke and Mill, as for later liberal thinkers, this criterion provides a barrier to entry to a whole variety of social types and classes. It is Mehta's point to show how in the colonial situation the representation of natives as either 'child-like' or 'inscrutable' provided the grounds for their exclusion. For us, it is now possible to look back upon Mill's description of those aspects of character that would *disqualify* a society from representative government, thus making it *eligible* for despotic rule, and recognize them as the socio-behavioural determinants of capacity for political participation passed down to him from Locke. Thus, at the heart of liberalism lies a fundamental presumption *against* political liberty for those who, by dint of their socio-behavioural capacities, are judged incapable of comprehending, aligning themselves with, or engaging in the elementary tasks of political participation. Had it not been for the demands of colonial rule, this doctrine of capacity might have remained (as in Locke) principally directed towards children and the circumscription of the political nation. With colonial rule, however, there arose a demand for a proper account of political exclusion and of despotic government, which Mill provides. Colonial rule also created the space, I will argue, for the constitution of a distinctive type of political subject, the colonial subject of exclusion.

Just how this colonial subject came to be constituted can only be touched on here (for a fuller discussion see Brown, 2005a). What made the colonial subject unique, however, and what made him or her distinct from the metropolitan subjects of an emerging British polity was a structure of obligations, rather than rights, upon which his or her relationship with the state rested. Whereas emerging civil societies at the metropolitan centre gradually extended different types or classes of rights to their political subjects (first civil rights, then political, later social), government in the colonial domain rode above native society and its subjects (as distinct from citizens) were admitted to civic and political institutions on a much more limited and contingent basis. Colonial government regulated access to these civic and political spheres through a structure of obligations – mainly virtues required of native subjects – that lacked counterpart rights. In this way colonial power worked to establish the conditions under which new forms of native subjectivity would be born. The obligation to which natives were subject was the obligation to be, to live, in a certain (new) way. Colonial subjects were thus constructed as *agents* of obligation rather than *recipients* of rights. The ethical characteristics required to fulfil these obligations, virtues such as obedience, rationality, responsibility, restraint, and so on, acted as a screen or precondition to the entry of natives into civic and political life. Where natives could demonstrate the requisite dispositions and capacities, they became eligible for entry into the sphere of rights that might be described as a kind of pre-citizenship. Colonial subjects were, as Mill had proposed, excluded as a matter of presumption; their inclusion followed only from fulfilment of an elaborate set of character- (or virtue-) based obligations. And the inclusion we are speaking of here was a distinctly limited form of political subjecthood. It was a highly circumscribed regime of rights and one, as the struggles of independence movements illustrate, that was designed to keep the colonial subject in a subordinate position to that enjoyed by the new metropolitan recipient of rights.

My argument concerning exclusion is thus twofold. First is the basic point that social and political exclusion is a central theme of liberal thought and doctrine. My aim in this section has been to demonstrate exactly how this is so, from the practical realm of parliamentary politics to the doctrinal liberalism of John Stuart Mill. My second point is that exclusion is two-tiered. There is, on the one hand, the boundary of political inclusion and exclusion in the metropolitan states of the West. This boundary is made possible by the restriction or extension of rights to different classes of the populace. On the other hand, there is a form of exclusion that was developed in the governance of colonial possessions. This type of exclusion places its subjects outside the political field of rights upon which metropolitan citizenship is founded. The colonial subject of exclusion must fulfil an obligation to demonstrate the requisite dispositions and capacities to participate in political life before entry into the field of rights (however circumscribed they might initially be) is granted. Just how this understanding of liberalism and its forms of exclusion can assist us in understanding recent turns toward penal severity, the rise of a new punitiveness in Western societies, will be the theme of the final section of this chapter.

Political exclusion and the new punitiveness

Quite a number of penal measures have been cited in this book as evidence of an emerging new punitiveness. These range from the criminalization of 'nuisance' behaviours, through more targeted police and prosecution policies, to a variety of tougher sentencing schemes, including mandatory sentences, three-strikes statutes, and community notification measures. The situation is similar in discussions of exclusion. Exclusion has been held to include policies that limit or make difficult access to housing, goods, or services (Social Exclusion Unit, 2002), barriers to accessing credit (Rose, 2000), and criminal justice measures like zero-tolerance policing (Young, 1999). My suggestion in respect of both exclusion and a new punitiveness is that the terms are at risk of becoming so broad as to limit their analytic usefulness and that there is very substantial overlap between the two ideas. My aims in this section are twofold. First, I want to develop more clearly a definition of the new punitiveness – what criteria allow us to classify a strategy or policy as part of the new punitiveness? Crucial to this taxonomic exercise will be an understanding of the forms or grades of exclusion provided for within the political structure of liberalism previously discussed. Here I will distinguish between what might be described, after Foucault (1977), as an 'economy of suspended rights' and the radical forms of exclusion developed through colonial power and, arguably, re-entering the political frame in recent times.[3] Secondly, having established this classification scheme I will apply it to a number of contemporary penal developments. In doing so I hope to show that while the idea of a new punitiveness has considerable value, if it is to be taken seriously and used to mark out radical departures from established norms, then it will be found that the extent of the trend is in fact not so great and wide ranging as might first have been supposed.

Defining the new punitiveness

If the idea of a new punitiveness is to have analytical value, it must satisfy two principal demands. It must, first, be capable of coherent conceptual description. That is to say, we must be able to describe what the new punitiveness is, what it is not, and how it differs from its conceptual or empirical neighbours, like 'populist punitiveness' (Bottoms, 1995), 'new penology' (Feeley and Simon, 1992), and the periodic rises and falls in punitive sentiment that characterize most jurisdictions over time. Second, we must be able to derive from this definition some criteria that will allow us to classify new 'cases' of punitiveness as belonging to or outside of our category. These criteria must allow for reliable classification and for the accurate discrimination of valid from invalid cases.

What, then, is the new punitiveness? It is, in my view, a new way of using punishment, a new form of penal power. It is marked out by sanctions or strategies that represent a radical departure from previous trends in punishment. It is characterized not by a whole range of new practices and measures but by a few enormously important reconfigurations of the state–subject relationship achieved through novel forms of punishment. The new punitiveness displaces penal subjects from the field of political citizenship. Such displacement is a new effect of punishment, for previously punishment has worked only to achieve the *attenuation* of political subjects' rights. Foucault (1977) viewed this as one of the central features distinguishing the prison from the bloody forms of punishment it replaced: 'From being an art of unbearable sensations', he argued, 'punishment has become an economy of suspended rights' (p. 11). My argument is that, to this day, most punishments have remained faithful to the basic structure that Foucault identified: a limited suspension or attenuation of the liberty rights that inhere with political citizenship. But in recent times we have begun to see a radical departure from this structure. In what can best be described as a reprising of the techniques and strategies of colonial power, Western governments have moved to excise a limited number of citizens from the field of political citizenship. Like the colonial subject, these new penal subjects are placed outside the rights-based sphere of citizenship and are made subject to requirements and obligations that no ordinary citizen could be made to assume. Where the colonial subject was required to develop and display a complex set of virtues as qualifications for entry *into* a domain of rights, the new penal subject is displaced and excluded from this domain on the basis of his or her incapacity to function properly as a political subject. This disability is indexed by the very virtues, those '*dispositions* or *capacities* to act, respond and feel' (O'Neill, 1996: 138; original emphasis), that were required of the colonial subject: obedience (to law), rationality, responsibility, restraint, and the like. I will describe in a moment how this is evidenced in certain radical penal measures, measures that I believe mark out the emergence of a new punitiveness. Before doing so, however, I wish to describe how the new punitiveness differs from other analytical categories and to consider whether or not we can describe some criteria that will allow instances of the new punitiveness to be recognized and correctly classified.

For a number of reasons it is in fact relatively easy to differentiate the new punitiveness from notions like populist punitiveness (Bottoms, 1995) or the new penology (Feeley and Simon, 1992). One is that both the latter are essentially process descriptions: on the one hand, of policy-making, and on the other of the machinery of justice. It is quite possible that the observations about both trends could be correct, but that the specific impacts of either upon the basic structure of Western punishment practices described above would be quite small. So another ground upon which the new punitiveness can be distinguished from these undoubtedly important analytical categories is that the notion of new punitiveness is focused on the specific point of application of penal power. It is focused on the point where punishment intersects with the field within which political subjects are constituted. The new punitiveness is also focused on transformation or radical departures from past practice at this point of intersection. This special focus ensures that the new punitiveness is distinguished from the change and flux in penal practices that are inevitable in any large system over time.

But the principal criterion that allows us to distinguish instances of a new punitiveness from traditional punishment practices centres on the distinction that was key to understanding colonial forms of exclusion. It can be put in the way of a question: 'Does this penalty or measure tinker with the rights of political subjects, or does it radically transform the status of the individual, thus revising their relationship with the state into one structured around obligation'? This is a single and simple criterion, but its simplicity belies its importance. Recall that liberalism extends citizenship rights in principle to all, even if certain specific groups may have certain specific rights withheld during defined periods or under defined conditions. Citizens are *recipients* of the liberty right to vote, for instance, whether or not they are *currently* eligible to vote by dint of age (youth) or by dint of its temporary suspension (during imprisonment in some jurisdictions). But, once of age, or once released from prison, the liberty right of franchise is reinstated as a matter of course: it does not need to be re-earned, for it inheres naturally to political citizenship. Contrast this with the colonial subject. This person was not constituted as a recipient of rights but an agent of obligation: first and foremost, in other words, the colonial subject and the new penal subject must demonstrate capacity in order to (re)enter or fully participate in civic and political life. So what forms of punishment or exclusion might meet this criterion?

The new punitiveness in practice

At least three penal innovations of recent years can usefully be understood as reflecting a colonial form of exclusion: civil commitment statutes, sex offender registration and notification schemes, and mass imprisonment (Brown, 2005a). Each is a different and special example of how an individual or, in the case of mass imprisonment, a whole community, may be radically excluded from society and the rights-based realm of political citizenship. But the present effort to define the new punitiveness and invoke a specific criterion for its classification allows for a more detailed and defensible account of how this works. My strategy here will be to elaborate a case for civil commitment as an instantiation of the new punitiveness, followed then by a suggestion as to what other penal forms might be similarly classified, finishing with an indication of which nominally severe penal practices do not fit with this classification and why. Before moving into this analysis, however, I should make one important point of clarification. The aim of what follows is not (or not only) to show that contemporary strategies of exclusion have distinct similarities to strategies developed in the colonial domain. Interestingly, there are indeed continuities in the shape and form of modes of exclusion across time. But what I seek to demonstrate here is something more significant. It is that certain contemporary penal practices render individuals or, in the case of mass imprisonment, groups, outside the realm of political citizenship. It might even be said that these practices represent something like a hangover of medieval 'civil death', wherein individuals were stripped of all rights so as to be effectively legally dead, that has travelled through some wormhole within the structure of liberalism, appearing again first in colonial practices and now in an emerging set of contemporary penal strategies.[4]

Civil commitment statutes, otherwise often known as sexual predator or sexual psychopath laws (see Janus, 2000), are an archetypal case of the new punitiveness. They remove from society an offender who has completed a finite sentence of imprisonment and committed no further crimes. They are civil rather than criminal. But they invoke basic criteria – or virtues – against which the individual is held to fail and, by so doing, prove themselves unfit to participate in society. In most cases this involves some measure of the individual's capacity to check their own behaviour, to comprehend legal prohibitions and, under pains of previous punishment, to modify their conduct accordingly. Terms such as 'psychopathy' or 'volitional dysfunction' provide the background to debate about whether or not the individual retains the minimum dispositions and capacities to live freely in society – to enjoy, in other words, the fundamental liberty rights of citizens. Looking beyond the legalese of terms like volitional dysfunction, we find debates unfolding about the basic capacities of certain individuals to function autonomously, to exercise choice, and to take responsibility seriously. In the landmark case of *Kansas* v. *Hendricks* (1997), for example, the court heard Hendricks explain that when he 'get[s] stressed out' he 'can't control the urge' to sexually violate children and that the only way he could foresee stopping such conduct was for him 'to die' (p. 3). Though there remains considerable debate among jurists as to the value of the concept of volitional dysfunction (see, for example, *In re Linehan*, 1996, Minnesota), its use has become widespread in the United States due to its key role in shoring up the constitutionality of statutes whose aim is the permanent removal of citizens from society.

Once civilly committed under these laws, it is very difficult for an individual to imagine returning to society, for society now effectively reverses the burden of proof required to achieve freedom. While the procedure of commitment requires states to establish a strong case that the liberty rights of the prisoner should be curtailed through transfer to a form of civil quarantine, and while the burden of demonstrating a continued need for commitment rests with the states, in effect the onus is shifted to the offender, for it is he or she who must prove that some change in his or her dispositions and capacities has in fact occurred. Thus, on the basis of evidence that individuals are of a certain type – a kind of atavistic pre-citizen, either incapable or unwilling to establish the basic dispositions of self-government, freedom, autonomy, and responsibility – the state removes them permanently from society, reinstating the colonial structure of obligation. Under this structure a high bar is placed before committed offenders. They must prove to a court that they possess the elementary character traits and aspects of human virtue common to 'normal' citizens if they wish to be reinstated or re-elevated to the rights-based realm of freedom and political citizenship.

Sex offender registration and notification schemes seem similarly to satisfy the criterion that measures under the scheme restructure the penal subject's relationship with the state into one characterized by obligations that carry no counterpart rights. Notified sex offenders may be required to undertake a variety of tasks (advising the state of their movements, avoiding certain areas) and so to demonstrate certain capacities, or ways of living and being, for which they receive no recipient rights. The liberty rights of full citizens would prohibit the arbitrary imposition of such obligations, but in sex offenders they become permissible not because they are an element of punishment but because the *character* of sex offenders lies so much in doubt. To be sure, unlike the penal subject of civil commitment, registered sex offenders are at large in the community, but it is a highly circumscribed freedom. Why notified sex offenders are to be viewed as agents of obligation, rather than simply citizens with circumscribed rights, lies in the fact that things are required of them: they are required to perform in certain ways, and so we will tend to characterize them as we do colonial subjects, first as agents of obligation and second as recipients of limited rights.

But rights may also be limited in a less direct fashion and they may be limited for groups as well as for individuals. Colonial governments became adept at thinking of and managing their subjects at the level of whole communities or geographical tracts. A significant feature of contemporary penal strategies is the way the prison has come to be utilized in a similar fashion, as a tool for the governance and management of 'suspect' communities. Mass imprisonment as a phenomenon has begun to attract attention in recent times as imprisonment rates in the US have climbed to record levels (e.g. Garland, 2001). But as any scholar of minority imprisonment will tell, national imprisonment rates pale in comparison to those of indigenous and minority groups. It is estimated in the United States, for example, that approximately one in every eight young black men is in prison on any one day (Harrison and Karberg, 2003). In Australia, where the national rate of imprisonment stands at around 150 per 100,000 of the imprisonable age population, the rate of indigenous imprisonment hovers around 1,900 per 100,000 of the imprisonable age indigenous population (Brown, 2005b). Similar trends may also be observed among migrant communities in Europe and elsewhere (Junger-Tas, 1997). At one level, each of these prisoners is simply subject to the ordinary restrictions associated with punishment by the state. But what makes the strategy of mass imprisonment distinctly colonial is the way in which whole communities, as distinct from their individual members, may be excluded from the benefits and access to participatory institutions of civil society by dint of this technique. Loic Wacquant (this volume) has argued forcefully for a broader view of punishment, one that examines its 'extra-penological' functions, and has proposed a crucial role for the prison in the permanent subordination of black Americans. In the Australian context, historical scholarship by Hogg (2001) and also by Finnane and McGuire (2001) has shown how the imprisonment of Aboriginal Australians developed as a strategy of governance to replace what were coming to be seen as outmoded and anti-modern techniques based around reservations or 'missions', removal of children from their families, and forms of bonded labour. It is deeply ironic that as the recipient rights of Australian Aborigines were expanded through the grant of full citizenship rights in 1967, the prison emerged as a new strategy of control that would continue to limit and erode the capacity of Aboriginal Australians to participate fully as civic and political subjects.

Beyond this point, most other recent penal innovations, from zero-tolerance policing through boot camps to mandatory sentencing and penal austerity measures, can be seen as no more than the partial, temporary, and occasional suspension of citizens' liberty rights (see Zimring and Hawkins, 2004; Jacobs, 2004). They are part of what Foucault referred to as an 'economy of suspended rights', but they fail to confer special obligations upon their subjects and so must be seen as continuous with the broader disciplinary apparatus that was so much the centre of Foucault's attention. No great consideration has been paid to how the rights of serious or dangerous offenders, and their attenuation, should be dealt with in a formal sense. One exception is Bottoms and Brownsword (1983), who set out three main theories of rights that might provide a principled approach to the withdrawal and restitution of rights. The detail of their argument is not crucial here. What is important is the recognition they give to the main argument I have sought to develop here: that most punishments seen heretofore, even those pertaining to dangerous offenders, rest upon the suspension of the liberty rights of political subjects so that the main 'issues' raised by the punishment have to do with justifications for suspension and presumptions regarding their restitution.

Conclusion

This chapter began with a simple premise: that liberalism, though sorely misunderstood, could provide an explanation for the rise in recent times of a new punitiveness in Western societies. I therefore dwelt at some length upon the character, structure, and goals of liberalism in the hope that I could provide a detailed and informed understanding of the role of exclusion within liberal practices of government. It was only after this rather long detour that the chapter turned back to the issue of recent shifts in punitiveness in the West. Following from my analysis of liberal exclusions I have tried to argue for a strong definition of a new punitiveness, one that distinguishes the new punitiveness from both neighbouring concepts (like penal populism) and weaker varieties of punishment (those that attenuate rather than remove political rights). The effect of this has been to limit the apparent extent of this trend toward a new punitiveness in contemporary Western societies. But the flip side of that limitation of extent is that the forms of punishment and exclusion that may be labelled instances of a new punitiveness are *radical* departures from the political norms of punishment that *radically* reconfigure the relationship of penal subjects to the state. And it is these characteristics that make the new punitiveness revolutionary.

Notes

1   Sections of this outline of British liberalism's emergence, particularly with respect to the notion of character, draw upon Bellamy (1992), especially chapter 1.
2   I do not wish in any way to encourage the view that Mill's liberalism is synonymous with British liberalism, but to suggest that for current purposes the account he developed is sufficient for a reader to gain an understanding of the general *structure* of liberal doctrine. It also provides a basis for understanding how important contemporary critics drawing inspiration from different liberal traditions, such as James Fitzjames Stephen, came to view his account as so deeply flawed. I give some account of the important debate between Mill and Stephen in Brown (2004); see also Stokes (1959).
3   This section expands on an idea I noted, but was unable to develop, in Brown (2005a).
4   The notion of 'civil death' has recently reappeared in the United States in debate over felony disenfranchisement laws that bar felons and ex-felons from voting for life. A number of states retain such laws on their statute books. Their origin seems to lie in the 'Jim Crow' laws of the nineteenth century and the racial gerrymander established as America sought, on the one hand, to enfranchise its 'colonial subjects' – slaves – while, one the other, tightly circumscribing their access to the rights-based domain of civic and political citizenship. Such laws commonly barred voting, office holding, property ownership, and the right to make a will. A clear modern analogue of this, but one that is unfortunately beyond the scope of this chapter, is the 'non-citizen' status accorded to refugees and asylum seekers.

References

Bellamy, R. (1992) *Liberalism and Modern Society: An Historical Argument*, Cambridge: Polity Press.

Bottoms, A. E. (1995) 'The Philosophy and Politics of Punishment and sentencing', in C. Clarkson and R. Morgan (eds) *The Politics of Sentencing Reform* (pp. 17–49), Oxford: Oxford University Press.

Bottoms, A. E. and Brownsword, R. (1983) 'Dangerousness and Rights', in J. W. Hinton (ed.) *Dangerousness: Problems of assessment and prediction* (pp. 9–22), London: Allen and Unwin.

Brown, M. (2002) 'The Politics of Penal Excess and the Echo of Colonial Penality', *Punishment and Society: The International Journal of Penology*, 4: 403–423.

Brown, M. (2004) 'Crime, Liberalism and Empire: Governing the Mina Tribe of Northern India', *Social and Legal Studies*, 13: 191–218.

Brown, M. (2005a) '"That Heavy Machine": Reprising the Colonial Apparatus in 21st Century Social Control', *Social Justice* (forthcoming).

Brown, M. (2005b) 'Corrections', in D. Chappell and P. Wilson (eds) *The Australian Criminal Justice System*, Sydney: Butterworths.

Capaldi, N. (1998) 'John Stuart Mill's Defence of Liberal Culture', in E. J. Eisenach (ed.) *Mill and the Moral Character of Liberalism* (pp. 77–114), University Park, PA: State University of Pennsylvania Press.

Dean, M. (1999) *Governmentality: Power and Rule in Modern Society*, London: Sage.

Dean, M. (2002) 'Liberal Government and Authoritarianism', *Economy and Society*, 31: 36–61.

Eisenach, E. J. (1998) 'Introduction', in E. J. Eisenach (ed.) *Mill and the Moral Character of Liberalism* (pp. 1–12), University Park, PA: State University of Pennsylvania Press.

Feeley, M. and Simon, J. (1992) 'The New Penology', *Criminology*, 39: 449–74.

Finnane, M. and McGuire, J. (2001) 'The Uses of Punishment and Exile: Aborigines in Colonial Australia', *Punishment and Society*, 3: 279–98.

Foucault, M. (1977) *Discipline and Punish: The Birth of the Prison*, Harmondsworth: Penguin.

Garland, D. (ed.) (2001) *Mass Imprisonment: Social Causes and Consequences*, Thousand Oaks, CA: Sage.

Hallsworth, S. (2000) 'Rethinking the Punitive Turn: Economies of Excess and the Criminology of the Other', *Punishment and Society*, 2: 145–60.

Harrison, P. and Karburg, J. (2003) 'Prison and Jail Inmates at Midyear 2002', *Bureau of Justice Statistics Bulletin*, Washington, DC: US Department of Justice, Office of Justice Programs.

Hogg, R. (2001) 'Penality and Modes of Regulating Indigenous People in Australia', *Punishment and Society*, 3: 355–79.

Holmes, S. (1993) *The Anatomy of Anti-Liberalism*, Cambridge, MA: Harvard University Press.

Jacobs, J. B. (2004) 'Prison Reform and the Ruin of Prisoners' Rights', in M. Tonry (ed.) *The Future of Imprisonment* (pp. 179–96), Oxford: Oxford University Press.

Janus, E. (2000) 'Civil Commitment as Social Control: Managing the Risk of Sexual Violence', in M. Brown and J. Pratt (eds) *Dangerous Offenders: Punishment and Social Order*, London: Routledge.

Kansas v. Hendricks (1997) 117 S.Ct 2072. Accessed at: http://supct.law.cornell.edu/supct/html/95-1649.ZO.html

King, D. (1999) *In the Name of Liberalism: Illiberal Social Policy in the USA and Britain*, Oxford: Oxford University Press.

In re Linehan (1996) 557 N.W. 2d 171 (Minn.)

Junger-Tas, J. (1997) 'Youth Justice in the Netherlands', in M. Tonry (ed.) *Crime and Justice: A Review of Research*, Chicago: University of Chicago Press.

Mehta, U. S. (1999) *Liberalism and Empire: A Study in Nineteenth Century Liberal Thought*, Chicago: University of Chicago Press.

Mill, J. S. (1972) *Utilitarianism, Liberty, Representative Government, including Selections from Auguste Comte and Positivism* (H.B. Acton, ed.), London: J.M. Dent and Sons.

O'Malley, P. (1992) 'Risk, Power and Crime Prevention', *Economy and Society*, 21: 252–75.

O'Malley, P. (2004) 'Penal Policies and Contemporary Politics', in C. Sumner (ed.) *The Blackwell Companion to Criminology* (pp. 183–195), Oxford: Blackwell Publishing.

O'Neill, O. (1996) *Towards Justice and Virtue: A Constructive Account of Practical Reasoning*, Cambridge: Cambridge University Press.

Rose, N. (1996) 'Governing Advanced Liberal Democracies', in A. Barry, T. Osborne and N. Rose (eds) *Foucault and Political Reason* (pp. 37–64), London: UCL Press.

Rose, N. (2000) 'Government and Control', *British Journal of Criminology*, 40: 321–39.

Social Exclusion Unit (2002) *Reducing Reoffending by Ex-Prisoners*, London: Author.

Stephen, J. F. (1873) *Liberty, Equality, Fraternity*, London: Smith Elder and Co.

Stokes, E. (1959) *The English Utilitarians and India*, Oxford: Clarendon Press.

Valverde, M. (1996) '"Despotism" and ethical governance', *Economy and Society*, 25: 357–72.

Young, J. (1999) *The Exclusive Society: Social Exclusion, Crime and Difference in Late Modernity*, London: Sage.

Zimring, F. E. and Hawkins, G. (2004) 'Democracy and the Limits of Punishment: A Preface to Prisoners' Rights', in M. Tonry (ed.) *The Future of Imprisonment* (pp. 157–78), Oxford: Oxford University Press.

17. Rethinking narratives of penal change in global context

Wayne Morrison

This chapter has a simple argument: our narratives of penal change must be reassessed and complemented by analyses that adopt a self-conscious global context. I want to suggest that most analyses of the new punitiveness have tended to misunderstand the terrain of analysis, being unduly constrained by an implicit identification of society, or community, with notions of self-sustaining systems. Put simply: in modernity no 'society' or 'nation-state' should be treated as if they were a self-sustaining system; all are part of a global entity. However, it is precisely such an awareness that is excluded from much of our everyday analysis and consciousness; further, the extent to which the local is a product of the global and their interconnections is downplayed in modernity in order to construct and preserve ideologies of 'doing justice' or striving to balance competing rights. The relationship between conceiving global justice and modern forms of development is problematic, and one may suspect that a global justice is precisely what modernity is *not* orientated towards. In contrast, what this chapter tries to highlight is that the biggest non-punitive area we inhabit is the global international system. The century just concluded perhaps saw the greatest amount of inter-human slaughter, rape, and destruction of property of any century; in partial recognition of which we even created a new crime, genocide, but in the face of which extremely few persons were ever punished. Our focus on specific sites of punitiveness needs to be complemented by recognizing an irrational non-punitiveness also operating outside the specific terrains we focus upon. Moreover, that may aid in better identifying the forms of power at work on both sides of the supposed divide.

A punitive or a non-punitive world: which terrain, whose control, which analysis?

To orientate this discussion I begin with a concrete example: a report by A.G.N. Ogden, the British Counsel-General in Shanghai, to the British Ambassor in Nanjing in mid-1947.

It had been announced that the two Japanese were to be paraded in Chinese carts, but possibly owing to a delay at the start, the procession actually consisted of military motor vehicles, with the Japanese in an open truck under a heavy armed-guard. Crowds estimated at about 150,000 in all shouted and cheered as the parade passed and it is said that at some points stones were thrown at the condemned men, who presented a stolid and unmoved attitude throughout, although they had refused a narcotic injection offered to them before the procession set out. (quotations and material adapted from Sellars, 2002: 47–8)

Six months earlier a Chinese military tribunal had found Yonemura Haruchi (the 'Wolf of Changshou') guilty of burying Chinese victims alive and Shimoto Jiro (the 'Tiger of Kiangyin') guilty of torture, rape, and plunder, sentencing them to death. Now they were driven along the Bund and Nanjing Road in Shanghai, where dense crowds had gathered to watch, then shot at the Kiangwan Execution Grounds witnessed by a large throng.

For Ogden this display was a relic of the past. Shanghai's foreign-language newspapers, he reported, had condemned the public parade and execution and deplored 'the fact that such proceedings should still be regarded as natural and unobjectionable by the Chinese authorities'. He also charged the Chinese as applying a double standard:

> It is interesting to compare the relentless attitude of the Chinese authorities towards Japanese accused of war crimes and Chinese 'traitors', with their complacency regarding the continued presence in this country of certain Germans who, although objectionable on political grounds, were granted exemption from deportation presumably because they were regarded as being useful in post-war trade activity.

When forwarded to London, Ogden's report received a concise rebuttal from Frederick Garner in the Foreign Office's War Crimes Section:

> As a matter of fact the Chinese have been quite moderate about Japanese war criminals. Considering the immense amount of crimes committed they have executed very few. They have preferred to make a public example of notorious cases rather than execute large numbers privately. I do not consider that the Chinese have behaved any worse than many European countries – in fact they have I think behaved better … As regards letting useful Germans stay on in China what about von Paulus in Russia and the German 'rocket' scientists in the USA and in this country?

What are we to make of this exchange? It could, for example, be seen as material for one of the central narratives of penal development, that of the civilizing process (Elias, see Pratt, this volume). But this is somewhat disorientated, for Ogden's comments, those of a Western male in government service judging the application of the civilizing tendency towards another country, cross boundaries. The rebuke they drew brought out a shared assumption of elite power, namely, that 'they' (i.e. the political authorities in China) actually had the application of penality under control. That penality was primarily a political matter to be massaged and theatrically applied by the political-administrative elite was simply assumed as the natural course of events for 'such proceedings'.[1] But what exactly was the nature of those proceedings and how did that differ from the normal application of penality – the subject of penology and criminology?

Garner described the proceedings as dealing with 'war criminals', and the response to the 'immense amount of crimes committed' was to publicly execute a few; in other words only to punish a small symbolic token of the immense amount committed. War is perhaps the single greatest organizing force, historically determining national boundaries, making social allegiances, and almost as quickly turning strategic friends into foes. If the world can be considered as a set of processes linking and co-constituting the local and global, the concept of war should be crucial. However, what sort of images do we find when we consider criminological and penological material? Not only are the realities of war, genocide or other state-sponsored massacres not usually included but it is difficult to see the question of the co-constitution of the local and the global posed at all. Rather we find concepts such as society, state, community, usually with some assumption of a system that makes these relatively sustaining. Among other effects, this results in instability in determining the location of analysis.

David Garland's *The Culture of Control* (2001), a key text orientating this book, is a case in point. Subtitled 'crime and social order *in contemporary society*' (emphasis added), it veers between stating that it is limited to an analysis of the US and UK to statements that it deals with 'contemporary society', the collapse of 'modern crime control' (p. 72), late-modern society (p. 73), and modernity itself. To what does this term 'contemporary society' refer? Are not the Democratic Republic (DR) of Congo, Chechnya, or Bangladesh also examples of contemporary society? When the text refers to 'the coming of late modernity' (e.g. p. 75), there is uncertainty whether late modernity is a global phenomenon impacting upon the US and UK or whether late modernity spreads outwards from the US and UK. A question such as 'so how did the social changes of late modernity come to impress themselves upon the field of crime control and criminal justice?' (p. 103) seems without boundaries but is meaningless in that text if read that way. And why is the crucial referent, namely the 'effect of making crime more salient as a social or cultural fact' a part of 'modern consciousness' (pp. 147–8), only drawn from the author's reading of the US and UK? Is it because of the text's neo-positivism in which the surely much greater crimes in the DR Congo, Chechnya, or Bangladesh cannot count as, there, crime is too prevalent to count, or must be placed outside the view of the 'field' in case any comparison would upset the framework of analysis as to what makes for 'modern crime control'? No criteria to settle the meaning of the crucial referents are offered, they are simply assumed. The text is a contribution to a conversation within a particular community; it takes a context which, however, is analysed as if it were the paradigm of the modern or the late-modern, as if the terms used were incontestable and normal; as indeed they may appear to the majority of the intended readership. Structuring this text and the interaction with the intended readership, are assumptions and realities as to power, inclusion, and exclusion, of what processes drive and count as contemporary society and modern forms of social life (one may suspect this is a text written within the shadow of a new imperium). I would, however, agree that 'our textbooks need to be rewritten and our sense of how things work needs to be revised' (p. 5).

We work for the most part within a positivist tradition, in other words we work with the data that have been made visible and presented for analysis. We read these data as the key to social forces that we cannot immediately see (post-Durkheim) and usually what cannot be so linked is unverifiable, called metaphysical, certainly not the subject of scientific analysis. But we may learn more in this field from what is not presented, from what is avoided, than from what is presented. Consider recent data on penal trends, specifically the use of imprisonment in different states.

According to the United Nations *Global Report on Crime and Justice* (1999), chapter 4 on 'Punishment', prison is the universal sanction for serious crimes, applied more than any other punishment and regardless of the type of legal system or level of development of a country. The report, however, states that globally there is no overall trend towards a major increase in prison population, with slightly more states reporting increased use of imprisonment than those showing less use. While there are considerable differences among states in the use of prison, prison rates do not appear to be dependent on the amount of crime in a state, nor does greater use of non-custodial sanctions lead to less use of prison, or vice versa.

Turning to the *International Comparisons of Criminal Justice Statistics 2000* (Barclay and Tavares, 2002), we find that some jurisdictions have seen reductions in the prison population. One notes Turkey but most obviously Northern Ireland, which experienced a 42 per cent reduction in the period 1990–2000, compared with a 44 per cent increase for the larger jurisdiction of England and Wales. In both Turkey and Northern Ireland the answer is political: the decline is to do with the release of individuals whom many considered to be 'political prisoners' (though achieving that label was denied them by the government until recently). The link between the political and penality thus seems clear, but, would run a standard response to including this data, you cannot include these as they are exceptional cases, not the norm.

Can we learn from the exceptional? Taking the *World Prison Population List* (Walmsley, 2003), we find details of the numbers of prisoners held in 205 independent countries and dependent territories in 2001. Over 9 million people are held in penal institutions across the world, mostly as pre-trial detainees or having been convicted and sentenced. About half of these were in the United States (2.03m), Russia (0.86m), and China (1.51m plus pre-trial detainees and prisoners in 'administrative detention'). The list shows that the United States has the highest prison population rate in the world at 701 per 100,000 of the national population, followed by Russia at 606. However, it also shows that prison population rates vary considerably between different parts of the world and between different parts of the same continent. Countries and dependent territories are listed, with rates from Indonesia at 29 to the United States at 701; with one exception: *Rwanda*. The prison population rate for Rwanda is not calculated since it would be so far above the others it would skew all analysis. The problem is that Rwanda, with a national population of 8.1m, has 112,000 persons in prison, but this 'total includes 103,134 held on suspicion of participation in genocide'. It would, to put it simply, be much easier for criminological analysis if

Rwanda did not hold persons in prison in connection with genocide. As a result, Rwanda cannot be counted because it has broken a key unwritten rule of the positivist criminological game – do not count state-sponsored crime.[2]

This avoidance occurs so regularly that it is unexceptional, an example being *A General Theory of Crime* (Gottfredson and Hirschi, 1990). The authors expressly argue that their theory 'can encompass the reality of cross cultural differences in crime rates' (p. 175). They also expressly state that 'a general theory of crime must be a general theory of the social order' (p. 274; although they said that lack of time and space prevented them from pursuing this latter issue further). Combining 'classical' conceptions of crime, and 'positivist' analysis of criminality, the authors argue that 'Nearly all crimes are mundane, simple, trivial, easy acts aimed at satisfying desires of the moment, as are many other acts of little concern to the criminal law' (p. xv). They defined criminality as a matter of the level of self-control an individual possesses. Low rates of self-control also mean that the offender is less likely to hold a steady job, more likely to have drug or other addiction problems, and more likely to be involved in accidents. Individuals differ in the amount of self-control they possess and 'self-control is presumably a product of socialisation and the current circumstances of life' (p. 179).

There have been many attempts to apply this theory, and some criticism, but nowhere has the theory been confronted with the 'facts' of state-sponsored massacres and genocide. In many such cases the perpetrators have a job (in the army or intelligence services), do not get involved in accidents (which would be prejudicial to the performance of their function), and would probably score high on whatever self-control test that could be devised to empirically operationalize the theory. The decision to engage in genocidal actions may be wholly rational, as with the 1971 decision to cleanse the nationalists and those elements perceived as not Islamic enough from the population of East Pakistan to ensure greater ease of governability from the power centre in West Pakistan. In some other cases they well fit the picture outlined in the theory. The theory may well benefit from such an engagement. The point is that such events are simply not regarded as providing any facts that a 'general theory of crime' should consider. Yet the figures for state-sponsored massacres or other forms of deliberate death in the *twentieth century – excluding military personnel and civilian casualties of war* – are usually regarded as between 167 to 175 million people (Rummel, 1994; Smith, 2000).

What then were the technologies of data collection Gottfredson and Hirschi relied upon to give them 'cross-cultural crime rates'? They were of course the state-sponsored forms of objectifying the commission of crime and the related indices linked to state practices of punishing. Given that the vast majority of the people who caused the deaths of the 167–175 million persons mentioned above were not subjected to criminal justice processes or penality, a data-collection procedure tied to the state institutions must result in a specific picture of crime and criminality oblivious to their existence. But consider the effect on crime rates as revealed in recording practices if one included 'genocide'. Three examples will illustrate: Cambodia, Rwanda, and Bangladesh. In the case of Cambodia, a conservative estimate for the number killed between 1975 and 1979 in the Pol Pot 'auto-genocide' is 2,000,000. This represented around 25 per cent of the then population. In the Interpol International Crime Statistics for 2000, Cambodia, with a greatly expanded population of 11,304,084, recorded 553 'voluntary homicides' or 'murders'.[3] On these figures it would take 3,616 years of 'normal' homicide to equal three years of the exceptional. For Rwanda the accepted figure for the six months of genocide in 1994 is 800,000+, while in the 2000 Interpol statistics 3,606 voluntary homicides were recorded. Thus it would take around 222 years of 'normal' homicide to equate to six months of the exceptional. A figure of 1,500,000 would be a conservative figure (the Bangladesh government claims 3 million) for the numbers killed in the nine months from March to December 1971 out of a population of 75 million from the West Pakistani military actions (widely called attempted genocide) and disease that resulted from the dislocation of the population and associated political and ethnic cleansing in what was then East Pakistan (now Bangladesh). In contrast, 3,539 voluntary homicides were recorded for Bangladesh in the 1998 Interpol figures (the latest available) for a population of 127,400,000. Again it would take around 424 years of the normal for this much larger population to give nine months of the exceptional.

But it may be said these are not the cases of advanced, civilized Western societies, such as the US or Russia; there, no such comparison can be made. Take Russia, which throughout the 1990s has the highest registered homicide rate – with totals between 26,000 and 29,000 per annum. As stated later in this chapter, the Caucasus area has seen the most intensive projects of civilizing from the Russia centre. In 1994, Russian President Boris Yeltsin launched an invasion of Chechnya, a republic within the Russian union. The invasion was a planning disaster that led to immediate military setbacks that resulted only in an intensification of the violence unleashed. During 1994–96 over 80,000 Chechens, mainly civilians, including over 27,000 in the capital Grozny alone, were killed. In the face of the resistance from Chechen fighters, mostly lightly armed, Russian forces resorted to mass artillery, rocket barrages, and air strikes to smash Chechen villages and towns; Grozny was left razed. While some military commanders were sacked for incompetence, there were no trials for the vast killing and maiming of civilians or the virtual destruction of a country. Moreover, independent observers have little doubt that there was no justification for the invasion and that the reason was a search for an impressive military victory to store up symbolic images of the Russian state after the collapse of the Soviet Union. Yeltsin's actions may have been called a crime by the tiny minority of the civilized world that read the accounts of the few journalists that managed to get information out or the Amnesty International reports (for example, Amnesty International report, 1996; Margolis, 1999; BBC television, 1999), but there is no realistic chance of anyone facing penal actions for events that resulted in civilian deaths equalling in number the official homicide totals for the entire Russian state that are called upon to justify (partially at least) its high imprisonment rate.

Now consider the US. The homicide statistics for the US in the twentieth century are usually divided between the 1900–50 period, where fewer than 300,000 were recorded, to the 1950–2000 period, where 805, 830 were recorded (source: FBI Uniform Crime Reports). On 6 August 1945 US forces dropped an atomic bomb called 'Little Boy' on the Japanese city of Hiroshima; on 9 August another, called 'Fat Man', on Nagaski. By the end of 1945, less than six months later, the Hiroshima bomb had caused 140,000 deaths, with 70,000 from the Nagaski bomb. Five years later the totals were 200,000 and 140,000. At the Tokyo International Military Tribunal (IMT) an attempt was made at including many countries in the judgment process. Thus there were 14 judges as opposed to the four at the IMT at Nuremberg. The only judge with any previous experience of 'international law', the Indian judge Radhabinod Pal, issued a full dissenting judgment, refusing to accept the prosecution of the Japanese defendants as he considered that the Allies too should be tried and punished for crimes committed during the war, in particular for the dropping of the atomic bomb. Who was responsible? How much deliberation went into this decision? In US President Truman's memoirs, 561 pages are given to 1945, with the decision to use the atomic bomb briefly explained on page 491 (Glover, 2001: 104). We learn that there was little deliberation and a small group involved, though the decision was Truman's with the British Prime Minister Churchill also in favour if it could end the war sooner (a very contestable proposition). This one decision and action caused a death toll which considering the Anglo-American common law definition of homicide (death following within a year and a day of the action) amounted to almost as many deaths as the first half of the century's state-counted homicides for the US.

Truman was not of course prosecuted, though Sellars (2001: 66, relying upon the biography of Truman written by his daughter) relates a stag dinner hosted by Truman in early 1953. Churchill had the bad manners to ask Truman if he had his response ready for when they both were to stand before St Peter and be asked to justify using the bombs. The shock to the dining group this suggestion caused was alleviated when a mock trial of Churchill followed in which Truman was the judge and the jury of Churchill's peers consisted of the US Secretary of State and other close US colleagues and generals. Acquittal resulted, though Sellars could not find in Margaret Truman's account the reason; perhaps, Sellars surmised, 'they sensed that their own hands were dipped in blood. Or perhaps, they reasoned that it did not matter anyway. After all, even in real life tribunals, no one ever punishes a victor.'

What of today? The total for 1950–2000 coincides with the 800,000 figure usually taken as the conservative estimate for the 1994 Rwandan genocide, widely accepted as the most easily preventable genocide of the twentieth century. The causes of the genocide are traced back to the tactics of first German and the post-World War I Belgian imperial rule with the artificial distinction employed between Tutsi (whom they used as an administrative class) and Hutu. At independence the Belgians did an about-turn and handed power over to Hutu officials; post-independence ethnic conflict resulted in periods of semi-civil war. With French military forces backing the Hutu army in the early 1990s, groups around, but not including, the Hutu president resolved to find a way to remove Tutsi from Rwandan society. Their chance came with the shooting down of the president's plane. Having prepared the ground already by a campaign that blamed the Tutsi for the economic and political problems of Rwanda, the genocidal actions were first conducted by the army and a paramilitary set of groups numbering perhaps up to 50,000 armed with knives and machetes. Marchak (2003: 208) summarizes:

> Hutu moderates, carefully listed in advance, were the first victims. The next victims were the Tutsi leadership and rank and file of opposition parties, the prime minister, and other high-ranking officials who might have intervened

or sympathized with the Tutsis. After the decimation of the leaders, Tutsi civilians and thousands of Hutu who were not extremists were slaughtered. Churches and mission compounds in which Tutsis and moderate Hutus had sought refuge became killing grounds … Throughout the attacks, the government-owned radio station and a private station, Radio Mille Collines, urged the killers on.

There were UN peacekeepers on hand and their commander had been desperately sending warning messages to his superiors and to the UN, urging a strengthening of his mission. It would be inconceivable for the French military advisors not to know something was about to happen. When the first killings began, ten Belgian UN soldiers were killed with the 'result' that the UN withdrew the mission and all attempts to get intervention failed in particular because of US reluctance, caused in part by the previous killing of 18 US servicemen in Somalia. The subsequent official US line was that they did not have proper information; they did not appreciate the full picture. We now know that they knew fully what was going on and that President Clinton had ordered that the term 'genocide' not be used as that might trigger calls for the US to intervene, not to mention the quasi-legal obligation to take action as a country that had ratified the Genocide Convention (see for example, 'US chose to ignore Rwandan genocide', *The Guardian*, 31 March 2004). Thus deliberate US inactivity was one of the crucial factors that condemned to death the equivalent of the US homicide total for 1950–2000. It would be literally unthinkable for President Clinton to face penal sanctions in connection with these deaths. He was, however, pursued by extremely expensive legal proceedings (costing more than a UN force that would have deterred or at least stopped the main killings of the genocide) for most of his second term in office. The question to be ascertained in those proceedings, which included impeachment hearings, was whether he committed a crime or mis-demeanour when he stated that an activity with a certain female intern at the White House, later found to be an oral sexual act, did not constitute 'sexual relations'. He was acquitted.

And so the twentieth century ended as it began. For it had been born with the ongoing genocide in the then Congo Free State, a huge parcel of land given by the Berlin Treaty of 1884 (that drew up the map of Africa and allocated the tracts to the European powers) to King Leopold II, the King of the Belgians. Under Leopold's system of exploitation and plunder (which he called his 'Civilizing Mission') perhaps as many as 10 million Africans died and practices of mutilation were introduced that continue today (Ascherson, 1963; Hochschild, 1999; Morrison, 2005, chs 5 and 6). When Leopold died in 1909 a scandal erupted that dismayed the Belgian people; it was over his young mistress. The fact that he was said, by foreigners, to have the blood of millions of people, themselves foreigners, directly on his hands was of little consequence. Today the DR Congo is one of the places from which it is accepted that criminological data cannot be taken (it is termed the world's 'forgotten war' or 'state of constant rape and plunder' with a UN-estimated 3.5 million people dead from the period 1996 to the present). Along with Chechnya, it is seen as closer to what Hobbes once described as a permanent state of 'warré' or a 'melee' rather than social order. As with Leopold's regime, there have been no prosecutions – although the first appointed Prosecutor to the new International Criminal Court has stated that investigating the situation in the Congo will be his first priority. That may be in the future; but at present we inhabit the great divide. How did we get into this situation? We must look to the founding structures of modernity itself.

The founding of modernity: the case of Thomas Hobbes and the beginnings of the great divide

It is a commonplace that Hobbes provides a crucial focal point for analysing modernity and that much of social theory is an attempt to address the Hobbesian problem; namely, how can social order be constructed and maintained in the face of randomness and subjective rationality (see for example, Bauman, 1991)? In *Leviathan* (1651) Hobbes draws his readers into agreeing with him by two main tactics. First, henceforth we will analyse humans and frame controversial issues in the terms of a scientific discourse that will enable us to reach agreement on the terms of the discussion, if not the outcome. Second, we can locate ourselves in history by reference to a narrative that depicts the past (in his case presenting a natural or pre-social human condition), by reference to which we contrast our social interaction and use as a constant reminder of failure. Hobbes presented the natural condition of mankind as a state of 'warre' of all on all, where reason-guided conduct has little chance against the violent passions of man; left to his own subject desires – and the picture of man given by Hobbes' science is of a creature motivated by subjective desire – the life of man is 'solitary, poor, nasty, brutish and short'. Fear, tied to the desire for life, rescues humanity from this condition. Fear of death drives man to act rationally and combine, forming a strong, even totalitarian government, through accepting that power – might – lies at the heart of social organization. I simplify somewhat, but there is no denying the extent to which he places the achievement of security – the pacification of violence – before all else and the extent to which performability (the power to enforce or to make a predictable, repeatable occurrence) is given a practical epistemic warrant. Concentrating, however, upon power and the need to perform may blind us to three key elements: the theatricality of state power, the need to control discourse (or put more aptly, the need to provide authorities and rules and create canons for different sets of discourse), and the need to fashion a set of constraints that both allow subjective desire to act as a productive force and yet provide a set of channels for its organized expression.

The goal is civilized space, a realm of civil society where a civilized humanity can flourish beneath the watching gaze of the sovereign (one entity that is the representative of all). Social violence was to be controlled. Hobbes postulated the basis of the social bond – in place of dynasties, religious tradition or feudal ties – as rational self-interest exercised by calculating individuals. As bearers of subjective rationality, individuals were depicted as forming the social order and giving their allegiance to a government, a sovereign, because it was in their rational self-interest to do so and the metaphor for the social bond was contractual, not traditional. The sovereign was now to have a particular *territory*, which many have rather loosely termed the 'nation-state'.[4] This paradigm of civilised space is also a duality. Within the civilized space granted by the power of the sovereign the necessary reference points for social intercourse – expectations, contracts, and the truth of speech – are secured. Outside may lie a world of darkness. Beyond the reach of the sovereign's guarantees lies the land of the 'other'. But we do not see it. It is, however, an invisible presence. Contained in fear, in dreams, in stories told by travellers, the realm of the other is there but unacknowledged. It is to be mastered or kept at a safe distance.

The key to ruling is the proper channelling of the subjective desires of the subjects of rule. As later writers, including Weber and Freud, have stressed, interests, desires, and ideals establish 'society' as a symbolic order that is larger and more powerful that any of its members. In order for an entity we call society to exist at all, it must succeed in channelling their desires away from self-destructive ends. Thus the achievement of Hobbes' imagery: sublimating their violence towards one another, the members of society endow a single object with symbolic powers over them. The subsequent history of successful rule lies in the trick of controlling the fears of the subjects and allowing the games of what Hobbes calls 'felicity', the ongoing and perpetual arousal of desire and satisfaction of it through consumption, innovation, and cultural style.

The narratives of penality refashioned in global awareness, or the great forgetting

The games of felicity require that the subjects perceive the civilized space as secure. Garland's (2001) picture of a penological consensus existing in the 1970s and early 1980s mirrors Giddens' picture of a sociological orthodox consensus. The nation-state was perceived as a contained social entity subjected to processes of continuing rationalization and civilization (for the impact of postmodernity on this picture, see Bauman, 1991). My argument in outline is that, viewed globally, both were continuations of the Europeanization of the world, a project dating back several centuries. Postmodernity is also post-Europeanization. Garland expresses surprise at the new punitiveness, stating that no reading of Marx, Durkheim, Elias, or Foucault could have predicted it. My point here is that any reading of them undertaken to support an evolutionary predictability as to 'social development' of penality within an extracted 'contemporary society' is a reading constrained by the great divide and distorted in its focus upon analysis of the circumstances of the civilized space. The processes operating internal to this image of protected space link with other processes that cross boundaries and are far more difficult to see, but equally effective (for a reading of the inter-relationship of the civilized spaces of Brussels and the de-civilized spaces of the Congo, see Morrison, 2005, ch. 6). There are other ways of reading them more open to global factors.

Consider Marx. Most readings of Marx concentrate upon his analysis of capitalism as it works itself out in the confines of a territorially bound nation-state. A close attention to Marx, by contrast, shows the extent to which he identified the tendency to abstraction and various devices that hide the reality of social connectedness as key elements of the capitalist world system. Marx was for most of his writing a strict modernist, analysing the conditions of the present to build the future; his dismissal of the 'past' was, however, modified in his later writings where he realized the interdependency of modern methods and relations of production in the civilized high centres of global capitalism on the traditions and resources of the other lands. Contemporary European modernity was in large part a consequence of the domination of the outside, a domination that had to be ideologically interpreted in such a way that it was brushed out of everyday consciousness.

Although the centrality of the capitalism he observed was 'the fact that the workman sells his labour-power as a commodity' (Marx, 1867: 571), this ideological subject, the 'isolated individual', the ideal subject of the modern world, is in reality a product. 'The *sine qua non* of capitalist production' is 'this incessant reproduction, this perpetuation of the labourer' (1867: 571); this social reproduction is more important than the material production, for the mode of material production may change, as may the commodities produced, but the creation and re-creation of this 'social relationship', the isolating of the human unit and centring of this entity is the central focus in understanding the political.

Among the features therein pushed out of analysis is global violence. And for all Marx's late injunction that 'force is itself an economic power' (1867: 751), the violence involved in the creation of modern capitalist Western societies, and the violence perpetrated outside the nation-state focus of analysis, is huge. Moreover, the violence inherent in the state system is glossed over and fades from thought – the linkage between control of the imagery of threat and security and the use of violence by the powerful elites (so amenable to Weber's analysis and definition of the state or of the command theorists of law) fades as modernist jurisprudence, to take one example of contemporary discourse, gives us an image of law as an interacting body of rules and principles (such as in the mainstream disputes between H.L.A. Hart and R. Dworkin). Yet Marx reminds us that we are in a game of forgetting the foundational injustice or non-justice of the system, as when a particular social violence was legalized in Britain whereby in the eighteenth century the law itself (under the guise of the Parliamentary Acts of Enclosure) became 'the instrument of the theft of the people's land', on top of which 'bloody legislation against the expropriated' had for several centuries previously penalized vagrancy, forcing the dispossessed 'onto the narrow path of the labour market' (1867: 724, chapter 28).

We need to note what is focused upon and what is taken up as the accepted legacy of vision bequeathed by Marx. Concentrating upon the measures taken by the British state in the bloody legislation of the sixteenth century through the eighteenth and nineteenth centuries against vagrancy, begging, idleness, and petty forms of theft brings out the aim of preventing any alternatives to wage labour, but this should be placed along with an 'external' element wherein 'the treasures captured outside Europe by undisguised looting, enslavement and murder, floated back to the mother country and were there turned into capital' (1867: 753–4). Marx, writing for a predominantly European audience, focused on the role this had for European economic transformation; thus global colonialism provides 'one of the principal elements in furthering the transition from feudal to capitalist mode of production' (1865: 332; 1867: 756–7); but we should not thereby be blinded to the consequences elsewhere. 'The rosy dawn of the era of capitalist production' was made possible by 'the discovery of gold and silver in America, the extirpation, enslavement and entombment in mines of the aboriginal population, the beginning of the conquest and looting of the East Indies and the turning of Africa into a warren for the hunting of black-skins' (ibid.). The subsequent history of capitalism and liberal economic analysis must render the subjects of such awareness as 'externalities'. But they are not. The war on drugs, which legitimates the imprisonment of over one-third of the inmates in US prisons, also creates a paramilitary apparatus and direct military involvement in Colombia, among other countries, and provides a ready supply of income in countries whose economy is devastated by foreign intervention, such as Afghanistan and Chechnya.

Consider Elias:

> In the midst of a large populated area which by and large is free of physical violence, a 'good society' is formed. But even if the use of physical violence now recedes from human intercourse ... people now exert pressure and force on each other in a wide variety of different ways. (Elias, 1982: 270–71)

Two crucial factors need emphasizing: one is the process of pacification of the territory, the freeing of the populated area from physical violence; the other is group conflict. Globally the pacification of territory has been hidden in concepts of civilization, development or subduing the barbarians, but we now realize it was neither a particularly pretty image nor a 'just' one. In the post-colonial era it becomes a central question for the history of many nation-states, as in Australia, to be repressed by central authorities who do not wish for the justice of the conceptual link between current crime and punishment to be questioned.

Contemporary Chechnya would provide an arresting case study for Elias' civilizing/decivilizing process sociology. The Muslim world was a principal target of nineteenth- and twentieth-century Europeanization, with the majority of France's, Holland's, and Russia's colonial subjects and almost half of Britain's being Muslim. The Muslim people of the Caucasus repeatedly tried to revolt against the repressive rule of imperialist Russia and under the socialist modernity of Stalin the repression turned into near genocide. In the early 1940s some 14,000 Chechens and Ingush were shot and killed by Stalin's secret police in order to destroy political and intellectual leadership, while in 1944 Stalin forcibly relocated almost the entire Chechen and Ingush populations (over a million persons) to special camps in Central Asia. In some accounts nearly one-third of those transported – over 250,000 people – died. In 1957 the Chechens and other exiled groups were officially rehabilitated; reformed, they were returned to their republics, where they found that their land had been Russified. Hundreds of thousands of Russian farmers had been brought in to work the land and now made up over a quarter of the population of the Caucasus. Chechen customs and language were repressed and over 800 mosques and 400 religious colleges had been closed. Only in 1978 did Soviet authorities in the Caucus allow around 40 mosques to reopen, staffed by less than 300 registered *ulema* (Damrel, 1995). The present tragic position reflects a failed attempt by successive ruling elites from a central power base to control a process of pacification of territory and transformation of social mores.

That may seem extreme and any attempt to apply Elias beyond the European states that provided his arena is problematic (but worthwhile). However, we should remember that in his analysis of European states Elias concentrates on the central role of courtly society for enforcing tacit rules of conduct, regulating manners, and controlling social aggression. The members of the court came to be identified according to an ethical norm, constructing an exclusionary opposition in which 'high society' was the 'good society'. The psychological subject created in the civilizing process reflects the graduations of taste and class extending outwards from this courtly society now embedded in a 'social subject' that is both an acute observer of the social behaviour of others and the object of a similar intense scrutiny and social/ethical positioning from others. Elias social world, the civilizing world, is a social order of hierarchies and the constant reinforcing of notions of taste and appropriate social manners. We should not airbrush away that we are talking of group conflict in the positioning of the subject in the symbolic order of 'society', seen as the universe of shared meaning that the subject accepts.

Here we may wonder, and it can be no more than that at this stage, if the postmodern communication society marks the final (at least in urban settings) stage in the freeing of that subject desire from the moorings of 'organic forms' surviving from 'traditional societies' that appeared in 'the rituals of everyday intimacy' and the 'periodical festivals in which the community manifests itself'. For Lacan (1977), we had 'levelled down' and replaced hierarchy with a 'democratic' anarchy of the passions and desires. We may suspect that law-and-order campaigns enter into the games of excitement and boredom played out in the hyper-civilized areas of urban mass consumers with all their cultural dialectics of taste, power, identity, and status. At the level of channelling desire we find the neoliberal state divided, and in key areas the state and the market pull in opposite directions; the reassertion of 'rational' law-and-order control by a neo-Leviathan state (Garland, 2001) fights the constant invocation of excitement that is now a vital part of the market-driven culture (Presdee, 2000; Hayward, 2004; Ferrell *et al.*, 2004). When, however, we read key participants in the conservative analysis for asserting penal control (for example, Murray, 1999) it becomes clear that we are talking of real group battles over social norms and manners, for which the trope of the 'underclass' functions as a container of values itself to be contained (see Wacquant, this volume). In conditions where desire has an (over)abundance of bearings the subject is doomed to ever more intense games of felicity. Therein 'society' and 'civilized social values' as a locus of seduction for the included, and repression and constraint for the 'other' as opponent must be constantly invoked, else the conditions for enforcing minimal conditions of identity vanish. The politics of recognition – a struggle for differentiation and recognition in a world where rigid hierarchies have broken down – is no tame affair.

Conclusion: remarks on Foucault and the art of judging totality

There is one final theorist to consider: Foucault. Foucault engaged in a diverse set of readings on the power of recognition and placement in the order of things.

Discipline and Punish (1977) begins with a transformation from the public spectacle of the death of Damiens to the installation of discipline in the 'case'. Few commentators note that Damiens attacked the role of Louis XV in putting forth a particular view of religious authority. In fact Damiens was defending a similar position to that held by the majority of the judiciary of the time. This was a clear example of the threat of subjective rationality that Hobbes warned against. In the interrogation and execution, Damiens was erased from consideration as an individual; he could not be accepted as the bearer of any rationality contrary to that espoused by the governing authority. Damien's punishment – the same meted out to Ravaillac, the successful assassin of Henry IV in 1610 (in addition to the torture and execution his house was destroyed and his immediate family were exiled for life; see Chevallier, 1989) – as well as the rhetorical presentation of his life were in part designed to remove any status of martyrdom from him. The symbolic representation of the investigation and execution was a ceremonial affirmation of a totality in which his presence was only as an object, not subject. In contemporary etchings officially published to circulate the spectacle beyond those physically present, we find a balance expressing what Foucault terms *'la liturgie de la peur'*. Writing after the French Revolution, Joseph de Maistre (1971) highlighted how torture and execution reflected a total world view in which the executioner was seen as a key figure mediating between man and God. Crime springs from human corruption, its punishment from God's justice: punishment must follow to ensure we live in an ordered world with a meaningful history. Many today do not share de Maistre's particular grand narrative of a meaningful history; but what can we then say to those in Bangladesh who tell that no persons ever faced trial or 'justice' for the mass killings, rape, and destruction in the events of 1971 that gave birth to their 'nation-state', in large part because the US exerted pressure to prevent them, thus ensuring that (West) Pakistan was thanked for being an intermediary in the opening up of China to US diplomatic relations? Who can answer Anthony Mascarenhas, the Pakistani journalist who did so much to bring the horrors of 1971 to world attention, that 'machination and murder have been the curse of Bangladesh – its legacy of blood. It will not end until public accountability and the sequence of crime and punishment is firmly established' (1986).[5] After the largely unpunished history of political assassinations and endemic corruption, the official criminal statistics do not reflect the journalists' accounts of rapes, murders, politically motivated assassinations, bombings, acid attacks against women, pillaging of villages, and the rise of Islamic fundamentalists that made the *Far Eastern Economic Review* question whether Bangladesh is becoming the next 'cocoon of terror'? (See for example articles at www.worldpress.org.) Or as one activist put it to me during a visit in 2003:

> if the world tells us that the powerful should not be punished, whatever their 'crimes', how can I succeed in arguing for the detection, apprehension and punishment of men who throw acid in the face of women who refuse to marry them, or are deemed not to be properly covered by the head scarf? (see Morrison, 2005: chapter 9)

I also doubt that Foucault can be applied as a prophet of penal development: he was more a deconstructionist, demonstrating webs of power and by implication contingencies and relativism. His penological enterprise aimed also to upset the power of judging guilt and innocence, of calling into question the 'order of things' into which the 'case' was to be inserted. In the twentieth century looking at the few 'International Tribunals' that have taken place can show how absurd judging and enforcing the order of things can seem; take the contrast between the statuses of the two IMT after World War II. Today the holocaust assumes the role of the icon of Nazi crimes, but it is well to remember that it was not a direct subject of the IMT trial at Nuremberg (Bloxham, 2001). That the Jews were a minor figure of victimhood at those trials reflected their then (and now) vastly diminished presence in post-war Europe. Hitler's victory in ethnically cleansing continental Europe of the Jews gave them little political presence in a trial that increasingly took place in a Europe striving for civilized recovery and normalcy. The IMT at Nuremberg, organized and divided up by the four Allied powers, was dominated by the charge of waging aggressive war – it was a tribunal enforcing an ethos of governing as between sovereigns. If we remember it well it is as much to do with the subsequent history of Europe, that of a desire for civilized space, for a peaceful cooperative enterprise, in which the IMT serves as an educative lesson in the perils of decivilizing forces.

By contrast, the IMTFE (the Tokyo IMT) was dominated by the US in its planning and operation, received little attention from the press and governments and very little academic study since. Its claims to rational justice only work at the cost of sealing off proceedings from the outside, for at the same time as the Western powers were trying Japanese leaders for attempting to conquer East Asia, they were forcibly re-imposing their will in places such as the Dutch East Indies (Indonesia) and French Indochina (particularly Vietnam). Moreover, the very title of the Pacific War for the events it followed, so called to demonstrate that the US was the dominant force, downplayed the wars of China and India. When it came to judgment time, Judge Radhabinod Pal was denied the right to read out his dissenting judgment. But in inviting him to participate, the constituting powers had misjudged the operation of this spectacle, for while Pal, for example, was moving across to take up his appointment, a well published trial was taking place in India of nationalists who had fought with Japan against the British army, with Nehru as one of the defence counsel. At the Tribunal avoidance was the name of the game, only a handful of people were prosecuted, and whole areas of victimhood were forgotten, such as the sexual exploitation of the comfort women system. The British policy of burnt earth of spring 1942 that had been aimed at making Japanese expansion into what is now Bangladesh more difficult, along with subsequent incompetence, indifference and class bias, had condemned 2–3 million Bengalis to death from starvation, but this could not be raised as a crime, either of intention or ommission. It was best to also avoid, as has continued, the Japanese medical experiments, which could go unpunished as long as the US could take the findings.

Perhaps we should also remember that all the defendants found guilty and sentenced to imprisonment at the major trial or the subsidiary ones at Nuremberg were released by the 1960s, with only Hess as the exception. The politics of the new world order, the Cold War, meant that denazification would suffice. In any event most came to agree that no justice could be found for the scale of the crimes, such as the holocaust, although some have seen this in Israel a sovereign state to ensure that the Jewish people have civilized, protected space. Others see in Israel the proof of Hitler's victory; denazification cannot return Jewish communities to Europe. When the Cold War ended, the great crimes of Soviet modernity went almost all unpunished. In stark opposition to the law-and-order criminology of the domestic space, the crimes were seen as the product of the system; hence it was enough to change the system.

If we are now surprised that politicians have discovered crime and punishment, I have argued that the political is inherent in penality and becomes clearly visible when we try and contrast two areas of penality, one inside the confines of the nation-state, the other outside those confines in the realm of the 'international'. We have been mistaken in looking to the modernist narratives of penal development as if they could be abstracted from globality, as if they reflected modern forms of crime control. In global terms we have lived through and continue to inhabit a remarkably non-punitive world. In the twentieth century mass rape, torture, killing on a scale unimaginable in earlier centuries were tolerated and went unpunished. Of course there were also games where participants played by the rules of discourse, it was best to label those you raped, killed, or tortured as terrorists, sub-humans, criminals, insurgents, animals, rebels ... It was usually best to kill them away from the eyes of journalists – usually, but not always – for if the journalists were from your own civilized space they might well be trusted to share your perception of the situation. As we seek to understand the sites of the new punitiveness we also need to have in mind the reality of the modern global community, a 'community' that both does not or cannot punish its criminals. Adopting a global awareness may then also enable us to realize a different social solidarity in which the rhetorics and intolerances at play in localities find themselves confronted by a broader conception of the stakes at issue.

Notes

1   One may note that the seven defendants sentenced to death by the International Military Tribunal Tokyo were hung at Sugamo Prison on 20 December 1948, with only military personnel and press present to verify, as per the orders of General MacArthur (Horowitz, 1950, p. 573).
2   By comparison 16 persons are detained at the UN *ad hoc* tribunal costing several millions of dollars which has so far tried less than ten persons. The Rwandan internal figure is reducing through death faster than prisoners can be processed by their local tribunals. At the end of 1998, 125,028 person were listed as officially detained on suspicion of participating in genocide; in 1998 several thousand detainees died as a result of AIDS, malnutrition, dysentery, and typhus. During the month of November 1998 alone, 400 prisoners died from typhus in the Rilima prison alone (Reyntjens, 1999: 14).
3   Source, Interpol International Criminal Statistics on the web. Accessed in 2003; as part of the anti-terrorist measures these figures are no longer available to the public!
4   The 'legal' origins of the nation-state are usually linked in the literature of political relations and 'International Law' to the Treaty of Westphalia in 1648, often referred to as a 'tyrants' charter' as it allows rulers to literally get away with murder if they shelter behind the cloak of 'state sovereignty'.

5 At the present time the two main political parties in Bangladesh are headed by women who have survived the assassination of their husband while president (General Zia), in one case, and the killing of their whole family except the two daughters who were in Europe, in the case of the death of the first Prime Minister and widely called 'Father of the Nation', Sheikh Mujibur Rahman. Their politics are marked by intense personal dislike and mistrust; in part because without trials or proper investigations there is no secure knowledge as to who was involved in the various coups, assassinations, and movements to secure the state or destabilize it.

References

Amnesty International (1996) *Brief Summary of Concerns about Human Rights Violations in the Chechen Republic*, London: Amnesty International.

Ascherson, N. (1963) *The King Incorporated: Leopold the Second and the Congo*, London: George Allen & Unwin.

Barclay G. and Tavares, C. (2002) *International Comparisons of Criminal Justice Statistics 2000*, London, Home Office: Research Development & Statistics Directorate.

Bauman, Z. (1991) *Intimations of Postmodernity*, London: Routledge.

Bloxham, D. (2001) *Genocide on Trial*, Oxford: Oxford University Press.

Chevallier, P. (1989) *Les Regicides: Clement, Ravaillac, Damiens*, Paris: Fayard.

Damrel, D. (1995) 'The Religious Roots of Conflict: Russia and Chechnya', *Religious Studies News*, 10(3), September.

De Maistre, J. (1971) *The Works of Joseph de Maistre* (trans. Jack Lively), New York: Schocken.

Elias, N. (1982)*The Civilising Process* (trans. E. Jephcott), Oxford: Blackwell.

Ferrell, J., Hayward, K., Morrison, W. and Presdee, M. (2004) *Cultural Criminology Unleashed*, London: Glasshouse.

Foucault, M. (1977) *Discipline and Punish*, Harmondsworth: Penguin.

Garland, D. (2001) *The Culture of Control*, Oxford: Oxford University Press.

Glover, J. (2001) *Humanity: A Moral History of the Twentieth Century*, London: Pimlico.

Gottfredson, M. and Hirschi, T. (1990) *A General Theory of Crime*, Stanford: Stanford University Press.

The Guardian (2004) 'US Chose to Ignore Rwanda Genocide', 31 March.

Hayward, K. (2004) *City Limits: Crime, Consumer Culture and the Urban Experience*, London: Glasshouse.

Hobbes, T. (1991 [1651]) *Leviathan* (edited by Richard Tuck), Cambridge: Cambridge University Press.

Hochschild, A. (1999) *King Leopold's Ghost*, New York: Mariner.

Horowitz, S. (1950) 'The Tokyo Trial', *International Conciliation*, 465: 473–584.

Lacan, J. (1977) *Ecrits* (trans. Alan Sheridan), New York: Norton.

Marchak, P. (2003) *Reigns of Terror*, Montreal and Kingston: McGill-Queen's University Press.

Margolis, E. (1999a) 'Following in Stalin's Footsteps', *Toronto Sun*, 31 August.

Margolis, E. (1999b) 'US Aids Russia's Crimes in the Caucasus', *Toronto Sun*, 12 October.

Margolis, E. (2000) 'Forgotten Chechens Face Extermination', *Toronto Sun*, 23 January.

Mascarenhas, A. (1986) *Bangladesh: A Legacy of Blood*, London: Hodder and Stoughton.

Marx, K. (1865) *Capital*, Vol. 3, Moscow: Progress [1971 reprint].

Marx, K. (1867) *Capital*, Vol. 1, London: Lawrence and Wishart [1967 reprint].

Morrison, W. (2005) *Criminology, Civilisation and the New World Order*, London: Glasshouse.

Murray, C. (1984) *Losing Ground*, New York: Basic Books.

Murray, C. (1999) *The Underclass Revisted*. American Enterprise Institute for Public Policy Research: Papers and Studies. http://www.aei.org/ps/psmurray.htm

Presdee, M. (2000) *Cultural Criminology and the Carnival of Crime*, London: Routledge.

Reyntjens, F. (1999) 'Talking or Fighting? Political Evaluation in Rwanda and Burundi, 1998–99', *Current African Issues*, no. 21. Nordiska Afrikainstitutet.

Rummel, R. (1992) *Democide*, Transaction Press, New Brunswick, NJ.

Rummel, J. (1995) *Death by Government*, Transaction Press, New Brunswick, NJ.

Sellars, K. (2002) *The Rise and Rise of Human Rights*, Phoenix Mill: Sutton.

Smith, R. (2000) 'Human Destructiveness and Politics: The Twentieth Century as an Age of Genocide', in I. Wallimann and M. Dobkowski (eds) *Genocide and the Modern Age*, Syracuse: Syracuse University Press.

Walmsley, R. (2003) *World Prison Population List* (5th edn), London: HMSO.

Index